Guide to Burma

2nd edition

Nicholas Greenwood

Bradt Publications, UK
The Globe Pequot Press Inc, USA

First published in 1993 by Bradt Publications.
Second edition published in 1995 by Bradt Publications,
41 Nortoft Road, Chalfont St Peter, Bucks SL9 0LA, England
Published in the USA by The Globe Pequot Press Inc, 6 Business Park Road,
PO Box 833, Old Saybrook, Connecticut 06475-0833

Reprinted with amendments February 1996

British Library Cataloguing in Publication Data
A catalogue record for this book is available from the British Library
ISBN 1 898323 21 6

Library of Congress Cataloging-in-Publication Data
Greenwood, Nicholas
Guide to Burma / Nicholas Greenwood. — 2nd ed.
  p. cm.
Includes bibliographical references and index.
ISBN 1-56440-704-7
1. Burma—Guidebooks. I. Title.
DS527.3.G74 1995
914.9104'5—dc20   95-5015
                                                                    CIP

Photographs Nicholas Greenwood and Jongdech Nantidoi
Cover photographs Nicholas Greenwood
Front Buddha image in the 'earth witness' posture,
Peik Chin Myaung Caves, Maymyo
Back Hermit ('yathe'), Myohaung, Arakan State
Illustrations Rebecca de Mendonça
Maps Steve Munns

Typeset from the author's disc by Patti Taylor, London NW10 1JR
Printed and bound by Grafo SA, Bilbao, Spain

'... I pass in the spirit amid the courts of the great golden pagoda in Rangoon, and hear the monotonous chant of the worshippers as they bow themselves before a mighty brass image, that gleams out of a dim shrine by the light of a hundred tiny candles guttering on the ground. In the warm and dream-like dusk the smell of incense is wafted to my nostrils, and the fragrance of the frangipanni perfumes the air like scent. I could go on with a hundred of such scenes, all different, and all indelibly impressed on my brain; for the charm of the most fascinating country in the world, the country of Burma, has laid hold upon me and will be with me to the end.'

A Bachelor Girl in Burma, Geraldine Edith Mitton, 1907

This book is dedicated to Daw Aung San Suu Kyi, the Nobel Peace Prize Laureate, whose indomitable spirit and devotion to her people serve as an inspiration to all.

'They say that beyond all countries you hear Burma a-calling, and it is named the Land of Regrets because people who have been there are never the same afterwards; there lives in their hearts always a tiny ache of regret for the land they have left.'

G E Mitton, 1907

ABOUT THE AUTHOR

Since first setting foot in Pagan in November 1990, Nicholas Greenwood has sought to improve his knowledge and understanding of Burma, its peoples, culture, history and politics. He has been the first Western traveller to visit all areas of the country for over 30 years and is the author of the travelogue *Bound Tightly With Banana Leaves: A South East Asian Journal* (Right Now Books, 1992) and the first edition of *Guide to Burma* (Bradt Publications, 1993).

ACKNOWLEDGEMENTS

To Anna Allott, Senior Research Fellow, School of Oriental and African Studies, University of London, for her endless patience, incalculable assistance and wise counsel.

To Ko Zar Ni, formerly of Mandalay University, for inspiration and friendship.

Thanks are also due to Patricia Herbert, Head of the Southeast Asia Section of the British Library's Oriental and India Office Collections, Hugh Davies of Shan Travels & Tours, Jasper Young, Jean-Louis Vangeluwe, Thanomsil Khiansua, Jongdech Nantidoi, Russameeh Petcharaburi, the countless *hsaik-ka* drivers of Burma and Clio Press Limited of Oxford.

To my sister Caroline and my dear friend Judith, for putting up with my travel whims, to my publisher Hilary Bradt for the fortitude of a Burma Airways' timetable compiler, to my editor, Tricia Hayne, and to all my friends in Burma, whom I cannot mention personally, *tjay-zu timba-deh*.

CONTENTS

Introduction   **xi**

'Visit Myanmar Year 1996': the state's viewpoint
by **Dr Naw Angelene**   **xii**

Chapter One   **General Facts**   **1**
Geography, climate, time, days and dates 1, History
and politics 4, Press, TV and propaganda 30,
Economy 33, Population and people: the ethnic
groups 36, Religion, pagodas and temples 38,
Festivals 42, Language 45, Burmese names: old and
new 48, Burmese personal names 50, Food and
drink 53

Chapter Two   **Burmese Culture** *by* Ko Zar Ni   **59**

Chapter Three **Before You Go**   **68**
Visas 68, Inoculations and health problems 70,
Currency, black market 77

Chapter Four   **Getting There and Away**   **79**
Tour operators 79, Travel restrictions 82, Airlines 83,
Border crossings 85, Arrival and customs 86,
Departure 87

Chapter Five   **Practical Information**   **88**
Getting around 88, Useful addresses 91,
Accommodation 92

Chapter Six   **Rangoon and Vicinity**   **94**
History and general description 94, Where to stay 97,
Where to eat 97, Entertainment and shopping 99,
Sightseeing 103, Shwedagon Pagoda 103, Sule
Pagoda 105, National Museum 105, Other attractions
107, Beyond Rangoon 109, Syriam 109, Twante 110,
Pegu 111, Shwemawdaw Pagoda 111, Shwethalyaung
112, Other places of interest 114

Chapter Seven **Mandalay and Vicinity**   **117**
Mandalay and vicinity 117, Getting there and
around 117, History and general description 120,
Where to stay 125, Where to eat 126, Entertainment

and shopping 127, Mandalay Hill and environs 128, Other attractions 132, Amarapura 136, Getting there 136, History 136, What to see 138, Ava 139, Getting there 139, History 139, What to see 140, Sagaing 142, Getting there 142, History 142, What to see 142, Mingun 145, Getting there 145, What to see 145, Maymyo 148, Getting there 148, History 148, Where to stay and eat 148, What to see 149, Monywa 151, Getting there 151, History 151, Where to stay and eat 151, What to see 151, Kyaukse and vicinity 153

Chapter Eight   **Pagan and Vicinity**   **155**
Getting there and around 157, General description 157, Where to stay and eat/shopping 158, Pagodas and temples 159, Archaeological Museum 167, Mount Popa 167

Chapter Nine   **Prome and Shwedaung**   **172**
Prome 171, History 171, Getting there 172, Where to stay and eat 173, What to see 173, Shwedaung 176

Chapter Ten   **Inle Lake Region**   **178**
Getting there 178, Kalaw and the hilltribes 178, Pindaya 180, Inle Lake 181, Taunggyi 183, Heho 186, Thazi 186

Chapter Eleven   **Other Destinations**   **188**
Upper Burma 188, Mogok 188, Meiktila 190, Toungoo 191, Pakokku 192, Magwe 193, Taungdwingyi and Beikthano 194, Shan State 195, Kengtung 195, Getting there 195, Where to stay and eat 195, What to see 195, Lashio and vicinity 197, Getting there 198, Where to stay and eat 199, What to see 200, Hsipaw 201, Lower Burma 201, Moulmein and vicinity 201, Getting there 202, Where to stay and eat 202, What to see 204, Kyaiktiyo and vicinity 207, The Irrawaddy Delta: Bassein 210, Getting there 211, Where to stay and eat 211, General description 212, History 212, What to see 213, Chaungtha 216, Getting there 216, Where to stay and eat 216, What to see 217, Henzada 217, Where to stay and eat 218, What to see 218, Arakan State 219, Sandoway and Ngapali 219, Getting there 219, Where to stay and eat 220, What to see 221, Akyab 222, Getting there 225, Where to stay

and eat/shopping 225, What to see 226, Myohaung 229, Getting there 231, Where to stay 231, What to see 231, Kachin State 235, Myitkyina 235, Getting there 236, General description 237, Where to stay and eat 238, What to see 238, Bhamo 240, Getting there 240, Where to stay and eat 242, What to see 242, Putao 243, Getting there 244, General description/ where to stay and eat 245, What to see 246, Kayah State 246, Loikaw 246, Getting there 247, General description, 248, Where to stay and eat 248, What to see 248, Tenasserim Division 249, Tavoy 249, History 249, General description 251, Getting there 252, Where to stay and eat 252, What to see 252, Mergui and the Archipelago 254, History 254, Getting there 258, Where to stay and eat 259, What to see 260

Further Reading   **265**

Postscript   **273**

Burma Directory   **273**

And finally...   **277**

Index   **279**

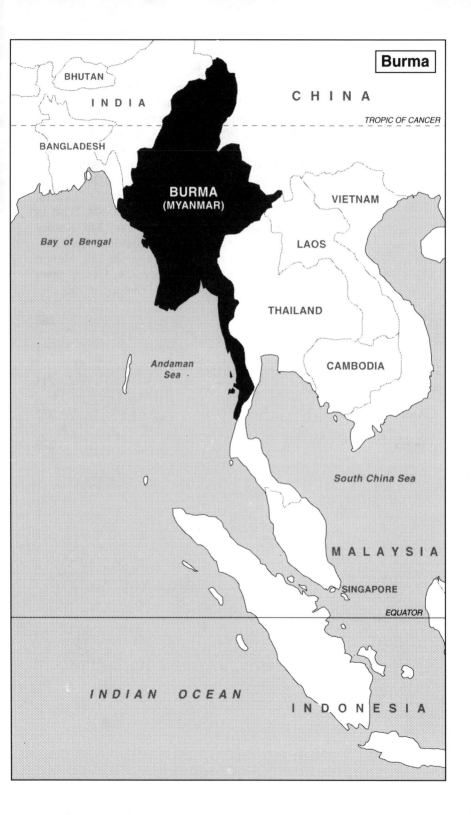

Introduction

'The land of our love and service has, for the moment, become *terra incognita*. Yet there are those who, wistfully watching for the turn in the fortunes of war, and dreaming and planning for the Burma that shall be, cherish memories of which the war cannot despoil them.'

Clement H Chapman, *Glints of Gold (Burma)*, 1943

Burma (the name in English was changed to Myanmar by the military government in 1989) is an extraordinary country. The very moment you touch down at Rangoon's Mingaladon Airport on your flight from Bangkok, you set your watch back 30 minutes and your life back at least 30 years. For Burma is caught in a singular time-warp having been cut off from the outside world since General Ne Win seized power in a *coup d'état* in 1962. Once the richest nation in Southeast Asia, Burma is now one of the poorest lands in the world. It lies practically untouched by modernisation, stifled by an inept military dictatorship, yet is home to the kindest and friendliest people you could ever hope to meet. It is the country of Pagan — the 'Land of 2,000 Temples' — of Mandalay and Moulmein, the revered Shwedagon Pagoda, the astonishing Golden Rock Pagoda, merchant adventurer Samuel White's Mergui and of 'the sunshine an' the palm-trees an' the tinkly temple-bells'. One-time port of call for Kipling, Conrad, Orwell, Saki, Malraux, H G Wells and Somerset Maugham, Burma is truly a unique and remarkable land.

'VISIT MYANMAR YEAR 1996': The state's viewpoint

by Dr Naw Angelene

At last the doors to Myanmar, the magic golden land, are widely opened to the outside visitors around the world. All out efforts are now made to create Myanmar a destination for international travellers.

The real excitement began with the announcement of 1996 as Visit Myanmar Year at the first meeting of the Tourist Industry Development Management Committee which was held on 1 May 1994. Lieutenant-General Khin Nyunt, the Secretary-1 of the State Law and Order Restoration Council, leads the committee as the chairman and Lieutenant-General Kyaw Ba acts as the vice-chairman while other ministers are members.

When the second meeting of this Tourist Industry Development Management Committee was held on 17 May, all the members reported the plans and preparations for the year.

More sub-committees were formed and the chairman urged all members to prepare for sufficient accommodation, facilitation of air and road transport, installation of modern telecommunications, provision of adequate electricity, setting up markets for convenient purchase of food and proper health care and so on.

Since the designation of Visit Myanmar Year 1996, both local and foreign journalists, correspondents and travel news writers have been contacting the Ministry of Hotels and Tourism asking for information about the Year. Many pointed out the need for better infrastructure, accommodation, transport, tourist facilities, etc.

Undeniably, decades of isolation has held back the economic and material growth of Myanmar and thus there is much to be done for the celebration of Visit Year in 1996. Now all the requirements are being seriously discussed and plans are underway for the expected 500,000 or more tourists to arrive. While the Ministry of Transport is buying additional aircraft and planning for the construction of new roads and airports, the Ministry of Rail Transportation is buying new trains for the convenience of the travellers.

And while the Mayor of Mandalay is trying his best to make Mandalay, the last capital of the Myanmar King, the most attractive destination for historical and cultural tourists, the Mayor of Yangon is also very much occupied with his plan for the creation of Yangon as the Garden City of Asia. Big signposts can now be seen at the crossroads of Yangon, calling for efforts to make Yangon the cleanest and most beautiful city in 1996.

Especially since tourism development of Myanmar is based on the country's diverse culture, historical, archaeological and religious monuments and varied natural environment, all the ministries concerned are seriously involved. Meetings are being held for the performances of cultural and traditional dances of the many different national races in Myanmar for the entertainment of foreign travellers. At the same time primary archaeological sites like Bagan, Mandalay, Bago, Myauk-Oo and Pyay will be undergone intensive improvements.

Promotion programmes to make Myanmar an attractive and well known tourist destination are being undertaken by the Ministry of Information.

As tourism development is interrelated with other economic sectors, Ministry of Hotels and Tourism has to cooperate with all government and private sectors to improve tourism infrastructure, while cooperation is also made with media at home to let the world know about the uniqueness of Myanmar.

The forceful drive for the holding Visit Myanmar Year 1996 is gaining momentum. Whatever the purpose, the spinoff effect of the preparation for the Visit Year is apparent. The encouragement and activities for the development of Myanmar as an international tourist destination surely will make a substantially greater contribution to the country's economic and social development. Roads will be wider, lights will be brighter, tours will be cleaner, grass will be greener and with more job opportunities, people will be happier.

With all those expectations, let us whole-heartedly invite tourists all around the world to our beautiful Golden Land and welcome the Visit Myanmar Year 1996.

Author's note
As a result of the government's declaration of 1996 as 'Visit Myanmar Year', a haphazard programme of development is taking place throughout the country. Visitors should also be aware of changes in timetables and, because of rampant inflation, price fluctuations.

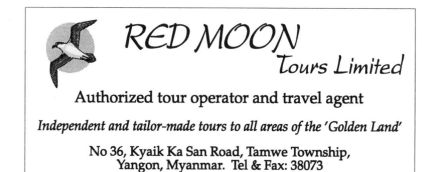

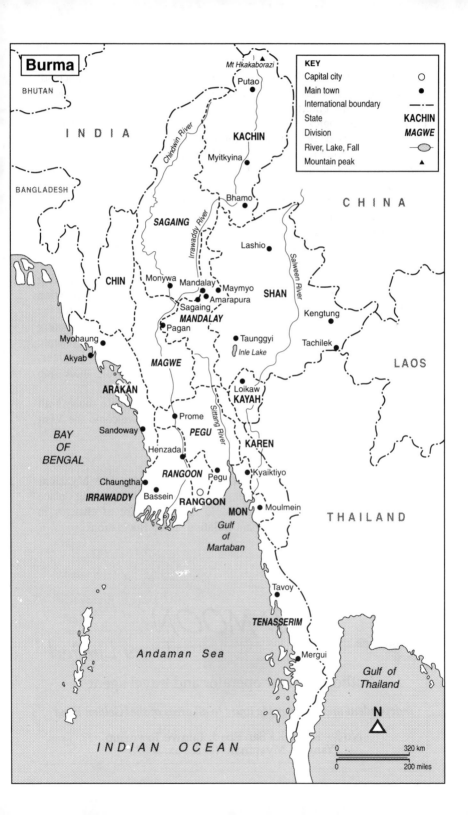

Chapter One

General Facts

GEOGRAPHY, CLIMATE, TIME, DAYS AND DATES

'The country known by the generic name of Burma, including in that title both the old British provinces and Upper Burma, our latest acquisition, has an area of about 230,000 square miles, an area that is, about twice as large as that of the United Kingdom, of which the old provinces contain about 90,000, and Upper Burma about 140,000. The river par excellence of Burma is the Irawadi. This great stream, which is navigable by steamers drawing five feet of water as far as Bhamo, 900 miles from its mouth, and its largest tributary the Kyendwin, form in Upper Burma several fertile plains, producing rice, cotton, wheat, and other valuable crops, while in the lower part of its course, in conjunction with the river Sittang, it forms a splendid delta, which is the main source of the world's supply of rice. The vast expanse of delta, nearly 100 miles each way, appears, indeed, one immense rice-field, stretching away illimitably, level as the sea. The aspect of this plain is changeful. In midsummer, after the first heavy rains, an unbroken sheet of water, it becomes carpeted, as the rice plant grows, with brightest green, which turns, ere December arrives, to waving gold, and then, after harvest, to a dreary grey flat of sun-baked mud, over which the smoke of the burning stubble hangs like a pall. Out of it rise, visible to great distances, the mighty masses of the great pagodas of Rangoon and Pegu, as changeful in their golden sheen of light, and yet as unchanging, as the wide plain over which they have looked for so many centuries.'

J Annan Bryce, 1886

Burma, the second largest country in Southeast Asia, covers an area of 676,552 km², 261,218 square miles or 167 million acres (roughly the size of Vietnam and approximately the size of France and England combined). It is bordered by India and Bangladesh in the northwest, China (and Tibet) and Laos in the north and northeast and Thailand in the east and southeast. Burma's west coast is contiguous to both the Bay of Bengal and the Andaman Sea and totals about 2,000 miles. The greatest length of the country from north to south is about 1,300 miles, and the greatest width from east to west is about 600 miles.

The country's major waterway is the Irrawaddy River, derived from the Hindu *airavati*, meaning 'elephant river'. The Irrawaddy has its confluence at Myit-hson in Kachin State, where the Mali Hka and Nmai Hka Rivers converge. Uncertainty exists as to where these two rivers actually rise. However, as Euan Cox wrote in *Farrer's Last Journey: Upper Burma 1919-20*:

> 'The area north of the confluence of the two main streams, the N'mai hka and M'li hka, that form the Irrawady, is... a geographical tangle of mountains and valleys... We thought vaguely that it would be pleasant to spend a season on the frontier range which divides Burma from a little offshoot of Tibet that runs southward between Assam and China, the range on which the M'li hka rises... No one can play pranks with the N'mai; as far as its junction with the M'li it carries with it some of the dour ferocity of the Tibetan alps which give it birth.'

The Irrawaddy's biggest tributary is the Chindwin which runs from the northwest, converging in central Burma. The country's other significant (and longest) river, the Salween, has its source in central Tibet as the Dngul Chu River, flows through eastern Tibet, then enters Burma and flows across the Shan Plateau to its mouth at Martaban. The Mekong River forms the border between Burma and Laos.

Burma consists of seven states and divisions: Arakan, Chin, Kachin, Karen, Kayah, Mon and Shan States, and the Irrawaddy, Magwe, Mandalay, Pegu, Rangoon, Sagaing and Tenasserim Divisions. According to 1993 estimates, the most densely populated are: Mandalay (5,716,000), Rangoon (4,943,000) and Sagaing (4,802,000) Divisions. The least populated is Kayah State with 223,000.

Burma has a tropical climate with three general seasons. The rainy season during the southwest monsoons from mid-May to mid-October, the dry cool season from mid-October to mid-February and the hot season from mid-February until the onset of the rains in May. It can be exceptionally cold in the north where there are snow-capped mountains (Burma's highest peak, and the highest in Southeast Asia, Mount Hkakabo, known as Hkakabo Razi, reaches 5,887m or 19,314ft) and quite cool in Shan State. In the rainy season about 200 inches of rain fall on the coastlands, about 100 inches in the Irrawaddy Delta and about 80 in the hills, but in the dry central zone only about 25 to 45 inches. Immediately before the rains begin the temperature reaches 100°F or more in the Delta and the dry zone. The coolest months are December and January, when in southern Burma the maximum temperature does not fall below 60°F.

Burma is a forest-clad mountainous country. Three parallel chains of mountain ranges run from north to south: the Western Yoma (*Yoma* literally means backbone) or Arakan Yoma, the Pegu Yoma and the Shan

Plateau. They begin from the eastern extremity of the Himalaya mountain range. These mountain chains divide the country into three river systems: the Irrawaddy, Sittang and Salween. The Irrawaddy and its major tributary, the Chindwin (600 miles long), constitute the greatest riverine system in the land. As it enters the sea, the Irrawaddy forms a vast delta of 150 miles by 130 miles.

According to these mountain chains and river systems, the country can be divided into seven major topographic regions: the Northern Hills, the Western Hills, the Shan Plateau, the Central Belt, the Lower Burma Delta, the Arakan Coastal Region and the Tenasserim Coastal Strip.

Burma lies on an earthquake fault: there were major quakes in 1838 (Mingun), 1912, 1917, 1930 (all around Pegu) and 1975 (Pagan). The most recent tremor in May 1994, 140 miles west-south-west of Mandalay, measured 6.2 on the Richter scale.

'The one thing that a Burman can be relied on not to do is to adhere to a time schedule and we were obviously in for a long wait. Masses of Burmese onlookers were there sitting on their haunches, quite content as usual to wait endlessly and without complaint. But Brownlow and I, standing there under the burning sun without any shade and rather nervous about what was going to happen, got hotter and hotter.'

A J S White, 1991

Burma is 6½ hours ahead of GMT (as opposed to BST which, according to the locals, stands for 'Burmese Standard Time' or BAST — 'Burma Airways Standard Time'), and thus half an hour behind Thailand, the country from which the majority of tourists arrive. A number of travellers come from Singapore which is 1½ hours ahead of Burma in time, but probably 100 years ahead in terms of development.

The Burmese date is 638 years after the Christian era. Therefore, in order to obtain the Burmese year, you have to subtract 638 from the Christian date. In practice, both eras are used: to distinguish one from the other the word *Thekkayit* is placed before the Burmese date. Often both the Burmese date and the English date are used together, in that order, in official documents (without *Thekkayit*).

The Burmese month is divided into two parts, *la-zan* (the waxing) and *la-byee-gyaw* or *la-zok* (the waning). The full moon (*la-byee*) falls on the 15th of the waxing, the *la-gweh* (hidden moon) on the 14th or 15th of the wane. The days of worship are the full moon, eighth of the wane, the hidden moon and the eighth waxing.

HISTORY AND POLITICS

'SAVANNA-BHUMI (sic) — "Land of Golden Hues", — so the earliest recorders named the land of Burma some two thousand years ago. The name was to be truer than they knew. Yesterday, the waving fields of her golden grain, the sheen of her gilded pagodas, the saffron robes of her countless monks, the orange glow of her passionate sunsets these, all, bestowed on her a title of which Burma was justly proud. The very word "shway" (gold) is, perhaps, one of the most common in her speech.'

Clement H Chapman, 1943

Owing to the lack of reliable records, very little is known about Burma's early history. Legends relate that a king of the Mons, a people who had apparently migrated into Lower Burma from the southeast, built the Shwedagon Pagoda on the site of modern Rangoon during the lifetime of the Buddha (c 6th century BC). Another legend, that the 3rd century BC Indian Emperor Ashoka (or Asoka), a devout Buddhist, sent monks to Thaton, a Mon settlement in Lower Burma on the Gulf of Martaban, suggests that they had early contacts with the Indian subcontinent by sea. Indian ships docked at Thaton, Pegu and other Lower Burma ports, and the region became an outpost of Indian civilisation. India's chief contribution to Burmese culture was Buddhism, and over the centuries it was the axis around which Burmese life and national identity evolved.

Chinese records from the 3rd century AD mention a people known as the Pyu who lived in the central Irrawaddy River area of Upper Burma, having apparently migrated into the region from the Tibetan Plateau. Chinese Buddhist pilgrims of the 7th century AD describe a Pyu city-state, known as Sri Ksetra (the 'Pleasant' or 'Fortunate Field'), near the modern town of Prome on the banks of the Irrawaddy. Sri Ksetra consisted of over 100 monasteries and its finest monument still in existence today is the 200ft high Bawbawgyi Pagoda, constructed of brick in Indian style. According to Burmese chronicles, the Pyu gained supremacy over the Mons, sent ships to India, Ceylon (Sri Lanka), the Malay Peninsula and Indonesia and claimed tributaries as far afield as Sumatra and Java. According to records, the Pyu Kingdom came to an end in AD 832.

Another group of states was established as early as the 4th century AD in what is now Arakan State, on the Bay of Bengal. The Arakanese were related to the Burmans of Upper Burma and, because of their location on the coast, had close sea links with India.

The Burmans, a people akin to the Pyu, founded settlements at Pagan on the banks of the Irrawaddy River in Upper Burma as early as the 2nd century AD (the first known date for the establishment of Pagan is AD 849). Strategically located on the north-south and east-west trade routes and close to the irrigated plain of Kyaukse, which produced an abundance of rice, Pagan provided an economic base upon which a mighty kingdom was to evolve.

The founder of the Pagan Dynasty was King Anawrahta (1044-77) and he was the first to bring Lower and Upper Burma under unified rule. Starting from Pagan, at that time merely a cluster of small villages, he conquered the neighbouring principalities of the central Irrawaddy valley. In 1057 he captured Thaton, gaining control over Lower Burma and bringing back to his capital the Theravada scriptures in Pali, a large number of Buddhist monks and artists and craftsmen of every description. From the Mon monks the Burmese received their alphabet and religion. Thus it was from this momentous date that there began the extraordinary architectural and artistic activity which, in a little more than two centuries, covered the city and its surrounding areas with hundreds of magnificent monuments.

Kyansittha (1084-1113), the second great king of Pagan, continued the work of Anawrahta, reunifying the kingdom after a series of uprisings, fending off foreign invaders and maintaining diplomatic and ecclesiastical ties with Ceylon. Though influenced to a certain extent by Hinduism, Kyansittha considered himself primarily a Buddhist king and indeed was responsible for the construction of the Ananda Temple, deemed the finest example of Burmese religious architecture.

Pagan flourished for more than two and a half centuries before it was overrun by the Mongol armies of Kublai Khan, who invaded Upper Burma from China in 1287. From the 14th to the mid-16th centuries, Upper Burma came under the control of Shan princes in what was a period of disunity and foreign domination. Burman kings, however, ruled at Ava (near Mandalay) as Shan tributaries. In Lower Burma, a Shan named Wareru (1287-96) established a kingdom at Martaban in 1281, subsequently gaining control of much of the Lower Burma region. There followed a golden age of Mon culture. Binnya U (1353-85) set up a new capital at Pegu. Dhammazedi (1472-92), a former Buddhist monk, was a model Buddhist king who promoted the reform of the *sangha* (monkhood) through the introduction of orthodox ordination rites from Ceylon.

In the 16th century, a resurgence of Burman power took place at Toungoo on the Sittang River. In 1280 a fortified town had been established there which subsequently became a political centre of some significance. After the capture of Ava by a Shan prince in 1527, many Burmans sought refuge in Toungoo. Tabinshwehti (1531-50) founded the second unified Burmese dynasty known as the Toungoo Dynasty. Tabinshwehti conquered Pegu in 1539, extending his control to Martaban and the coastal area as far south as Tavoy. He seized Prome from the Shan forces and in 1546 had himself consecrated King of Burma with Pegu as his capital. In 1548, however, he overstepped himself by attempting to invade Siam (now central Thailand) and he was assassinated two years later. Following a subsequent revolt in central Burma, his brother King Bayinnaung (1551-81) captured Ava in 1555,

thus uniting Upper and Lower Burma. He then marched against the Shan
principalities in eastern Burma and parts of what today are Thailand and
Laos, and in 1569 captured the Siamese capital of Ayutthaya. However,
during the reign of Bayinnaung's son Nanda Bayin (1581-99) the
Toungoo Dynasty began to wane: Siam reasserted its independence and
an Arakanese fleet laid siege to Pegu, capturing it in 1599. Later King
Thalun (1629-48) moved the capital northwards from Pegu to Ava, thus
withdrawing effective Burman power from Lower Burma. Eventually in
1752 a Mon named Binnya Dala deposed the last Toungoo monarch, who
was brought back (along with as many as 30,000 prisoners) to Pegu.

However a new leader, Maung Aung Zeya, appeared in Shwebo in
Upper Burma and within eight years unified Upper and Lower Burma.
He defeated Binnya Dala's troops and proclaimed himself king of Burma,
assuming the title Alaungpaya, 'the embryo Buddha'. Alaungpaya
founded the Konbaung Dynasty which ruled the country until the late
19th century. He captured Ava in 1753 and two years later brought his
forces down the Irrawaddy River in a large flotilla and occupied Dagon,
the site of the greatly revered Shwedagon Pagoda. There he established
a new town called Yangon, meaning 'The End of Enmity/Hostility',
known by the English as Rangoon, the future capital of colonial and
independent Burma. In 1756 Alaungpaya captured Syriam, Lower
Burma's main trading port, and the following year took Binnya Dala's
royal capital Pegu. Even the then Shan Kingdom of Chiang Mai was
brought under his control.

Alaungpaya demanded that the king of Siam recognise his status as an
'embryo Buddha'. When the monarch refused, he laid siege to
Ayutthaya, the Siamese capital, but the siege was cut short when
Alaungpaya was struck down with fever. As a consequence his troops
made an orderly retreat back to Burmese territory, but the king died in
May 1760.

Ayutthaya, alas, was not safe from eager Burmese hands, for in April
1767 Hsinbyushin (1763-76), the Konbaung Dynasty's second great king,
completely destroyed this once great city, killing the king of Siam in the
process and leaving behind a legacy of hatred of their Burmese
neighbours which the Thais have not thrown off to this day. Having re-
established Ava as his royal capital, Hsinbyushin proceeded to become
embroiled in numerous entanglements with a much larger and more
serious enemy, the Chinese, who were disturbed by Burmese expansion
into the Shan States, Chiang Mai and Laos which bordered their
southwestern province of Yunnan. Hsinbyushin's final years were
marked by few accomplishments and he died in 1776, only to be
succeeded by his son Singu Min who ordered the withdrawal of Burmese
armies from Siamese territory.

Singu Min ruled until 1781 when he was assassinated. His successor
Maung Maung fared even worse, surviving for only seven days before

King Bodawpaya (1782-1819), the fourth son of Alaungpaya, seized power. Believing himself to be the Buddha reincarnated, Bodawpaya had many of his royal rivals massacred. He was responsible for the construction of the extraordinary Mingun Pagoda and the casting of the vast Mingun Bell. He conquered the Kingdom of Arakan and established a new capital at Amarapura (near Mandalay) in Upper Burma.

The megalomaniac Bodawpaya's harsh policies in Arakan, including the drafting of thousands for forced labour in Upper Burma, drove large numbers of refugees across the Naaf River into what was by that time British territory. Rebels used the Bengal side of this loosely defined border as a staging area for raids on Burmese garrisons in Arakan. The Burmese, claiming the right to cross the Naaf in hot pursuit of insurgents, caused increasing apprehension in the British and Burmese-British relations steadily deteriorated.

Bodawpaya died in 1819 and was succeeded by his grandson Bagyidaw. Like his grandfather, Bagyidaw continued to rile the British by pursuing aggressive policies both in the kingdoms of Assam and Manipur and on the Bengal border. Burmese forces marched into Assam, intervening in a succession struggle, which placed the British in a delicate position since both pretenders to the throne sought protection on British soil and organised resistance movements. Manipur was also invaded because its raja was reluctant to become a vassal of the new Burmese king. Beset by refugees from Manipur, the raja of yet another state, Cachar, fled to British Indian territory. In 1823 the British declared Cachar and a neighbouring state Jaintia protectorates. On the India-Arakan border, Burmese troops seized East India Company personnel and an island in the Naaf River claimed by the British.

In January 1824 Burmese forces marched into Cachar and fought British troops, and warring resumed on the Naaf River. Worried by the Burmese attempts to seize Bengal, the British governor general Lord Amherst ordered his forces by sea to Lower Burma, and captured Rangoon on May 10. The Burmese were thus obliged to forsake Arakan and return to Upper Burma.

The First Anglo-Burmese War lasted from 1824 until peace was restored with the signing of the Treaty of Yandabo on February 24 1826, providing for the cession of the territories of Arakan and Tenasserim to the British, an end to Burmese suzerainty over the Indian hill states of Assam and Manipur, an indemnity of £1 million to be paid to the British for the costs of the war, and the exchange of diplomatic representatives between Burma and British India. British troops left Rangoon in December 1826 after full payment of the indemnity; the treaty, however, was a shattering blow to Burmese pride. When representatives were exchanged, Bagyidaw tried to negotiate the return of Tenasserim, but in vain.

In 1837 Bagyidaw, growing increasingly insane and incompetent, was overthrown by his brother Tharrawaddy, but political stability was further undermined by revolts among the Shans in Lower Burma during the period of 1838-40. Tharrawaddy reneged on the Treaty of Yandabo and in 1839 formal diplomatic relations were severed. The king died seven years later, to be succeeded by his son Pagan Min, a wholly ineffective and corrupt monarch. Government in both Upper and Lower Burma steadily began to crumble, whilst unrest continued apace in the Shan States.

In 1852 the Second Anglo-Burmese War broke out over a dispute involving two British merchants who had been arrested by the Burmese Governor of Rangoon for evading customs duties. Britain, keen at this time to extend her empire and to put down what they deemed to be 'inferior natives', sent an armed naval escort to Rangoon to demand compensation and the removal of the Rangoon governor. The British further insisted that an indemnity of £100,000 be paid and that the king himself should apologise personally. By October, the British had seized Rangoon, Martaban, Bassein, Pegu and Prome. On December 20 1852, it was announced that Lower Burma would be annexed as a province of British India.

Following a revolt by his half-brother Mindon Min at Shwebo in December 1852, Pagan Min was deposed and forced into retirement in February 1853. The new King Mindon refused to recognise the annexation of Lower Burma, but did not resume hostilities.

A peaceful, intellectual[1] ruler and devout Buddhist, King Mindon exercised a conciliatory attitude towards the British and extended diplomatic contacts with other Western countries. Like the monarchs before him, he also moved his capital, this time from Amarapura to a site a few miles away at the foot of Mandalay Hill. In 1861 he constructed a teak palace enclosed by square walls 2km long on each side.

King Mindon died on October 1 1878 and was succeeded by his 19-year-old son Thibaw. A weakling, he was shrewdly manipulated by his 'secondary queen' Supayalat, the Central Palace queen's second daughter. She ousted her elder sister as Thibaw's chief queen and even undermined the position of her mother. Thibaw himself was a heinous monarch: he disposed of over 80 relatives (the most important princes

---

1 'Intellectual' may be a matter of some dispute. Sir George Scott — alias Shway Yoe — referred to King Mindon as being 'kindly and ignorant'. He relates an episode when, in 1874, Mindon heard the news that Gladstone had lost the election and was to be replaced by Disraeli. The King is alleged to have sighed and said, 'Then poor Ga-la-sa-tong is in prison, I suppose I am sorry for him. I don't think he was a bad fellow, and I gave him the Fifteen-string Salwe (the Burmese Order of Knighthood) a year or two ago'.

and princesses) by having them sewn up in sacks of red velvet and clubbed to death, or trampled upon by the royal elephants.

'When the foundations of the city wall were laid, 52 persons of both sexes, and of various ages and rank, were consigned to a living tomb. Three were buried under each of the 12 city gates, one at each of the four corners, one under each of the palace gates... and four under the throne itself. Along with the four human beings buried at the corners of the city were placed four jars full of oil, carefully covered over. These were examined every seven years by the royal astrologers, and as long as they remained intact the town was considered safe.'

Sir George Scott

At the third examination in 1880, it was found that the oil in two of the jars had dried up. This discovery coincided with various other incidents of ill omen, including an outbreak of smallpox. The astrologers advised Thibaw to change the capital, but he refused. The astrologers held another meeting and decided that the only alternative was to offer propitiatory sacrifices and that the number should be the highest possible: 100 men, 100 women, 100 boys, 100 girls, 100 soldiers and 100 foreigners. This Thibaw agreed to and a royal mandate was signed and arrests began. A terrible panic spread in Mandalay and there ensued a mass exodus from the city. The announcement of the impending massacres caused an outcry in England, and Thibaw's ministers took fright. The mandate was countermanded, though it is widely believed that out of the 100 already arrested, some were secretly buried alive under each of the posts at the 12 gates as a compromise between the fear of the spirits and the fear that the English troops would cross the border.

Thibaw's fatal blunder, however, was to seek an alliance with the French (already at that time involved in a war with China over Vietnam whilst extending her influence into Laos) as a counterbalance to the British. He signed a contract which was to allow France to build a railway to Mandalay and to place a flotilla on the Irrawaddy. A strong French presence in Upper Burma was perceived as a strategic threat to India, which the British could not tolerate. Britain, herself, was eager to annex Upper Burma for that would open up the supposedly rich markets of southwestern China.

And so eventually British forces sailed from Thayetmyo further up the Irrawaddy in a flotilla of steamboats on November 17 1885. The Third, and final, Anglo-Burmese War had begun. The capital Mandalay fell on November 28 and an armistice was hastily drawn up. King Thibaw (caught napping in the royal bathing-pool when General Prendergast entered the palace, demanding his instant surrender and abdication) and Queen Supayalat refused to flee and were banished to India. Thibaw never saw his native country again, dying in exile at Ratnagiri on the

A Burmese princess

Bombay coast in 1916, though Supayalat was allowed to return to Burma on a yearly stipend of £1,800 before her death in Rangoon in December 1925. In February 1886 Burma became a directly administered province of British India.

'An extremely bad government Theebau's undoubtedly was, and he is, of course, responsible for its crimes, but there is good reason to think that he never instigated, and was often remorseful for them. After the execution of his brothers, he for a time drank heavily, and I was told at the time that this began in an attempt to drown his remorse. The habit was encouraged by men who had designs upon his life and throne — their subsequent execution was called a massacre — but he had long entirely abandoned it. Personally, Theebau always appeared to me — and I saw him a number of times — a stupid, rather sensual-looking, but amiable young man. He had a particularly soft and sweet voice, a very unusual thing for a Burman.'

J Annan Bryce, 1886

By 1890 there were some 60,000 British troops and police in Burma, their responsibility being to suppress the large numbers of armed bandits and insurgents in the land. There was unrest throughout the country, exacerbated by the fact that the British recruited Karens to fight Burmans. By 1889 the Shan States were brought under British rule.

During this period, however, swift economic progress was taking place: the development of efficient steamship transportation, the opening of the Suez Canal in 1869 and the construction of railways (reaching Mandalay by 1889, Myitkyina by 1898 and Lashio by 1902) all drew the country more tightly into the international economic system in ways that would have as far-reaching consequences as had the extinction of the Konbaung Kingdom in 1886. Between 1870 and 1926-27 the value of exports increased 20 times and the value of imports 15 times. Modern, large-scale Western enterprise was firmly established: teak, rice, mining (rubies), tin, tungsten and petroleum were all exploited to the full. Land under cultivation grew by 145,300 hectares between 1861 and 1870 and between 1890 and 1900 rice land increased by 943,900 hectares. In the early 1870s the annual average of rice exported was 732,000 tons; by 1900 this had become 2.5 million, by 1920 3.6 million.

All this required extra labour and though there was some Chinese immigration after 1852, the vast majority of immigrants during the late 19th and early 20th centuries came from the regions of Bengal and Madras in India. Indeed by the end of the 19th century, India was supplying most of the workers for Lower Burma's rice-mills and dockyards and for the other burgeoning industries. The total was further swelled by natural disasters in Madras and Bengal which drove more and more immigrants into Burma. The Indian population of Lower Burma increased from 297,000 in 1901 to 583,000 30 years later. By 1918 around 300,000 labourers had come to Rangoon: 13 years later the city's population consisted of 50% Indian, but only 36% Burmese, with lower percentages of Chinese, Indo-Burmese, Eurasians and Europeans. English and Indian, rather than Burmese, were the languages most often spoken in the streets and offices.

All the while, however, resentment on behalf of the Burmese was growing, mainly over nationalist issues but also over economic hardship. By 1930 there were mounting communal tensions as Burmese cultivators found themselves at the mercy of Chettiar money-lenders and as labourers in the port cities competed with Indian immigrants for jobs which were becoming increasingly scarce. In May 1930 there was a riot in Rangoon involving Burmese and Indian dockworkers, and indeed throughout the 1930s there were sporadic outbreaks of violence against the Indian and Chinese communities. In July 1938 renegade Buddhist monks led Burmese mobs through Rangoon on a rampage of killing which resulted in the deaths of around 200 Indians.

Further unrest amongst the Burmese stemmed from a variety of causes, but essentially it was the desire to rid themselves of British colonial rule. This had been simmering ever since the annexation of Upper Burma, particularly in the rural areas where a 'saviour king', or Setkya Min, had promised to liberate the people from the colonialists. The most widespread of these movements first appeared in 1930, when in October of that year Saya San, a traditional Burmese physician and member of an organisation called the General Council of Burmese Associations (GCBA), formed in 1919-20, proclaimed himself king, setting up a palace with royal insignia in Tharrawaddy District north of Rangoon. The rebels, however, armed just with spears and swords, were no match for the superior British forces and the uprising was subdued by 1932.

During the 1930s nationalists were divided as to whether Burma should continue to remain part of India or separate from it. Those against separation argued that Burma would not be able to profit from further political reforms taking place in India unless it were granted self-governing dominion status, which the British were not prepared to accord. The British Parliament, however, voted for separation and approved a new constitution for Burma in 1935 over the spirited opposition of many nationalists. Under the new system a British governor of Burma still retained extensive powers, though a nine-member cabinet was appointed by the governor in consultation with an elected House of Representatives. Elections were held in 1936, and when the new constitution was implemented the following year, Dr Ba Maw, leader of the Sinyetha (Poor Man's) Party, was chosen Prime Minister by a coalition of parties. Ba Maw, the self-styled *A-na-shin* or 'dictator', was half-Armenian, with an alleged doctorate from Bordeaux University.

The *Dobama Asi-ayone* (We Burmans Association) had emerged in 1930-31 during the Saya San rebellion in part as an urban response to what was essentially a village phenomenon. Its members drew attention to themselves by calling each other *thakin* or master. This was an act of defiance, because the word was customarily used by Burmese as a respectful term of address to the British, like the term *sahib* in India. The founders of the association claimed that the Burmese must develop a 'master mentality' as opposed to the 'slave mentality' which the British had imposed. Their choice of the term *thakin* was viewed as a first step in this direction, and they were soon known to the general public as Thakins, gaining national prominence through Rangoon University. In the autumn of 1935 Maung Nu and Aung San were elected president and secretary respectively of the Rangoon University Student Union (RUSU).

Aung San was born on February 13 1915 in the township of Natmauk in the oil-fields of Yenangyaung, central Burma. His father was a moderately prosperous landowner. A grand-uncle on his mother's side had been a prominent leader of the resistance movement in Upper Burma after it was annexed by the British in 1885-6. He was educated at the local vernacular school, the Yenangyaung High School, and went up to Rangoon University with the intention of trying to join the Indian Civil Service. The university was a hotbed of nationalist politics and Aung San soon plunged into the students' political movements. He became editor of *Oway* magazine, the organ of the All-Burma Students' Union, and the union's second and third president. He was known as a taciturn, strong-willed and capable president, who seemed to think and act in sudden bouts of violence. Some students were afraid of him, others worshipped him. He was rusticated for an article in *Oway* and this led to the country-wide students' strike of 1936. The quarrel was patched up, but before leaving the university Aung San was again threatened with expulsion for his political activities. He obtained his BA degree in history and political science, but never completed the law course which he had intended to do. In October 1938 Aung San joined the Thakin Party, became its organising secretary, and after three months its general secretary.

The Thakins succeeded in having two of their members elected to the legislature in the 1936 election. They were among the first groups to force the issue of outright independence, expressed by the rural followers of Saya San, into the urban and university arena. And in particular it was Aung San who proposed independence in terms of 'Burmese' rather than 'Burman' nationalism. Permeated with an ultra-nationalist spirit, the Thakins had no single, consistent political ideology — their statements had a vaguely Communist basis, their emblem was the hammer and sickle. As general secretary of this party, Aung San helped to organise the strikes and disturbances of 1938-9 and for a time was detained in gaol.

Short, wiry, sallow, with fine eyes and a commanding presence, Aung San himself assumed the responsibilities of the nationalist revolution. A man of sudden impulses and a terrible temper, he had little knowledge of and not much liking for social reform. His greatest contribution to Burmese nationalism was the decisive cast he gave to it, repeating continually that freedom on paper was less valuable than real freedom.

In February 1939 Ba Maw was replaced as prime minister by Tharrawaddy U Pu. In September of that year, as war broke out in Europe, Ba Maw's *Sinyetha* Party joined forces with the Burma Revolutionary Party, a Thakin group formed by Kodaw Hmaing (a former Buddhist monk and writer and one of the founders of the Dobama Asi-ayone) and Aung San, to form the Freedom Bloc, a coalition committed to total independence. Aung San became acting secretary of this Freedom Bloc. In September 1940 U Pu's government was replaced by one formed by U Saw, head of the *Myochit* ('Party of Patriots' or 'Lovers of their Country') Party, who attempted to suppress the Freedom Bloc and to persuade the British to grant Burma full self-governing or dominion status.

Increasing Japanese interest in Burma at this time stemmed not only from the fact that the country was rich in strategic resources (such as oil), but also because the Burma Road provided a route through which the Allies could supply the Chiang Kai-shek government in Chongqing. Its severance would hasten a successful conclusion of the war with China. In 1939 Japanese agents contacted Ba Maw who, the following year, discussed the possibility of obtaining Japanese support for independence with his ally Aung San. In August 1940 Aung San and a fellow Thakin were smuggled out of Burma on a ship bound for Amoy, subsequently reaching Tokyo, to lay the groundwork for the armed struggle against the British in concert with Japanese advances into Southeast Asia.

An intelligence organisation, the *Minami Kikan*, was set up by the Japanese military to coordinate operations in Burma. Aung San returned home, contacted the Thakins and arranged to smuggle a small group of men out of the country. Together the so-called 'Thirty Comrades' — as they came to be known — received military training from the Japanese on Hainan Island off the south coast of China. They formed the core of the Burma Independence Army (BIA), established in Bangkok in late December 1941, whilst underground movements were being organised within Burma itself. When Japanese forces began the invasion of the Tenasserim area along the Andaman Sea and other parts of Lower Burma in January 1942, the BIA aided their advance, occasionally engaging retreating British forces in combat. One of the 'Thirty Comrades', Thakin Shu Maung, infiltrated Rangoon in early February and organised sabotage activities. This man, who was born near Prome on May 24 1911 and who had started his career as a humble postal clerk, was to become better known by his *nom de guerre* Ne Win (meaning 'brilliant like the sun'). Rangoon fell in March 1942, British troops withdrew to and evacuated Mandalay, and in May the Burma Road was cut off.

When most of Burma was in Japanese hands, Ba Maw was made prime minister (in August 1942) and Aung San commander of the 4,000-strong Burma Defence Army, the successor of the BIA. In January 1943 the Japanese Prime Minister Hideki annnounced that independence would be granted by the end of the year. In August Ba Maw was proclaimed head of state in a ceremony in Rangoon that recalled the traditions of Burmese kingship. He assumed the title of *Adipadi* or 'Head of State'. *Bo-gyoke* (General) Aung San was appointed Minister of Defence and Commander of the new Burma National Army (BNA), and Thakin Nu, Minister of Foreign Affairs. In reality Ba Maw's government had very little actual power: norminally independent, Burma was seen by Tokyo as an economic and strategic component of its all-out war effort, a fact of which Aung San was fully aware. All the while he was secretly organising resistance plans against the Japanese, incorporating, amongst others, such diverse groups as the Karen National Organisation, the Japanese-sponsored East Asia Youth League, former associates from *Dobama Asi-ayone* days, and the leftists.

Lord Mountbatten, head of the South-East Asia Command, agreed to cooperate with Aung San. The 1944 Japanese offensive into India through Manipur had failed, and by the end of January 1945 Allied troops had reopened the Burma Road and captured Myitkyina. On March 27 Aung San, receiving a signal from Mountbatten, led a revolt of the BNA, which began attacking Japanese units. Rangoon was captured in early May, though hostilities continued in various parts of the country up to and even after the Japanese surrender on August 15 1945. At the end of May 1945 the BNA was officially recognised as a component of Allied Forces and renamed the Patriotic Burmese Forces (PBF).

But if, in return for aiding the British, General Aung San was to expect the immediate granting of Burmese independence, he was to be disappointed. On May 17 1945, the Churchill Government issued a white paper proclaiming a very conservative programme: the 1937 constitution, with its elective prime minister, was to be suspended and the governor, appointed by London, would retain all authority. Although what the British called 'Burma Proper' (a term used by the colonialists to describe the central region of the country), where the population was predominantly Burman, would be given 'full self-government within the Commonwealth' after 1948, the Shan States and the other border regions inhabited by non-Burman minorities would remain under British rule indefinitely. Thus in essence it granted Burma less than the Japanese had, even though Ba Maw himself had only been a puppet leader.

Aung San initiated a campaign against the white paper at a mass meeting in Rangoon on August 19 1945, demanding that independence be granted immediately. There was universal discontent: a general strike broke out in September 1946 and the country rapidly degenerated into chaos. The British governor, Hubert Rance, with few troops at his disposal, was forced to comply with Aung San's demands. A new executive council was formed; Aung San served as deputy chairman, and six of its 11 members were supporters of the Anti-Fascist People's Freedom League (AFPFL). The general strike ended on October 2 1946. In December of that year, Labour Prime Minster Clement Attlee invited Aung San and other political leaders to London. On January 27 1947, Attlee and Aung San signed an agreement calling for full independence within a year, elections for a constituent assembly within four months, continued British aid, British sponsorship of Burma to membership of international organisations and, most significantly, the promise that the border areas would be included within the boundaries of the new nation.

In April 1947 elections were held for the Constituent Assembly. There were a total of 255 seats, Burma Proper being allotted 210, of which 24 were reserved for the Karens and four for Anglo-Burmans, and the border areas were apportioned 45. The AFPFL won an overwhelming victory, returning 248 representatives, most of whom were socialists or members of the People's Volunteer Organisation (PVO), which was in effect the private army of the AFPFL. The assembly met on June 9, and Thakin Nu was chosen as its president.

On the morning of July 19 1947, a mere 40 days later, gunmen entered the Secretariat building in central Rangoon and assassinated Aung San and seven of his ministers. The general concensus was that U Saw, left out of the political process after the January 1947 Attlee-Aung San agreement, had plotted the murders, apparently nurturing the desperate hope that with Aung San out of the way, the British governor would turn to him to lead the country. It was possible that he was also planning a takeover by force. But the crime was carelessly conceived: the assassins were traced to U Saw's house by the police, and U Saw and his accomplices were immediately arrested.

An unpredictable but complex character, U Saw was an immensely wealthy Burman from the Irrawaddy Delta who had been educated partly in Calcutta in 1919-20 during the years when Gandhi's non-cooperation movement was beginning, and partly at Cambridge. With his own private aeroplane, he clearly represented the interests of the rich rice-owners, having played a minor role in the short-lived rebellion of 1930, when Saya San had led a vast movement of protest against the dominant forces. Saya San, known as *Galon* after the bird of the Indian fable that could kill snakes, was later executed in Tharrawaddy gaol; U Saw thereupon began to call himself Galon U Saw, and to regard himself as the leader of the movement of resistance. He was not a very successful leader. In 1932 he was arrested for sedition; in 1933 he became a member of the Corporation of Rangoon and the editor of *The Sun*, a leading daily newspaper. During the following year he began his interest in Japan. He flew to Tokyo, travelled through Korea and Manchuria, and was given to understand that in the event of war breaking out he would be given important positions. He wrote a guide to Japan, and returned to Burma, where he was again sentenced to imprisonment in 1937. Twenty days after his release he received the important portfolio of Minister of Forest Lands. In 1940 he became premier and visited Britain as Burmese prime minister the following year. However, he was rebuffed by the government and was arrested and interned in Uganda on his way home. Seven years later — in May 1948 — U Saw (and his associates) would be executed for the murder of Aung San.

The sudden, violent death of Aung San, the architect of Burma's independence, at the age of just 32 stunned the nation. In spite of his youth and lack of any political philosophy, Aung San had kept the strings together in a single hand. He was unlike any leader the Far East had thrown up, remininiscent in some ways of the Argentinian Perón. 'The Burmese,' Aung San once said, 'will have no hesitation in using force if the demand for independence, desired by all of them, is not met.'

All that had been carefully constructed now seemed on the verge of collapse. Governor Hubert Rance, however, wisely showed no inclination to use the assassination as a pretext to delay the independence process. He appointed Thakin Nu, president of the Constituent Assembly and vice-president of the AFPFL, prime minister forthwith.

On September 24 1947, the Constituent Assembly approved the constitution of the independent Union of Burma. It provided for a parliamentary system of government and a bicameral legislature. The Upper House, the Chamber of Nationalities, had strong minority representation (72 out of 125 members were non-Burman); the Lower House, the Chamber of Deputies, was elected from geographical constituencies defined by population. It nominated the prime minister, who in turn was responsible to it, whereas the president of the Union of Burma had only formal powers as head of state. Shortly afterwards there followed the creation of the Shan and Kachin States and later also the Karenni (Kayah) State. The Chins of the western border were not granted a state, but a Chin Special Division was established. Although a Karen State was not set up, a referendum on this issue was promised and the Karen Affairs Council was created to 'aid and advise the Union Government on matters relating to the Karens'. On October 17 1947, Prime Ministers U Nu and Clement Attlee signed a treaty formally recognising the independence of the Union of Burma. The British agreed to cancel a £15 million debt and provide a military mission. The Burmese government claimed the right to expropriate British properties, though with adequate compensation for the firms involved. On December 10 1947, the British Parliament (despite spirited opposition from Churchill's Conservative Party) passed the Burma Independence Act and January 4 of the following year was set as the date for the transfer of power.

'When we left in January 1948, the future of Burma looked bright. If things have turned out, as alas they have, not to have that gleam that once we believed in, it is because civil war between the Burmese and Karens followed upon dissension amongst the Burmese themselves. We can but hope these troubles will soon cease and that there will be a true union of her peoples. This will be necessary if — as is likely — she is overwhelmed by a greater power.'

F Tennyson Jesse

Taking full advantage of Burma's newly created independence, various factions began to stir up trouble throughout the country: communists, Muslim rebels, Karen leaders (embittered by what they perceived as British desertion of their people and disillusioned with the non-creation of a Karen State) and Kachin commanders attempting to suppress the communists in central Burma, all instigated disorder. By 1951 a government minister actually admitted that less than half the country was under effective state control, and in many areas its authority was limited to the daylight hours. To compound matters, a new threat had surfaced in 1949 as the Chinese Civil War spilled over on to Burmese territory. After Yunnan Province in southern China was taken over by the communist People's Liberation Army, Nationalist (Kuomintang) forces crossed the border into Burma and began using the frontier area as a base from which to attack the communist forces. Before long these troops (numbering as many as 12,000 by 1953 and known as the Chinese Irregular Forces, the CIF) had entrenched themselves in Shan State. From fighting the communists, they turned their attention to establishing a lucrative opium export business, extending their control over most of the eastern part of Shan State. Here a system of 'war-lordism' flourished which gradually spread into western Laos and northern Thailand, creating the infamous 'Golden Triangle'. By 1953 over 80% of the Burma Army was occupied in fighting CIF groups, which they were never to succeed in dislodging from their Shan State stronghold.

For ten years from the granting of independence, Burmese politics was dominated by the AFPFL, whose popular support was assured through its historical role as the party of *Bo-gyoke* Aung San, though it remained a coalition of diverse individuals and groups. U Nu's chief economic policies consisted essentially of land reform, nationalisation and the establishment of a socialist welfare state, but these were never going to be easy goals to achieve. The government found itself increasingly dependent on foreign aid (such as Japanese war reparations, the equivalent of some US$250 million, grants from the United States and long-term loans from the World Bank); even the Soviet Union and other communist countries donated gifts and loans and agreed to purchase surplus Burmese rice. By 1960 many sectors of the economy had not even returned to pre-war levels: petroleum and teak exports, for example, were down to 52% and 39% of pre-war levels. Burma's position in the international economic system was rapidly deteriorating, necessitating the government to change tack and to emphasise instead the development of the economy through encouragement of the private sector. This notion, proposed in the Four-Year Plan of 1962, was to have dire consequences, for it aroused the discontent of those military officers (most notably Ne Win) committed to a socialist policy. Ne Win, in fact, had previously served as caretaker prime minister (proposed, ironically as it turned out, by U Nu himself) from October 1958 until February 1960, since U Nu, desperate to resolve an increasingly worsening situation, had requested the army to assume temporary control. (It now seems that the 1958 military takeover was also a *coup*.)

In February 1960 Ne Win began the process of reinstating a civilian government by holding elections for parliament. For the first time in Burma's history more than half the electorate (59%) turned out to vote and U Nu won a landslide victory. U Nu reorganised his party and renamed it the *Pyidaungsu* (Union League) Party, but not even a change of name could bolster the party's internal divisions and U Nu was forced to relinquish his post as party president. Both the effectiveness of the government and the economy were on the wane: the time was ripe for Ne Win to step in once again. On March 2 1962 the petty postal clerk from Prome who had renamed himself 'brilliant like the sun' seized power in a military *coup*. The 1947 constitution was suspended, parliament dissolved and several eminent political figures, including U Nu, were arrested.

The date of April 30 1962 is one remembered with trepidation by many Burmese, for it was the day that Ne Win's newly formed Revolutionary Council (consisting of high-ranking military officers) announced 'The Burmese Way to Socialism'. This resulted in political alignment with the socialist bloc, closing the country to the West, censorship, driving out Indians and Europeans and civil war.

For 12 years Burma faltered, languished and declined. In April 1972 Ne Win and 20 other military leaders resigned their commissions, though Ne Win remained as prime minister and head of the Burma Socialist Programme Party (BSPP, or *Lanzin* in Burmese). A new constitution was announced on January 3 1974; two months later the Revolutionary Council (Ne Win's 'flagship') dissolved itself and power was transferred to the newly elected People's Assembly (*Pyithu Hluttaw*). Ne Win proclaimed himself president and the 'new' Socialist Republic of the Union of Burma was created.

For seven years, from 1974-81, Ne Win's continued reign was dominated by strikes, student unrest, insurgency, massive inflation, declining exports, smuggling, opium trafficking, and complete isolation from the outside world.

In August 1981 at the Fourth Congress of the BSPP, Ne Win stunned the Burmese nation by announcing his intention to retire as president following the October elections to the People's Assembly. In November he was succeeded by San Yu, the former BSPP general secretary, though he retained his post as leader of the BSPP. A complex and unpredictable character, Ne Win differed from other modern-day dictators (like Ceaucescu or Honecker, for example) by consistently and single-mindedly placing enormous emphasis on astrology and numerology. For years Ne Win hid himself away in a luxurious, heavily guarded villa by Inya Lake in Rangoon; on the other side of the lake on University Avenue, as irony would have it, lay the home of Daw Khin Kyi, widow of Burma's independence hero *Bo-gyoke* Aung San and mother of Daw Aung San Suu Kyi.

Daw Aung San Suu Kyi was barely two years old when her father died, yet, despite spending much of her early life out of the country, she never forgot her background and heritage. Cultured, elegant, charismatic — and always 'Burmese' — Suu received her university education at St Hugh's College, Oxford, where, perhaps somewhat surprisingly in the light of subsequent events, she rarely took an active role in politics. And yet before her marriage to British Tibetologist Michael Aris in 1972, she was known to have remarked, 'The day might come when my country may need me as it had needed my father'.

Maybe it was fate, then, that brought Daw Aung San Suu Kyi back to Burma in April 1988, though the actual reason was for Suu to look after her mother Daw Khin Kyi, who had suffered a severe stroke (and who was to die just eight months later on December 27). The country by now was in deep decline and on the verge of ripping itself apart. Ne Win's idiosyncratic management of the economy had resulted in dire financial consequences, the final, damning indictment of which came on December 11 1987 when Burma was granted the UN-afforded status of Least Developed Country (LDC). Foreign debt had reached a massive US$3.5 billion at the same time as foreign exchange reserves had shrunk to US$20-30 million. Burma's per capita income had slipped to below US$200 and manufacturing was at less than 10% of the GDP. In the 1970s Burma prided itself on its high literacy rate (it won a UNESCO prize for this), and in order to obtain LDC status it had to fiddle the literacy figures (some say from as high as 81%) to make them appear low enough to qualify.

It had been a sorry degeneration into poverty and civil discontent, but not wholly unpredictable if one examines Burma's turbulent past. Nonetheless, Ne Win's rule was characterised by bizarre moves and punctuated with singular, seemingly illogical acts. On September 5 1987, for example, Sein Lwin (secretary of the State Council) decreed that all 25, 35 and 75 kyat banknotes were to be demonetised without compensation (the 75 kyat note had been introduced by Ne Win himself to celebrate his 75th birthday). In a trice, 80% of the country's money in circulation was wiped out, and many students found themselves far from home and penniless. Instead of bolstering the economy, this action had exactly the opposite effect: it created massive inflation, increased still further the already rampant (and illegal) black market activity and caused profound resentment and distrust amongst the student population.

'The Burman is easygoing, casual and satisfied with a little. When a great increase of the population of Burma has rendered the struggle for existence much more urgent than it is now, the Burman will either have to bestir himself or go to the wall.'

W R Winston, 1892

This latest economic move was too much for the students to take: over 500 spilled out on to the streets of Rangoon destroying government vehicles in a Bacchanalian rampage. The state responded by immediately closing all the universities and colleges. In another bizarre twist the following month, new banknotes were issued in the denomination of 45 and 90 kyat. In reality this was quite typical of Ne Win: both 45 and 90 added up to and were divisible by nine, Ne Win's lucky number.

The year 1988 began just as 1987 had ended, with a floundering economy and massive discontent amongst the student population. Following a minor incident in a tea shop, on March 13 students clashed with the elite death squad *Lon Htein* (riot police); three days later the scenes became even uglier. The *Lon Htein* gunned down a number of students in cold blood: one of the most brutal periods in Burma's history was just dawning (a period recently documented in John Boorman's film *Beyond Rangoon*). The following day at least 1,000 students were arrested and taken to Insein gaol, north of Rangoon.

On March 18 ('Bloody Friday') thousands of students converged on the Sule Pagoda. Under the command of Sein Lwin, thereafter known as the 'Butcher of Rangoon', the *Lon Htein* and *Tatmadaw* (military) moved in and scores of demonstrators were murdered.

Two months later, on June 20, over 5,000 students staged a peaceful protest in Rangoon; the following day hordes of students marched towards central Rangoon chanting slogans. Once again the *Lon Htein* intervened and around 80 protesters were massacred. The state responded by announcing a 60-day ban on public gatherings and imposing an 1800 to 0600 curfew in Rangoon. However, on June 23 the students established a strike centre at the Shwedagon Pagoda. In Pegu, meanwhile, 80km northeast of the capital, there were further bloody clashes and at least 70 people were shot.

Exactly one month later, the Burma Socialist Programme Party (the BSPP) convened a special session which was attended by over 1,000 delegates. Ne Win appeared, closely shadowed by his most loyal subject Khin Nyunt, and began a 30-minute address. To the surprise of those present, Ne Win put forward a proposal for a new parliament and for the creation of a multi-party system (thus, in theory anyway, making Burma the first so-called 'socialist' country to permit a multi-party system; but, as time was to show, little would come of the motion). It was, though, what Ne Win didn't say that caused more consternation — or rather what was announced on his behalf by Htwe Han, the BSPP Central Committee Headquarters secretary. Since Ne Win felt in some small measure responsible for the tragic events of the previous two months and since he was now advancing in years, he had decided to quit as party chairman and party member. More was to follow: not only would Ne Win resign, but so too would San Yu, the BSPP's vice chairman and state president, BSPP General Secretary Aye Ko, Defence Minister Kyaw Htin, Finance Minister Tun Tin, and Joint Secretary General Sein Lwin. Indeed the very core of Burma's military leadership was apparently resigning *en masse*. In reality, Ne Win had absolutely no intention of relinquishing power (most political observers agree that he never has had).

Three days later the Central Committee of the BSPP held a meeting, choosing Sein Lwin as Ne Win's successor. The following day Sein Lwin was elected chairman of the Council of State. No move could have been better calculated to enrage the students, for Sein Lwin (a subordinate of Ne Win in the Fourth Burma Rifles) had, of course, acquired the nickname the 'Butcher of Rangoon' for ordering the *Lon Htein* to cut down the demonstrators in the spring. In fact, Sein Lwin's record of anti-student violence stretched back over a quarter of a century as he had also been responsible for student deaths at the hands of the military and the dynamiting of the Rangoon University Student Union building in 1962; he had also played a part in brutally suppressing the student demonstrations in 1974 at the time of the funeral of former UN Secretary General U Thant.

July 28, one of the holiest days in Burma's calendar, was the Full Moon Day of *Wa-zo*, the beginning of the Buddhist Lent, and a number of students and anti-government protesters congregated at the Shwedagon, Rangoon's most sacred pagoda. Four days later an underground student organisation, the All-Burma Students' Union (*Ba ka tha*) brazenly distributed leaflets calling for a national strike on August 8, which was a highly auspicious day in the Burmese calendar (8s were said to be lucky for the opposition, whereas 9s were favourable to Ne Win; this was 8.8.88). Symbolically, it was also the date of the fall of the Ava Dynasty according to the Burmese era, 888 BE (AD 1526). On August 3 the government declared martial law; 10,000 demonstrators defied the ban, however, and marched through the centre of Rangoon. From August 3 until the proposed day of the general strike, hundreds of protesters were arrested for flouting martial law.

At precisely eight minutes past eight o'clock on the morning of August 8 1988, the dockworkers in the port of Rangoon walked out. The strike was on. Monks, women, students, people from all ethnic groups marched through the city waving portraits of Aung San, demanding democracy and economic reform. All over the land they demonstrated: from Mandalay, Sagaing and Shwebo in the north to Bassein in the Irrawaddy Delta, from Pegu, Toungoo, Pyinmana and Minbu in the central plains to the towns of Yenangyaung and Chauk along the Irrawaddy River, from Moulmein, Mergui and Tavoy in the south to Taunggyi, capital of Shan State, even as far north as Myitkyina, the capital of the northern Kachin State.

In Rangoon, meanwhile, the *Tatmadaw*, anxious and unsure, waited in the wings. At 5.30pm Rangoon's commander Myo Nyunt ordered the crowds to disperse or face the consequences. Instead, more people joined in and the throngs swelled. At 11pm hordes of demonstrators still remained outside the Sule Pagoda; all of a sudden, trucks of soldiers appeared from behind the City Hall. Monks, women, children, schoolgirls and students fled, terrified, in every direction as they tried to escape the bursts of gunfire. No one knows the exact number who perished, nor how many were massacred in pagoda-studded Sagaing the following day where countless unrecognisable bodies were dumped into the Irrawaddy River.

'Tell my sons, that when they come of age and join the army, they must understand that the army is the best training school that can produce men of virtue and valour.'

Rangoon Commander, Myo Nyunt, October 21 1993

It was now four months since Daw Aung San Suu Kyi had returned to Burma to care for her ailing mother. No longer could she bear to watch her countrymen and women suffer: she was under pressure from students and friends to assume the mantle of her late father Aung San. On August 26 a large crowd, many of them merely curious, turned up at the hallowed Shwedagon Pagoda. They had come to catch their first glimpse of the daughter of *Bo-gyoke* Aung San, whose huge portrait had been placed alongside a resistance flag of World War II above the stage where she was to speak.

'A number of people are saying that since I've spent most of my life abroad and am married to a foreigner, I could not be familiar with the ramifications of this country's politics. I wish to speak out very frankly and openly. It's true that I've lived abroad. It is also true that I am married to a foreigner. But these facts have never, and will never, interfere with or lessen my love and devotion for my country by any measure or degree. People have been saying that I know nothing of Burmese politics. The trouble is I know too much. My family knows better than any how devious Burmese politics can be and how much my father had to suffer on this account... The present crisis is the concern of the entire nation. I could not, as my father's daughter, remain indifferent to all that was going on. This national crisis could, in fact, be called the the second struggle for independence.'

With these words, delivered in flawless Burmese, Daw Aung San Suu Kyi won over the hearts of the people, and at the same time set herself on a fateful collision course with U Ne Win.

Burma remained in a state of chaotic uncertainty until, at 1600 on September 18 (after 37 days under the leadership of another of Ne Win's allies, Dr Maung Maung), the music programme of the BBS (Burma Broadcasting Service) was interrupted by the following announcement:

'In order to bring a timely halt to the deteriorating conditions on all sides all over the country and in the interests of the people, the defence forces have assumed all power in the state with effect from today.'

This was the birth of the 'State Law and Order Restoration Council' (the 'SLORC'), another of Ne Win's military ruling groups. Ostensibly under the command of General Saw Maung, one of Ne Win's staunchest allies, the SLORC imposed a curfew on Rangoon from 2000 to 0400 and banned all gatherings of more than five people. The Burmese term for the 'SLORC' is *Na-Wa-Ta aso-ya*; *Na* = *Naingngan-daw* (State); *Wa* = *nyein-wut pi-pya-hmu* (Law and Order); *Ta* = *ti-hsauk-yay* (Restoration). The term for 'Law and Order', *nyein-wut pi-pya-hmu,* means 'quiet and subdued' or, literally, 'quiet, bowed down, pressed upon and flattened' and was used 100 years before.

On September 20 General Saw Maung pronounced himself prime minister, foreign minister and defence minister all at the same time. But both he and the 'State Law and Order Restoration Council' were soon to realise (most reluctantly) that the Burmese people would and could never accept or tolerate a one-party state. Concessions would have to be made to save the country from plunging even further into civil unrest and bankruptcy. Multi-party democratic elections were promised, and thus four days later Brigadier-General Aung Gyi (who had twice been imprisoned for his opposition to Ne Win in 1965 and 1973), General Tin U (likewise in 1976) and Daw Aung San Suu Kyi set up the National League for Democracy (NLD), which was registered as a political party on September 27.

Daw Aung San Suu Kyi, likening this struggle to Burma's earlier struggle for independence, threw herself wholeheartedly into the political fray. Tirelessly she toured the country, drawing vast crowds wherever she went. On one occasion, within a period of 13 days, she visited more than 50 towns and villages in Pegu, Magwe, Sagaing and Mandalay Divisions, as well as the Shan, Kayah and Karen States. Wherever she travelled, she was harassed and provoked by the SLORC and the

Tatmadaw and vilified in the state-run national press. Not once, however, did she flinch nor weary in her struggle to win democracy, respect and reforms for the Burmese people.

Eventually on February 16 1989 the BBS announced that elections would be held the following spring. Saw Maung was desperate to prevent further unrest and was convinced that the outcome of any election would reveal a hopelessly splintered opposition. But Daw Aung San Suu Kyi continued her campaigning throughout the land, constantly defying the authorities, until finally, as far as the SLORC was concerned, she overstepped the mark. Her outspokenness and honesty proved her undoing in June that year.

> '"U Ne Win", she daringly proclaimed, "is one of those that caused this nation to suffer for 26 years, U Ne Win is the one who lowered the prestige of the armed forces. Officials from the armed forces and officials from SLORC, I call upon you to be loyal to the state. Be loyal to the people, you don't have to be loyal to U Ne Win."'

Fearful and timorous, both the *Tatmadaw* and the SLORC remained loyal to Ne Win and, on July 20, Daw Aung San Suu Kyi was placed under house arrest.

> 'The possession of power is ruin to the Burmese character; so much so, that the governors and the governed seem to possess almost different natures. It is rare to find a man in authority who is not oppressive, corrupt, crafty, and cruel. A plebeian advanced to power leaps from one nature to the other at a bound, and exercises the pride and tyranny of office with as much apparent ease as if it had been his birthright.'
>
> *The Prisoner in Burmah*, Henry Gouger, 1860

Elections did eventually take place on May 27 the following year (the numbers of that date, of course, adding up to and being divisible by nine). The previous January, however, Rangoon's Elections Commission had banned Daw Aung San Suu Kyi from standing for election. Not that it made a jot of difference either to the result or to the SLORC's subsequent reaction to the outcome. Daw Aung San Suu Kyi's National League for Democracy captured 392 out of the 485 seats contested (81%) in the 492-member assembly (elections in seven of the constituencies were postponed for 'security reasons'). The National Unity Party (NUP), formerly Ne Win's Burma Socialist Programme Party, won a meagre ten seats.

The SLORC never handed over power to the people of Burma, claiming, amongst other things, that since Daw Aung San Suu Kyi was married to a foreigner, state secrets were at risk:

'Today, perhaps there may not be any problems here, but there are in Yangon and other places, regarding that young woman... Leaking of state secrets is not permissible in any way. This young woman can never be a leader of the country...'

Saw Maung, Letkhokkon, December 1990

The SLORC proceeded to wipe out all opposition.

'It is my responsibility to crush all internal as well as external enemies and insurgents... I am not a king, but the chairman of the SLORC. However, I have the sole responsibility for Myanmar... I am no king. It is not good for a king to be too severe. However, if a king is too lenient, others step on him. I cannot allow such a recurrence in my country.'

Saw Maung, September 1990

Having made almost all political activity impossible, the SLORC waged war on the country's ethnic groups and minorities. They sold logging concessions to the Thais which resulted in the wholesale destruction of the world's last remaining teak forests, yet amassed them some US$1 billion in hard currency. They peddled jade and gems, accumulated vast sums out of opium trafficking and continued to spend an estimated 60% of the nation's annual budget on defence. They acquired tanks, aircraft and military supplies from Belgium, Canada, China, Germany, Japan, Malaysia, Pakistan, Poland, Portugal, Sweden, Switzerland, the former USSR and Yugoslavia to suppress their own people. They used chemical weapons against the Kachin, Karen and Mon, forced thousands to flee their own homeland and persecuted the Muslim Rohingyas of Arakan State. As *Asia Watch* reported in December 1993:

'The SLORC government in Burma has engaged in its own version of ethnic cleansing. Official discrimination against non-Burmans goes back to the citizenship law of 1982, which gave full citizenship only to Burmese who could trace the families of both parents back to pre-1824 Burma. Some ten percent of the population who could not meet this criterion were considered non-nationals and classified as "associate" or "naturalized" citizens. The purpose was to deny full citizenship to ethnic minority groups. SLORC has also engaged in systematic persecution of non-Burman ethnic groups, including the Muslim Rohingya, over 300,000 of whom have fled to Bangladesh.'

'The shot-wound festered — as shot-wounds may
In a steaming barrack at Mandalay.'

The Ballad of Boh Da Thone, Rudyard Kipling, 1888

The SLORC raided Buddhist monasteries in Mandalay. In scenes reminiscent of the Khmer Rouge in the days of Pol Pot, they forcibly relocated hundreds of thousands of people from the towns to the countryside in order to disperse dissenters. They employed forced labour on projects throughout the land, from dredging the moat at Mandalay Palace to the extension of the runway at Putao Airport in northern Kachin State.

'We are angry that we are being ordered to do this terrible work. It is dangerous for me to say these things to a foreigner, but I am so upset that I do not care. We must use our hands to take this filthy, smelly dirt from the bottom of the moat. I have seen women collapse from the heat. And for this, the government pays nothing.'

> 50-year-old shop owner, Mandalay, August 1994

They are also extending the Ye-Tavoy railway line in Tenasserim Division, hacking through virgin forest and malaria-infested swamps. As Maung Aye, a 28-year-old farmer reports:

'It was the third time I was forced to work on the railway. There were soldiers everywhere but we had run out of food. We tried to steal some of theirs but we were caught and 26 of us were shot. I got away. They shot at me but the bullets went through my shirt, here and here. At my site, there were at least 4,000 people, men, women and children. We worked up to 18 hours a day. If we stopped or worked too slow, the soldiers would beat us with a bamboo rod or a metal pipe. I saw several people beaten. They were coughing up blood. Some didn't get up. I also saw many people die from sickness and starvation. When the soldiers come to collect labourers no one wants to go. But if we don't, they beat us or worse. My own family also had to suffer. The SLORC soldiers hit my wife's stomach with a rifle until she vomited blood and they kicked my son into the fire. His face was burnt. They punished them because I had escaped.'

'Voluntary' labour was also used on the construction of the Loikaw-Aungban railway, which was inaugurated on March 27 1993.

In its report of February 1994 entitled *A Swamp full of Lillies: Human Rights Violations Committed by Units/Personnel of Burma's Army, 1992-1993*, Project Maje of New Jersey, USA, reveals:

'April 18-19, '93; Mon; Waeng Patoke village, Thanbyuzayat Township, Mon State... Nai Sein Aung Kyi arrested as supporter of NMSP, "severely tortured by the troops". His wife, Mi Le, went to plead for him the next day and was raped in front of him... July 4 '93; Mon; Thanbyuzayat Township... Drunken soldiers, Saw Maung Maung and Moe Nyo raped Mi Aye Wan, a 13 year old schoolgirl, while her father was tied up in a plantation hut... Sept. 11 '92; Kachin... Troops led by Than Lain killed N'dau Gumja, a 45 year old man who did errands and odd jobs in a town, "because he was speaking Jinghpaw (a Kachin dialect) after the curfew at night"... First week of Feb '92... Demawso Township... Troops "seized a villager while cooking rice", accused him of being a rebel agent and interrogated him, tied him to a tree, called villagers to watch as he was disembowelled/killed. The same day, soldiers abducted five girls from the village and raped them.'

All the while, the West tut-tutted in mild disapproval. ASEAN (The Association of Southeast Asian Nations: Brunei, Indonesia, Malaysia, Philippines, Singapore and Thailand) merely responded with what it referred to as 'constructive engagement'. Senior officers in the Thai army, it is alleged, have extensive logging and mineral interests in Burma, and there is a growing two-way trade between the two countries that Thailand is eager to foster. Other ASEAN nations, such as Singapore, Burma's leading trading partner, Malaysia and Indonesia, also have growing commercial links with Rangoon.

'... we will not tolerate any foreign interference. The people who genuinely love Burma are the Burmese people; no foreigner will ever love Burma. It is all very clear. It is something to think about when foreigners say that they love Burma.'

Khin Nyunt, Chief of the Military Intelligence (MI),
Rangoon, July 1990

In December 1990, certain opposition politicians took to the jungle to evade capture and torture, and set up a provisional National Coalition Government of the Union of Burma. Their headquarters were at Manerplaw in the eastern border area of the country about 130 miles southwest of Chiang Mai, under the control of the Karen Liberation Army, who had themselves been waging a 40-year-old guerrilla war against the Burmese authorities (Manerplaw was eventually to fall to the SLORC on January 26 1995). At the beginning of December 1991 Saw Maung suffered a nervous breakdown and was replaced on April 23 1992 by Than Shwe, yet as a foreign diplomat remarked:

'Ne Win still pulls the strings. The military chiefs run things day by day but go to him before making any important decisions. He appointed them all and they owe their loyalty to him. He is the ultimate arbiter of power.'

On October 14 1991 Daw Aung San Suu Kyi was awarded the Nobel Peace Prize. The SLORC ignores all pleas for her release. In 1992 U Aye, of Burma's Foreign Ministry, was known to remark 'You can forget about that individual, she's finished', whilst Colonel Kyaw Win, deputy director of the Defence Service Intelligence, commented 'We cannot release her... because we are afraid that some unscrupulous elements might manipulate her and destabilise the situation.' In July 1994

Burmese Foreign Minister U Ohn Gyaw stated 'The time will come to talk (to her) or meet her, but we are in a process of democratic development so we have to show caution in every move.'

The visit in February 1994 of US Congressman Bill Richardson temporarily raised hopes that Daw Aung San Suu Kyi might soon be released, but these were swiftly quashed both by Kyaw Win, who announced that the Nobel Peace Prize winner 'will not be freed until at least the middle of next year (1995)', whilst Secretary-1 of the State Law and Order Restoration Council Khin Nyunt, when asked whether Daw Aung San Suu Kyi would soon be released, replied, 'I cannot answer the question... because my answer would be misleading, but we will deal with it by the existing law without making another law.' Daw Aung San Suu Kyi has never been tried or charged; she has been detained under a 1975 law designed for 'Safeguarding the State from Dangerous Subversive Elements'.

Eventually, on September 20 1994, Daw Aung San Suu Kyi was permitted to leave her house for the first time since July 1989 to attend a meeting with Senior General Than Shwe and Secretary-1 at the No 1 Defence Services Guest House in Rangoon. A second meeting between Daw Aung San Suu Kyi and Khin Nyunt took place at the Tatmadaw Guest House on October 28 1994.

'... Even the smallest light cannot be extinguished by all the darkness in the world because darkness is wholly negative. It is merely an absence of light. But a small light cannot dispel acres of encircling gloom. It needs to grow stronger, to shed its brightness further and further. And people need to accustom their eyes to the light to see it as a benediction rather than a pain, to learn to love it. We are so much in need of a brighter world which will offer adequate refuge to all its inhabitants.'

Daw Aung San Suu Kyi, 1993

Those *au courant* with Burmese politics believe recent changes to be purely cosmetic — particularly in light of the fact that in a subsequent state shake-up, all the top posts of the new 18-man constitutional commission went to senior figures in the armed forces. In addition few Burmese commentators have taken seriously the so-called (and hitherto long drawn-out) National Convention, assembled in January 1993 and chaired by Major-General Myo Nyunt.

'"For genuine party democracy to flourish in Burma," announced Myo Nyunt, "it will be necessary to work hand-in-hand with the military. To put it frankly, the maintenance of national stability, peace and tranquility without the participation of the Tatmadaw is extremely risky and dangerous."'

To cite the words of Brother Patrick of De La Salle Institute, Twante, back in 1947:

> 'Unless we know where we are going there is not much consolation in being told that we are on the way and travelling fast.
>
> 'It is futile to indulge in vague dreams and restless aspirations after something else merely because of political catchwords which identify autocracy with tyranny, or democracy with liberty. In this age of supposed enlightenment, it is distressing to see how easily people are carried away by mere names, and the claptrap of corrupt politicians. Their only salvation is to start thinking for themselves.'

Daw Aung San Suu Kyi was finally released from house arrest on July 10 1995. To end this section on a note of optimism, I shall quote from Clement Chapman's wonderful book *Glints of Gold (Burma)*, 1943:

> 'Burma was waking to find herself strategically important on the world map of conflicting forces. The young Burman idealist of but yesterday was setting out on the bewildering task of seeking to discover the Burmese soul which, he thought, had been overlaid. He desired that his people should stand among the nations of the earth in their own right, and with their own distinctive contribution.
>
> 'To-day we think of those who trusted in us to deliver them — in whom hope deferred might even fail like a candle in the wind. The tide will turn...
>
> 'And those who know her best will bear witness that Burma's dawns are as beautiful as her sunsets.'

PRESS, TV AND PROPAGANDA

The military-run Burmese media offer practically no news or information to either locals or tourists, but provide plenty of unintentional light-hearted entertainment. Fortunately most Burmese can tune into the BBC's World Service so they are well aware of developments both at home and in the world outside.

To confound the SLORC, in 1992 the National Coalition Government of the Union of Burma began broadcasting under the name Radio Free Burma; the DVB (The Democratic Voice of Burma) broadcasts from Oslo, along with Voice of America (VOA), All India Radio (AIR) and a rapidly increasing number of satellite dishes (bringing the BBC into Burmese hotels, guesthouses and homes of the affluent). Also in the pipeline is Radio Free Asia, built by the US at an estimated cost of US$39 million and structured on the model of federally funded and independently run Radio Free Europe and Radio Liberty.

The state's main English-language paper is *The New Light of Myanmar* (*Myanma Alin*) established in 1915. The former *Working People's Daily* (*Lok-tha Pyei-thu Nei-zin*) was set up in 1963 on a socialist model. Once 'socialism' had been jettisoned, the SLORC wanted a more respected title, so the *Working People's Daily* was renamed *The New Light of Burma*. As with its predecessor, it is often to be found lining hotel wardrobes and cupboards. In many ways it resembles the daily newspaper that used to be published in the former German Democratic Republic. The items of western news tend to be disasters (such as plane crashes), trivia (in the style of the British tabloids) or blatant anti-West propaganda, eg: 'Most Japanese distrust Clinton'. Local news revolves around the great achievements of the military. Headlines include: 'Onion Cultivators Co-operative Societies formed in Magway Division', 'South West Command Commander inspects protective measures taken against bank erosion in Nyaungdon' and 'Wall clock donated for No 2 Military Hospital'. Foreign headlines are even more informative: 'Man kills neighbour because dog wet on newspaper', 'World's biggest toad dies' and 'Woman kills mountain lion with kitchen knife'.

'Although they have abolished the one-party system in Burma
We still live in a single paper dictatorship
Where the *Working People's Daily*
Leaves a bitter taste in our mouths.

Some people say that
There is not a single true news item
In the *Working People's Daily*.
But it's really not that bad.
There is some news which is fifty percent true
(I'm only talking about the weather forecast, of course).
And once a month there is 100% reliable information
(When they announce the lottery winners).'

What Has Become of Us, Min Lu, translated from Burmese, 1992

A typical day's programme on TV Myanmar

1730	Martial Music
1740	Songs in honouring the 49th Anniversary Armed Forces Day
1750	Song Variety
1800	'Chit chit ah-tweh sling bag' — 'The sling bag is for my darling' (Starring: Kun Thee, Aye Yu Thandar) (Directed by Thet Naung)
1815	Song Variety
1900	Peter Pan & The Pirates: *Wind and the panther*
1920	Songs Variety
1930	Songs in honouring the 49th Anniversary Armed Forces Day
2000	News
	International News
	National News

Weather Report
Derrick: *The Third Victim*
Next Day's Programme

Radio Myanmar
0830	News
0840	Slogans
	Music Now To Nine
1330	News
1340	Slogans
	Lunchtime Music
2100	Spotlight on a star
2115	Perspectives
2120	Weekly News Review
2130	Vocal Gems
2145	News
	Slogans
2200	Portfolio for Easy Listening

Book and magazine publishing in English

There are practically no English-language books of any worth printed in Burma. Those which are for sale tend to be English-Burmese phrasebooks of appalling quality both in paper and text (eg: *Letters For Everyone* by U Tint Win Naing, Rangoon, 1993). This book includes, for example, a bizarre exchange of letters between the fictitious Ko Chit Yin and Ko Thein Zaw:

'Dear Sir,

I am sorry to have to make a complaint, bat (sic) for serveral (sic) nights past I have been unable to get a wink of sleeping owing to the constant barking of your dog. It would be a great kindness to me if you could control the dog. I have not been well lately, and my nerves are a bit overstrung; I am so sure you will understand my desire for quite (sic) at night.

Aplogizing (sic) for troubling you with this matter.

Yours fruly (sic),
Chit Yin'

'Dear Ko Chit Yin,

I am truly sorry that my dog has been disturbing your sleep. I am afraid he has been a bit noisy lately — perhaps on account of the full moon. I will certainly do my best to stop the nuisance, and will keep him indoors at night in the future. I hope you will not have to complain again.

Yours truly,
Thein Zaw'

In an attempt to promote 'Visit Myanmar Year 1996', a number of tourist magazines have suddenly appeared. *Today* (*THE MAGAZINE ON TOURISM AND BUSINESS IN MYANMAR*), published by Today Media & Information Ltd, was launched in December 1993 but is little more than the mouthpiece of the Ministry for Hotels and Tourism. It is handed out free of charge at Mingaladon Airport. *Myanmar This Month*, published by MacComm PR Advertising (Singapore and Myanmar) and also endorsed by the Ministry, is a very slim version of *Today*. *Golden Myanmar*, a quarterly publication, is indistinguishable from *Today* and costs US$2 or K200. *Myanmar Visitor's Guide*, *Panorama* (K45) and *Yangon Business Pocket Guide* (K90) are of the same ilk. Further publications can be expected.

All books and magazines printed in Burma are subjected to 'scrutiny' and require permission to be published. Many contain the following announcement:

'Non-disintegration of the union   Our cause
Non-disintegration of national solidarity   Our cause
Consolidation of national sovereignty   Our cause

Safeguard National Independence
Observance Of Discipline Leads To Safety
Keeping To The Rules Ensures Safety

Emergence Of The State Constitution is
The Prime Task Of All Union Nationals'

A studied and accurate assessment of the press and censorship in Burma is given in Anna J Allott's superb book *Inked Over, Ripped Out: Burmese Storytellers and the Censors* (PEN American Center, New York, 1993; Silkworm Books, Chiang Mai, 1994).

Perhaps the saddest form of propaganda has been the attempted brainwashing of Burma's teachers. To quote a Western diplomat in Rangoon:

'Burma's military junta has dismissed hundreds of teachers who failed a re-education course... Sources said that teachers on the course, which included training in discipline, law and moral studies, were made to shave their heads and given military indoctrination.'

ECONOMY

In terms of natural resources, Burma is potentially one of the richest countries in Asia. Gems (mainly rubies and sapphires from Mogok, northeast of Mandalay — see *Chapter Eleven*), jade (from Mogaung in Kachin State), gold, silver, zinc, tin (in Tenasserim Division), lead, antimony, petroleum (though drilling results have proved disappointing and some firms have decided to pull out), natural gas, prolific land resources (rice, fruit, sesame, pulses, beans, groundnuts, cotton, maize, sugarcane, wheat, sunflower, rubber, tobacco, jute), a multitude of fruits, teak, hardwood and vast unexploited fisheries and seafood should all, in theory, add up to a healthy and vibrant economy. However, due to the government's ineptitude and the fact that most of the profits from the country's wealth merely fund the 300,000-strong *Tatmadaw*, purchasing arms and military aircraft, Burma is bankrupt. The former 'Golden Land' (*Shwe Pyidaw*) now ranks as one of the poorest nations on earth and survives by means of widespread black market trading, gem peddling and opium trafficking. Opium production in 1991 stood at 2,350 metric tons, twice the output of 1988 when the SLORC took over and enough to supply 60% of the world market. According to the US International Narcotics Control Strategy, Burma produced approximately 2,280 tons of opium on 153,710 hectares in the 1991-92 crop season, the chief growing area being the Shan Plateau which extends almost the full length of the mountainous Shan State.

Border trade with Thailand provides funds for the smugglers and the SLORC with the six major crossings being at Mae Sai, Mae Hong Son, Mae Sariang, Mae Sot, Kra Buri and Ranong. Figures are naturally imprecise, but in 1982-83 it was estimated that some K920 million (or 51%) of all black market goods were smuggled through the Thai border. Thailand provides textiles, plastic products, medicines, machinery and spare parts, chemicals, electrical goods, foodstuffs and watches, whilst in return Burma trades timber (as a result of these massive teak and logging concessions to the Thais, Burma now has the fifth highest deforestation rate in the world), gems, jade, gold, tin, tungsten, livestock, opium and heroin, marine products, rice, rubber, industrial art objects and antiques. All this is known euphemistically as Burma's 'Informal Trade'.

Border trade via the southern Chinese province of Yunnan supplies not only Burma, but also Vietnam and Laos — though Burma is far and away the leading beneficiary. In 1993, trade rose 26.5% to 2.87 billion yuan (US$330 million), of which 2.57 billion yuan (89% of the total) was two-way trade between Burma and China. Cross-border trade is currently estimated at US$800 million per annum, about 40% of Burma's total trade. As Victor Mallet reported in the *Financial Times* of February 8 1994:

'Few business activities are as challenging as trading with Burma. The country is short of foreign exchange, is burdened with foreign debt payment arrears of about $1bn. and has an official exchange rate, the kyat, at 20 times its black market rate.

'... the generals have... encouraged border trade with China, welcomed

Aspects of Burmese Buddhism. Top left: The Snake Pagoda at Paleik Top right: Guinea-pig, Friday-born's prayer corner

Bottom left: Lord Buddha as a child, Mergui Bottom right: Chinese image, Nga Htat Kyi, Rangoon

Burmese novice monks. Top: Collecting donations, Lashio Railway Station

Bottom: Examination time in Tavoy

more tourists and courted foreign investors from Thailand, Singapore and further afield.

'Barter, or countertrade, is playing an important role... Swapping products allows traders to bypass problems caused by the overvalued official kyat, and many Burmese and foreign import-export companies have found themselves reluctantly involved in barter deals.

'... One of the most prominent barter arrangements in Burma is the deal between the ministry of forestry and Turnkey Contracts and Consultancy, a Singapore company, for construction of the recently opened International Business Centre, Rangoon's first modern office block.

'Diplomats in Rangoon say the multi-million dollar prestige project, in which companies such as Sumitomo and Texaco have already provisionally booked space, was paid for in Burmese logs.

'Asked whether he was paid in cash or trees, Mr Bernard Kwek, managing director of the Singapore company, said "a bit of each" and described the deal as "pretty complicated".'

As far as 'Formal Trade' is concerned, Burma's economy continues to rely heavily on agriculture which contributes 46.5% of the GDP and provides employment for 68% of the labour force. Rice is vital to the country's economy and rice cultivation is a way of life for about 70% of the population. It contributes 40 to 50% of 'official' export earnings and provides employment to about 65% of the labour force. Indeed, rice takes up nearly half the total cultivated area of 25 million acres. Prior to World War II Burma was the largest rice exporter in the world, contributing roughly half of the world's total rice exports, but this figure has dropped steadily: today Burmese rice is of very poor quality, fetching prices much lower than those prevailing in the world market. It is simply not possible any more to process high quality rice owing to the old and outdated rice mills from the pre-war days. Nor is it possible to increase rice exports because of Burma's growing population and the lower level of resources allocated to the agricultural sector.

Oil exploration, though strategically important and financially essential to the country, has proved almost fruitless to foreign enterprises. However, oil companies remain Burma's biggest investors, having provided some 65% of foreign investment since 1988. Over US$400 million have been ploughed into oil exploration in the past five years, from which the SLORC takes between 70-90% of the profits.

One of Burma's most valuable assets is the forests which cover 57% of the total land and produce about 75% of the world's teak resources. Fish and fishery products also have a high export potential, but have been badly mismanaged over the years, whilst beans and pulses (which form the third largest group in terms of export earnings after rice and timber), and oil cakes (eg: sesame cakes, groundnut cakes, cotton cakes and coconut cakes) are other major earners.

Tourism is potentially Burma's most lucrative source of income, but the industry has already been badly mishandled. Some may say this is hardly surprising as the Ministry of Hotels and Tourism is headed by an army officer, Lieutenant-General Kyaw Ba, who has no experience whatsoever of tourism.

'For Lieutenant General Kyaw Ba — a tough stoutly built professional soldier in his fifties — it was not a knowledge of tourism or the hotel business that made him Minister for Tourism... "I knew nothing of tourism," he confessed...

'Before his ministerial appointment... the general was a commanding officer of the Northern Military Division based at Myitkyina, capital of the hilly Kachin State in north Burma. "I had to do a lot of touring as commanding officer," he said, "and on one of these tours I came upon Lake Indawgyi, and... put up a proposal to the government to develop it into a tourist resort, with water skiing as a special attraction.

"That was how I became the first minister of the newly-created Hotels and Tourism Ministry of Myanmar."'

In 1990 Thailand attracted some five million tourists, Burma a paltry 8,806, raising a mere K25.54 million for its flailing economy. By 1993, the number of tourists had risen to only 22,363 (compared to 41,645 in 1986-87). As a result, Kyaw Ba has declared 1996 'Visit Myanmar Year' (postponed from 1995), opened up new areas, granted licences to private tour operators and hoteliers and extended tourist visas from two to four weeks. This is all part of Burma's so-called 'Market Economy System', inaugurated on October 29 1988. In fact, the upshot has been an Asian free-for-all with countries like Singapore, Thailand, Hong Kong, China, Japan, South Korea and Malaysia rushing to build hotels in Rangoon and Mandalay, and the contented Kyaw Ba has attracted over US$700 million in hotel construction from foreign companies.

POPULATION AND PEOPLE: THE ETHNIC GROUPS

'Happy by temperament, fortunate in his religion — for Buddhism is eminently suited to his race and character — inhabiting a country that is not overpeopled and that provides most of what he requires, the Burman is to be envied amongst the peoples of the East.'

W Harris, 1929

The population — 68.96% of whom are Burman — was estimated at 42.33 million in 1992-93, comprising as many as 135 ethnic groups. Most live in the central belt (Sagaing, Magwe and Mandalay Divisions), the delta region and the Shan Plateau. The Kachins live in Kachin State and Northern Shan State, the Karens mainly in Karen State, the Chins in the Chin Hills and in the dry zone west of the Irrawaddy, the Mons mainly in the southeast. The Arakanese have their own state which lies in the coastal region of the Arakan Yoma, the western range. The Shans live mainly in the Shan Plateau area.

Shan Around 7% of the population. They are Buddhist and have the same origins as the Thais (from Yunnan Province). At the collapse of the Pagan Dynasty at the end of the 13th century, a wave of Shan immigrants flooded into Burma and for the next 250 years they played an important role in the country's history. They have their own language and written script and a history and literature dating back centuries. In appearance they are often much fairer skinned than the Burmese.

Arakanese About 3.8% of the population who live in Arakan State on the west coast and bordering Bangladesh. They are roughly 30% Muslim and in appearance usually more dark skinned than the Burmese. In origin Tibeto-Burman, they speak a dialect of Burmese.

Karen Around 6% of the population, comprising at least 11 different tribes and groups including the Kayah, Pa-O and Padaung (the so-called 'giraffe-necked' women), though they are generally divided into two main groups: Pwo and Sgaw. The Karenni (Red Karen or Kayah) are ethnically and linguistically distinct from the Karen. Their small state, adjoining the southern Shan State, retained its autonomy even during British rule, and only became part of Burma after independence (the KNPP, the Karenni National Progress Party, was founded in 1948 in protest at being coerced into joining the Union of Burma). The Karen are 80% Buddhist (animist) and 20% Christian (Baptist). Their language is tonal and is thought to be of Sinitic origin. All Karen men are called *Saw* and the women *Naw*. *Saw* is the equivalent of *Maung*.

Kachin Around 2.3% of the population. Of Tibeto-Burman ethnicity, they are Baptist/Roman Catholic. The original name of the race was Jinghpaw or Singhpo, which was of Tibetan origin, being derived from the Tibetan term *sin-po* meaning cannibal. Kachin is interesting in that it never had a written language, and today uses Latin characters introduced by the missionaries. They say that when the 'Great Spirit' called all the nations together to give them letters, their race received theirs written on a buffalo-hide. However on the way home they got hungry, so hungry that they cooked and ate the hide, letters and all! In Kachin, 'hello' or 'how are you ?' is *kaja-ee*, 'thank you' is *cheju-kaba-sy* and 'goodbye' *wah-sa-na*.

Mon Around 2.3% of the population. They came into Burma from Eastern Tibet before the 5th century by which time they had spread over the Tenasserim coast founding a Buddhist kingdom at Thaton.

Linguistically Mon is related to Khmer, and is a totally different language from Burmese. Formerly referred to as *Talaings* (a derogatory term) or Peguers/Peguans, their main settlement areas are around Moulmein and the former capital of Pegu.

> 'They (the Burmese) are self-respecting, have good manners, always willing to help, delighted to see a foreigner, never encroaching... and withal as jolly and laughing as possible.'
>
> A Boger, 1936

RELIGION, PAGODAS AND TEMPLES

> 'Burmese Buddhism... is a world strange for the most part to Western perceptions... one almost from another planet... one of karma, merit, endless rebirths, "nats", and pagodas.'
>
> W L King, 1990

Theravada Buddhism (the original or 'pure' school of Buddhism) is the dominant faith, practised by over 80% of the population. Known as the 'Doctrine of the Elders', it is the oldest form of the Buddha's teachings, handed down by means of the Pali language. According to tradition, its name is derived from the fact of having been fixed by 500 holy Elders of the Order, soon after the death of the Buddha. Theravada Buddhism is sometimes referred to as Southern Buddhism or Pali Buddhism and is also practised in Sri Lanka, Cambodia, Laos and Thailand.

> '... he finds no god in Rangoon, but only the placid, unwinking, half-smiling image of Gautama Buddha, who, five hundred years before Christ, attained to Nirvana, and whose image is to-day worshipped by one-third of the human race.'
>
> Dr F E Clark, 1910

Burmese Buddhists are followers of Siddhartha Gautama, the Buddha (though not the first), who lived in north India in the 6th century BC. The Buddha, whose name derives from the Sanskrit word meaning 'enlightened', was concerned with the amount of suffering that he saw around him and was determined to find its cause. After much searching amongst the religious and philosophical sects of his day, he attained Enlightenment under the Bo (Bodhi) tree at Bodh Gaya, when he recognised that the cause of suffering was desire and attachment.

You can eliminate desire, lust and attachment by following the noble eightfold path of:

Right Views — the knowledge of suffering, the arising of suffering, the ending of suffering and the way leading to the ending of suffering.
Right aim or aspiration — the being set towards renunciation, non-resentment and harmlessness.

Right speech — abstinence from lying speech, from back-biting and abusive speech and idle chatter.

Right action — abstinence from taking life, from taking what is not given, from wrongdoing in sexual matters.

Right livelihood — gaining a livelihood in ways not injurious to others.

Right effort — inhibiting the arising of evil and immoral states of mind not yet arisen, getting rid of evil, immoral states of mind that have arisen, causing good states of mind to arise, establishing good states of mind.

Right mindfulness — regarding the body, feelings, perceptions, and activities and thoughts, self-possessed and recollected, and controlling the covetousness and dejection that are in the world.

Right contemplation or meditation.

For an excellent account of meditation, consult *Journey into Burmese Silence* by Marie Byles. In her foreword, the author writes:

'This is the account of the search for a quiet retreat in which to learn the art of meditation, that is, of how to still the thoughts and find the insight that lies beyond intellect. It tells of the ultimate finding of such a retreat at the Maha Bodhi Meditation Centre in Burma, and of life at this and other Burmese meditation centres...

'The type of meditation practised in Burma is known as Vipassana or insight meditation...'

Readers interested in Vipassana Meditation should contact the Venerable Sayadaw U Janakabhivamsa (in Burmese, U Zanaka — he speaks English) at the Chanmyay Yeiktha Meditation Centre, Kaba-Aye Pagoda Road, Rangoon. Alternatively, consult his 73-page booklet *Vipassana Meditation: Lectures on Insight Meditation*. This booklet contains lectures given at a ten-day retreat held at the Malaysian Buddhist Centre in Penang in April 1983.

The five great commands of the Buddha are:

To kill no living thing
Not to steal another's property
Not to commit any sexual crime
Not to speak what is untrue
Not to drink intoxicating drinks

The highest and ultimate goal of all Buddhists is to achieve nirvana (*nibbana*), which literally means 'extinction' or 'freedom from desire'. In Buddhist terminology, this constitutes the absolute extinction of that life-affirming will manifested as 'Greed', 'Hate' and 'Delusion', and therewith the ultimate and absolute deliverance from all future rebirth, old age, disease and death, from all suffering and misery. 'Extinction of greed, extinction of hate, extinction of delusion: this is called Nibbana', or, to put it another way, 'the absence of hatred, greed, delusion, suffering, and narrow individualized existence'.

Every Burmese Buddhist boy is expected to become a monk for a period (the ordination ceremony, a grand event where the head is shaved, robes given and vows taken, is known in Burmese as *shin-pyu* or 'Making a Holy One'), which may vary in length from a few days to a whole lifetime. In a similar ceremony, little girls (would-be nuns) have their ears pierced (*na-htwin*). Monks (*phongyi*) who renounce worldly goods are only allowed to possess eight articles: three pieces of cloth which form their robes, a begging bowl (*thabeik*), a mat, a blade, a needle and a water strainer.

Hinduism and Islam also have substantial numbers of followers in Burma, the latter particularly in the Arakan State. Many Karens, Chins and Kachins are Christian (there are over one million in Burma) and animist beliefs persist in certain areas, mainly amongst the hilltribes who still cling to their ancestral gods. The nature of their beliefs and the form in which they express them are of great importance, for these beliefs (animism) exert a powerful influence over their day-to-day lives. In all animist areas the spirits are deemed to have the same characteristics as human beings, the same tendency to be good to those they like and to frustrate and pester those who earn their displeasure. Acting on the logical assumption that these spirits are just as amenable to threats and flattery as their human counterparts, animists, through their religious ritual and sacrifices, do what they can to appease and placate the spirits.

The most celebrated group worshipped by the Burmese are the *nats*, a bizarre collection of mischievous spirits, and there are *nat* shrines throughout the country. There are 37 inner *nats* (those allowed into the precinct of the pagoda) and images of the 37 can be seen at the Shwezigon Pagoda in Nyaung-U, near Pagan. These are the spirits of named people, many of whom died a violent death. There are hundreds of outer *nats*, including natural *nats* of rivers, trees and special places. The most important place for *nat* worship is Mount Popa, 50km southeast of Pagan (see *Chapter Eight*). *Nats* are supposed to have supernormal powers, but it does not follow that all are good — goodness and power do not always go hand in hand in the world of *nats* as anywhere else. Nor are they immortal, though their lifespan is much longer than a human being's. They, too, are on the journey of birth and rebirth; they, too, are subject to death, decay and misery.

'Burma without its "Nats" would lose much of its interest and some of its charm. Their presence adds a zest to life, an addition to its "chances and changes". I should like to see a "Nat" colony introduced under the trees of

Kensington Gardens. It would be nice to watch little English children placing their posies of flowers in the tiny shrines and propitiating the "Nats" of the Round Pond and the Albert Memorial.'

East For Pleasure, Walter Harris, 1929

Alongside *nat* worship stand astrology and fortune-telling. Many a pagoda precinct is home to a Burmese astrologer, numerologist, palm-reader or fortune-teller. Pious Buddhists would not think of undertaking any important business without consulting their horoscopes or an astrologer to determine the most auspicious occasion. Indeed Burma's Independence Day was set only after careful astrological calculations.

Pagodas consist mainly of two types. The first is a bell-shaped stupa of solid brickwork raised on a series of receding terraces and crowned by a finial. The term *zedi,* which is derived from the Pali word *cetiya,* is applied to such structures. They were erected either to enshrine some relics of the Buddha, or of a Buddhist saint, or else to commemorate a sacred spot. Each has, therefore, a sealed-up chamber, often in the basement and sometimes in the *dhatugabbha* (meaning a shrine for relics) which lies between the bell-shaped section and the finial. The second type is a hollow vaulted temple mainly for enshrining the Buddha image. It is square in plan, sometimes with projecting porches or vestibules. A series of receding roofs rise above the chapel and finally a bell-shaped stupa or a curvilinear finial tops the structure. On these general types are evolved various forms of pagodas and temples by introducing different architectural and decorative features. Pagodas are not merely places for prayer and religious offering, they are also centres of social activity and an exciting destination for family outings and picnics. Burmese rarely go on seaside holidays; instead they visit famous (distant) pagodas. Every pagoda has an annual festival, which serves as both a trade fair and a clan gathering. Traders and pilgrims contribute voluntary funds to the pagoda; in this way, good business is done and at the same time, merit is made.

Most of the pagodas are built of brick and stucco while some are of stone. The images of the Buddha themselves are either of marble, alabaster, bronze or even of bricks and mortar. The smaller ones are sometimes made of gold and silver. They may even, rarely, be hollow, of lacquer (for example the large one in the British Museum).

Generally in Burma there are four conventionally accepted postures of the Buddha image: standing, seated (two postures), and recumbent (reclining). The standing image represents the Buddha teaching, with the right hand raised. The first posture of the seated image represents the Buddha in meditation, with the hands one upon the other resting near the navel, and the second, Enlightenment, with the Buddha seen cross-legged and the left hand open on the lap. The right hand is calling the earth to witness (at the moment of Enlightenment) and is usually touching the

Buddha image in the posture of Enlightenment

earth. The recumbent (reclining) posture is that of the Buddha at the time of entering nirvana, lying on his right side, the head in the right hand and the left arm lying on the left leg.

FESTIVALS

(See also Chapter Two, *Burmese Culture*)
Some Burmese festivals (*pwe*, pronounced *pweh*) have fixed dates; others vary from year to year according to the full moon days.

January
Independence Day (January 4), Karen New Year (January 12).

February
KNU Day (February 5), Shan National Day (February 7), Union Day (February 12) and Mon National Day, inaugurated in 1947 and celebrated in Mergui (February 15).

The full moon (in the lunar month of *Tabo-dweh*) is the time of the rice-harvesting festival *Htamane*, when food of the same name, consisting of sticky rice (*kaukhnyin*) mixed with sesame, peanuts, ginger and coconut, is offered. It also marks the enshrinement of eight sacred hair-relics of Buddha in the Shwedagon Pagoda more than 2,500 years ago.

March

Peasants' Day (March 2) and Armed Forces' (Defence Services') Day (March 27). The full moon day of *Tabaung* is when there are special alms offerings to monks, and fairs are held at the temples.

April

Burma's Buddhist New Year *Thingyan*, celebrated over three or four days around the middle of the month, is a joyous and exceedingly wet occasion. Buddha images are ceremonially bathed and monks are lavishly entertained. The word *Thingyan* is derived from a Sanskrit word meaning 'the entry of the Sun to any of the Twelve Signs of the Zodiac'. Gifts are offered to parents and teachers.

May

The full moon day of *Kason* honours the day on which, in different years, the Buddha was born, achieved Enlightenment and died. Processions are held in temples, Buddhists pour water on the sacred banyan tree and rituals are enacted at the Shwedagon and other pagodas. The annual Festival of Spirits takes place some time during May-June. May 1, May Day, is also celebrated as the Workers' Day.

June

On the full moon day of *Nayon*, student monks are examined on their knowledge of the *Tripitaka* religious texts.

Karenni National Day (June 21)

July

The full moon day of *Wa-zo* marks the beginning of the three-month period of Buddhist Lent, a time monks spend in retreat in their monasteries. Gifts of everyday necessities and robes (known as *Kathein-thingan*) are offered to help them through their spell of deprivation. During Lent there are no weddings and no courtships, and no Burmese would even contemplate moving home. This is the most common period for young men to enter the monkhood temporarily.

Martyr's Day (July 19) is dedicated to the memory of *Bo-gyoke* (General) Aung San, Burma's independence hero. Wreaths are laid at the Martyrs' Mausoleum near the north entrance of the Shwedagon Pagoda.

August

Taungbyon *nat-pwe* (32km north of Mandalay) is held from 10th waxing of *Wa-gaung* to the 15th of the full moon. One week after Taungbyon, Yadanagu *nat-pwe* in Amarapura is held from the 8th waning of *Wa-gaung* to the 14th of the hidden moon.

September/October

September and October (when the rain is dying off, but the river level is high) are the months when boat races are held on rivers and lakes throughout Burma. The most spectacular festival takes place in October at the Phaung-Daw-U Pagoda on Inle Lake near Taunggyi. At this splendid event, four of the five Buddha images, originally of sandalwood, but now covered so thickly by gold leaf applied by pilgrims that they appear to be rather shapeless objects of pure gold are placed on the Royal Barge (the fifth is left to take care of the monastery). The barge takes the shape of a bird, the *Karaweik* ('a mythical bird with a sweet voice'), and a procession takes place around the lake, stopping at each large monastery and village to spend the night before moving on the following morning to the next village (these visits represent those made by King Alaungsithu several centuries ago). At Yaunghwe they spend three nights and then they return to the pagoda via the right-hand side of the river. On the last day of the festival, which lasts nearly three weeks, there is a boat race. This consists of long boats, three at a time, each containing around 100 people who row with their legs (on both sides).

The Buddhist Lent (*thadin*) ends on the full moon day of Thadin-gyut, when the Buddha's return from Heaven[1] is celebrated with the 'Festival of Lights', involving all manner of lights, lamps, candles and fireworks. The poorest Burmese have some candles burning, even if they cannot afford paper lanterns or electric lamps. Dancing and various forms of entertainment take place and, as with most festivals, people gather ⌐ pagodas all over the land.

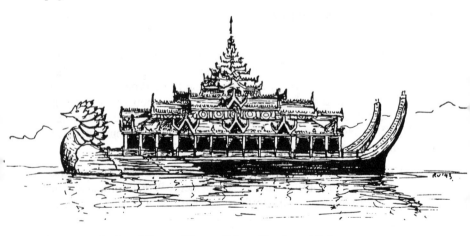

Rangoon: the Royal Barge ('Karaweik') on Kandawgyi Lake

[1] Buddha had spent three months in the abode of the *nats* and *devas* preaching to his mother.

November

The full moon day of *Tazaung-mon* is also an occasion for a festival of lights (see *Chapter Ten* on Taunggyi), as well as a Weaving Festival in which young girls engage in weaving competitions, making new robes for the monks by the light of the full moon. At the Shwedagon there is an all-night weaving-contest, the results of which are donated to the monks and to the Buddha images.

Shan New Year (November 22).

December

The *Nadaw* full moon is a time for honouring the spirit world and *nat* festivals (*nat-pwe*) are held in many parts of the country. Christmas Day is also a public holiday. December is writers' month, a time for open air talks and lectures.

Finally, there is another kind of festival which does not really fall within the usual confines of the term 'festival' but which marks the death of a *sayadaw*, the abbot of a monastery, or of a very famous monk. More accurately it is a funeral festival (known as *phongyi-byan*) lasting a number of days. The body is generally embalmed and lies in state for three days. There are two catafalques, specially erected, one in which the body actually lies in state and another duplicate token one. At the latter, professional mourners extol the virtues of the late *sayadaw* in song and word. On the actual day of the cremation, which takes place on a lavishly and colourfully decorated pyre, thousands of devout men, women and children gather to pay homage, an occasion which bears all the hallmarks of a pagoda festival.

LANGUAGE

More than 100 indigenous languages (excluding English, Chinese and Indian) — as distinct from mere dialects — are spoken in Burma, most of them by hill peoples. The common language is Burmese, spoken by (most of) the peoples of the plains and the hills. All these languages belong to only three groups. The Burmese language, and most of the other languages, belong to the Tibeto-Burman group — a sub-group of Sino-Tibetan. The Shan language belongs to the Tai language family; the language of the Mons of Lower Burma, and the Was and Palaungs of the Shan Plateau, belong to the Mon-Khmer language family (a sub-group of Austro-Asiatic). Karens are racially and linguistically Tibeto-Burman. As you would expect of a former British colony, many of the older generation of Burmese speak English; however, as a result of the junta's isolationist and xenophobic policies, the majority of the youth can manage little English. Tourist guides, taxi and trishaw drivers, though, speak English and sometimes French, German and Italian.

Burmese (*Bama zaga*) is the official language of Burma, and is spoken (*Bama-lou*, in the Burmese fashion) by at least two-thirds of the population. The most important regional tongues are Shan, Kachin, Chin, Karen and Mon. Hindi, Bengali and several Chinese dialects are also spoken among the various communities found mostly in the large towns and border areas adjoining India, Bangladesh and China.

Written Burmese, which to the outsider looks like a series of bubbles and circles from which various lines emanate, is based on a modified version of the old Mon alphabet which, in turn, is derived from south Indian alphabets. Street and town names, as well as the names of railway stations, are often written only in Burmese.

Burmese is monosyllabic and agglutinative (which means it combines simple words without a change of form in order to express compound ideas): it has neither conjugation nor declension, so that, in almost every instance, its composite words can be taken to pieces and the meaning of each part clearly shown. Burmese has three tones: an ordinary (unmarked) tone, an abrupt tone and a stressed or 'heavy' tone. It has 32 consonants, most of which occur only at the beginning of a syllable, eight vowels and four diphthongs. Only 25 of the consonants are used in Burmese words, but all 32 are required for words borrowed from Pali. The verb always comes at the end of the sentence, there is no definite article ('the'), and it is essential to use the special counting words when talking of numbers of things (eg: 'woman three person', not 'three women'). The Burmese alphabet consists of 44 letters and the script is written and read from left to right, top to bottom; there are no capital letters and just two main punctuation marks (comma and full stop).

Below are some basic Burmese phrases; for those interested in a quick stab at the language, I recommend John Okell's *First Steps in Burmese* (School of Oriental and African Studies, University of London, 1989), which consists of five cassettes and an informative accompanying text. Those who want to study Burmese fully should obtain Okell's superb four-volume course (see *Further Reading* for details).

Everyday phrases

Guide to pronounciation:
'K' as in English, eg: king, cat; (K with no following 'h')
'Th' as 'th' in English 'thin'

Hello (lit. 'good omens', 'auspiciousness')	*Min-gala-ba* (for the polite form, men add *k'in-mya**, women, *shin*)
How are you?	*Nay kaun la?*
I am fine	*Nay kaumba-deh*
Thank you	*Tjay-zu timba-deh*
You're welcome	*Ya-ba-deh*

I'm sorry	*Taung-bamba-deh*
How much?	*Beh-lauk-leh?* (*Beh-laulleh* is how it actually sounds)
Can I have the bill?	
(lit. how much for all this?)	*Beh-lauk tja-thaleh?*
How much is that one?	*Da beh-laulleh?*
What is that?	*Da ba-leh?*
Please take it	*Yu-ba*
Too expensive	*Zay mya-deh (Zay mia-deh)*
I'm going now (ie: goodbye)	*Thwa*-ba-ohn-meh*
OK, fine (ie: goodbye)	*Kaum-ba-bi*
See you again	*Twe-dhe-da-baw*
See you tomorrow	*Neq-p'an twe-dhe-da-baw*
What is your name ?	*Nammeh beh-lo khaw-thaleh?*
My name is...	*Tjanaw (tjama* for women) *nammeh...*
How old are you?	*Athet beh-lauk shi-bi-leh?*
I am... old	*Tjanaw/tjama* (plus number) *hnit* (= years)
Where do you come from?	*Beh-ga la-thaleh?*
I come from Mandalay	*Mandalay-ga (la-ba-deh)*
Where do you live?	*Beh-hma nay-dhaleh?*
Where are you going?	*Beh thwa-maleh?*
I am going to the market	*Zay thwa-meh*
I want to go to the Shwedagon Pagoda	*Shwedagon-p'aya thwa-jin-deh*
Where is the toilet?	*Ein-dha beh-hma-leh?*
I'm not very well	*Theiq nay-makaun-ba-bu*
I'm going to take a photograph	*Daq-poun yaiq-meh*
You don't mind, do you?	*Ya-deh-naw?*
I don't mind	*Ya-ba-deh*
I don't understand	*Na maleh-ba-bu*
I don't understand Burmese	*Bama-lo na maleh-ba-bu*
Do you speak English?	*Khin-mya ingaleiklo/ingalayllo/pyaw-tat-thala?*
What did you say?	*Ba pyaw-deh?*
No problem/never mind	*Kayt-sa mashi-ba-bu*
Do you know?	*Thi-dhala?*
I do know	*Thi-ba-deh*
I don't know	*Mathi-ba-bu*
Don't have/there isn't one	*Mashi-ba-bu*
Do have/there is one	*Shi-ba-deh*
Yes, it is so	*Houq-keh-*
No, it's not	*Mahouq-pa-bu*

Numbers

Zero	*Thoun-nya*
One	*Tiq*
Two	*Hniq*
Three	*Thoun*
Four	*Le* (Lay, as in Mandalay)
Five	*Nga*
Six	*C'auq*
Seven	*K'un-hniq*
Eight	*Shiq*
Nine	*Ko*
Ten	*Tas'eh*
Eleven	*S'eh-tiq*
Twelve	*S'eh-hniq*
Twenty	*Hnas'eh*
Twenty one	*Hnas'eh-tiq*
Thirty	*Thoun-zeh*
Forty	*Lay-zeh*
Fifty	*Nga-zeh*
Hundred	*Taya*
Thousand	*Tat'aun*

'"U" is a useful word in Burmese. It means egg, and uncle (term of respect), and the bow of a boat, and one's intestines, and a headland, according to how you say it. I said it in all the different ways I could, and they apparently guessed that I was more likely to need eggs than elderly gentlemen or bowels. I felt rather proud.'

Major R Raven-Hart, 1946

NAMES: OLD AND NEW

Burma, Bama, Myanmar or Myanma?

'Measures are being taken for the correct use of Burmese expressions. For example, our country is officially called Pyi-daung-su Myanma Naing-Ngan and is expressed in English as "Union of Burma". "Burma" sounds like mentioning Bama. In fact, it does not mean the Bama (Burmese nationals), one of the national racial groups of the Union only. It means Myanma, all the national racial groups who are resident in the Union such as Kachin, Kayah, Karen, Chin, Mon, Rakhine Bama, and Shan nationals. Therefore to use "Burma" is incorrect and Myanma should be used instead. Accordingly "Union of Myanmar" will be used in the future.

'Furthermore, measures are being taken for using words such as Yangon, Pyi, Sittwe, Mawlamyaing and Pathein in place of Rangoon, Prome, Akyab, Moulmein and Bassein respectively.'

Excerpt from SLORC press release, May 26 1989

'The terms *Myan-ma* (or *Myama*) and *Bama* are two forms of the same word, used with two meanings: (a) "pertaining to (the whole country of) Burma (including all ethnic groups: Karen, Shan, Kachin, Burmese, and so on)" and (b) "pertaining to the Burmese ethnic group (as distinct from the other ethnic groups)". In general, the form *Myan-ma* is preferred in formal and official contexts. The form *Bama* is preferred in conversation, written dialogue and personal letters.

'A similar distinction is made with the name for the country: *Myan-ma Nain-ngan* ("Burma-country") and *Bama-pye* (also "Burma-country") both mean "Burma". The former is the version preferred in formal discourse, and the latter is used in conversation and chatty writing.

'The English name for the country, Burma, was clearly taken from the more colloquial form of the Burmese name. The earlier English spelling "Burmah" was probably meant to reflect the stress pattern of the Burmese word *Bama*, and it looks as if later on people who read the word without having heard it properly pronounced gave it its present pronunciation "Burma" (with the stress on "Bur-" instead of on "-mah"), and so eventually the "h" came to be dropped from the spelling.

'"Myanmar" and "Burma". In the past some English speakers have tried to disambiguate meanings (a) and (b) above by using "Burmese" for "pertaining to all Burma" and "Burman" for "pertaining to the Burmese ethnic group alone", but this convention has not been universally adopted. In June 1989 the State Law and Order Restoration Council launched a new solution. It announced that the formal version *Myan-ma* (or *Myama*) was to be used for the whole country, including all the races, and the informal name *Bama* was to be restricted to the Burmese ethnic group (as distinct from the other races). This innovation was also to be reflected in English and other foreign languages also: the nation including all races was to be called *Myanmar*, and the Burmese race was to become *Bamar*.

'*Myan-ma* and *Bama* are adjectives in Burmese, and you usually find them used to qualify something else. This is why calling the country plain *Myanmar* sounds incomplete, and you will often find English-language sources in Burma using *Myanmar Naing-ngan* ("Burma state/country") instead.'

Abridged excerpt from John Okell's
Burmese: An Introduction to the Spoken Language, 1994

Names	**Officially decreed spelling after 1989**
Burma	Myanmar
Union of Burma	Union of Myanmar (Myanmar Naing-Ngan)
Burman	Myanmar
Burmese	Bamar
Arakan	Rakhine
Arakanese	Rakhine
Karen	Kayin
Tenasserim	Tanintharyi

Akyab	Sittwe (Sittway)
Amherst	Kyaikkami
Ava	Inwa
Bassein	Pathein
Haka	Hakha
Henzada	Hinthada
Kengtung	Kyaing Tong (Chiang Tung)
Magwe	Magway
Martaban	Mottama
Maymyo	Pyin U (Oo) Lwin
Mergui	Myeik (Beik)
Moulmein	Mawlamyine
Myohaung	Mrauk-U
Pa-an	Hpa-an
Pagan	Bagan
Pegu	Bago
Prome	Pyay (or Pyi)
Rangoon	Yangon
Sandoway	Thandwe
Syriam	Tanyin
Tavoy	Dawei
Twante	Twantay
Yaunghwe	Nyaungshwe
Chindwin River	Chindwinn River
Irrawaddy River	Ayeyarwady River
Salween River	Thanlwin River
Sittang River	Sittoung River
Burma Airways	Myanma Airways
Diplomatic Stores	Tourist Department Stores
Hotel and Tourist Corporation	Myanmar Hotels and Tourism Services
Tourist Burma	Myanmar Travels and Tours

BURMESE PERSONAL NAMES

Many foreigners are confused by the names of Burmese people. Wives and husbands have different names and the wife's name does not change after marriage. Children's names often bear no relation to that of their parents, for, in traditional Burmese circles, there is no such thing as a family name or surname but there are a number of rules governing name selection.

The first thing to note are the titles: you should refer to an older man as *U*, a man of similar age as *Ko* and a boy as *Maung*. Older ladies should be called *Daw* and girls of a similar age *Ma*. A teacher should be referred to as *Saya* (male), *Saya-ma* (female), a monk as *Ashin-p'aya* and an abbot as *Sayadaw*.

The names themselves are primarily chosen from two sources: the day of the week on which the person was born, and the various astrological influences. However, these rules are not always adhered to.

In Burma there is no such thing as a first, personal name and a family name or surname. Each person has their own personal given name, consisting of from one to four syllables. So Mrs Margaret Hilda Thatcher is not equivalent to Daw Khin Htay Yu. This is particularly confusing when it comes to Burmese telephone directories or aeroplane tickets — Daw Khin Htay Yu would be listed in the directory under 'Kh', as 'Khin Htay Yu' and should be on an airline ticketing computer system as such. However, you may well find that the computer operator, unaware of the Burmese system, has listed the lady in question as Mrs K H Yu — or some bizarre combination of *Daw*, 'Khin', 'Htay' and 'Yu'. This becomes even more complicated when a Burmese has just one name, for example, *Thiha*, meaning 'Lion'. He could be listed correctly as Thiha/Mr, or incorrectly as Ha/T Mr.

Thus the Burmese have no surnames. Take the name U Tin Myint Zaw, for argument's sake. Though there are three elements to his name — excluding the honorific U — he will always be referred to as 'Tin Myint Zaw'. He would not be called 'Tin' nor 'Mr Zaw'. He would also not pass on his name to his wife or children — she could be Daw Nwe Yin Win, and his sons Than Soe Lin and Tun Aung Kyaw, his daughters Kyi Kyi Swe and Than Than Aye. A further degree of confusion is added by the fact that some Burmese have the element *Ko* or *Maung* as part of their name already, eg: Maung Maung Sein or U Ko Ko.

A Burmese name consists of between one and four elements, from Ko Han to Daw Nan Aye Aye Myint. Each element is usually monosyllabic (though Pali words like *Thiha*, *Thida* and *Myitzu* have two syllables) and generally has a meaning of some sort. Below is a list of some popular elements with their meaning:

Aung	successful
Aye	calm, peaceful
Chit	loving
Gyi	big
Hla	beautiful, handsome
Htun	shine
Htut	apex
Khin	loving, friendly
Ko	elder brother
Kyaw	famous
Kyi	clear
Lay	little

Ma	mother, elder sister
Maung	younger brother
Min	prince, ruler
Mya	emerald
Myat	noble
Myint	noble
Myo	race, breed
Naing	victor
Ngwe	silver
Nu	soft, youthful
Nyein	calm
Nyo	brown
San	unusual, outstanding
Sein	diamond
Shwe	gold
Suu	gather together, collect
Than	million
Thaung	10,000
Thein	100,000
Thiha	lion
Tin	place upon
Win	radiant

Astrology is a key factor in name selection. In Burmese astrological terms there are eight days in a week, as Wednesday is divided into two — the morning (which retains its own name), and the afternoon, *Rahu*. The 33 letters of the Burmese alphabet are divided into eight groups and each group is assigned to one day. In choosing a child's name, the parents, an elder or preferably an astrologer, must first ascertain on which day of the week the child was born, and then select a suitable letter which corresponds with the day in question. For example, were the child to be born on a Monday, the astrologer has a choice of five letters — *ka* being one — and one of these letters will then be chosen to form the first element of the name. In this way, the astrologer may decide to call the child *Kyaw* (famous). The second element may start with a letter chosen from the day of birth, from the following day or from a day which is 'friendly' (*meik hpet*) to the first. It may also be a repetition of the first name, eg: 'Kyaw Kyaw', may come from the succeeding day, eg: 'Sein Win' (Tuesday and Wednesday), or a so-called 'friendly day' (determined by the astrologer, perhaps by rhymes or mathematical formulae), or simply be for euphonious reasons.

Each day has its own planet, birth sign and cardinal point. There are eight cardinal points marked by posts (*gyo-daing*) which are to be found at major pagodas, where the person will pay obeisance, make offerings and appease their guardian spirit, represented by a planet and an animal.

Monday	Moon, tiger, east — *Kyaw*, *Ngwe*, etc.
Tuesday	Mars, lion, southeast — *Sein*, *Hsan*, etc.
Wednesday am	Mercury, elephant with tusks, south — *Win*, *Wun-na*, etc.
Wednesday pm	*Rahu* (mythical planet), elephant without tusks, northwest — *Hla*, *Ri*, *Yo*, etc.
Thursday	Jupiter, rat, west — *Min*, *Bo*, etc.
Friday	Venus, guinea-pig, north — *Thein*, *Thiha*, etc.
Saturday	Saturn, *naga* (dragon), southwest — *Tin*, *Ne*, etc.
Sunday	Sun, *galon* (mythical bird), northeast — *Aung*, etc.

As you will have gathered, Burmese names are — at least for foreigners — especially confusing. For those with a particular interest in the subject, I recommend Gustaaf Houtman's *Burmese Personal Names* (Department of Religious Affairs, Rangoon, 1982).

FOOD AND DRINK

'Elsewhere we see shelves laden with fish of different kinds, obtained from the streams and estuaries in the neighbourhood. Their local names are peculiar, and therefore a few may be enumerated. — including, as they do, carp, hilsa, prawns, dog fish, cat fish, butter fish, mud fish, cock up, sable, and so on.'

Our Trip to Burmah, Charles Gordon, 1877

Surgeon-General Gordon may have been a dabhand with the old scalpel, but evidently not much of a pisciculturist.

Burmese cuisine has been influenced by its neighbours China, Bangladesh, India and Thailand, but unfortunately Burma seems to have come off worst. China and India have had the strongest impact, yet it is practically impossible to find a decent (and authentic) Chinese or Indian restaurant throughout the land.

Curries, soups, noodle dishes, rice and raw or cooked vegetables form the basis of most (all?) meals. The omnipresent curry can be made from chicken, duck, beef, pork, mutton, seafood or fish (in the Inle Lake region there is a particularly wide variety: catfish, eel, mudfish, featherback, mugel and small shrimps). Vegetarians can choose from egg curry or a wide selection of omelettes. Common spices include chillies (though the food is less hot than in Thailand), coriander, turmeric, cumin, ginger, galangal, lemon grass, tamarind and garlic. Vegetables include onions, spring onions, aubergines, courgettes, mange-tout, potatoes, beans, maize, cauliflowers, cucumbers and tomatoes. There is also a wide diversity of fruit: numerous types of bananas, pineapples, custard-apples from Prome, mangoes, mangosteens, tangerines, lemons, limes, watermelons, rambutans, lychees, durians ('like eating a bad egg over an open sewer'), avocados, coconuts, papayas, apples, pears, pomelos from Moulmein and even strawberries from Maymyo. You will find, however, that the reply to your order will invariably be *mashi-bu* — 'don't have'. So always carry a bunch of bananas around with you just in case. Incidentally, the Burmese tend to eat with their hands, but you'll be given a spoon and fork.

Myitkyina (in Kachin State) has arguably the best cross-section of fruit: oranges, apples, grapefruit, American limes, pineapples, pomelos, limes, avocados, giant oranges called 'Washingtons' and *teh-thi*, a fruit peculiar to Burma (though originating in China) which is red and has the consistency of an apricot. Among Myitkyina's other 'delights' are a plethora of vegetables of all shapes and sizes, giant carp, and frogs (*hpa* — heavy tone, as opposed to *hpa* — level tone — which means 'prostitute'). From Myohaung, in Arakan State, comes the most delicious of all Burmese fruit, *shau-cho-thi*, which literally means 'sweet lemon' but in fact is a kind of mini-orange.

Burma's national dish is *moun-hin-ga*, a curry-flavoured fish soup. Traditionally this is eaten with noodles and garnished with chopped onion, extra chillies, lemon or lime wedges or crispy fritters. Another popular dish, which emphasises the Chinese connection, is Shan noodles (Shan *khauk-hsweh*) stir-fried with pork, spices, onion, tomato, strips of omelette and topped with a few chopped chives and a squeeze of lime. The Southeast Asian influence is evident in the use of *ngapi*, Burmese fermented fish paste. The most celebrated variety *seinsa ngapi* comes from Tavoy and Mergui, though many a traveller has been put off by the foul smell.

'Food arrived, and I drank tea and ate rice and fish-stew, and what Nyo insisted was ngapi, that "half-pickled" and "half-putrid" fish. If so, it was a special sort, since its smell did not throw the other dishes off the table, nor break a hole up through the thatch to escape.'

Major R Raven-Hart, 1946

Lap'et is a peculiarly Burmese dish, regularly offered to guests (when it will often be presented in a lacquer box). Shredded fresh ginger is mixed into fermented green tea leaves and is served with peanuts and deep-fried dried beans. A multitude of other ingredients can also accompany *lap'et*: butter beans, chick peas, garlic, toasted sesame seeds and dried shrimps with dried shrimp powder. Burmese fare can also include *hincho* (clear soup with powdered shrimp and vegetables), *hsan byoke* (a boiled rice dish), *oh-no khauk-hsweh* (curried chicken in a coconut flavoured sauce with noodles), *wet-tha-ni* (reddish pork curry), *taung-bho-hmo* (Burmese mushrooms), and *nga let-thok* (fish salad).

On your travels you may also stumble across *pazun asein-gyaw* (prawns and vegetables fried), *ganan-hin* (crab curry, a speciality from

Arakan State), *cha-zan-hinga* (special chicken-bone soup with mushrooms and glass noodles), *ameh-tha-don-gyaw* (minced pork with onions and chillies), *ngapi-gyaw* (fish paste with chillies, garlic and onions), *wet-u-gyaung-gyaw* (a type of fried sausage), *kyet-tha-lon-gyaw* (fried chicken ball made from minced chicken, flour, egg, pepper, onion, garlic and ginger and looking like a chipolata), *ameh-tha-thok* (beef salad, known as *hlyan-phyan* in Chinese), *ka-kadit-gyaw* (fried perch), *mon-la-ywet-gyaw* (fried radish leaves), and *leik-u* (turtle's eggs) — not forgetting, of course, the stir-fried grasshoppers, beetles and sparrows.

'Being already a favourite, I was permitted to gratify my curiosity by tasting one of the most suspicious-looking dishes. It was a kind of sand-cricket fried crisp — nice enough, except in name, as a condiment, with boiled rice. Another favourite insect with the Burmese — though I did not see it among the King's dishes — is one which I would not offend the stomach of my reader by calling it a maggot, if I could find another word equally appropriate. It somewhat resembles a nut-maggot, magnified to three or four inches long, and is found embedded in every joint or sprout of a species of palm, close to its insertion into the main trunk of the tree. When fried and spread on a toast, it is not to be distinguished from marrow, though I could never altogether overcome my repugnance to its shape and large black head, with which it was brought to table entire in undisguised hideousness.'

Henry Gouger, 1860

A celebrated Burmese dessert is *sanwin-makin*, a semolina-based pudding made with coconut milk and baked in a large, shallow, stainless steel dish. When the top becomes golden brown, it is served on to a glossy banana leaf and neatly folded into a parcel. *Moun-baun* (at least what I sampled) is an Arakanese pudding made from coconut, sugar and rice, though one dictionary, which lists no less than 41 different kinds of *moun* (snack), describes it as a kind of spongy cake; elsewhere it is described as 'rice sponge cake'. Jaggery is the cooked sugar juices of the palmyra palm. It is supposed to have a purging influence and be good for constipation. Apparently it also has a soothing effect on the stomach and intestinal linings. I am reliably informed that Burmese fried bananas are delicious.

'Htun La came to the rescue, and bought some Chinese biscuits from the eating-house opposite. My first bite brought to life a juicy maggot which blinked its eyes as it saw light, the first for many a long day. Still, better a whole maggot than half a one! I threw the biscuits away, contenting myself with a few bananas.'

Stanley Short, 1945

Drink

'What! beer manufactured in Rangoon? Yes: and very good beer too, in so far as colour, flavour, and creaming qualities are concerned.'

C Gordon, 1877

The brand Surgeon-General Gordon was referring to must remain forever a mystery, since his trip to Burma took place some 12 years before the celebrated Mandalay Beer first appeared on the market. A tradition since 1886, Mandalay Beer still keeps most visitors going (when it's available), though there are a variety of stronger alcoholic beverages, notably Mandalay Rum. Johnny Walker Whisky is to be found in most places.

For teetotallers, bottled water may be the wisest option, particularly as pH7 Drinking Water produced by Ministry of No (1) Industry, Myanma Foodstuff Industries, claims:

'* EVERY HEALTHY AND STRONG PERSON ALWAYS PREFERS THIS DRINKING WATER.
* IT'S GOOD FOR KIDNEY, CAN REMOVE FATIGUE, AND SUMMON UP ENERGY WITH TEN KINDS OF BENEFITS, GOOD APPETITE, CLEANLINESS, BEAUTY ETC.
* IT CONTAINS ESSENTIAL MINERALS FREE FROM COLOUR, ODOUR AND OTHER IMPURITIES.
* IT IS WELL STERILIZED BY ULTRA-VIOLET RAY, SO IT SERVES AS MEDICINE.
* IT IS AN IDEAL WATER FOR ALL PEOPLE AND ALL AGES TO INCREASE INTELLIGENCE AND MAKE THE BODY HEALTHY AND VIGOROUS. AS ONE NEEDS 2.74 LITRES PER DAY FOR DRINKING.
* TESTED MONTHLY BY THE NATIONAL HEALTH LABORATORY, MINISTRY OF HEALTH, MYANMAR.'

An alternative to the above is Shwe Wut Yee Aqua Drinking Water, which should be stored 'IN A CLEAN AND COOL PLACE, AVOID EXPOSURE TO SUNLIGHT AND STRONG SMELLING OBJECTS'. It is also 'GOOD FOR KIDNEY, CAN REMOVE FATIGUE AND SUMMON UP ENERGY WITH TEN KINDS OF BENEFITS, GOOD APPETITE, CLEANLINESS, BEAUTY ETC'. It is 'WELL STERILIZED BY ULTRA-VIOLET RAY, SO IT SERVES AS MEDICINE' and is an 'IDEAL WATER FOR ALL PEOPLE AND ALL AGES TO INCREASE INTELLIGENCE AND MAKE THE BODY HEALTHY AND VIGOROUS'.

If that fails to convince you, the following beverages are also available: soda water (with bizarre, copied logos such as 'Singapore Mineral Water Rangoon' with a logo of Singapore Airlines on the oft re-used bottle), orange and lemon pop (known as 'lemon sparkling' or simply 'sparkling'), sugar-cane juice (*kyan-yay*), Chinese, Burmese plain tea and 'English' tea (the last-named is even sweeter than the dreaded lemon barley, as it's made with condensed milk heaped thick with spoonfuls of sugar), and, of course, coffee ('Nescafé', allegedly). Burmese plain tea (*yay-nway-gyan*) is always given free with cups of 'English' tea or coffee to clean the mouth afterwards. It tastes like slightly bitter hot water and is the safest drink everywhere. Other recommendations would be *ziphaw-yay*, plum juice, which is very refreshing, grapefruit juice (known as *grapefruit phaw-yay*), or strawberry milkshake, particularly in Maymyo.

Western drinks have arrived in Burma, so you can also choose from Pepsi, Seven Up (Sprite) and Sunkist (orange — curiously enough the Burmese refer to what we think of as an 'orange', with a thick, hard skin, as a 'Sunkist'. The Burmese use the word 'orange', *lein-maw-thi*, for what we call 'mandarins').

Bottled water and soft drinks vary in price from K6 up to K85 (depending on the whim of the vendor) and beer anything up to K100 (including imported beers such as Heineken and Tiger). 'English' tea costs around K4-5 per cup, but as a result of massive inflation can sell for K30 per cup in some places (eg: Mogok). Tap water is OK for brushing your teeth and washing, but should only be drunk in emergencies. On your travels you will come across earthenware pots (with one communal cup) by the roadside, which contain 'drinking' water for all — again, only sample it if (a) you are dying of thirst and (b) you have been inoculated against hepatitis A and all other contagious diseases.

Food and drink list
Snacks

Spring roll	*Kaw-byan-gyaw*
Noodles	*Khauk-hsweh*
Rice noodles	*Moun-di*
Transparent noodles	*Kya-zan*
Salad	*Athok*
Fish soup, eaten with noodles	*Moun-hin-ga*
Samosa	*Peh-byok*
Parata	*Pala-ta*
Pudding (like set custard)	*Pu-din (moun)*
Buttered bread	*Paun-moun htaw-bat-thok*
Buttered Indian bread	*Nan-bya htaw-bat-thok*
European-style cake	*Keik-moun*
Biscuit, cookie	*Bi-sakut-moun*
Ice cream	*Yay-geh-moun* (lit. 'water solid snack')
Yoghurt	*No-gyin*

Restaurant dishes

Food, cuisine	*Asa-asa*
Rice (cooked)	*Htamin*

Pork	*Wet-tha*
Chicken	*Kyet-tha*
Beef	*Ameh-tha*
Fish	*Nga*
Prawn	*Pazun*
Crab	*Ganan*
Duck	*Beh*
Egg (chicken)	*Kyet-u*
Egg (duck)	*Beh-u*
Bean curd	*Peh-bya*
Mushroom	*Hmo*
Aubergine	*Khayan-thi*
Tomato	*Khayan-chin-thi*
Potato	*A-lu*
Fried	*Gyaw/kyaw*
Steamed	*Paung/baung*
Stewed	*Chet/gyet*
Curry	*Hin*
Dressed salad	*Thok*
Sour	*Chin*
Hot (spicy)	*Sat*
Sweet	*Cho*
Stew	*Satu*
Roasted, toasted	*Kin/gin*
Sweet and sour	*Cho-chin*
Vegetables	*Hin-thi hin-ywet*
Clear soup	*Hin-gyo*
Sour sauce	*Achin*

Drink

Cold drink	*A-aye*
Water	*Yay*
Iced water	*Yay-geh-yay*
Cold boiled water	*Yay-gyet-aye*
Plain tea	*Yay-nway-gyan*
Tea (with milk and sugar)	*Lap'et-yay (acho)*
Coffee	*Kaw-hpi*
Milk	*Nwa-no*
Juice	*Ayay*
Orange juice	*Lein-maw-yay*
Lime juice	*Thanbaya-yay*

Chapter Two

Burmese Culture

by Ko Zar Ni, ex-University of Mandalay

To attempt to encapsulate Burmese culture in a chapter of this length is to invite strong criticism, particularly from Western-educated Burmese and non-Burmese citizens of Burma. The readers therefore are forewarned that the Burmese culture as portrayed in the following pages is how an urban-educated Burmese experiences and perceives it. Thus the snapshot of my culture may not necessarily be the culture familiar to other indigenous peoples such as Karen, Mon, Shan, Kachin and so on. Nor may it be the culture experienced by rural folk. Nonetheless, there are essential elements that constitute cultural experiences of the bulk of the Burmese people, if not of other groups with distinctive traditions, cultures and languages. Cultural attributes such as respect for one's elders, hospitality, generosity, *Ah-na-deh* and *nat* worship are several examples in this regard. Seen in this light, the chapter can be a valuable vehicle which will take even the casual observer through the typology of the Burmese cultural landscape.

Theravada Buddhism is the predominant religion of the country. Buddhism was initially introduced into Burmese society in the Pagan period by King Anawrahta, the founder of the first unified Burmese kingdom. Prior to the spread of Buddhism, the practice of spirit (*nat*) worship was prevalent among the Burmese. This practice was so strong that even after Buddhism became the major philosophical system, spirit worship came to be incorporated into Buddhist traditions and this holds true to the present day. Over the course of time, Burmese embodied spiritualistic elements into Buddhism.

The concept of the *nat* (spirit) is an important component in understanding Burmese Buddhist cultural rituals. Most Burmese believe that there are *nats* everywhere, dwelling in both animate beings and inanimate objects. According to the Burmese belief system, everyone has his or her own personal guardian spirit whose duty is to record and regulate one's conduct, thoughts and behaviour. This *nat* is a special and personal kind of *nat* and is known as *Ko-saung-nat*, one's own inner guardian spirit. Huge plants, rivers, forests, houses, streets, villages, lakes, fields, towns and cities all have *nats* that guard and protect them.

It is not in one's interests to do things that might displease the *nats*. In rural areas, for instance, many people still believe that urinating against a big tree would upset the *nat* which guards the tree. Such behaviour might provoke the *nat*, which as a result might punish that person. Punishment may take a minor form like making the offender lose his way home. There was a famous incident that took place near Mandalay some years ago on a mountain named *Thakinma Taung* (Mistress Mountain), regarded as the place where the celebrated *nat* Mae Oo resides. One day, a young couple from Mandalay was found dead on that mountain. What was interesting was that their bodies were attached to each other through their genitals; in other words, they seemed to have died during sexual intercourse. People wondered if it was due to the guardian *nat* Mae Oo, who presumably did not approve of such behaviour on her mountain range.

There are two kinds of *nats*: good and evil. The good *nats* are believed not to do harmful things to human beings. In fact the good ones may even bring good fortune to people who live their lives according to Buddhist principles. The bad *nats* can cause trouble in people's lives. Many Burmese fear the evil *nats* more than anything else in the world. There is a story that tells how a young man was taking a walk by the Royal Lake in Rangoon one day when he perceived he was being followed by a green spirit (*nat sein*). In Burmese culture, when a person dies an unnatural death, such as in a car accident, he or she becomes a green spirit. The green spirits are out on the streets wandering about and haunting the passers-by. Anyway, the young man was so afraid of the green spirit that he began reciting Buddhist prayers, as any Burmese might do under similar circumstances. Saying prayers didn't do anything to stop the green spirit following him and the young man began sweating with fear. All of a sudden, he conceived of a brilliant idea. He spoke to the green spirit. To his great relief, not only did the green spirit stop pursuing him, but it was scared right away. From that day hence, the young man was never followed by the same green spirit when he took his stroll by the Royal Lake. Friends, curious to discover what it was the young man had said to the green spirit to frighten it away, were told, 'I asked the green spirit if it wanted to join our Burma Socialist Program Party?'. The scary green spirit had finally met something scarier than itself!

Nat festivals are very popular in Burma. Two of the best known are *Yadanagu* (Treasure Cave) Festival and Taungbyon *Pwe* (*Pwe* means festival), both held near Mandalay. During Taungbyon *Pwe*, believers from all around the country come to Mandalay by train, car and plane. The actual site of Taungbyon *Pwe* is located in a small village called Taungbyon, about 12 miles north of Mandalay. Taungbyon has numerous cannibalistic features. While it attracts many *nat* believers from among different social strata, those who like festivities go there simply to enjoy dancing, drinking and having a good time. Usually those who earn a living out of spiritualism and Burma's supernatural subculture derive a sizeable income from these festivities. The interesting thing is that many Burmese believe that they belong to certain *nats* (*nats* have names like people), and the association is to be known through family history. For example, a household may belong to two *nats*: one from the husband's kinship lineage and the other from the wife's side. These ancestral *nats* are known as *Mi-zaing-hpa-zaing* (parentally associated *nats*). Believers are supposed to honour their ancestral guardian spirits by offering, amongst other things, food, money and wine. Annually or once every two years, a member of a given family would go to honour the *nat* to which they belong. Failure to do so, many of our elders believe, is likely to result in a decline of the family business, demotion or stagnation in one's professional career, or simply physical dangers. In these *nat pwes*, *natkadaws* (wives of the *nat*) dress up like old Burmese princes or princesses and the arcane royal court language is used. There are also male *natkadaws* who are gay. The *nat*, acting as a major source for psychological security, fulfils lay people's need to be dependent upon some kind of supernatural power. It is interesting to note that in Burmese Buddhist culture, while Buddhist teachings essentially exhort individual liberation through self-reliance (in theoretical Buddhism the Buddha is not a saviour nor god), many Burmese find a safe haven in the practice of *nat* worship. Every year, people of different age groups go to these makeshift *nat* shrines, and drink and dance like mad. The music, known as *nat-hsaing*, is extremely lively with the beating of powerful Burmese drums and cymbals. As the music plays, throngs of people dance, many intoxicated, on drugs or possessed by the *nat*. The crowd becomes increasingly excited and rowdier and fights usually break out. Annually there are fights which result in the death of one or more people. These fatalities occur during the heat of passion, and often the victim and the killer never know each other. All the while on stage, where the spirits possess their respective *natkadaws*, the arcane royal court language is relayed between the spirit worshipper and the spirit. Amongst the crowd, however, the most obscene language is heard, particularly by the male *pwe*-goers. While it is not overtly endorsed by the public, such obscenities are tolerated as a feature of the Taungbyon *Pwe*.

Burma's most famous festival is *Thingyan* or the Water Festival, which falls during the month of April. According to the Burmese lunar calendar, it marks the Burmese New Year's Day. Usually it begins on April 13 and lasts about four full days. Perhaps this is the best time to be in Burma. Throughout the land, rich and poor, Buddhist and non-Buddhist, participate in this society-wide festival. It is said that in the days of the monarchs, people gently poured water on one another. Some would put perfume in the water in a silver bowl, dip a bunch of *Padauk* flowers into the scented water and gently shake the flowers over a friend. Not so gentle these days!

In major cities like Mandalay and Rangoon, the gentleness with which *Thingyan* originated has long gone. Powerful water hoses, plastic water balls, steel, bronze and plastic water pistols have replaced the silver and gold bowls of old. For a month or two prior to the actual water festival, people intending to take part in the various festive activities start practising their acts. Many women join dance troupes, while their male counterparts memorise verses in preparation for *Than-Gyat Athin*. *Than-Gyat* is a kind of chorus used to deliver social and political criticism against the whole year's social and political wrongs, usually committed by those in high office. Within the confines of the three or four days of *Thingyan*, the authorities are (or more accurately, used to be) lax to the criticisms directed at them.

Unlike a *nat pwe*, during the *Thingyan Pwe*, the more religious go to the monasteries and pagodas to listen to sermons from learned monks and spend the entire Thingyan period there. Some may return home at the end of the day. One is not supposed to pour or throw water on these monastery-goers, who can be distinguished by their brown *longyi*, *eingyi* or beads they wear around their neck and wrists. Or they may simply say 'We are going to the monastery'. One immediately understands that these people are one of a group of several on to whom water should not be thrown (the others include police and postmen).

Pouring water on one another has a symbolic meaning attached to it, though the extreme heat of April (usually about 100°F in Mandalay) may have something to do with it. Water symbolises the purification of past mistakes and wrongs. In our childhood we were told that the guardian spirit of the sky (whose residence, according to Buddhist cosmology, was in the celestial abode higher than the mundane world of human beings) toured the human world, observing us all the time. Names of naughty children were entered into his leather-bound book and punishment meted out to them. We kids were really frightened of this. Our parents told us that if we did not behave well or obey them, our own names would be put on the list of this all-powerful spirit. Being a rebellious child myself, it scared the hell out of me and, needless to say, I was uncharacteristically (and regretfully!) obedient around this time of year.

At the end of the *Thingyan* Festival comes the Burmese New Year's Day. On New Year's Day there is no more water throwing and hordes of people across the country flock to the pagodas and monasteries to offer food, flowers, gold leaf, candles and money to the Buddha. Social organisations found in many residential quarters sponsor activities called *Thet-gyi-pu-zaw-pwe*, or honouring the elderly. The oldest members of the community are singled out and given donations. Elderly ladies who have become less mobile have their hair washed and nails cut, whilst other tasks are carried out by the village or city youths as symbolic gestures, showing that society still cares about the elderly, who have given their wisdom and labour for the betterment of the community.

Thingyan is the most inclusive of all the festivities in Burmese Buddhist culture. It is the *Thingyan* Festival that every ethnic, racial and religious group takes part in and becomes one with the indigenous culture. You find people from all walks of life, laughing, joking and exchanging smiles. In these joyous and festive days, the divided community in Burma finds something in common that they all love, removing the status distinction derived from wealth, race, ethnicity and religion, and finding instead the beauty of free spirit and light-heartedness, qualities all Burmese treasure.

Burmese are fun-loving people. One of the highlights of Burmese cultural life is the *pwe*. There are essentially two kinds of *pwe*: *zat-pwe* and *anyeint*. The former is Burma's equivalent of an opera or play and you have to pay to get in. There are seating arrangements called *Hpya-Nay-ya* (literally 'mat place': one's designated seat). *Anyeint* is a street concert which begins at around 2030 and lasts until 0130. Usually a well-to-do family hires a reputable *anyeint* troupe to celebrate a successful business deal, a monk's novitiation ceremony, and so forth. Word of mouth relates where and when the *pwe* will take place. Or one can simply observe the arrival of a *pwe* from the makeshift wooden stage at a street corner or at the street-side. In Mandalay, with the end of the rainy season (August) comes the *pwe* season. For most Burmese (who lack the western habit of hanging around bars), nightlife usually involves going to a *pwe* or sitting at a teashop.

Unlike the more formal *zat-pwe*, the *anyeint* is free of charge and accessible to the public. The audience is seated on the streets in front of the stage where the *pwe* is to be performed. Seating is very much on a 'first come, first served' basis, so those who plan to attend the *pwe*, go and mark their own 'seats' by leaving some used bamboo mat, chair or bench on the day of the *pwe*. The *pwe* troupe consists of three comedians, a dancer and a musical band. The first part of the *anyeint* programme is a combination of joke-making (many with a sexual innuendo), singing and female dancing. The dancer, known as *min-thami* (king's daughter), dresses up like a princess, while the three comedians wear the old Burmese costume of a jacket, long *longyi*, shirt and head-dress. These people have to be very witty, well-versed in Burmese language and able to improvise, since the *pwe* was originally a form of entertainment with royal patronage. Like other cultural activities, royal patronage was vital in promoting the *pwe* in the kingdom, since the royal court was the cultural centre of the land. With the fall of the final Konbaung king in 1885 and the disappearance of the royal court, Burmese cultural life declined under British colonial rule. *Anyeint* and *zat* artists, dancers and musicians still use court language spoken at the time of the Burmese monarchs. This has now become standard practice in Burmese theatre.

Burmese are taught to treat their elders with great respect — in theory, you must show respect to someone who may be just one day older. Status, wealth and position of authority also determine the amount of respect shown to another individual. When a Burmese meets a (Burmese) stranger, he judges the other's age and status and addresses him accordingly. A Burmese in his or her 50s would address a person of college-going age as *Tu-maung* (nephew) or *Tu-ma* (niece), while the latter would use words like *U* (uncle) or *Daw* (aunt). A young civil servant may be addressed as '*U* so and so' (male) or '*Daw* so and so' (female) by his or her subordinates. If appropriate, their title (captain, doctor, chairman or secretary) will also be used.

To Burmese, age is a really important cultural concept which regulates how one interacts with others. Honorific terms or prefixes such as *U* or *Daw*, egalitarian terms such as *Ko* or *Ma* or subordinate terms such as *Maung* or *Ma* are used during face-to-face interactions. A person's standing is never fixed: take the fictitious case of a 30-year-old trishaw driver by the name of Kyaw Soe Tun. He would usually be addressed as 'Ko Kyaw Soe Tun' by his not so close peers and co-workers, while his superiors in the trishaw union might address him as 'Maung Kyaw Soe Tun'. In both cases the prefixes *Ko* and *Maung* may be dropped depending on how close the person is to Kyaw Soe Tun. In that case the driver will simply be addressed as 'Kyaw Soe Tun'. Nonetheless, it is important to note that the Burmese consider it rude to address people whom they don't know well enough (or have just met) without using honorific terms like *Maung*, *Ko* or *U* (if it is a man) or *Ma* and *Daw* in the case of a woman.

The concept of age regulates not only how one interacts verbally with others, but also one's manners and demeanours. Bowing slightly in front of an older person, though different from Japanese-style bowing, is customary. When receiving an object from an older person, the younger one would take it with two hands instead of one, or at least with the right hand, supported at the elbow by the left. Touching the head of an older person is considered extremely rude, since different parts of the body are deemed differentially sacred, starting from the foot to head in order of sacredness. In many Burmese homes, except on cement floors, people prefer guests (as well as members of the family) to remove their shoes. In religious compounds, temples, pagodas, monasteries and congregation houses, 'foot wearing' — as the signs say — is strictly prohibited. This must be taken seriously and complied with, since for the Burmese, wearing shoes in these places constitutes a major insult. In colonial days, British officials refused to take off their shoes when entering religious compounds and this stirred up considerable anti-British feeling among the Buddhist population.

Boys from Buddhist families are supposed to enter the Buddhist Order for a period of time as young novices. Many adolescent boys are anxious to be novitiated, as the ceremony is believed to mark their entrance into manhood. Parents feel an absolute necessity to have their sons novitiated in a monastery and they strive hard to achieve this cultural and spiritual need. Once the boys enter the Buddhist Order, for however long a period, they become sons of the Buddha. This is the most important symbolically sacrificial ritual that parents can do to express their devotion to the Buddhist teaching. By having their children enter the Holy Order of Monks — even if only temporarily, as in most cases — parents also assume the patronage for the promulgation of Buddhism. Novices are considered to occupy a spiritually higher position than their lay parents and it is common practice throughout the land to see parents kneeling before their own children and paying them obeisance.

The age for novitiation varies depending on the circumstances, though the ceiling is considered to be 20 years from the time one is born. Buddhists include the nine-month period inside the womb when calculating the age of would-be novices. From the day the baby celebrated his or her first birthday, he or she will therefore be deemed to be two. Impending novices are warned to take extreme care of themselves, as evil spirits are likely to attempt to make the novitiation unsuccessful, as legend relates they tried to do in the case of the Buddha on his way to becoming the Enlightened One. I recall being asked not to engage in hazardous activities such as climbing a tall tree or swimming, since the evil spirit might push my back and make me fall off the tree or drown in the river.

Perhaps the most noticeable aspect of Burmese culture is people's extreme reluctance to hurt the feelings of others. This characteristic is universal among Burmese nationalities, as well as amongst the Chinese and Indian for whom Burma has become their permanent home. In this context you will often hear the phrase A-na-deh. In Burma people are almost more afraid of losing face than anything else. Burmese culture may be said to be shame-based rather than guilt-built. A famous Burmese adage relates that 'One lives not on the basis of one's biological life but on the basis of whether or not one loses one's face'. By and large Burmese don't like saying 'No'. The popular expressions *Asbet Hkweh* (losing face) and *Asbet mashi-bu* (lacking shame or unashamed) indicate that our culture is shame-based. The concept of A-na-deh appears to be connected to the fear of losing face or possibly offending others. This can result in problems in interpersonal communication among individuals since there is a degree of culturally conditioned inexpressiveness. While it may be a charming custom for those unfamiliar with Burmese culture, it causes, over a period of time, strain in human relationships.

Dating in Burmese culture is a radically different affair compared to Western dating customs. The co-education type mingling of man and woman is not encouraged. Rather, proximity between man and woman is seen as dangerous and likely to result in sexual tension and hence intercourse. Domino and ballroom dancing are deemed very un-Burmese and considered to be the influence of Western cultural decadence since Western-style dancing involves holding hands or being in each other's arms. Physical distance is very important in gender relations. In the old days, the distance between two lovers who were not yet married was said to be an arm's length. After World War II this shrank a bit, yet the time required to get to know one another was set at about three years (or three rainy seasons as we say in Burma). Unlike in Western societies, Burmese men and women do not hug, for there is supposed to be little or no physical contact between the sexes. A Burmese man should not enter the bedroom of a woman, not even that of his own sister.

Sexuality is a curious thing; there certainly exists a kind of double standard. Virginity is highly valued and pre-marital sex is still unacceptable, although an increasing number of lovers appear to engage in this activity. This is particularly so in major urban centres like Rangoon and Mandalay. If a man fools around, sleeps with prostitutes and has extra-marital affairs, the social ramifications are not as strong as they would be in the case of a woman. Polygamy is legal in Burmese society, yet there remains strong social pressure against it. The overwhelming majority of couples is monogamous.

Some Burmese psychologists, like Dr Sein Tu of Mandalay University who studied with Cora Alice DuBois and Margaret Mead, have observed that in Burma homosexuality is highly repressed. Although homosexual jokes abound among males, it is not uncommon to find men holding hands as in many Arab countries. Physical proximity between the same sex is deemed normal, yet the opposite is true between man and woman.

Unlike in neighbouring Thailand, prostitution is illegal. Nonetheless one would find brothels in major cities such as Rangoon, Mandalay and Taunggyi operated with the collaboration of government officials. In Ne Win's time there existed a notorious brothel called *Nay-Pyi-Daw* (Royal City) run under the auspices of an ex-colonel, who was chairman of the regional party (at state level) of the Burma Socialist Program Party. It was well known among Mandalayians that the party chairman was rewarded by his brothel-owning friend with 'fresh materials' for turning a blind eye to this illegal business.

The Burmese term for prostitute is *Pyi-daza*, and the history of prostitution predates the founding of the first Burmese Kingdom of Pagan in 1044. *Pyi-daza* literally means 'One who is the treasure of the entire society'; the woman deemed the most beautiful was declared society's treasure. Her beauty was such that no single man was allowed to possess her as mistress or wife — she was to be shared by all men (primarily the wealthy and powerful, who thereby accorded her prestige and held her in high esteem). Unlike society's treasure of old, her counterparts in Burma today are an exploited group forced to sell their bodies to earn a living at the very bottom of the social hierarchy. The spread of AIDS

By the banks of the Irrawaddy River

Chicken stupa, Pegu, one of the 547 previous incarnations of the Lord Buddha

and the forced sexual labour of Burmese, Shan, Karen and other women by both Burmese and Thai men in the sexual marketplace of Thailand and Burma have thrust society's 'treasures' into an altogether more sinister arena.

A famous Burmese writer once remarked that the Burmese are not racists but cultural chauvinists. I concur with her assessment of our Burmese Buddhist attitude towards others. Buddhism as understood in the Burmese context is indisputably the basis of Burmese culture. You will often hear the expression that to be Burmese is to be Buddhist; hence Buddhism is coterminous with 'Burmeseness'. Nothing excites a Burmese more than the sight of a foreigner clad in Burmese *longyi* and speaking broken Burmese. That, to a Burmese, is the acceptance of Burmese cultural superiority by the white-faced Westerners, and affirmation of his belief that Burmese Buddhist culture is holier and better. The worst crime a born Buddhist Burmese can commit is to convert to another religion, for then the convert would no longer be considered a true or authentic Burmese.

Chapter Three

Before You Go

VISAS

Tourist visas are valid for a stay of 28 days and must be used within three months of being issued. Extensions, in theory, are not permitted; however there have apparently been cases of extensions being granted by the immigration authorities at a cost of US$35 a day (but don't bank on it). There is no limit to the number of times you can re-enter the country, provided you have a valid visa obtainable from one of the embassies or consulates listed below. According to the authorities 'those arriving without visas, if required, will be reported (deported?); children over 7 years mentioned in the passport of a parent must hold a separate visa; a transit visa is valid for 24 hours only'.

The London and Bangkok Embassies — which charge £12 and 470 baht respectively — require the applicant to complete two application forms and one immigration form, along with three photographs. More obscure embassies (eg: Dhaka, Jakarta, Kathmandu) may ask you to fill out up to eight forms.

Essentially there are three types of visa: 'FIT' (Foreign Independent Traveller), 'Package tour' and 'Business'. The first-named is the one embassies are most keen to issue, because with FIT stamped in your passport, you are obliged to change a minimum of US$300 (or 'equivalent acceptable currency') on arrival at Rangoon Airport in exchange for Foreign Exchange Certificates (FECs).

'Those visitors holding Entry Visa Tourist (FIT) must change on arrival a minimum of US$300 or other equivalent acceptable currency with Foreign Exchange Certificates 300 units. This is the minimum amount to be spent by a tourist during his/her stay in the country. Any unused Foreign Exchange Certificates out of this amount will not be reconverted. If a tourist has exchanged in excess of US$300, any unutilized balance of the Foreign Exchange Certificates will be reconverted at the time of departure on presentation of the 'Foreign Exchange Certificates Voucher' at the Exchange Counters. Children up to 12 years and members of the Package Tour Groups are exempted.'

The 'Package tour' visa will be issued to an individual or group who has proof (ie: a letter or fax of confirmation from a licensed tour operator in Rangoon or elsewhere), that they have already paid for a tour. A 'tour' can consist of just one person and last anything from three days to four weeks. With a 'Package tour' visa, no money need be exchanged on arrival, though some eager Burmese officials may demand otherwise. 'Business' visas (800 baht in Bangkok) can be obtained on receipt of a letter of invitation from an approved Burmese organisation. Depending at which Embassy you apply, visas can be issued within ten minutes (Bangkok, for example), or a maximum of two days.

With 1996 — 'Visit Myanmar Year' — very much in mind, Kyaw Ba, Minister for Hotels and Tourism, is contemplating relaxing visa restrictions still further and allowing 'Package tour' visas (on pre-arranged tours but not FITs) to be issued on arrival. This will make chaotic Mingaladon Airport, Rangoon even more chaotic.

NB: Some of the embassies in remoter climes — like the Burmese Embassy in Dhaka or Kathmandu — may not have been informed that tourist visas have been extended. In addition, some will only issue 'Package tour' visas to those with a letter from one of the companies on their list of state-approved tour operators — a list that was published over three years ago when private (ie non-governmental) agencies were not permitted.

Embassies/Consulates

Australia 22 Arkana St, Yarralumla, Canberra, ACT 2600; tel: (6) 2733811; fax: (6) 2734357

Bangladesh 89(B) Road No 4, Banani, Dhaka 13; tel: (2) 601915; fax: (2) 883740

Canada 85 Range Rd, Suite 902-903, The Sandringham, Ottawa, Ontario, K1N 8J6; tel: (613) 232 6446; fax: (613) 232 6435

China No 6 Dong Zhi Men Wai St, Chaoyang District, Beijing; tel: (1) 5321584; fax: (1) 5321344

Czech Republic There used to be an Embassy in Prague, but that is now closed. There may be one in Bratislava since the Czechs handed their Rangoon Embassy over to the Slovaks and left Burma in 1993.

Egypt No 24 Mohamed Mazhar St, Zamalek, Cairo; tel: 3404176; fax: 202 43 16793

France 60 Rue de Courcelles, 75008 Paris; tel: (33) 42 25 56 95; fax: (33) 42 56 49 41

Germany Schumannstrasse 112, 5300 Bonn 1; tel: (228) 210091; fax: (228) 219316

Hong Kong Room 2424, Sun Hung Kai Centre, 30 Harbour Rd, Wanchai; tel: (852) 827 7929; fax: (852) 827 6597

India 3/50 F Nyaya Marg, Chanakyapuri, New Delhi 110021; tel: (11) 600251; fax: (11) 6877942

Indonesia 109 Jalan Haji Agus Salim, Jakarta; tel: (21) 327684; fax: (21) 327204
Israel 12 Zalman Schneor Street, Ramat Hasharon 47239, Tel Aviv; tel: (03) 5400948; fax: (03) 5493866
Italy Via Vincenzo Bellini 20, Interno 1, 00198 Rome; tel: (6) 8549374; fax: (6) 8413167
Japan 8-26, 4 Chome, Kita-Shinagawa, Shinagawa-ku, Tokyo 140; tel: (3) 3441 9291; fax: (3) 3447 7394
Laos Sok Palaung Rd, PO Box No (11), Vientiane; tel/fax: (21) 2789
Malaysia No 5 Taman U Thant Satu, 55000 Kuala Lumpur; tel: (3) 2424085; fax: (3) 2480049
Nepal Chakupat, Patan Gate, Lalitpur, Kathmandu; tel: 521788; fax: 523402 (850 rupees)
Pakistan No 12/1 Street No 13, Sector F-7/2 Islamabad; tel: (51) 822460; fax: (51) 820123
Philippines 4th Floor, Basic Petroleum Building, 104 Carlos Palanca Jr. St, Legaspi Village, Makati, Metro Manila; tel: (2) 817 23 73; fax: (2) 817 58 95
Russian Federation 41 Ul Gertsena, Moscow; tel: (95) 291 05 34
Singapore 15 St Martin's Drive, Singapore 1025; tel: (65) 734 2637; fax: (65) 235 5963
South Korea 723-1, 724-1 Hannam-dong, Yongsan-ku, Seoul; tel: (2) 792 3341; fax: (2) 796 5570
Sri Lanka 17 Skelton Gardens, Colombo 5; tel: (1) 587608; fax: (1) 580460 (1,000 rupees)
Switzerland 47 Avenue Blanc, 1202 Geneva; tel: (22) 731 7540; fax: (22) 738 4882
Thailand 132 Sathorn Nua Rd (corner of Thanon Pan), Bangkok 10500; tel: (2) 234 4698; fax: (2) 236 6898 (470 baht)
United Kingdom 19a Charles St, London W1X 8ER; tel: 0171 499 8841, 0171 629 6966, 0171 629 4486, 0171 629 9531; fax: 0171 629 4169 (£12)
USA 2300 S St N W, Washington DC 20008; tel: (202) 332 9044; fax: (202) 332 9046; 10 East 77th St, New York 10021; tel: (212) 535 1310; fax: (212) 737 2421
Vietnam Building No A-3, Ground Floor, Van Phuc Diplomatic Quarters, Hanoi; tel: 253369; fax: 252404
Yugoslavia Kneza Milosa 72, Belgrade; tel: 645 420; fax: 235 1802

INOCULATIONS AND HEALTH PROBLEMS

The following immunisations are recommended by the British Airways Travel Clinic in London, tel: 0171 831 5333. Up-to-date information is available by calling either the MASTA Travellers Health Line on 0891 224100 or the Travel Clinic Healthline run from the Hospital for Tropical Diseases on 0839 337733.

Polio Within 10 years

Tetanus Within 10 years

Typhoid fever Three different immunisations are available. Injectable Vi (single dose) and the older typhoid vaccine (two doses) both last three years. Oral typhoid capsules require boosting annually.

Hepatitis A Significant risk if antibody negative. For regular travellers the new hepatitis A vaccine (Havrix, given as a course of two doses one month apart to protect for one year; a booster at six to 12 months will increase that to ten) gives long-term protection, doing away with the need for repeated gammaglobulin injections. As it is a dead vaccine, it may be given in any relationship to any other vaccine. It is not required if you have had the infection in the past or have been shown to have antibodies already in your blood. Rumours that the AIDS virus may be passed with the gammaglobulin injection are completely unfounded for vaccine manufactured in the UK.

The following may be considered optional but you should take into account the comments in reaching a decision with your doctor:

Rabies Within one to three years depending on exposure to risk. Three injections are needed, at one, seven and 28 days. Protects for two years, but if you are bitten by any animal suspected to be a rabies carrier, further treatment is still needed. Beware of dogs (Orwell's so-called 'pariahs') and don't be fooled by the friendliness of the celebrated Burmese cats, which were actually bred in Thailand, or by the plethora of monkeys around Mount Popa and the Hpo-win-taung Caves (Monywa).

Hepatitis B Transmission is through sex or contact with contaminated blood, needles and syringes. The vaccine is available on private prescription or through British Airways Travel Clinics.

There is a new potentially fatal hepatitis C virus (HCV) which causes cirrhosis and liver cancer. The only known treatment for HCV is Interferon, which costs about £3,000 for a three-month course and has been a success with only 20% of people who have hepatitis C.

TB Children should be immunised at any age; less important for adults. A skin test (Heaf) is available if you are in doubt about your immune status.

Diphtheria Within 10 years

Cholera Reports of epidemics in Rangoon, identified as a new strain (Vibrio cholerae 0139, 'Bengal cholera'), should not worry travellers unduly, so long as they ensure strict food and water hygiene. Immunisation against cholera — which in any case only offers 60%

protection for three to six months and is unlikely to be effective against this new strain — is not generally recommended.

Seasonal Diseases

Seasonal diseases normally only occur during the months shown below. The requirement for immunisation depends on the areas you visit and your living conditions.

Japanese encephalitis From June to September. Immunisation should be considered if travelling during these months, though the risk is confined to rural areas where the mosquito vector breeds in rice fields. Three jabs, days one, seven and 28 give two years' protection.

Dengue fever From June to October. This viral disease is endemic in many areas and is spread by daytime biting mosquitoes (*aedes aegypti*) who breed, for example, in water-storage containers, flower vases, etc. Prevention entails avoidance of mosquito bites. At present there is no vaccine available.

Malaria
'IF....

If you can use intelligence and reason,
When listening hard to what the doctors say,
And realize that in the rainy season,
You have GOT to fight mosquitoes every day;

If you can bear to hear the fools who chatter,
(Of course, you know, I NEVER use a net!)
And tell you that it really doesn't matter,
Yet still obey the orders that you get;

If you believing others may be slacking,
Can go and watch the doings of your men,
And finding that some discipline is lacking,
Can give a talk about it there and then;

If you will try to minimize infection,
By thinking what to do about the drains,
And then ensure by personal inspection,
That everything is right before the rains;

If you will rub the ointment with your finger,
On portions of the body that are bare,
And when the evening cometh never linger, -
For then it's time for trousers everywhere;

If you can chide the other silly buffer,
Who sits about with shorts above the knees,
And tell him what you think he ought to suffer,
For giving chances to anopheles:

If you can bear in mind the orders given,
And never stint that flitting with your gun,
Till all mosquitoes from your tent are driven,
YOU'LL NEVER GET MALARIA, MY SON!'
Army in India Training Memorandum, No 25, July 1944

Malaria is a protozoal disease, the protozoa being carried from person to person in the gut of around 70 different species of anopheles mosquito. The female anopheles mosquito attacks between dusk and dawn; the males are benign fruit eaters. There are several different form of malaria, the two most important being vivax and falciparum. The other minor varieties are similar to vivax. Vivax is rarely fatal but can lie up in the liver and recur over months and sometimes even years. Though benign in relation to falciparum it is hell — an experience well avoided. Falciparum (cerebral malaria) is much more dangerous and can be fatal. Local populations build up some resistance to malaria, though much of this is because the vulnerable have already perished as children. Infant mortality is very high in malarial areas. The traveller, on his or her part, can have built up no such immunity and is at an increased risk. Beware of 'old hands' who tell you that they were in the jungle for 20 years and never had malaria once. They have either been extremely fortunate or are economic with the truth. Malaria affects over 270 million people in over 100 countries. A million people die of it every year. More than 10,000 travellers from Europe return with it annually, of whom an increasing number die.

Malaria is a risk throughout Burma except in Rangoon and areas above 1,000m. It is most intense during the months of March through to December in Arakan, Chin, Kachin, Kayah, Mon States, Pegu Division and Hlegu, Hmawbi and Taikkyi Townships of Rangoon, from April through December in the rural areas of Tenasserim Division, from May through December in Irrawaddy Division and the rural areas of Mandalay Division, and from June through November in the rural areas of Magwe and Sagaing Divisions. In Karen State it is present all year round. Exposure to the risk of malaria infection is almost unavoidable in areas where vector mosquitoes are difficult to control, such as valleys with *anopheles minimus* breeding in streams and forests, with *anopheles dirus* breeding in shaded pools and wells (in Mudon and the vicinity of Moulmein, for example), and coastal marshes with *anopheles sundaicus* and DDT-resistant *anopheles annularis*.

The recommended prophylactic is proguanil (Paludrine) 100mg twice daily and chloroquine (Nivaquine/Avloclor) 150mg (base) twice weekly. Tablets should be started one week before entering a malarial zone and continued regularly for at least four weeks after leaving the last zone. An alternative for journeys of less than three months is mefloquine (Lariam) 250mg once a week. If you intend taking mefloquine, go and see your GP: it's only available on prescription and can have serious side-effects. In addition, mefloquine is only licensed in the UK for journeys of up to three months, though the drug is considered to be safe to use for up to 12 months. Some strains of malaria are proving resistant to all drugs (in localised parts of Burma, resistance to mefloquine is already as high as 70%), so prevention (mosquito nets, coils and repellents and clothing which covers all the body) is strongly recommended.

The best advice for travellers to Burma at present is as follows: if a measured fever of 38°C or greater develops seven days or more after arriving in a malarious area, immediate medical help should be sought. If suitable help is unavailable (as is likely to be the case in Burma) or your condition deteriorates, self treat with Halfan (or quinine plus Fansidar, 500mg sulfadoxine and 25mg pyrimethamine) without further delay and get to a doctor (preferably in Thailand or Singapore) as soon as possible. For Halfan (halofantrine hydrochloride), which should not be taken with food, take two tablets six hourly for three doses and repeat one week later. As these tablets may be difficult to obtain abroad, ask your clinic doctor for a supply to take with you.

Malaria is transmitted by mosquito bite, so:

- Use insect repellent on exposed skin between dusk and dawn.
- Remember that the risks of being bitten are much greater in a rural, rather than a built-up area. You can reduce the risk of being bitten in a rural area by visiting only in the day, when mosquitoes rarely bite.
- Wear long-sleeved clothing and long trousers after sunset, avoiding dark colours as these attract mosquitoes.
- Wear repellent-soaked wrist or ankle bands between dusk and dawn.
- If your accommodation is not protected against mosquitoes by, for example, screened windows and/or airconditioning, then do the following:
  - When entering a room at night use a fly killer spray to kill any mosquitoes which have entered the room.
  - Always sleep under a mosquito net. Make sure that there are no holes in the net and that it is tucked under the mattress. You can increase the effect of the net by soaking it in an insecticide such as permethrin.
  - If you think mosquitoes can enter your room at night, use an electric mosquito killer or burn a mosquito coil. 'Buzzers' (sold in pharmacies and supermarkets all over the world) are useless.

AIDS AIDS is posing a major health, social and economic problem for Burma. Infection with HIV (the virus that leads to AIDS) has spread rapidly in the country since 1989, particularly among illegal drug injectors. This followed the spread of heroin injecting in Burma and neighbouring countries from the 1970s onwards; Burma is believed to have the highest HIV infection rate in the world among intravenous drug addicts. HIV and AIDS are now found throughout the country and among many different groups in the population, including blood donors, military recruits and women. In Rangoon about 74% of all drug addicts are HIV positive. In July 1993, a Harvard AIDS specialist estimated that between 300,000 and 400,000 people in Burma were infected with HIV. Until the end of 1992 condoms were not officially allowed in Burma. Those available on the black market are often past their 'use by' date.

For another angle to the AIDS epidemic (Burma now has the third highest HIV rate in Asia after India and Thailand), consult *A Modern Form of Slavery: Trafficking of Burmese Women and Girls into Brothels in Thailand*, published by Asia Watch and The Women's Rights Project (divisions of Humans Rights Watch) in December 1993.

'Thousands of Burmese women and girls are trafficked into Thai brothels every year where they work under conditions tantamount to slavery. Subject to debt bondage, illegal confinement, various forms of sexual and physical abuse, and exposure to HIV in the brothels, they then face wrongful arrest as illegal immigrants if they try to escape or if the brothels are raided by Thai police. Once arrested, the women and girls may be subjected to further sexual abuse in Thai detention centers. They are then taken for deportation to the Thai-Burmese border where they are often lured back into prostitution by brothel agents who play on their fear of arrest on return to Burma.

'Thai police and border patrol officials are involved in both the trafficking and the brothel operations, but they routinely escape punishment as, for the most part, do brothel agents, owners, pimps and clients.'

General health precautions

If you are in luck, you may be able to obtain a copy of a wonderful book entitled *On duty under a tropical sun. Being some practical suggestions for the maintenance of health and bodily comfort and the treatment of simple diseases; with remarks on clothing and equipment for the guidance of travellers in tropical countries*, published in London in 1883 and written by no less a duo than Major S Leigh Hunt (Madras Army) and Alexander S Kenny (Senior Demonstrator of Anatomy at King's College, London). It is a gem. The preface states:

'The suggestions in the following pages are offered with a view to assisting those whose duties may necessitate a temporary residence in the East, but who, from lack of previous experience, may not be aware of the simple means of counteracting and palliating many of the petty annoyances and personal discomforts which are attendant upon residence in tropical climates. The compilers have limited themselves to suggestions which have arisen solely in their personal experience in Egypt, India, Burmah, Australia, and elsewhere, and they have every reason to believe that they will be found practically useful.'

This extraordinary tome covers everything from 'Burmese Ringworm' to 'Egyptian Blind Boils', from 'Flatulence' to 'Inflammation of the Testicle' ('brought about by a blow, or, in some instances, from over-exertion in the saddle'), from 'Prickly-pear Thorn-wounds' to 'Wounds from Poisoned Arrows' ('Owing to the advance of civilisation, and the adoption by native races of European weapons, wounds from poisoned arrows, or spears, are much less frequently met with than they were formerly'). It also covers 'Restoration after Drowning', 'Native Servants' ('Do not expect too much at the hands of a native servant, for, in such case, your expectations are not likely to be realised. Under kind, but consistently firm treatment, a native servant will generally serve you satisfactorily') and the 'Revolver'. If your servant doesn't come up to scratch Major Hunt and Senior Demonstrator Kenny 'can confidently recommend Adam's Patent Double-action Central-fire, Breech-loading Revolver, 4.50-inch bore'. Incidentally, 'Burmese Ringworm' — a disease I am not personally familiar with — 'frequently occurs in contiguous parts'. For treatment, the writers recommend 'Goa powder' (whatever that may be), 'Two drachms of carbolic acid, about half an ounce of glycerine, and four ounces of water, or some tincture of iodine painted over the part', or simply 'sulphur and vinegar'.

Loath that I am to contradict such experts as Hunt and Kenny, my advice would be as follows: don't drink tap water, avoid ice and ice-cream, unpeeled fruit, raw vegetables[1], salads, crab, lobster and cold meat dishes and be careful in some of the restaurants. The food has often been hanging around all day (just as it has been in the markets) pestered by flies.

It can get swelteringly hot in Burma (particularly in Prome, Pagan and Mandalay) so take precautions against the sun. Around some of the temples and pagodas you may see a snake, but it is most unlikely. Many travellers to Burma have an illogical obsession with snakes and are convinced they plague the entire country. However, as J K Stanford

---

[1]There is one wonderful root vegetable called *sein-za-u* ('succulent, edible tuber' or, literally, 'raw-eat-root') of the climber 'Pachyrizus angulatus' (*peh-sein-za-bin*) which you can eat raw. It is often sold in bunches when the train stops at railway stations. You don't need to wash it; just peel off the skin, a bit like a turnip. The flesh is juicy, crunchy, very refreshing — and cheap.

wrote in his marvellous book of 1944 entitled *Far Ridges: A Record of Travel in North-Eastern Burma 1938-39*:

> 'Here was a jungle that ought to be alive with snakes, and the only one I had seen in the last three months was the corpse of a fierce-looking green one which I had bought off a Lashi hurrying over the pass to a fair two days' journey further on.'

In his wonderful book of 1877 entitled *Our Trip to Burmah*, Surgeon-General Charles Alexander Gordon (and he ought to know) lists all the poisonous snakes (land and water) in Burma — a sum total of just ten. Gordon relates a bizarre tale of a certain Major Richardson:

> 'I have often, when out shooting, seen a man catch a large snake by the tail and whirl it round and round until the snake stretches itself out straight, when he slips the disengaged hand along its body and catches it round the neck, letting it run away, and continuing the performance until at last the snake refuses to move at all. One I saw thus treated was over twelve feet in length — a large python.'

Happy hunting!

The worst thing you'll probably contract is diarrhoea or possibly dysentery. In any case, always carry a strong all-purpose antibiotic with you (eg: Erythrocin/Erythromycin or Distaclor, which are available without prescription in Thailand). If you're worried, seek treatment in Bangkok or Singapore.

CURRENCY, BLACK MARKET

The Burmese unit of currency is the kyat (pronounced 'chat'), divided into 100 pyas. Unless the SLORC demonetises the currency again, the present kyat bills in service are: K500, 200, 100, 90, 50, 45, 20, 15, 10, 5, 1 and 50 pyas. The K500, 100, 50, 20 and 50 pyas notes were introduced on Armed Forces' Day, March 27 1993 'for easy handling in line with the new market-oriented economic system', according to Finance Minister Brigadier-General Win Tin. Analysts, however, believe that the new notes reflect Burma's massive inflation which requires K500 notes, though the new notes themselves may well encourage further price rises. The K100 and 50 had originally been recalled way back in May 1964, and it is now planned to stop printing the K90 and 45 notes. The introduction of the 50 pyas note is quite bizarre. Since the black market rate is roughly US$1 to K100 (the official, ie: state, bank or hotel, rate is approximately US$1 to K6), 50 pyas is worth less than a ½p.

The other legal form of currency in Burma is Foreign Exchange

Certificates (known as FECs), which were introduced on February 4 1993. According to the 'Programme for the issue and use of Foreign Exchange Certificates' issued by the Central Bank of Myanmar (Ministry of Planning and Finance of the Government of the Union of Myanmar), the following regulations apply:

1. Foreign Exchange Certificates (FECs) are issued by the Central Bank of Myanmar for the convenience of tourists visiting Myanmar.

2. Foreign Exchange Certificates (FECs) are issued in three denominations:
   FEC equivalent to US Dollar Ten
   FEC equivalent to US Dollar Five
   FEC equivalent to US Dollar One

3. **Exchangeable currencies**. Foreign Exchange Certificates are exchangeable with the following currencies:
   US Dollar
   Pound Sterling and other major foreign exchanges

4. **Travellers cheques**. The acceptable travellers cheques:
   Master Card Traveller's Cheque
   American Express Traveller's Cheque
   Bank of Tokyo Traveller's Cheque
   CITI Corp Traveller's Cheque
   Visa Traveller's Cheque
   Bank of America Traveller's Cheque
   National Westminster Bank Ltd Traveller's Cheque
   First National CITI Bank Traveller's Cheque
   Swiss Bankers Traveller's Cheque
   Commonwealth Bank of Australia Traveller's Cheque

5. **Exchange rates**. The exchange rates of Foreign Exchange Certificates are as follows:
   US Dollar (one) = Foreign Exchange Certificate (one) unit
   Pound Sterling is to be changed at the daily cross rate notified by the banks.

6. The fractions of the Foreign Exchange Certificates calculated at the daily cross rate will not be exchanged.

Remember that all tourists with FIT stamped in their passport must change a minimum of US$300 (or other acceptable foreign currency) on arrival. Others with the 'Package tour' or 'Business' visa need not; what you do with your money after leaving Mingaladon Airport is entirely up to you.

Chapter Four

Getting There and Away

'I met the Dacres at Marseilles. They are on their way to Nice and have taken the villa there we had last year, and they were so astonished to see me; and would not believe me when I said I was going to Burma. Eveleyn — you know what stupid things she always says — pretended she had never heard of Burma and wanted to know if it was the same as Bermuda, as she once had a cousin there, she said. I simply ignored her.'

Elizabeth Visits Burma, 'Jeff', 1910

TOUR OPERATORS

'There is no restriction whatsoever for tourists, however, they are required to get permission from the ministry if they wish to visit remote areas in the north and south.'

Kyaw Ba, October 28 1994 (see next section)

According to the latest government figures, 22,363 tourists visited Burma in 1992-93 raising K68.03 million. The greatest number of visitors in recent years was 41,465 in 1986-87 (K40.53 million). In 1992-93 Germany provided most tourist arrivals (at Rangoon) with 1,265, followed by Americans (1,209), Italians (1,172), Japanese (1,028) and Koreans (834). The UK was seventh on the list with 791 tourists.

Travellers intending to visit Burma can choose from the following options:

* Contact one of the UK-based operators specialising in Burma
* Contact a travel agent in Bangkok, Singapore, Hong Kong or Kuala Lumpur (the main points of entry to Rangoon)
* Contact a private tour operator directly in Rangoon
* Simply turn up at Mingaladon Airport, Rangoon as an FIT (Foreign Independent Traveller), change your US$300 and hope for the best

UK

Until October 1992 all British travel agents were forced to book tours to

Burma through the state-run Myanmar Travels & Tours (MTT, formerly Tourist Burma) and consequently their programmes were both heavily restricted and hugely expensive. The easing of these restrictions by granting licences to private tour operators in Burma, establishing private hotels, guest and resthouses, the opening up of numerous 'new' destinations and the extension of tourist visas have changed the picture quite dramatically. Nonetheless, it must be borne in mind that in Burma there is no such thing as a 100% 'private' hotel, guesthouse, tour operator, etc in the Western sense of the word; all Burmese enterprises are subject to varying degrees of SLORC control. Below are two UK-based companies who can help with your travel to Burma:

Mergui Travels & Tours, 36c Sisters Avenue, London SW11 5SQ; tel/fax: 0171 223 8987, part of Right Now Books & Tours (Burma). Advice on all aspects of travel both to and within Burma.

The Travel Trading Company, Trofarth, Clwyd, LL22 8BW, Wales; tel: 01492 650225; fax: 01492 650093. Independent, tailor-made and group tours.

There are other UK-based tour operators who offer standard, set tours to Burma, but their programmes are limited and overpriced. Firms like Asia Voyages (now known as Asia World Travel), who allegedly invested an abortive US$8.9 million in the SLORC for charter flights to Pagan and Mandalay, are therefore not recommended.

North America
Shan Travels & Tours, Tour Consultants (Burma), 14312 90A Avenue, Edmonton, Alberta T5R 4XR, Canada; tel/fax: (403) 483 7493 (a wide variety of independent, group and tailor-made itineraries organised by an experienced Burma traveller).

Thailand
Those who wish to travel to Burma independently from Bangkok or on a non-government tour (and have not organised a schedule beforehand) are advised to contact the helpful, efficient and English-speaking:

Pan House Travel, 2 Lard Prao Road, Choke Chai 4, Bangkok 10310; tel: 538 0335, 538 3705, 538 3491; fax: 538 2465; telex: 20333

If you choose to make your reservation in Bangkok, the mark-ups tend to be ludicrously high — so steer well clear of firms like Skyline Travel Service (MTT's Bangkok arm), Diethelm, MK Ways, Exotissimo Travel, etc, and all those who advertise regularly in various Thai publications. Most of these agents book either via Skyline in Bangkok or Myanmar Travels & Tours in Rangoon and only offer standard tours at exorbitant prices. It makes more sense to contact a company like Pan House Travel, which deals directly with private tour operators in Rangoon.

Singapore/Hong Kong/Malaysia

Although there is no first-rate tour operator in Singapore who deals with Burma, the country does boast Southeast Asia's outstanding airline, SilkAir, a subsidiary of Singapore Airlines, which flies daily to Rangoon (see *Airlines* page 83). Tickets for SilkAir can be purchased at any travel agent.

SilkAir's office in Singapore is located at 77 Robinson Road, #10-03 SIA Building, Singapore 0106; tel: 322 6881/2, 229 7134/5; fax: 222 7028.
In Rangoon: 537 Merchant St; tel: 84600, 82653; fax: 83872.

Myanmar Airways International's office in Singapore is at 1 Scotts Road, #22-04 Shaw Centre, Singapore 0922; tel: 735 7315; fax: 735 6188.

As far as Hong Kong is concerned, again there is no one travel agent I can recommend. However, Myanmar Airways International flies from the colony to Rangoon on Mondays and Fridays. Tickets can be obtained from:

MAI, Room 2201, Asia Standard Tower, 59-65 Queen's Road, Central, Hong Kong.

In Malaysia, contact:

Maple Travel (M) Sdn Bhd, General Sales Agent, 2.46-2.49, 2nd Floor Wisma Stephens, 88 Jalan Raja Chulan, 50200 Kuala Lumpur; tel: 244 3077/3101; fax: 242 9392. Penang: tel: 635880; fax: 631405; Johore: tel: 3325218; fax: 3324715.

Rangoon

The 1992-93 Rangoon Yellow Pages listed 23 travel agents, the 1994-95 Trade Directory of Myanmar no less than 146. Locals say the total is now well over 200. Booking directly through one of these licensed ('private') Burmese tour operators is the cheapest (if not always easiest) way of arranging a trip to Burma. The drawback is that communications are poor — fax lines tend to be frequently engaged — and much of the business is still conducted via telex. It should also be noted that, although theoretically 'private', all travel firms must pay a minimum of 25% of the tour price to the SLORC.

Emperor Travels & Tours, No 47, Room 13, Bogalayzay Street, Rangoon; tel: (95-1) 96103; fax: (95-1) 89960 (clearly marked for the attention of 'Emperor Travels & Tours'); telex: 21201, 21236 (again, the communication must be marked specifically for 'Emperor'. Both fax and telex numbers belong to a communal state bureau).

Red Moon Tours Ltd, No 36, Kyaikkasan Road, Tamwe Township, Rangoon; tel/fax: (95-1) 38073; telex: 21201, 21236 (AMH 2167).

Since Rangoon has very few fax machines — Mandalay appears to have just one — and many companies share the same number, the best way to make contact is via telex or express mail. Booking is fairly straightforward (and avoids middlemen and travel agents' commissions): send a fax (if you can get through), telex or letter to Rangoon (make sure you address the letter 'Yangon, Myanmar' or the Military Intelligence will either open it or simply refuse to deliver it) requesting your tour or suggesting an itinerary of your own. The company will reply with a price quote and you then either transfer the funds to their bank account in Rangoon or pay them on arrival. Remember, if you wish to obtain the 'Package tour' visa and thereby avoid having to change US$300, you will have to take a letter/fax of confirmation to the Burmese Embassy of your choice.

Since many travellers are keen to explore newly opened areas, and are therefore requesting tailor-made itineraries, a complete list of tours would be impossible. Suffice it to say that programmes are available from three days to four weeks: Emperor's prices start at US$127 and go up to US$2,256 for their set tours. Prices do not include airfares, airport taxes, entrance and visa fees and insurance.

NB: Allow at least a month's notice if you decide to book through Rangoon.

Travel restrictions: where you may or may not go

It is not possible to give hard and fast rules: areas in Burma oscillate between being 'on' and 'off' limits for a number of reasons. However the following list will give some indication as to where tourists may travel (see page 85 for border crossings).

Areas accessible without permission (no guide required)

Rangoon and environs
Syriam
Twante

Pegu

Mandalay and environs
Amarapura
Ava
Sagaing
Mingun
Maymyo
Monywa
Kyaukse

Kalaw
Pindaya

Pagan and environs
Mount Popa
Meiktila
Thazi

Inle Lake and environs
Taunggyi
Heho

Prome
Shwedaung
Toungoo
Pakokku
Magwe

Areas accessible with permission (no guide required)

Moulmein and environs	Sandoway
Kyaiktiyo	Ngapali
	Akyab
Bassein	Myohaung
Chaungtha	

Areas accessible with permission (guide required)

Kengtung	Myitkyina
Lashio	Bhamo
	Putao
Mogok	
Loikaw	Tavoy and environs
	Mergui and the Archipelago
Henzada	

Airlines

The following airlines fly to Burma:

Myanmar Airways International (MAI, airline code UB)

Daily to Rangoon from Bangkok: UB 222 departs Bangkok at 1835 and arrives at Rangoon at 1915. UB 221 flies daily from Rangoon to Bangkok, departing at 1600 and arriving at 1740.

Daily except Friday, UB 226 leaves Bangkok at 1035, arriving Rangoon at 1115; UB 225 departs Rangoon at 0800, arriving Bangkok at 0940.

Four times a week (Tuesday, Thursday, Friday and Sunday) to Rangoon from Singapore: UB 232 departs Singapore at 1345 and arrives at 1510. UB 231 leaves Rangoon at 0815 and arrives at 1235.

Twice weekly (Monday and Friday) to Rangoon from Hong Kong: UB 238 leaves Hong Kong at 1315 and arrives at 1500. UB 237 departs Rangoon at 0730 and arrives at 1210.

Twice weekly (Wednesday and Saturday) to Rangoon from Kuala Lumpur: UB 234 leaves KL at 1845 and arrives at 1945. UB 233 departs Rangoon at 1345 and arrives at 1745.

Once a week (Wednesday) to Rangoon from Dhaka: UB 252 leaves Dhaka at 1015 and arrives at 1230. UB 251 departs Rangoon at 0800 and arrives at 0915.

New routes include Kunming and Dhaka.

Myanmar Airways International is a US$10 million joint venture between Burma's former domestic and international carrier Myanma Airways and Highsonic Enterprises Private Limited of Singapore (originally with significant financial backing from Brunei). Myanma Airways stopped flying internationally on August 14 1993, when MAI took over with one Boeing 757, wet-leased from Royal Brunei Airlines. Owing to a disagreement with Brunei, Myanmar Airways

International handed back their sole 757 and instead leased a 146-seater Boeing 737-400 from Malaysia Airlines under a two year contract. The new MAI 737 had its maiden flight on August 13 1994.

MAI's inflight service is good — infinitely better than that of the former Myanma Airways — but, alas, they only have two planes (the second Boeing 737-400 arrived on December 7 1994), which fly non-stop between Rangoon, Bangkok, Singapore, Hong Kong and KL without adequate maintenance, and tickets can only be purchased in the countries they serve. In Thailand, I would recommend Oriental Travels, Charn Issara Tower, 942/47 Rama IV Road, Bangkok; tel: 234 9387-9; fax: 236 5503. MAI (next door) may well sell you a return ticket for 5150 baht (if you ask nicely).

SilkAir (MI)
Daily to Rangoon from Singapore: MI 512 departs Singapore 0810 and arrives at 0930; MI 511 leaves Rangoon at 1025 and arrives in Singapore at 1445.

SilkAir flies a Boeing 737 and, for me, ranks as the outstanding carrier in Southeast Asia.

Thai Airways International (TG)
Twice daily to Rangoon from Bangkok: TG 305 leaves Bangkok at 1450, arriving at 1540. TG 306 departs Rangoon at 1630 and arrives Bangkok at 1810.

Since Thai Airways increased its number of flights to Rangoon — which are always jam-packed — the service has deteriorated alarmingly. The 70-minute flight is a scramble as the surly staff hands out insipid meals and the assorted Burmese immigration and customs forms (if they remember to stock them). Oriental Travels sells a return ticket for 5,550 baht. Outside Thailand, tickets can be purchased from any Thai office or agent: in the UK the price is around £150 (depending on the value of the £ and whether or not you are flying Thai into Bangkok). If you fly Thai to Bangkok, onward return tickets to Rangoon are cheaper, as indeed they are if acquired via an agent.

Other airlines
Air China (CA) and Biman Bangladesh (BG) fly once a week to Rangoon from Kunming and Bangkok respectively (on a Wednesday and Thursday). Neither can be recommended, however, owing to their poor service and unreliability.

New routings are Calcutta (on Indian Airlines), Karachi (on PIA) and Vientiane (on Lao Aviation).

Bangkok Airways (PG)
Bangkok Airways, which used to fly from Chiang Mai to Mandalay and Pagan, and the SLORC have been quibbling over various fees and charges imposed by the military upon tourists arriving in Mandalay and will not recommence flights until these have been resolved.

Air Mandalay

Air Mandalay, which belongs to the Singapore-based Techmat Holding Pte's Air Mandalay Holdings Pte Ltd, currently flies daily from Rangoon to Mandalay, Pagan and Heho. Air Mandalay also flies to Sandoway and, internationally, links Chiang Mai with Rangoon and Mandalay.

Air Mandalay's fleet comprises two French-made ATR 72s — two more are in the pipeline — in a joint venture operation which is worth US$35 million. Air Mandalay holds 60%, Myanma Airways/SLORC 40%. Air Mandalay can be contacted at 146 Damezedi Rd, Bahan Township, Rangoon; tel: 35488, 30144, 82561; fax 35937. In Mandalay: Unit G-23, 82nd Street, Between 26th and 27th Streets; tel: 27439; Thailand: Mekong Land, c/o 399/6 Soi Thonglor 21, Bangkok 10110; tel: 712 5842/381 0881; fax: 391 7212; Singapore: MAS Travel Centre, 19 Tanglin Road, #04-15 Tanglin Shopping Centre, Singapore 1024; tel: 235 4411/737 8877; fax: 235 3033.

It is occasionally possible to fly by charter from Chiang Rai to Tachilek, Kengtung and Heho on Thai Flying Service. For details fax: Bangkok 258 6597 or Chiang Rai (053) 731441. There is also talk of air links between the Thai border town of Mae Sot and Moulmein in Mon State. On October 30 1993, Aeroflot dropped its weekly flight from Moscow-Bombay-Rangoon-Vientiane. However, rumours persist of a new air connection between Madras and Rangoon via Air India.

BORDER CROSSINGS

Depending on the whim of the Burmese, Chinese and Thai officials, the following border crossings are sometimes permissible. Before you attempt to enter Burma via one of these routes, however, it is advisable to check with the authorities concerned. They may be able to inform you (a) if the crossing is open to foreigners, (b) whether or not you need a visa, (c) how long you can stay and where you can wander, and (d) how much foreign currency you need to exchange.

Mae Sai (Thailand)/Tachilek/Kengtung/Jing-hong (Xishaungbana, China)[1]
Monglar (China)/Kengtung/Tachilek[1]
Lweje (China)/Bhamo
Muse/Namkham/Kyukoke
Muse/Lashio
Muse/Lashio/Mandalay/Rangoon
Namkham/Bhamo
Kunlone/Lashio
Mae Sot (Thailand)/Myawaddy
Three Pagodas Pass (Thailand)/Payathonzu
Ranong (Thailand)/Kawthaung

---

[1]Owing to periodic fighting between opium warlord Khun Sa and the SLORC, the Tachilek/Kengtung region fluctuates between being 'on' and 'off' limits.

At present, only those who have booked a state-organised package tour are permitted to travel all the way from Yunnan Province in China down to Rangoon and from Mae Sai in Thailand through to Yunnan. At Three Pagodas Pass/Payathonzu, you are required to leave your passport on the Thai side and pay 130 baht. The border is closed from 1800 to 0600 but there are no restrictions regarding the use of cameras, camcorders, etc. Once in Burma, you are greeted by a sign which reads 'DRIVE SLOWLY DRIVE RIGHT SYSTEM IN MYANMA'.

ARRIVAL AND CUSTOMS

To quote from the official regulations regarding 'Entry Procedure (Airport)':

1. To show your passport, entry-visa, disembarkation card and other relevant documents to the officers at the immigration counter (foreigners' section)
2. To exchange 300 US$ for FECs at the counter of Myanmar Foreign Trade Bank (MFTB)
3. To let customs officers examine your passport and declaration forms at the customs counter
4. To pick up your luggage taken in by the conveyor-belt
5. To declare, if any, electrical goods/camera/jewellery and foreign currencies at the customs counter
6. To settle customs duties, if required, through the red channel
7. To let customs preventive officers inspect your luggage
8. To let immigration officers reexamine your passport

Fine, in theory. In practice, you need to complete a pink (or grey) Thai-style arrival/departure card and two identical customs declaration forms (declare jewellery, camera and valuables) and you need only declare foreign currency in excess of US$2,000. You can also immigrate at the desk marked 'TOURISTS'. You only need to change the US$300 if you have 'FIT' stamped in your passport. Then collect your luggage, proceed through the green channel, hand over one of your customs declaration forms (retain the other half for departure) and you're in Burma!

Tourists are allowed to import two cartons of cigarettes or 100 cigars, two bottles of liquor and ½ litre of perfume. Passengers are also permitted to bring their personal pets on condition that they are accompanied with health certificates (the pets or tourists?). The import and export of kyat is prohibited.

DEPARTURE

1. To get your ticket confirmed at the airlines concerned
2. To pay the airport tax (6 US$ in cash or FECs) at the airport

3. To show your passport and airport tax receipt at the counter of the airline concerned so as to receive your boarding pass
4. To let the immigration officers examine your passport and embarkation card
5. To submit your passport and declaration form at the customs counter
6. To let the customs preventive officers inspect your luggage
7. To go through a body-search

You're out! In fact, the first thing to do is to pay your airport tax in US dollars cash or FECs — ALWAYS remember to retain US$6 for this — get your name crossed off the list and then check in. Your return ticket should have already been confirmed immediately AFTER YOUR ARRIVAL. The immigration officer will probably ask you one question: 'Where did you stay in Yangon?' and stamp your passport. Proceed through customs where a bored official will glance at your form and may ask to see the items you have declared. The luggage and hand baggage are then X-rayed: don't forget to remove your camera and films. The machine says 'FILM SAFE' but it isn't. Once you are through to the departure lounge there is just one grubby restaurant, which only accepts dollars (kyat cannot legally be taken out of the country). The authorities also state that 'Exports of antique and archaeologically valuable items are prohibited. Only gems, jewellery and silverware purchased at the authorized shops are allowed to be taken out'.

Chapter Five

Practical Information

GETTING AROUND

'We proceeded to charter one of the conveyances we found there waiting for
hire, a peculiar kind of vehicle, resembling in size and appearance a dog
kennel set on a pair of high wheels, and it proved a marvel of
inconvenience. You climb up with difficulty, thrust yourself through the
small aperture as best you can, for it is no easy matter, and then you stow
yourself away, sitting down on the floor of the conveyance with your knees
about your ears. It is quite impossible to preserve a dignified demeanour in
one of these bullock gharries, and yet, sad to relate, it was found that this
was the only kind of conveyance available for His Majesty the King, when
he was removed from the palace to the river on his way to India.'

W R Winston, 1892

More than one hundred years have passed since Winston penned these
words about his work as a Wesleyan Methodist missionary in Upper
Burma. Little has changed. Indeed Burma still has a quite extraordinary
array of vehicles, many quasi-prehistoric. There are trishaws (*hsaik-ka*)
and horse-carts, stagecoaches and riverboats, pick-ups, taxis and buses,
bicycles without brakes and jeeps without floors, Winston's abhorred
bullock carts, 'zed ferries' and something the Burmese call a 'trawler G'
— a sort of trailer drawn by a small engine. All are ancient and
tumbledown; all trundle along lugubriously at speeds varying from slow
to very slow and all break down.

By air
Myanma Airways (UB)
Myanma Airways — referred to universally throughout Burma by its
airline code 'UB' — operates a wholly unpredictable domestic schedule
with its 'fleet' (a veritable misnomer) of obsolete Fokkers (F-27 and F-
28); the F-27 (Fokker Friendship) dates back to November 24 1955 and
I think Myanma Airways (or UBA, Union of Burma Airways, as it was
then known) was the very first customer. Rumour has it that Myanma
Airways has placed an order for some new Fokkers, which it hopes will

be delivered in time for 'Visit Myanmar Year 1996'.

Burma has 21 domestic airports (including Rangoon) which are currently in service. There are innumerable grand schemes to build new ones and extend old ones: for example, since Rangoon International Airport cannot take a 747 — though Putao, in remotest Kachin State, can — they plan to construct 'Hanthawady International Airport' at Pegu, 80km northeast of Rangoon. On December 2 1993 'Commander Maj-Gen Soe Myint... called for concerted efforts in the making of a world class airport'. (*The New Light of Myanmar*)

Below is a list of airports served from Rangoon and Mandalay, the days of the week when the planes are supposed to depart (1 Monday, 2 Tuesday, 3 Wednesday, 4 Thursday, 5 Friday, 6 Saturday, 7 Sunday) and the cost for a one-way ticket (all tourists have to pay in US$). Prices vary as to whether the aircraft is an F-27 (twin-prop) or F-28 (jet). It is pointless giving flight times or numbers. Unless otherwise stated all prices are for an F-27. Sometimes UB switches from the F-27 to the F-28 without warning — in which case, tourists must pay the supplement in dollars on the spot.

From Rangoon to:
Bhamo (BMO): 3 (F-27 $130; F-28 $145)
Heho (HHO): 1,2,3,5,6,7 (F-27 $75; F-28 $85)
Kalemyo (KMO): 5,7 (F-27 $120; F-28 $130)
Kawthaung (KTH): 1,2,5 (F-27 $130; F-28 $145)
Kengtung (KTG): 1,3,5,7 (F-27 $105; F-28 $115)
Kyaukpyu (KPU): 3,7 (F-27 $70; F-28 $80)
Lashio (LSO): 2,3,5,6 (F-27 $110; F-28 $125)
Loikaw (LKW): 2,4,5,7 (F-27 $55; F-28 $60)
Mandalay (MDY): Daily (F-27 $90; F-28 $100)
Mergui (MYT): Daily (F-27 $90; F-28 $100)
Mong Hsat (MST): 2,7 (from HHO F-27 $50; F-28 $55. From KTG F-27 $25; F-28 $30)
Moulmein (MMN): 3,6 (F-27 $35; F-28 $40)
Myitkyina (MKN): 1,3,5,7 (F-27 $150; F-28 $165)
Pagan (PNU): Daily (F-27 $80; F-28 $90)
Putao (PTO): 1,3,5,7 (No price available from Rangoon, but from Myitkyina on F-27 $40; F-28 $45)
Sandoway (TTE): 2,4,6 (F-27 $50; F-28 $55)
Sittwe (STW): Daily (F-27 $80; F-28 $90)
Tachilek (TCL): 1,2,4,6,7 (F-27 $100; F-28 $110)
Tavoy (DWI): Daily (F-27 $65; F-28 $75)

From Mandalay to:
Bhamo: 7 (F-27 $50; F-28 $55)
Heho: 1,3,5,6,7 (F-27 $35; F-28 $40)
Hkamti (KTI): 1,4,7 (F-27 $80; F-28 $90)

Kalemyo: 1,3,4,7 (F-27 $50; F-28 $55)
Myitkyina: 1,5,7 (F-27 $70; F-28 $80)
Pagan: 2,3,4,7 (F-27 $35; F-28 $40)

If you choose to fly on Myanma Airways, remember that all timetables are unpredictable and confirmed flight reservations are forgotten or mysteriously disappear without explanation. There are no announcements to explain delays, nor any when (or, rather, if) a flight is about to depart, so keep a firm eye on your fellow passengers and chase after them if they appear to be heading towards an aeroplane. At domestic airports (other than Rangoon) the only way you know a plane is arriving is when you hear a 'clanking' sound, that is to say a piece of metal struck at least three times serving as an 'announcement'. If at all possible, only travel on Myanma Airways with hand luggage; this eliminates the probability of discovering that your flight has eventually departed without your luggage. Foreigners on domestic flights are required to register with immigration authorities on arrival, so keep your passport handy at all times. Due to the fear of hijacking, the state does not permit Burmese to carry lighters on board, whilst tourists — but not locals — ought not to bring batteries with them.

Checking in is an extraordinary performance. You are required to pass at least five different officials, all with nothing to do except stamp your ticket, pose pertinent questions like 'What is your father's name?' and 'What is your religion?' and even occasionally put you (along with your luggage) on the scales.

First choice for tickets goes to the military, second choice to VIPs, diplomats, businessmen and state officials, third choice to foreign visitors and group tours, fourth choice to tourists and fifth (and last) 'choice' to the Burmese people. If there are any tickets left for locals, these are drawn by lots, so you soon learn that it's impossible for the average Burmese citizen to plan his or her schedule in advance. Thus, either attempting to purchase an airline ticket for a local — or indeed trying to reconfirm one for a tourist — is sardonically referred to as 'all day sightseeing at UB office.'

Air Mandalay

On November 1 1994 Air Mandalay (a Singapore/SLORC joint venture) commenced flights from Rangoon to Mandalay; connections to Pagan were added subsequently. Other domestic routes are Heho and Sandoway; the only international destination is Chiang Mai.

Air Mandalay has direct flights from Rangoon to Mandalay, Pagan and Heho on a daily basis, and flies to Sandoway on Monday, Wednesday and Friday.

The fares are Rangoon to Mandalay US$105 one way, Mandalay to Pagan US$42, Rangoon to Pagan US$93, Mandalay to Heho US$42,

Rangoon to Heho US$93, Rangoon to Sandaway US$63, Rangoon to Chiang Mai US$123, Mandalay to Chiang Mai US$145.

By rail

Burma claims to have 2,270.41 miles of railroads. The main connections are Rangoon to Myitkyina (722 miles), Rangoon to Mandalay (385 miles, see *Chapter Seven*), Rangoon to Lashio (560 miles), Rangoon to Moulmein (178 miles) and Rangoon to Prome (161 miles).

USEFUL ADDRESSES

Embassies (all in Rangoon)

Australia 88 Strand Rd; tel: 80711, fax: 71434, telex: 21301
Bangladesh 56 Kaba Aye Pagoda Rd; tel: 51174, telex: 21320
China 1 Pyidaungsu Yeiktha Rd; tel: 21280, telex: 21346
Czech and Slovak 326 Pyay Rd; tel: 30515
Egypt 81 Pyidaungsu Yeiktha Rd; tel: 22886, fax: 22865, telex: 21315
France 102 Pyidaungsu Yeiktha Rd, POB 858; tel: 82122, fax: 87759, telex: 21314
Germany 32 Natmauk Rd, POB 12; tel: 53673, telex: 21401
India 545-547 Merchant St; tel: 82933, fax: 89562, telex: 21201
Indonesia 100 Pyidaungsu Yeiktha Rd; tel: 81714
Israel 49 Pyay Rd; tel: 22290, telex: 21319
Italy 3 Inya Myaing Rd, Golden Valley; tel: 30966, fax: 33670, telex: 21317
Japan 100 Natmauk Rd; tel: 52288, fax: 52530, telex: 21400
Korea (South) 97 University Ave; tel: 30655, telex: 21324
Laos POB 1550, A1 Diplomatic Quarters, Taw Win Rd; tel: 22482, telex: 21519
Malaysia 82 Pyidaungsu Yeiktha Rd; tel: 20249, fax: 21840, telex: 21321
Nepal 16 Natmauk Lane; tel: 50633, telex: 21402
Pakistan A4 Diplomatic Quarters, Pyay Rd; tel: 22881
Philippines 56 Pyay Rd, 6½ Mile; tel: 64010
Russia 38 Sagawa Rd, tel: 72427, telex: 21331
Singapore 287 Pyay Rd; tel: 33200, fax: 33129, telex: 21356
Sri Lanka 34 Taw Win Rd, POB 1150; tel: 22812, fax: 21509, telex: 21352
Thailand 91 Pyay Rd; tel: 21713, telex: 21341
United Kingdom 80 Strand Rd, POB 638; tel: 81700, fax: 89566, telex: 21216
USA 581 Merchant St, POB 521; tel: 82055, fax: 80409, telex: 21230
Vietnam 40 Komin Kochin Rd; tel: 50361
Yugoslavia (as was): 114A Inya Rd; tel: 32831

Tourism, transport

Myanmar Hotels and Tourism Services 77-91 Sule Pagoda Rd, POB 1398; tel: 83363, fax: 89588, telex: 21330
Myanmar Travels and Tours 77-79 Sule Pagoda Rd; tel: 86024, 85689, fax: 89604, 89588, telex: 21330

Myanma Railways Rangoon Railway Station; tel: 74027
Inland Water Transport 50 Pansodan St; tel: 83244
Myanmar Airways International 123 Sule Pagoda Rd; tel: 89772/4
Myanma Airways (domestic) 104 Strand Rd; tel: 82678
Thai Airways International 441/445 Maha Bandoola St; tel: 75936, 75988, 75167
SilkAir 537 Merchant St; tel: 84600, 82653
Biman Bangladesh 106 Pansodan St; tel: 75882
Air China 67 Pyay Rd; tel: 75714
Rangoon Airport; tel: 62811

Communications

Rangoon Central Post Office 39 Bo Aung Kyaw St (corner of Strand Rd); tel: 85499. Open Monday to Friday 0930 to 1630; postcards cost K3 to Europe, airmail letters K5, registered letters K14.
Telephone, Telex and Fax Overseas calls, telexes and faxes can be made/sent at major hotels and at the Central Telegraph Office 125 Pansodan St; tel: 81133. Public telephones are located at (some) airports, railway stations and department stores.

Emergency telephone numbers
Ambulance: 192
Fire Brigade: 191
Police: 199
Immigration: 86434

Hospitals and clinics

Rangoon General Hospital Bogyoke Aung San St; tel: 81722
Insein General Hospital Mingyi St; tel: 40132
Kandawgyi Clinic Natmauk Rd; tel: 50149
Lake View Clinic Kan Yeiktha Rd, 6½ mile; tel: 30083
Eye, Ear, Nose and Throat Hospital 30 Natmauk Rd; tel: 53955/53967
Central Women Hospital Minye Kyawzwa Rd; tel: 22811/22804
Aye Yeik Tha Polyclinic No 340 Shwe Bon Tha St; tel: 77242
Medicare Service Dr Khin Maung Thwin; tel: 20542

ACCOMMODATION

'The top floor of the Lee Min Hotel comprised the sleeping quarters. There were cubicles built round the sides and the central space was used as an overflow for late guests and as a communal wash room. There was no space in the cubicles in which to do one's toilet for there was only one foot leeway between the bedside and the clap-board partition. Everything had to be done in public. The place seemed a little overcrowded to Tozer and myself. One cubicle with a slightly larger bed housed four men and two girls. One of the girls was pregnant and the other had a six-months-old baby with her. The baby cried all night.

'... A languorous girl with a concave chest drooped over my chair breathing down my neck. She retched hoarsely and spat on the floor. A bright vermilion cry stabbed the still night air as someone killed a pig outside.

'... The air became hot and fetid like an unventilated cow stable... We decided to give up trying to write and retire to our respective cubicles. I opened the little trap door in the wall of mine that served as a window and breathed deeply of the fresh night air. I climbed into bed — a thinly-padded quilt laid on a solid wooden bedstead — but not to sleep. Long and loudly our fellow-guests advertised their somnolence. They snored and coughed and rent the night with raucous body noises. After one particularly sonorous belch I heard Tozer cry from his cubicle, "Have that one on me, old boy!"'

Red Moon Rising, George Rodger, 1943

The Lee Min Hotel on the Burma/China border may or may not still be standing, but it would not be atypical of Burmese accommodation outside Rangoon or Mandalay. 'The Gateway To The Land of Pagodas', the Strand Hotel, founded in 1901 by the Sarkies brothers (who also owned Raffles in Singapore and the E & O in Penang), is still very much standing. 'Upgraded' at a cost of approximately US$22 million, the Strand today charges up to US$650 a night, a good deal more than Rodger and Tozer paid at the Lee Min Hotel way back in the early 40s. And also more than the 11p (K15) a night I paid at the Sibin Rest House for government officials in Tavoy in 1994.

As of November 15 1994, Burma boasted 216 hotels, motels, inns and guesthouses, of which 37 were state-owned and 179 belonged (allegedly) to the private sector. The total number of rooms stood at 4,384.

Chapter Six

Rangoon and Vicinity

'The streets of the town are narrow, and much inferior to those of Pegu, but clean, and well paved: there are numerous channels to carry off the rain, over which strong planks are placed, to prevent an interruption to intercourse. The houses are raised on posts from the ground; the smaller supported by bamboos, the larger by strong timbers. All the officers of Government, the most opulent merchants, and persons of consideration, live within the fort; shipwrights, and people of inferior rank, inhabit the suburbs; and one entire street, called Tuckally (Tat-ga-le), is exclusively assigned to common prostitutes, who are not permitted to dwell within the precincts of the fortification.

'Swine are suffered to roam about the town at large: these animals, which are with reason held unclean, do not belong to any particular owners; they are servants of the public, common scavangers; they go under the houses and devour the filth. The Burmans are also fond of dogs, numbers of which infest the streets; the breed is small and extremely noisy.'

Thus described Colonel Symes Rangoon in his *Embassy to the Kingdom of Ava* way back in 1800.

History and general description
One hundred and forty-three years later, Clement Chapman, chairman of the Upper Burma District (Methodist Church), 'after trekking over the hazardous hills route, leading a convoy to safety in India 1942', portrayed Rangoon in a rather different light:

'The sun comes fitfully from under the lifting clouds, and shines on the ripples of the water. And then, for a moment, the pearl-grey mist is parted, and you gaze breathlessly on something suspended as it were in mid-air — the golden splendour of the Shwe Dagon, the queen of Buddhist pagodas! Up there, dominating the life of the city, the sheen of its gold, the grace of its poise, the shimmering of its tapering spire, all combine to make it what it is, an ethereal expression of the soul of a worshipping people. You may have crossed the seas in search of the harvest of Burma's rice-fields, the teak of her forests, the wealth of her oil. You will never know the land, never understand the wistful longings of her children, if you have looked on the Shwe Dagon pagoda with unseeing eyes.'

Nearly 200 years after Symes complained of prostitutes, pigs and pariahs — as indeed did Orwell in *Burmese Days* — and almost 50 years after Chapman eulogised the 'Shwe Dagon pagoda', little has changed in Rangoon. As capitals go, it is comparatively new, at least in historical terms. In other respects it's a crumbling, decaying, Dickensian yet alluring metropolis. It is quite unlike any other place in Southeast Asia.

From the middle of the 18th century, Rangoon steadily grew in importance, though it had no political status until after the annexation of Lower Burma by the British in 1852. Known as *Okkala* way back in the mists of time, and later *Dagon* (possibly from the Shwedagon Pagoda), it was renamed *Ran-kon* or *Yangon* meaning 'The End of Enmity/Hostility' after the conquest of Lower Burma by King Alaungpaya in 1755. The city then became Rangoon, an easy Anglicisation of Ran-kon.

For a long time Rangoon was little more than an oversized village, even when King Alaungpaya made it the principal port in preference to Syriam (just across the river), which formerly held pride of place. Rangoon, then, was merely a riverside village with a total area of not more than one-eighth of a square mile and with a circumference of just a couple of miles. It was after the British chose to make it their administrative centre that the present chess-board pattern city, planned by their engineers, emerged, the cross-streets being numbered in the American way.

Heavily battered during World War II, the essence of 'old' Rangoon today remains very much as it did then. There has been the odd lick of paint here and there, new hotels springing up, road widening, cutting down trees and building pedestrian bridges and a fortune (allegedly more than 350 million kyat) spent on the construction of a new pagoda. Known behind closed doors as the 'Socialist Pagoda', the *Mahawizayazedi* (Great Conqueror) stands gleaming, in the shadow of the Shwedagon, subsidised by funds appropriated by Ne Win solely to make merit for himself as a *hpaya-daga* (pagoda-builder) and to appease the *nats*. The lavish pagoda, heavily gilded, glistens in the heat, while the Burmese citizens, strolling by, muse how the money might have been more wisely apportioned. As George Orwell remarked in his novel *Burmese Days*: 'It was time now to be making ready for the next world — in short, to begin building pagodas.'

'When the Umbrella is crowned on the Indian Pagoda;
The Sun shall certainly disappear;
And the Moon will not rise up;
The Saturday-born King shall self-destruct.'

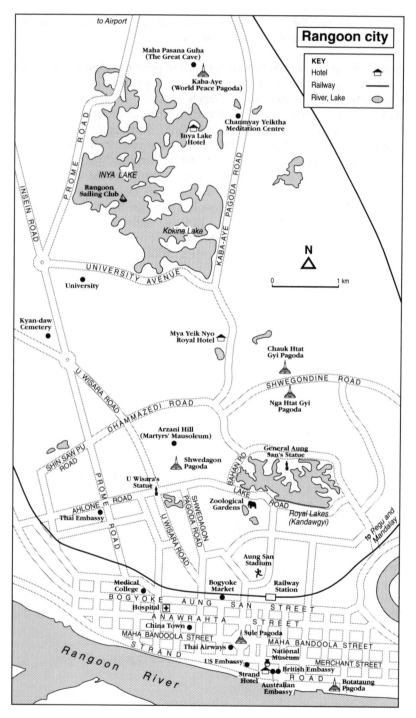

Where to stay

Forget the renovated colonial Strand Hotel, the hideous Russian-built Inya Lake, the rat-infested Thamada, the British-built Kandawgyi (which has had US$10.5 million pumped into it by the Thais), the Sakhantha (the Railway Hotel, 'thoroughly fitted with modern sanitation'), the Garden, Dagon and YMCA — all universally drab. Well-to-do foreigners these days head for the Mya Yeik Nyo Hotels Group ('Dusky Shade of Emerald'), comprising Mya Yeik Nyo Royal, Supreme and Deluxe. The Mya Yeik Nyo chain, which is owned by Zaykabar Company Limited, claims to be a private enterprise, but is in fact SLORC run. The service at least is above-average and the rooms are clean and well-equipped.

Mya Yeik Nyo Royal No 20, Pa-Le Rd, Bahan Township, tel: 38310 to 38319
Mya Yeik Nyo Supreme 23/25, Kaba Aye Pagoda Rd, Bahan Township, tel: 51464, 53818/9
Mya Yeik Nyo Deluxe No 16(B) Thukhawaddy Rd, Yankin Township, tel: 63196, 56529; telex: 21525.
Fax numbers for all three hotels: 65052 and 38318.

The Mya Yeik Nyo Royal is a veritable palace, situated on the second highest hill in Rangoon and affording superb views of the Shwedagon. 'Palace' is no misnomer, for in its previous incarnation, the Royal played host to state leaders the world over. Lying in grounds of more than six acres, it boasts a swimming pool and every luxury you couldn't possibly expect from a hotel in Burma. They will even stage a *pwe* on request. Prices start from US$120 (for a single Junior Suite), rising to a staggering US$420 for a so-called 'Mayor Suite' (all rates plus 20% tax).

The Supreme and the Deluxe are very much on a par with each other. Rates start at US$40 (plus 20% tax) for a single (US$60 plus taxes at the Supreme), rising to US$120 for a double suite. This should include a fruit tray on arrival, breakfast and complimentary tea and coffee. Late check-out incurs no extra charge.

Located within sight of the Shwedagon Pagoda, the **Alfa Hotel** (No 41, Nawaday Street, Dagon Township, tel: 70127-33, fax: 70134) merits a reserved recommendation in the mid-range bracket — prices 'officially' range from US$110-154, but travel agents' rates are US$60-85, including tax and breakfast. Facilities include a 24-hour coffee shop offering 'Casual European Cuisine', Lotus Restaurant ('Fine Myanmar Dining'), business centre and IDD telephone (which doesn't operate). The staff and management still have a lot to learn, but they mean well.

Where to eat

Alas the **New Delhi Restaurant** and its 'fighting balls' has gone downhill, so now the only decent Indian restaurant in Rangoon is **Simla**, No 222/224 Anawrahta St, between 31st and Bo Sun Pat Streets, tel: 71409. Possibly the noisiest place in town, it serves excellent chapattis but avoid the skinny chickens and other meat dishes. The city's one and only Thai restaurant is **Sala Thai**, 56 Saya San Rd, tel: 38661, which offers a comprehensive selection of Thai dishes. The food is much improved of late, but grossly overpriced.

Chinese restaurants abound: the **Panda** at No 205 Wadan St (at the corner of Keighley St and St John's Rd, tel: 21152) is one of the most expensive. Others are **Fu Sun**, located at No 160, Kokkine, Kaba Aye Pagoda Rd and **Nagani Garden Restaurant**, No 148, A-1 Compound, 8½ Mile, Prome (Pyay) Rd, tel: 60871. Steer clear of the Royal Garden Restaurant, Kandawgyi (near the Karaweik) — great views of the Shwedagon but shambolic service.

Two of the best local restaurants are the **Hla Myanmar**, No 27, 5th Street, West Shwegondine, Bahan Township, tel: 36822, and the **Mya Kan Tha**, No 70 Natmauk Lanthwe (corner of Po Sein Rd), whilst another Burmese restaurant I would recommend — owing to its pleasant location — is **Lone Ma Lay**, Bogyoke Aung San Park, Natmauk Rd, Bo Cho (2) Quarter, tel: 50357.

Acceptable Burmese fare can also be obtained from **Danubyu Restaurant**, No 170, 29th St, tel: 75397, while **Hi Top Cafeteria**, No 235 Prome (Pyay) Rd, offers excellent views of the Shwedagon Pagoda — and noodles. You could also try the **Holiday Restaurant**, No 51 Po Sein Rd and **Joy Restaurant**, 150(B), Kaba Aye Pagoda Rd & New University Avenue Rd, tel: 53281. The top seafood restaurant is the unfortunately named **Dolphin Restaurant** (no dolphin on the menu), Aquarium, Lake Road, Mingala-taung-nyunt Township, tel: 85084, which serves excellent lobster. **Smile World Restaurant**, Block (1), Roof floor of Theingyi Zay (C) Block, provides good food and the current fad — Burmese songstresses belting out the latest pop hits (much favoured by the Chinese). The most incongruous restaurant — and not one for the queasy — is the **Central View Revolving Restaurant**, Top Floor, Hledan Junction, Kamayut, tel: 35745. The Central View Musical Group Singers will entertain you on your one-hour 45-minute revolving trip around Rangoon. Nauseous, but popular with the affluent Chinese, Wa and Kokang fraternities.

For western food, try **Dream Burger & Snacks**, 161 Upper Keighley St, Lanmadaw Township, tel: 21911. In October 1994 Burma's first Singapore-style food centre opened at Bahan Sports Ground, Bahan Township, tel: 36916. The **M-3 Food Center** serves Burmese, Indian and European dishes.

My two favourite coffee shops are **Pearl** at No 5 York Rd (near the Thamada Hotel), which serves excellent plum cake and has expanded into the burger market (very popular with the locals), and the **Pepsi Shop**, 151, 46th St, Botataung Township, tel: 94258 (run by a delightful family). Try their strawberry ice cream and delicious home-made Burmese desserts. Strongly recommended.

Mandalay Hill at dusk, 'When the mist was on the rice-fields an' the sun was droppin' slow' ('Mandalay', Kipling)

Sagaing, 'crests crowned with pagodas, sides sprinkled with monasteries and sacred shrines'

Kyet-thindaing Pagoda, Tavoy, the unique Buddha image with six fingers on his left hand

Entertainment and shopping

'He (the true Burmese) is passionately fond of outdoor games. A wrestling-match or canoe-race in its way rouses as much enthusiasm, and gives rise to as much gambling, as a prize-fight did or a boat-race or cricket-match now does with us. His own so-called football is a sport requiring skill and agility, and he has taken kindly to the English game, as well as to cricket. He may be seen playing polo, learnt from his Manipuri subjects, in the streets of Mandalay, and the race-meetings in Lower Burma draw large and enthusiastic crowds of Burman spectators. But his energy is intermittent, and does not redeem his character from the charge of general indolence. He will abandon his work for a week to watch a regatta or a poay, for these poays or plays — performed either by actors in person or by marionettes worked by strings over a screen, and the Burmese show considerable skill in both forms — are as interminable as the Chinese dramas, though they are certainly more interesting to watch. The Burman, indeed, will have his holiday in season or out of season, and he endeavours with great success to make his life a perpetual picnic.'

J Annan Bryce, 1886.

Burmese theatrical performances are known as *pwe* or *pweh* (but not *poay* as stated by Annan Bryce in his talk entitled *Burma: the Country and People*, given at the Evening Meeting of the Royal Geographical Society on March 22 1886). They are the highlight of any trip to Burma and have been described by many a traveller in years gone by. In Chapter Two, Ko Zar Ni relates his experiences of the Spirit Festival (*Nat-Pwe*) of Taungbyon, near Mandalay. The most vivid account of a *pwe* is given by Shway Yoe in *The Burman: His Life and Notions:*

'There is no nation on the face of the earth so fond of theatrical representations as the Burmese. Probably there is not a man, otherwise than a cripple, in the country who has not at some period of his life been himself an actor, either in the drama or in a marionette show; if not in either of these, certainly in a chorus dance. It would be wrong to say that there is no other amusement in the country, but it is indisputable that every other amusement ends up with a dramatic performance. When a Burman is born there is a pwe; when he is named there is a pwe; when a girl's ears are bored; when the youth enters the monastery; when he comes out again; when he marries; when he divorces; when he makes a lucky speculation; when he sets up a water-pot; builds a bridge; digs a tank; establishes a monastery; dedicates a pagoda, or accomplishes any other work of merit; when there is a boat or horse race; a buffalo or cock fight; a boxing match, or the letting loose of a fire-balloon; a great haul of fish, or the building of a new house; when the nurseries are sown down, or the rice garnered in; whenever in fact anything at all is done, there is a theatrical representation. Finally, there is a pwe, as grand as his friends can make it, when the Burman dies.'

(Chapter 29 of Shway Yoe's book gives the best account of a Burmese *pwe*.)

The marionette shows Shway Yoe refers to are called *yoke-thay pwe* and were most famously staged in Mandalay and Pagan. After almost dying out, they have resurfaced (for the sole benefit of tourists) in Mandalay at the corner of 63rd and Aung Daw Mu Pagoda Street (K200 per person). Those interested in marionettes are strongly urged to read Ma Thanegi's wonderful book *The Illusion of Life: Burmese Marionettes* (White Orchid Press, Bangkok, 1994).

Most Europeans find Burmese music extremely difficult to grasp. It is certainly an acquired taste and quite different from anything you will have heard in the West. The ensemble or *hsaing-waing* (literally 'a circle of small drums suspended within a frame') comprises a bizarre collection of instruments:

pat-waing	a circle of drums; the largest piece of equipment
kyi-waing	brass gong circle
maung-zaing	'gong-chime', a set of graduated gongs
wa let-khok	bamboo clappers
hneh	oboe; two sizes *hneh-gyi*, big; *hneh-lay*, small
si	small pair of cymbals, held in one hand, for giving the beat
wa	two pieces of wood or bamboo, which function like a pair of castanets
si-do	short drum
lin-gwin	cymbals
sahkunt	double headed horizontal drum
chauk-lon-pat	a set of six drums that vary in size
pat-ma	large barrel drum suspended from a *Pyinsa-rupa* figure — an imaginary animal with the body of a snake, the antlers and hooves of a deer, the wings of a bird, the tail of a fish and the trunk and tusks of an elephant. It is the most striking item and the 'symbol' of the orchestra.

Other Burmese musical instruments include Burmese harps (*saung*), zithers, clarions, *pattala* (a Burmese xylophone), bamboo flutes, violins and cup-shaped bells. An ensemble would not, however, comprise a harp or pattala. Again, Shway Yoe's *The Burman* (chapter 31) is the book to consult.

There are eight, nine or even more members of a Burmese ensemble, as well as two jesters (*hsaing-nauk-hta*) who are also *wa let-khok* players and even vocalists (*hsaing-hso*). Most of the musicians don traditional formal Burmese dress: a *gaung-baung* (Burmese turban), *le-ga-don-eingyi* (stiff collar shirt), *longyi* (sarong) and *taik-pone* (jacket).

Pyinsa-rupa: the mythical animal and symbol of the Burmese orchestra

Karaoke predictably arrived in Rangoon a while ago, though under the following strict regulations:

1. No dancing allowed whatsoever.
2. Make no nuisance in the premises.
3. Refrain from causing disgraceful manners.
4. Don't exchange harsh words.
5. No annoyances to be caused.
6. Unbecoming behaviours are totally not entertained.
7. Actions infringing to the set rules of the state are not permitted.
8. No disturbances out of drunkeness or whatever.
9. Don't spit on the floor.
10. Please don't throw rubbish.
11. Staff members are strictly prohibited from participations.
12. Dress properly.

Rangoon boasts a superb collection of art galleries. I would particularly recommend the Lokanat Galleries, 62 Pansodan, Kyauktada Township, tel: 87506 (open Monday to Friday 0930 to 1630), which features the work, amongst others, of the late Paw Oo Thett, and GV Golden Valley Art Centre, 54 (D) Golden Valley, tel: 33830, which has a fine selection of oil paintings, watercolours, pencilling and pastel.

The most interesting bookshop in town is the Pagan Book House, No 100, 37th St, run by a wily old character U Ba Kyi, who sells (and buys) an intriguing collection of books on Burma. The shop is open daily. Cheaper books are available at countless street stalls. Many, however, are poor quality photocopies which sell for as little as K100 or US$1.

Bo-gyoke Aung San (formerly Scott) Market is the place to go for shopping; like so many Southeast Asian markets it's a vast, sprawling place selling the usual souvenirs plus goods smuggled in from Thailand, China and India. You will almost certainly be approached to change money on the black market — be discreet. Occasionally, you can purchase items in US dollars, Thai baht or other foreign currency (again, if you want to, do it surreptitiously). Always bargain. Scott Market was renamed Bo-gyoke Aung San Market in honour of Burma's independence hero, General (*Bo-gyoke*) Aung San.

I would not recommend buying your souvenirs in Rangoon since they are invariably more expensive than in their place of origin. Marionettes (*yoke-thay*) and tapestries (*kalaga*), for example, are best purchased in Mandalay, lacquerware in Pagan, umbrellas (*hti*) in Bassein, shoulder bags (with silver tassels) in Kachin State and *longyi* (depending on your preference) in Arakan or Mon States. Various wood and ivory carvings, jewellery, gems, jade and antiques (of dubious quality and authenticity) can be found throughout Burma. Buddha images (from sandalwood, teak and even from the wood of the jackfruit tree) are to be seen at the entrances to (amongst others) the three 'Gold' pagodas — the Shwedagon in Rangoon, the Shwemawdaw in Pegu and the Shwesandaw in Prome. Regarding gems and the like, forget it. These days a 'ruby' from Burma is almost as commonplace as a Burmese moggie, only marginally less genuine. In any case, gems, jade, jewellery and antiques cannot 'officially' be taken out of the country unless purchased from a SLORC outlet, such as the Diplomatic Stores (the Tourist Department Stores), where the prices are exorbitant and the 'guarantees of authenticity' worthless.

There are two stores which I can recommend, one for T-shirts of Burma, the other for cheroots. Zaw Winn Hlaing, No 7 Central Block, Bo-gyoke Aung San Market, is run by two charming ladies, Daw Khin Aye Myint and Ma Khin Hla Wai, who will be delighted to serve you. Bargain hard (and flatter them), and they should knock down the price for you. For an astonishing array of cheroots of all shapes and sizes, drop by Daw Aye Kywe's Daw Ohn Mai Cigar Factory, No 45, Nyaunbin St, Kemmendine.

You may like to take a stroll to the Zoological Gardens, located near the Kandawgyi Hotel. Inaugurated in 1906, the zoo is open daily from 0800 to 1600 (entrance fee K5). There is also the Hlawga Wildlife Park, Prome Rd, which is open from 0800 to 1700 (Wednesday to Sunday) and the Aquarium, Kan Rd, Mingala-taung-nyunt Township (0900 to 1630, closed Monday). Sadly, for equine enthusiasts, horse racing has been banned in Burma since Ne Win took over the reins of the country in 1962. It must have been fun, though, as Mi Mi Khaing recalls:

'Horse-racing in Rangoon was a foreign importation, but nevertheless the stadium was always filled, not only with the fashionable section in an enclosure but also with rows of four-anna spectators who had been collected from all the streets of the town by the privately-run Burmese buses which tore along on race days, with two "spares" (spare-men in addition to the driver) hanging out from the back step and shouting to all they passed: "Race-a-ko, Race-a-ko! Race-course, race-course".'

Burmese Family, 1946

A J S White relates an equally nostalgic tale of horse racing in Burma in the early 1920s:

'... ponies and jockeys arrived from far afield and three English bookies came up from Rangoon. There was no doubt a good deal of dirty work. I was Starter — on a borrowed police pony. I had, of course, a good deal of trouble with jockeys trying to get away with a false start — so as to be sure of carrying out their instructions not to win. One jockey who realised that his efforts to "hold" his pony were failing, fell off deliberately just before his pony galloped first past the winning post.'

Sightseeing
Shwedagon Pagoda

'It is always a delight to one's eyes to gaze upon its glittering spire, always a fairy study of artistic enchantment; but perhaps if it has a moment when it seems clothed with peculiar and almost ethereal, mystic attraction, it is in the early morning light, when the air has been bathed by dewdrops and is of crystal clearness, and when that scorching Eastern sun has only just begun to send forth his burning rays. I would say go and gaze on the pagoda at the awakening hour, standing there on the last spur of the Pegu Hills, and framed by a luxuriant tropical bower of foliage.'

G T Gascoigne, 1896

Towering over the city of Rangoon is the gold-encrusted Shwedagon Pagoda — Kipling's 'Winking Wonder' — the biggest Buddhist temple of its kind in the world. Heed Miss Gascoigne's advice and admire this wonderful structure in the early morning or perhaps at twilight. Or simply afar from the Royal Lake. If time permits, visit twice or three times to fully appreciate the wondrous splendour of the Shwedagon Pagoda. Walk up the first time, your shoes stuffed in a shoulder bag or — for a small fee — left with the flower seller at the bottom. You could buy some flowers to offer to the Buddha, but don't smell them or carry them with the blooms downwards!

Believed to have been constructed in 585 BC, the Shwedagon was originally a mere 27ft high, but was brought up to its present height of 326ft in the 15th century by Shin Sawbu, queen of Pegu. It commands veneration and worship not solely because it dates back 2,500 years, but because of the authenticity of its origin which finds support in Buddhist scriptures. It is thought that two Burmese traders, Tapussa and Bhallika of the Mon Kingdom of Okkala, who had journeyed to India by sea, met the Buddha and received a gift of eight hairs from his own hands. On their return, their sacred gift was enshrined by King Okkalapa in a golden pagoda on the Theinguttara Hill, the most natural location for a temple. It is also believed that the sacred relics of the three preceding Buddhas, which had been enshrined on this hill — a staff, a water dipper (filter) and a bathing garment (or portion of a robe) — were excavated and re-consecrated or re-enshrined along with the new relics, in effect giving the pagoda a fourfold religious significance. Kings, queens and commoners have, through the ages, bestowed gold, silver and a myriad of other gifts to embellish the pagoda. The gold-plating and the precious stones (rubies, sapphires and topaz) in the diamond bud and the vane and *hti* run into many millions of kyat.

There are four approaches to the Shwedagon with ascending flights of steps from all the four quarters: north, south, east and west, lined with vendors offering flowers, gold leaf, candles, books and an assortment of souvenirs. Entering via the western approach from the U Wisara Road, you will find on reaching the platform a figure of the founder King Okkalapa himself on the wall towards the west-northwest corner.

The base of the pagoda is 2ft 3in high with a perimeter of 1,420ft. On the platform are 64 smaller pagodas with four large ones right in the centre of the four cardinal points. There are *chinthe* (lion-like sentinels), innumerable shrines, *tazaung* (prayer pavilions) and *zayats* (resthouses built on sacred land/wayside resthouses for travellers). The platform itself is paved with marble and, whichever way you turn, you will find superb woodcarvings, floral designs, mosaic-wrought pillars along with numerous Buddha images, cast in alabaster and brass. There are the famous bells: the *Maha Ghanta* (Great Voice) Bell, 7ft high, 6ft 8in wide, 1ft thick and weighing 16 tons, a gift by Singu Min in 1778, and the *Mahatisadda Ghanta* (Great Sweet Sound) Bell which weighs 40 tons, is 8½ft high, 7ft 8in wide and 1ft thick. This was a gift from King Tharrawaddy in 1841 and is the second largest bell in the land.

Entering by the southern stairway, you find two huge *chinthe*, 30ft high, and statues of ogres. Once on the main platform looking up, you will see three terraces. Above the three terraces, you notice the *Khaung Laung Pone*, a bell-like shape which has a circumference of 442ft at the base and 192ft at the top, reaching a height of 70ft 4in. Then comes the inverted begging bowl (*thabeik hmauk*) bearing a decorative ring of flowers trailing down, the twisted turban (*baung yit*) which takes you another 41ft above; the lotus flower 31ft 5in high; the banana bud 52ft 11in high, the *hti* (umbrella) going up another 33ft (a donation of King Mindon), above that the pennant-shaped vane borne aloft and reaching towards the 76-carat diamond bud on top, a globe of gold, studded with precious stones. The weight of gold leaf on the pagoda is reputedly 60 tons, the number of diamonds on the gold and silver weather vane 1,100, and the number on the diamond orb 4,350.

'Hail, Mother! Do they call me rich in trade?
Little care I, but hear the shorn priest drone,
And watch my silk-clad lovers, man by maid,
Laugh 'neath my Shwe Dagon.'
                                    Kipling

At the foot of the hill, all around, lie many old and new monasteries, concealed by huge trees, palmyras and coconut palms. There are also a number of *zayat* for pilgrims and countless stalls selling food, drinks and souvenirs.

Independent travellers who visit the Shwedagon have to pay an entrance fee of US$5 and K5 for a camera. Most foreigners enter from the south; remove your shoes and socks at the bottom. There are two lifts to take you to the raised platform of the stupa. The pagoda is open daily from 0400 to 2100.

'Solitary at the foot of the column, the worshipping woman kneels, with an offering of flowers in her hands. The platform is deserted. These two are alone — the solemn pyramid so tremendous, the worshipper so little, the truth so imperial, the aspirant so lowly.

'The hum of the distant town has died away. The silence on the terrace is broken only by the murmur of her lips, and by the tinkle of the bells among the clouds high up on the pagoda's summit. And here, in the golden shadow there falls upon her troubled heart
    "The secret of the wordless calm."'
                                    Sir Frederick Treves, 1925

Sule Pagoda

Located in the centre of Rangoon and surrounded by shops with traffic whirling round it, the eight-sided Sule Pagoda reaches a height of 157ft. There are two accounts of the origin of the Sule, which dates back more than 2,200 years. One is that the Venerable Mahinda went to Sri Lanka (Ceylon) 236 years after the nirvana of the Buddha. As a compliment in return, three years later, the then king of Sri Lanka sent an eight-man delegation to Burma. The delegation, gifts and Buddha relics brought were received by Bhoga Sena, king of what is now Syriam. The construction of the present-day Sule Pagoda was entrusted by the king to his minister Athoke. In those days the pagoda was known as *Kyaik Kathoke* or *Kyaik Sura* (*Sura* meaning a 'hero', and *Athoke* was a celebrated hero). In due course, the pagoda became known as Sule.

National Museum

The National Museum was first inaugurated in June 1952 at the Jubilee

Hall, Shwedagon Road, and subsequently shifted to its present site, 24-26 Pansodan Street, formerly the Bank of India, in February 1970. It has a rich collection of antiques, cultural objects, arts and handicrafts of indigenous races, royal regalia, musical instruments, decorative arts and an art gallery. The artefacts are displayed in different showrooms in what is in truth a rather gloomy three-storey building.

On the ground floor, the first object that strikes you (and indeed the main attraction of the museum itself) is the *Thiha-thana Palin* (Lion Throne) which was presented by Lord Mountbatten in 1948. Built in 1816 during the reign of King Bodawpaya, it is the sole remaining throne of nine which were constructed: the other eight were destroyed by fire during World War II. Carved out of *yamanay* hardwood and finely gilded, it is flanked by royal regalia (all solid gold, including gold betel cups and vessels), silverware, artefacts, photographs, models and paintings of Mandalay Palace. You can also see various ceremonial robes, head-dresses, garments, girdles, divans and couches belonging to past members of the Burmese monarchy; even King Thibaw's state attire and ivory chair and Queen Supayalat's dressing table are on display.

National Museum, Rangoon: hintha betel container

There are opium weights, hilltribe costumes, paintings, woodcarvings, Buddha images from the Pagan period and tools dating back to neolithic times. Many of these displays are on the second and third floors of the museum which are easily missed. Most items are inadequately labelled and poorly displayed. The entrance fee is US$4 and it is open from 1000 to 1500 Monday to Friday.

Other attractions

Situated near the Rangoon River waterfront, east of the Strand Hotel and at the intersection of the Strand and Botataung Roads, is the **Botataung Pagoda** (Pagoda of a Thousand Officers). The pagoda was constructed in AD 997 (359 BE) on the orders of Okkalapa, King of Twante, on the spot where the body of his son Minnanda, who had been drowned in the Pegu River, was burned. Legend has it that 1,000 officers brought two hairs of the Buddha, which are displayed in a glass case in a hall on the right side in front of a stunning Buddha image. This image was donated by King Mindon in the middle of the 19th century and taken by the British at the end of that century. It was returned in 1951. The Botataung is a hollow pagoda with a zigzagging corridor with walls completely covered in mosaic mirror glass.

The **Chauk Htat Gyi** (Six-Storey) **Pagoda,** north of the Royal Lake on Shwegondine Road, houses the fourth largest reclining Buddha in Burma, 216ft long and 58ft high. The original was built in 1907 by an exceptionally rich Burmese gentleman, but was destroyed in 1957. Rebuilt in 1966, it was completed in 1974 at a cost of no less than K5 million (allegedly from public donations). Of particular interest are the feet of the Buddha which are inscribed with the 108 sacred symbols characteristic of an enlightened Buddha.

Nearby (and currently under renovation) stands the **Nga Htat Gyi** (Five-Storey) **Pagoda**, erected in 1900 by U Po Aung, a merchant of Rangoon and one of the trustees of the Shwedagon Pagoda. With its peculiarly shaped stupa, it houses a giant seated Buddha on a lotus throne, a footprint of the Buddha and a huge bell. There is also a silver stupa in the precinct. A beautiful *tazaung* with glass mosaic and woodcarvings on the wall and ceiling was donated by a rich Burmese lady and escaped the fire that destroyed much of the building. It is very peaceful early in the morning and at dusk when worshippers come to pay their respects. Next to the pagoda is a Chinese Temple.

The **Kaba-Aye** (World Peace) **Pagoda** was constructed in 1952 for the Sixth Great Buddhist Synod (1954-56). In 1948 a certain Saya Htay was meditating at the foot of Shin Ma Kyaung Hill near Pakokku when he was approached by an old man dressed in white. The old man gave him a bamboo staff inscribed with the Pali words *Siri Mangala* and asked him to present it to U Nu. He further requested that U Nu build a pagoda to secure and reinforce the foundations of the Buddha Sasana. U Nu selected a site on a hillock seven miles out of Rangoon, also called Siri Mangala. The pagoda has a circumference of 300ft and goes up to a height of 118ft, with a gilded finial. In the treasure vault is a silver image of the Buddha cast out of half a ton of silver and four hundred-weight of brass.

The **Mahapasana Guha** (Great Cave) nearby was also opened specifically for the Sixth Great Buddhist Synod on May 10 1954. The

Mahapasana Guha — a building in the form of a cave — serves as an assembly and ordination hall for abbots and monks. The cave — 455ft long and 370ft wide — cost over K9 million to construct.

The **Eindawya Pagoda** was built in 1846 by Yewun U Win, on the site of the residence of Pagan Min, when he accompanied his father Shwebo Min to Rangoon in 1841.

Near the airport at Mingaladon is the **Kyaik-kalo Pagoda** (also spelt Kyaik Ka Lawt), which has a *zaungdan* (a covered walkway along which to approach the pagoda) recently constructed by the SLORC. *Kyaik* is the Mon (Talaing) word for pagoda and *kalaw* means 'to do obeisance or revere'. According to tradition, an ogre did obeisance to Buddha Kakusandha on this spot. Close by (about a minute's drive away) is the **Kyaikkale Pagoda**, which also has a newly constructed *zaungdan*. In Mon *kale* means to disappear. Legend has it that the Buddha Kakusandha disappeared on this spot between the eyebrows of the ogre while playing hide and seek. In the pagoda precinct stands a statue of the ogre called Kaya Heindaka Bilu. The pagoda, which was repaired in 1897 and crowned with a *hti* in 1904, is surrounded by monasteries. In the precinct is a tall, standing statue of the Buddha making a prophecy.

About ten minutes' drive away stands the **Alein-nga-sint Pagoda**, built by a famous abbot Seiwunkaba Sayadaw. It is unique in style and quite peculiar. Inside is a green Buddha image called Maha-sandaw-shinmya-hpaya (The owner of the hair relics' emerald statue). The foundation stone of this pagoda was laid on April 22 1958 jointly by the abbot and the President of Burma, U Win Maung. In the four corners are staircases each with five tiers: the name of the pagoda literally means 'twist five layer'.

At North Okkalapa, five minutes from Mingaladon Airport, is the **Meilamu** (Meh-lamu) **Pagoda**, which boasts numerous vast Buddha images. Amongst the myriad of images are the Buddha on the way to Enlightenment, the Buddha preaching to his five disciples, the Buddha resting, four large images in different postures, a large image of all eight conquests of the Buddha, a reclining Buddha, three laymen offering *hsun* (food) to the Buddha, images of Shin Thiwali (the most fortunate disciple of the Buddha) and Shin Upagok (the most powerful of all the disciples), Lord Buddha's son Yahula asking for a legacy from his father, Lord Buddha surrounded by two rivals, Devadatta and a follower, two images of the Lord Buddha meditating, and a hermit called Thumayda prostrating himself as a bridge over a stream for the Buddha to walk over.

In the Thamaing area of Rangoon is the **Kyauk-waing Pagoda**, called Kyaik-waing-ut in Mon. In Mon *waing* means 'to play' and *ut* 'hide and seek'. According to tradition, Buddha Kakusandha played hide and seek with the ogre, the wager laid being that if the ogre was found by the Buddha, he should listen to his preaching, and if not found, the Buddha should be eaten by the ogre.

In the Thin-gan-gyun Township of Rangoon stands the **Kyaik-kasan Pagoda**, which is reputed to have been built in the 4th century BC by Sihadipa, king of Thaton, assisted by Yasa and seven other monks, over 16 hairs and 32 bone-relics of the Buddha. In Mon it is called Kyaik-Hasan, signifying the 'Pagoda of eight monks'. Golden statuettes of these monks were enshrined in the building.

In Yegyaw, Pazundaung Township, in East Rangoon is the **Shwephonebywint Pagoda**, where Buddhists meditate in order to attain Enlightenment. It contains a footprint of the Buddha, a small stupa and compound. For those interested in meditation, it is a fascinating pagoda: its name literally translates as 'Practise meditation and Enlightenment blooms here'. Indeed there are shrines of Enlightened persons and *nats* in the precinct. The pagoda was originally called Shwegyokpwint — 'Golden casket being opened'. The casket in question contained hair relics that were enshrined in the pagoda, which was founded by King Okkalapa after the Shwedagon.

In Sanchaung Township stands the **Kohtatgyi** (Nine-Storey) **Pagoda**, built by means of donations from a merchant named U Kyin, his wife Daw Ngwe Zan and son Maung Kyaw. Constructed on August 5 1905, it contains a giant seated Buddha, which is currently under renovation.

Situated about 21 miles (or 45 minutes) northeast of Rangoon is the **Htaukkyant War Cemetery**, said to be the resting place of 33,421 soldiers who perished in World War II.

BEYOND RANGOON

Syriam

Syriam (Tanyin) was Lower Burma's main trading port in the 18th century and an old Portuguese settlement. Today it is a dirty, ugly place which is reached either by ferry in about 40 to 50 minutes or by car in 30 minutes over the Yangon-Tanyin Tada (bridge), built with the aid of the Chinese and completed in November 1992. Syriam is home to two splendid pagodas: the **Kyaikkauk** and **Kyaikmawwin** (also known as the Kyauktan Yay-leh-hpaya, 'water middle pagoda').

Guarded by two massive *chinthe* with black beards (the head of the left *chinthe* is tilted to the right), the Kyaikkauk is located at Payagon. According to tradition, it enshrines one of the two hairs of the Buddha which were given by the sage to 24 hermits on his visit to Syriam at the invitation of Gavampati, the second being enshrined in Rangoon's Kyaik-kasan Pagoda. The pagoda, which is similar in size and design to the Shwedagon, has four pavilions with four seated Buddhas. In front of the pagoda lie the tombs of two celebrated Burmese writers, Natshinnaung and Padethayaza.

About two to three minutes' drive away is **Natsin-gone** ('hillocks where there are *nat* shrines') and a dilapidated stupa called Manawmaya-zedidaw. Alas, all of the *nats* have disappeared, but their names are written inside the shrines. There is a tomb of the abbot named Sayadaw U Dewataymiza who apparently lived until he was 109 and a marble footprint of the Buddha encircled by two dragons. There is also a monastery called Manawmaya.

Reached by boat, the **Kyauktan Yay-leh-hpaya**, meaning 'Pagoda in the middle of the water', is guarded by two colourful ogres. Legend relates that the water level never rises up to the pagoda precinct even if the surrounding area becomes flooded.

To make the journey to Syriam by ferry, you have to get to the Thidar jetty. The ferry actually crosses the tributary of the Rangoon River known as the Pazundaung-chaung. Be prepared for an unpleasant ride: you have to wait until the ferry is jam-packed before it moves off and if you want a wooden seat you will have to pay extra. The ferry stinks of urine and is full of hawkers selling everything imaginable: quail's eggs, pomelos, bananas, lemons, guavas, coconuts, sugarcane, buns, ice-cream, peanuts, newspapers, cigarettes, toys and results of the Burmese lottery. They even rent out Burmese comics for the trip. It's a dull crossing with little of interest, though when you reach Syriam you can take a horse-cart and explore a part of Burma which has probably only seen a handful of tourists in the past decade.

Twante

'Incidentally the police officer at Twante at this time was an Old Etonian named Blair... Blair, whom I saw something of later in Rangoon, became famous in due course as George Orwell, the writer.'

The Burma of 'AJ', A J S White

Orwell was posted to Twante in 1924 (before being sent to Syriam, which he loathed, the following year). According to his biographer, Bernard Crick, Orwell's sole interest in Twante was 'shooting imperial pigeons'. These days, Twante is a pottery town famed for its large earthenware jars, which are supplied to Rangoon and much of the delta, its freshwater fishery and turtle eggs.

Twante is also known for its **Shwesandaw Pagoda**, which, in days gone by, was an object of greater veneration to the Talaings (Mons) than even the Shwedagon, since it had never been renovated by the Burmans. It was erected in 577 BC by a husband and wife as a shrine for three hairs of the Buddha. The spot on which the pagoda stands was chosen by the Lord Buddha as it had been the site of two of his previous incarnations — one as an elephant and one as a *thamin* (a kind of deer). Twante occupies the site of an old Talaing town, the walls of which are still traceable. It was also the location of an ancient *nandaw* (palace).

Pegu

'... it is a great citie, very plaine and flat, and foure square, walled round
about, and with ditches that compass the walls about with Water, in which
Ditches are many crocodiles. It hath no Draw-bridges, yet it hath twenty
Gates five for every square in the Walls...'

Venetian traveller Caesar Frederick (1569) quoted in
an English translation of 1588 by Thomas Hickock, giving
perhaps the earliest description of Pegu by a European

Pegu is located some 50 miles to the northeast of Rangoon and takes
about two hours to reach. It is possible to go on your own by public bus
(hot, crowded, uncomfortable but cheap), train (the No 13-Up leaves
Rangoon at 1720, arriving Pegu at 2050; the No 14-Down departs Pegu
at 0550, arriving Rangoon at 0900) or by hiring a private car. There is
one tourist hotel, the insect-infested Shwe Wa Tun with air-conditioned
rooms from US$37 to $62 (breakfast included). Lousy.

Pegu was established as the capital of Lower Burma during the reign
of Binnya U (1353-85), and was conquered by Tabinshwehti (who
founded the Toungoo Dynasty) in 1539. Seven years later, Tabinshwehti
pronounced himself King of Burma with Pegu as his capital. In 1599,
however, towards the end of the Toungoo Dynasty, an Arakanese fleet
laid siege to the city and captured it. During the reign of King Thalun
(1629-48), the capital was moved back from Pegu to Ava. During Pegu's
golden years, around the time of 1519, it acquired the reputation as a
'rich city and international port'.

Legend, in fact, relates that Pegu's first historical period extended
from AD 573 to 1057. According to historical tradition, a king of Thaton
had two sons named Thamala and Wimala. They were about to establish
a town in the year 573 when they observed a sacred goose (*han-tha*) or
sheldrake building its nest on an island nearby. This was an auspicious
sign, and therefore they called their town Han-tha-wadi. But people
generally referred to it as Pegu (as indeed they do now) because it was
located on the Pegu River. Pegu's symbol today depicts these two
mythical *hintha* birds (the spelling and precise meaning of the word vary
according to which legend you believe), the smaller female perched on
the male's back. The name *hintha* derives from the Pali word *hansa*
which means a water bird. For another account of this story, see Khin
Myo Chit's *A Wonderland of Burmese Legends*.

Shwemawdaw Pagoda

'The celebrated temple of Shoemadoo, higher by thirty feet than the
Shoedagon, had long been conspicuous in the distance, towering above all;
and a noble feature it was, an emblem of stately and solitary grandeur...
Shoemadoo... was once, in point of sanctity, superior to all other temples
in Ava, and the natives declare it to be more than two thousand years old...

It was formerly gilded as highly as the Shoedagon pagoda, to which, in point of size and elegance of structure, it is superior...'

Capt F B Doveton, 1852

According to one legend — and there are many — the Shwemawdaw Pagoda 'derives its name from the Talaing (Mon) Hpoot-daw, which in Burmese is Bhoora-byan, flying or winged bhoora or pagoda. It is a pyramidal solid brick building rising to a height of 324 feet from an octagonal base, each side of which is 162 feet in length. It stands upon two terraces, one above the other; the larger and lower, about 10 feet from the level of the ground, being an exact parallelogram each of the sides of which is 1,390 feet long; the upper and the smaller terrace, of the same shape as the lower, is about 20 feet higher and has a perimeter of 2,735 feet; both are ascended by uncovered flights of stone steps. The base of the pagoda is surrounded by two tiers of smaller ones, the lower of which, six feet from the terrace, contains 75, each 27 feet high and 40 feet in circumference at the base; the upper tier contains 53.'

Two earthquakes (in 1912 and 1917) shook the pagoda, before another, even more devastating, brought it tumbling down in May 1930. It was reconstructed in 1952, and when the diamond-laden golden *hti* was placed on top in 1954, it reached a height of 374ft, 48ft taller than the Shwedagon. The Shwemawdaw Pagoda Festival is held annually each April.

Shwethalyaung

Hidden in the jungle for over a century following the sacking of Pegu in 1757, the Shwethalyaung (Giant Reclining Buddha) was discovered by chance in 1881 by engineers working on the extension of the railway line to Pegu. An Indian contractor for the supply of bricks and earth began digging the area for stocks when he came across a vast pile of brickwork, of which he decided to avail himself. However, storms of protests arose from fellow-workers conversant with the history of the image and the contractor was obliged to stop his work. The reconstruction of the holy image was started immediately and the once neglected crumbling image was restored to its former glory.

Built originally in AD 994 (on the death of King Anuraja) by King Migadhippa (the younger) to commemorate his conversion to Buddhism after years of spirit worship, this 180ft long reclining image is one of the most beautiful and sacred in Burma. Its dimensions are vast: it is 52½ft high, its face measures 22½ft, the palm of the hand 22ft, the sole of the foot 25½ft, the little finger 10ft and the great toe 6ft. It is protected by a huge steel *tazaung* erected in 1906.

Foreigners are charged US$2 to visit the Shwemawdaw Pagoda, the Shwethalyaung and the **Mahazedi Pagoda.** The Mahazedi (Great Stupa) was completed in 1560 by Hanthawadi Sinbyushin, known as King Bayinnaung to the Burmese and Braginoco to the Portuguese. Its

Guardian of the Shwethalyaung, the giant reclining Buddha at Pegu

construction was based on that of the Mahacheti stupa of Ceylon and is a beautiful bell-shaped structure. Over the years, the Mahazedi has suffered badly from both earthquakes and vandalism. The placing of the *hti* iron framework crest on top was celebrated in 1982 with festivals of music and dances.

Other places of interest

Pegu's two other pagodas of note are the **Shwegugyi** (Great Golden Cave) and **Shwegu-galay**. The former was built in 1476 by Dhammacheti, king of Pegu after the model of the Bodha Gaya Temple in India; the latter in 1494 by Hatthiraja or Byinnya Ran, also king of Pegu. The basement of the Shwegu-galay's shrine consists of ambulatory corridors containing 64 images of the Buddha, and its superstructure is a cylindrical pagoda.

The **Kalyani Thein** (*Sima* in Pali, meaning ordination hall) was first consecrated and built by King Dhammacheti (Dammazedi) in 1476. The original Sima was a prototype of the famous ordination hall of Ceylon but suffered from various earthquakes and fires subsequently. The present-day Sima was built in 1954 and stands on ground marked by white marble pillars, symbols of a consecrated place. Nearby are ten stone inscriptions in Pali and Mon relating the history of the monument as well as an account of the vicissitudes of the Buddhist Church in Burma and of the efforts made by Dhammacheti to reform and purify it. The Kalyani Thein was so called because the original monks were ordained on the banks of the Kalyani stream in Ceylon.

A few hundred feet off the Rangoon-Pegu Road, almost two miles out of town, stand the spectacular **Kyaikpun Pagoda** or **Images**. Built in 1476 by Dhammacheti, king of Pegu, there are four sitting images placed back to back and facing the four cardinal points, recalling the four-faced Brahma of India. Each image measures almost 100ft in height; the one facing west was destroyed in the 1930 earthquake and subsequently repaired.

The images are of the four Buddhas: Kaukathan (or Kakusandha, east), Gaunagong (or Konagamana, south), Kathapa (or Kassapa, west) and Gautama (north), who have each in succession attained Enlightenment in this world. Serenely they await the arrival of the fifth and final Buddha, after which this world cycle will be destroyed in universal chaos. As each Buddha saw his Enlightenment in this world, he left a relic at the Theinguttara Hill in Rangoon, which foretold his coming and which would now mark his attainment of wisdom — Kaukathan his staff, Gaunagong his water filter, Kathapa a portion of his robe, and Gautama his eight hairs which were enshrined in the first Shwedagon Pagoda after numerous perilous journeys.

In 1993, excavation work — resulting in the forced relocation of over 300 families — at the 16th century **palace of King Bayinnaung** unearthed six golden flowers of unique Burmese craftsmanship, 24 pieces of gold, ten polished rubies and three sacred statues which had been standing on a brick wall at what was believed to have been the altar wing of the Kambawza Thardi Palace. The palace was built in 1553 when the Mon king was at the height of his power. Excavation began in 1991, with funding assistance from UNESCO. The palace compound comprises many buildings, the major ones being the Audience Hall, King Bayinnaung's chamber, and the palaces of his two queens, Chantra and Kusuma. Five workmen also dug up 29 British gold sovereigns dating back to the 19th century at a rice-mill site.

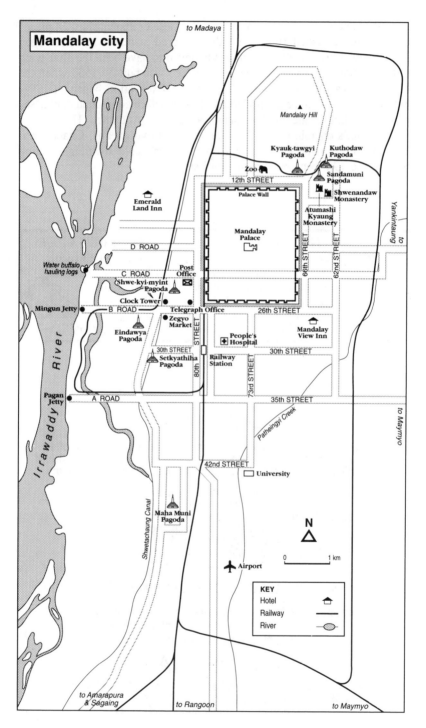

Mandalay city

to Madaya

Mandalay Hill

Kyauk-tawgyi Pagoda

Kuthodaw Pagoda

Zoo

Sandamuni Pagoda

12th STREET

Palace Wall

Shwenandaw Monastery

Emerald Land Inn

Atumashi Kyaung Monastery

Mandalay Palace

to Yankintaung

66th STREET

62nd STREET

D ROAD

Water buffalo hauling logs

C ROAD

Post Office

Shwe-kyi-myint Pagoda

Clock Tower

Mingun Jetty

B ROAD

Telegraph Office

26th STREET

to Maymyo

Eindawya Pagoda

Zegyo Market

80th STREET

People's Hospital

Mandalay View Inn

30th STREET

Setkyathiha Pagoda

30th STREET

73rd STREET

Railway Station

Pagan Jetty

A ROAD

35th STREET

Patheingyi Creek

Irrawaddy River

42nd STREET

University

Shwetachaung Canal

Maha Muni Pagoda

N

0   1 km

Airport

KEY

Hotel	
Railway	
River	

to Amarapura & Sagaing

to Rangoon

to Maymyo

Chapter Seven

Mandalay and Vicinity

'I was quite delighted at the idea of visiting a place I had heard so much of, and which (in name at least) is familiar to everyone, from Rudyard Kipling's famous song. I was looking out for all the things he mentions therein when we began to get near, and was so disappointed, Mamma, when Aunt told me that most of the song was absolute nonsense, and unintelligible to anyone who had ever visited the place. She said, too, that Rudyard Kipling evidently never could have seen Mandalay, or else he would never have written all the trash he did about the "flying fishes" of which there are, of course, none, and about "China cross the Bay." "What bay?" as Aunt remarked! Even I knew enough geography before I came to Burma to have told R.K. there was no bay at Mandalay, and no China either, as I find, unless he was thinking of China Street. But perhaps he got mixed up between Mandalay and Moulmein or some other place beginning with an "M"...

'Well, Mamma, although there were no flying fishes and no bay, there were plenty of "tinkly pagodas." R.K. was all right about these! And such pretty ones too...'

Elizabeth Visits Burma, 'Jeff', 1910

Getting there and around

'We spent that day crawling from station to station through the sunshine north of Mandalay. At intervals while Mr Holla was asleep, I borrowed "Lords of the Sunset" from him, and at other times I read the Burma Railway's Timetable, which had more in it than met the eye .. It was, for example, an offence to sell any part of one's return ticket, or to ride in or upon the engine or to extinguish the lamps. The latter in our carriage resembled, indeed, in the Irish R.M.'s memorable words, a gold-fish, and were "about as much use as an illuminant," and Heaven forbid that we should have extinguished any of them...

'... More seasoned travellers lighted spirit-stoves in the lavatory and beguiled the hours with tea and corned beef and cheese; they filled the wash-basin with ice and beer, which gave rise to that curious inscription on all of them, "DO NOT BREAK ICE ON BASIN." Years ago, in my young innocence, travelling through the dry zone, I had imagined from this warning that even on the Burma Railways it must sometimes freeze at nights.'

J K Stanford, 1944

The Rangoon to Mandalay line was opened for traffic in March 1889. The cost of constructing the line was estimated at a little over 'twenty millions of rupees'. These days passengers can travel on the thrice-weekly 'Dagon-Mann Special Express Rail Service (No 17-Up)' (and No 18-Down) under an arrangement made by Myanma Railways and the Dagon-Mann Company Ltd. This new train comprises the following: two upper-class special coaches with sleeping berths, three special upper-class coaches, two upper-class coaches, one first-class coach, two ordinary-class coaches, one restaurant car and guard's van (14 coaches in total).

The upper-class special coaches with sleeping berths have four four-passenger rooms each furnished with air conditioner, refrigerator, radio cassette and audio system. The upper-class coaches with sleeping berths have four four-passenger and two double-passenger rooms with air conditioner and audio system. The special upper-class coaches have 30 seats, each installed with air conditioner, video and audio systems. The upper-class coaches also have video and audio systems. The first and ordinary-class each have 60 seats also with video and audio systems. The restaurant has room for 27 people at a time and passengers can choose between eating there or 'room service'. All in all, the train can carry 406 passengers and is only supposed to stop at Toungoo and Thazi. You can't board at Toungoo, but you can get off; however at Thazi you can do both. The No 17-Up departs Rangoon every Sunday, Wednesday and Friday at 1515, arriving in Mandalay at 0520. The No 18-Down leaves Mandalay on a Monday, Thursday and Saturday at 1615, getting in to Rangoon at 0620. Tickets can be bought at Rangoon Railway Station four days in advance and cost US$50 (one way).

Regarding other trains, I suggest you consult J K Stanford's *Burma Railway's Timetable*, which may have looked something like this:

Rangoon dep 0600	Mandalay arr 2110	(11-Up, express)
Rangoon dep 0740	Mandalay arr 1825	(19-Up, express)
Rangoon dep 1145	Mandalay arr 0835	(1-Up, post)
Rangoon dep 1530	Mandalay arr 0700	(9-Up, express)
Rangoon dep 1700	Mandalay arr 0710	(5-Up, express)
Rangoon dep 1830	Mandalay arr 0820	(15-Up, special express)
Rangoon dep 1845	Mandalay arr 2135	(31-Up, parcel)
Rangoon dep 1930	Mandalay arr 1035	(3-Up, express)
Rangoon dep 2100	Mandalay arr 1130	(7-Up, express)
Mandalay dep 0550	Rangoon arr 1720	(20-Down, express)
Mandalay dep 0600	Rangoon arr 2130	(12-Down, express)
Mandalay dep 0650	Rangoon arr 0915	(32-Down, parcel)

Mandalay dep 0715	Rangoon arr 0400	(2-Down, post)
Mandalay dep 1515	Rangoon arr 0520	(6-Down, express)
Mandalay dep 1730	Rangoon arr 0730	(16-Down, special express)
Mandalay dep 1830	Rangoon arr 1000	(4-Down, express)
Mandalay dep 2030	Rangoon arr 1250	(8-Down, express)
Mandalay dep 2035	Rangoon arr 1135	(10-Down, express)

NB: It must be borne in mind that, because of the poor condition of the track, all journeys take a minimum of 14 hours despite what the timetable might say.

The alternatives for travellers are plane (Myanma Airways or Air Mandalay daily), private car or bus. The land route (often spending the night at Meiktila on the way) is no less tiresome than that by train. The road is bad — it was built in 1927 — and it can take anything up to 15 hours to reach Meiktila. Leaving Rangoon, you pass through **Pyu**, where roughly half of the population is Indian. Here you can lunch at the strangely named Academy Restaurant (Chinese), which has a wholly unacademic menu and an even less academic loo. Then it's on to **Toungoo**, where it would be sensible (and possible) to stop overnight, and Pyinmana. **Pyinmana** is quite a quaint town, famous for its three universities: the Institutes of Agriculture, Forestry and Veterinary Science, and for having Asia's only seed bank. It is also noted for its teak production and the celebrated Yezin Dam. Finally, some 14 or 15 hours later, you reach **Meiktila**. From Meiktila, it is another three hours to Mandalay.

For bus lovers, there are the private Rainbow Express and the government-run Trade Express. The former has air conditioning, reclining seats, costs K950 (including Burmese dinner and a snack) and is bookable one day in advance. The latter costs K1,100 with no food. The Rainbow Express leaves Rangoon and Mandalay 'every other day' at 1800 and arrives approximately 15½ hours later. The Trade Express has daily departures at 1900. Tickets for the Rainbow Express are available at No 96/98 Pansodan St, and for the Trade Express at No 200, 83rd Street, Between 27th & 28th Streets, Mandalay, or No 9 Yawmingyi Road, Dagon Township, Rangoon.

Transportation in Mandalay is as diverse as in Rangoon: your best bet, however, is to befriend a trishaw (*hsaik-ka*) driver and secure his services for the duration of your stay. Most understand English (some can even speak French, German and Italian) and all are absolutely charming. Don't forget to haggle over the fare: any currency or gift will do. It is a sad fact that, as a result of years of military rule, many of the trishaw drivers are actually graduates from Mandalay or Rangoon University.

Alternatives to the trishaw include horse-carts (always fun, except for the poor horse), buses (not recommended as they're always packed), jeeps, pick-ups or, if you're really energetic and don't mind the occasional crash or flat tyre, bicycles. Walking is not recommended: Mandalay is a vast, sprawling, hot and dusty city. It makes Bangkok seem like a pleasure park.

History and general description

'I wrote a song called "Mandalay" which, tacked, to a tune with a swing, made one of the waltzes of that distant age. A private soldier reviews his love and, in the chorus, his experiences in the Burma campaign. One of his ladies lives at Moulmein, which is not on the road to anywhere, and he describes the amour with some minuteness, but always in his chorus deals with "the road to Mandalay", his golden path to romance. The inhabitants of the United States, to whom I owed most of the bother, "Panamaed" that song (this was before copyright), set it to their own tunes, and sang it in their own national voices. Not content with this, they took to pleasure cruising, and discovered that Moulmein did not command any view of any sun rising across the Bay of Bengal. They must have interefered, too, with the navigation of the Irrawaddy Flotilla steamers, for one of the Captains SOS-ed me to give him "something to tell these somethinged tourists about it". I forget what word I sent, but I hoped it might help.

'Had I opened the chorus of the song with "Oh" instead of "On the road," etc., it might have shown that the song was a sort of general mix-up of the singer's Far-Eastern memories against a background of the Bay of Bengal as seen at dawn from a troop-ship taking him there. But "On" in this case was more singable than "Oh". That simple explanation may stand as a warning.'

From Kipling's unfinished autobiography *Something of Myself*, first published in 1937

So, alas, Kipling never made it to Mandalay; as his biographer Charles Carrington relates: 'Of Burma Kipling knew nothing at first-hand, until he called in a sea-going liner at Rangoon and Moulmein for a few days in 1889. Accordingly, we find his Burmese pieces somewhat remote and romantic.'

Towards the end of 1922, George Orwell boarded the Rangoon-Mandalay 'express', bound for the Burma Provincial Police Training School. Orwell referred to his time in Burma as 'five boring years within the sound of bugles' — the bugles, in fact, would only have been in the first year, while he was living in the cantonment in Mandalay. According to Bernard Crick — Orwell's biographer — 'The days consisted of cramming in the morning, drilling in the afternoon, and drinking at night.' Orwell's first posting took him far away from Mandalay to a place called Myaungmya in the Irrawaddy Delta. This was followed by postings at Twante, Syriam, Insein and Moulmein, before finally returning to Upper Burma (to Katha, 150 miles north of Mandalay) on December 23 1926.

Katha was clearly the setting for *Burmese Days*, though in the novel Orwell actually describes the city of Mandalay: 'Mandalay is rather a disagreeable town — it is dusty and intolerably hot, and it is said to have five main products all beginning with P, namely, pagodas, pariahs, pigs, priests and prostitutes'. Orwell's reference to the five 'Ps' of Mandalay is not wholly original. For in *Four Years in Upper Burma* by W R Winston, published in 1892, the author asserts: 'Mandalay has been said to be remarkable for three things, Phoongyees, Pagodas and Pariah dogs'.

Orwell's cynical sense of humour is best witnessed in a poem entitled *Romance*, which he wrote either whilst in Burma or shortly after leaving. It is clearly a parody of Kipling's *Mandalay*:

'When I was young and had no sense
In far-off Mandalay
I lost my heart to a Burmese girl
As lovely as the day.

Her skin was gold, her hair was jet,
Her teeth were ivory;
I said "For twenty silver pieces,
Maiden, sleep with me."

She looked at me, so pure, so sad,
The loveliest thing alive,
And in her lisping, virgin voice,
Stood out for twenty-five.'

Mandalay, indeed, is a city of many characters. Its evocative, romantic nature conjures up all manner of images: even Bertolt Brecht, who never even set foot in Burma, penned a song (with Kurt Weill) about Mandalay in his 'play with music' *Happy End*.

Mandalay was once the most beautiful city, the cultural heartland of Burma. But it was also a repressed, forlorn city, with a spirit stifled by a succession of battles, kings, fires and governments. It is a city that understandably clings on to its past, indeed, to a large extent, still lives in the past and accepts most grudgingly that it is today no longer the first city of Burma. Legend has it that when King Thibaw was forced to surrender to General Prendergast and was put on a ship to be exiled to India, old Mandalay wept and died. Trite as that may sound, it may not have been far from the truth. For decades Mandalay was stuck somewhere between the 19th and 20th centuries; a wonderful timelessness, almost decrepitude, pervaded the city.

Mandalay, alas, is no more the city of Kipling or Orwell, let alone King Thibaw. Locals sardonically refer to it these days as China's second city; old Mandalay has been bulldozed and sold off to the Chinese to make way for brothels, massage parlours, karaoke bars, night-clubs, hotels, restaurants, office blocks and spanking new motor cars. The streets of Mandalay are filled with the sound of Chinese music and karaoke songs.

As U Mya Maung, professor of finance in the Wallace Carroll School of Management, Boston College, wrote in May 1994 in his article in *Asian Survey* entitled *On the Road to Mandalay: A Case Study of the Sinonization of Upper Burma*:

'Rudyard Kipling poetically envisioned the road to Mandalay in British Burma as a place where "Flying Fishes Play and the Dawn comes up like Thunder outer China 'crost the Bay!" Under the present military rule, the road to Mandalay has become a place where hordes of economic dragons — traders and merchants — have been coming down like thunder from Burma's giant neighbor, China. Since 1988, Chinese traders, engineers, and trucks loaded with Chinese goods and modern arms have been traveling on the famous Burma Road that runs across the Shan state of northern Burma to the ancient "Golden City" of Mandalay...

'Since 1989, Mandalay's silhouette has been overshadowed by new, modern high-rise buildings, hotels, restaurants, shops, and homes owned and operated by ethnic Chinese and Yunanese merchants. Most of them are in the central sections of the city, stretching east to west, as well as in the sites of two famous markets, Zay Cho (the sweet bazaar) and Tayoke-tarn Zay (the China Town bazaar). During the 26 years of General Ne Win's rule when all private trade was banned, both bazaars served as black market centers for trading contrabands. During the past five years with the lifting of the bans on internal private trade and the legalization of border trade, the trading of all kinds of imported goods, legal and illegal, from China, Thailand, Japan, India, and elsewhere has proliferated. The China Town Bazaar is now the busiest and most expensive market, flooded with Chinese goods; the Sweet Bazaar is being reconstructed for sale by the military regime...

'According to the official census of 1993, Mandalay's population is over 653,000, with only 2,670 aliens. The unofficial estimates of the total population of Mandalay, however, are as high as 1 million because of a large number of unregistered illegal aliens. The majority of the alien population comprises foreign-born Chinese who reportedly have become Burmese nationals overnight by acquiring National Registration Cards (NRCs) in the black market. According to reports, many Chinese families from Yunan Province have crossed over the border to settle in a number of villages inside northern Burma. This virtual takeover of central Mandalay actually began with two devastating fires in 1981 and 1984 that destroyed sections of the downtown areas. In 1984, when Burmese businesses and residents could not finance the reconstruction of shops, buildings, and homes according to the specifications mandated by the military government, they were forced to sell their real estate to rich ethnic Chinese investors and merchants. Since then, Mandalay's native Burmese residents have gradually moved away from the center to the peripheral areas of the city...

'After 1989 and especially during 1990, the SLORC forced a massive relocation of Burmese Mandalayians to new satellite towns in the name of the City Beautification and Development Program. Its ostensible purpose was to attract foreign tourists and investors...

'... a different process of population relocation and restructuring of Mandalay took place. Real estate prices in central Mandalay have escalated to levels never seen before. The price of a small plot of land measuring less than 50 square feet at key sites in central Mandalay has climbed up to K50 million — $500,000 at the black market exchange rate of US$1 = K100. Aggressive and wealthy Chinese investors, ethnic Chinese Kokang and Wa drug warlords, and military "robber barons" have made wholesale acquisition of real estate and homes. By offering exorbitant prices to the Burmese landowners, they sharply accelerated the relocation process...

'... The road to Mandalay is no longer a quaint and romantic place of the glorious past as it has become a cruel playground built by the Burmese military regime for the economic dragons of China.'

The old city of Mandalay and all that surrounds it dates from the middle of the 19th century, though its royal culture is much older. Mandalay was the most Burmese of all cities and home of the most traditional Burmese music and dance. They say, too, that Mandalay was where they spoke the most eloquent Burmese. Together with Sagaing, it made up the religious heart of Burma, with its monasteries, *phongyi* and pagodas.

Mandalay is the city of King Mindon: 'His glorious and excellent Majesty, Lord of Elephants, Lord of gold, silver, rubies, amber, and the noble serpentine, Sovereign of the Empires of Thunapurtanta and Jambudipa, and other great Empires and countries, and of all the Umbrella-bearing Chiefs, the Supporter of religion, Descendant of the Sun, Arbiter of Life, King of Righteousness, King of Kings, and Possessor of boundless dominion and supreme wisdom'. There may be little left of the palace: some broken walls, some tombs, the moat, but round the 954ft high Mandalay Hill King Mindon's spirit lingers on, for it was he who sponsored the myriad of monasteries and pagodas that are the hallmark of Mandalay.

The city covers an area of 25 square miles, practically one-third of which was razed during World War II due to the principal offensive against the Japanese being centred in and around Mandalay Hill. With the loss of its palace and its magnificent woodcarvings, a part of Mandalay died. In 1981 a devastating fire destroyed much of the northwest of the town and left 35,000 people homeless. Mandalay is a veritable tinder-box: in recent years there have been countless fires, though not as ruinous as the one of 1981.

The city itself forms a near-perfect geometrical pattern, the roads cutting at right angles. The long, broad streets running east-west are

King Mindon, who established Mandalay as his new capital in 1857

alphabetically named (A, B, C, D, etc) and the cross-streets running north-south numerically, in the American style. Traffic can be chaotic (there never seems to be any order) and at times quite terrifying. Breakdowns are frequent and horns toot continuously.

'... Mandalay's preciousness lies in the fact that she is a record of late Burmese history. She typifies all the stress, nobility, aspiration, and decadence of a people hastening to a period of political extinction. Here are to be found all the elements of her ancient system, educational, social, and political. Symbols of religion are richer in Mandalay than in any other Burmese city unless we include places like Pagan that are virtually dead.'

W J Grant, 1940

Where to stay

Thankfully tourists are no longer obliged to stay at the dreary state-run hotels, comprising, amongst others, the large, colonial-style Mandalay Hotel (surly service), the decrepit Mya Mandala, with swimming pool but never anyone in it and the Innwa Hotel on Eastern Moat Road (two blocks to the north of the Mandalay Hotel) which some guidebooks and Burmese travel agents recommend, but which has a dodgy reputation and a bad security record.

Then there is the awful Manmyo Hotel by the Central Railway Station, the Kaung Myint Hotel (a veritable flea-pit) on 80th Street, Between 30th and 31st Streets, the Hotel Venus (misnomer) on 28th Street, Between 80th and 81st Streets, the Golden Express Hotel on 9th Street (bad location), the Tiger Hotel (ditto) on 82nd Street, Between 36th and 37th Streets and the Sabai Phyu (ditto) on 81st Street, Between 25th and 26th Streets. Nearby is the inexpensive but grubby Taungzalat Hotel (US$10 a single, $20 a double). The similarly priced Coral (Than Dar Aung) Rest House, which charges US$12 for a single, $18 for a double, is located at No 131, 80th Road, Between 27th and 28th Streets. The cheapest (but assuredly not the best) hotel for foreigners is the Si Thu Tourist Hotel, No 29, 65th Street, Between 30th and 31st Streets, where a single room costs US$6, a double $12 and a triple $18. The privately-run Yadanar Supon suffers from bad management and a poor location.

The new breed of Chinese hotels — such as the Silver Cloud on 73rd Street and the Palace on 80th Street, Between 32nd and 33rd Streets — are overpriced, offer poor service and are distinctly 'shady'. As the notice in the Palace Hotel states:

1. Please check up the roomwares when you first take a room. If something is in need or out of use kindly call the Reception desk.

2. The departure time is 12:00 noon. Daily at 12:00 noon is taken as one day stay.

3. It is restricted not to lodge more than accepted count in everyroom.

4. The cleaning service will take from nine to ten in the morning.

5. Please deposit all valuables and important papers at the reception desk when you leave the room during the stay.

6. It is not allowed to bring arms, drugs or black papers into the room.

7. It is strickly [sic] restricted to perform acts which are not accepted by authorities concerned.

8. Ask for help from the manager if there is any problem you face with the lodging.

The 'only problem faced with the lodging' is that the manager doesn't speak English, there is no cleaning service, Chinese 'guests' do bring in arms and drugs — I'm not sure about 'black papers' — and who knows which performing acts are acceptable or not?

The leader of the pack is now the **Emerald Land Inn**, No 9, 14th Street, Between 87th and 88th Streets, Pyigyiyanlone Quarter, tel: 26990/23578, fax: 35645, which offers exemplary service, swimming pool, garden and roof terrace with panoramic views of Mandalay Hill, complimentary fruit basket, tea and coffee, and satellite TV. Rates (excluding 20% in taxes, but including breakfast) go from US$30 to $80.

Not as luxurious as the Emerald Land Inn, but equally hospitable and with a more central location is the **Mandalay View Inn**, No 17/B, 66th Street, Between 26th and 27th Streets, tel: 22347. Rates — including taxes and breakfast — are US$36 for a single, $48 a double. The hotel has six double and two single rooms.

Where to eat

Perhaps the two best local restaurants are **Sakhan Thar**, No 24, 72nd Street, Between 27th and 28th Streets, Shwelan Quarter and **Daw Yi Yi Burmese Dishes**, 80th Street, Between 17th and 18th Streets. For Indian cuisine, try **Myoma Restaurant**, 27th Street, Between 80th and 81st Streets. Chinese restaurants are plentiful in Mandalay; for example the **Honey Garden Restaurant** at the corner of 70th and 29th Streets, which is very expensive, and the **Shwenandaw**, No 110, 73rd Street, at the corner of 29th Street. Of the two western restaurants, **Texas** ('Snack. Bar & Cold'), No 243, 80th Street, Between 31st and 32nd Streets, is infinitely better than 'BBB'.

The **Pyigyi-mun Restaurant** (Chinese) is situated on the moat opposite the Mandalay Hotel, but, owing to its splendid location, is extremely expensive. The Pyigyi-mun is in fact the Royal Barge which was constructed during the reign of King Bodawpaya, the founder of Amarapura, and it was used to transport the celebrated Mahamuni image, which had been brought over from Danyawady in Arakan State, from

Amarapura to its present site along the Nadi stream. The Royal Barge has been reconstructed at a cost of over K7,300,000 and, apart from serving as a restaurant, affords a superb view of Mandalay Hill.

A cheaper Chinese restaurant is **Min Min**, No 194, 83rd Street, Between 26th and 27th Streets, though I would be loath to recommend either the 'Pecking Roast Duck' or the 'Chicken State'.

The well known Burmese restaurant **Too Too** is on the south side of 27th Street, Between 74th and 75th Streets. For the cheapest and coldest Pepsi in town, try the **Pinya Cold Drink** on 74th Street, between 27th and 28th Streets, or **Min Yazar**, No 126 Hay Mar Zala, 27th Street, Between 76th and 77th Streets. For breakfast, there's **Shells Patisserie**, 26th Street, Between 81st and 82nd Streets or **Savoury Burger**, No 121, 37th Street, Between 77th and 78th Streets. The **Dawn Tea House**, near the railway station, is always packed and has a friendly atmosphere.

Entertainment and shopping

The Manmyo Tha-yar Recreation Centre — where locals belted out songs in Burmese, Thai and even English — used to stand on the moat by the palace, but the forced dredging of the moat has caused its temporary disappearance. Instead, there are puppet shows (at the corner of 63rd and Aung Daw Mu Pagoda Streets; K200 per person) and karaoke bars, and, if you're in luck, you may stumble across a *pwe* or *nat-pwe*. Otherwise for entertainment simply trundle around town in a trishaw (*hsaik-ka*) or horse-cart, take a stroll by the banks of the Irrawaddy (where you can watch exhausted water buffaloes hauling huge teak logs up the riverbanks) or enjoy a few Mandalay beers.

The celebrated **Zegyo Market** used to dominate the shopping in Mandalay. Situated in the town centre and overlooked by the Diamond Jubilee Clock (dating from Queen Victoria's reign), this vast bazaar was designed in 1903 by an Italian called Count Caldrari, first secretary of the Mandalay municipality. The original market has been pulled down and tawdrily rebuilt at a cost estimated to be no less than K124,000,000. It now occupies four floors, though shops and stalls on the fourth floor are not wanted by the traders owing to poor access (the escalators don't work during the frequent power failures!). In the old market, like goods were all sold in one place, now, in the modern four-storey concrete block, say the locals, it is difficult to find the shop and goods you want. Other markets include the Mingala Bazaar, near Mandalay General Hospital, the Bayagyi Bazaar, near the Maha Muni Pagoda (for religious artefacts), and the Nyaung Pin Bazaar for groceries fresh in from the Shan State.

A Burmese friend has asked me to include (and I quote): 'Please some more add: At present, you can possess such luxury "among many a Burma girl a-settin" in JERSO beauty parlour on St. 80 between St. 17 & 18, sipping with soft drinks to strong'. Make of that what you will.

Mandalay is famed for its ivory, gems, woodcarvings, tapestries, antiques, myriad Buddha images, silk and lacquerware. Touts will all too willingly escort you to 'their' shop, where they receive a sizeable commission. Ignore them and go alone to Law Ka Nat (Myanmar Handicraft Shop), No 85/2, 28th Road, Between 73rd and 74th Streets. Always bargain hard and, as ever in Burma, *caveat emptor*.

Mandalay also boasts an interesting array of Buddha image carvers. They carve the images out of stone, marble, alabaster, wood and ivory. Famed, too, are the gold-leaf makers and beaters and silk weavers. The Kyi Pwa Yay Press and Publishing House, belonging to the widely respected writer Ludu Daw Amah, is located at No 221, 84th Street. Established in 1938, this is the leading publishing house in Upper Burma — its first publication was a Burmese version of Maurice Collis' *Trials in Burma*, translated by Daw Amah.

Mandalay Hill and environs

'Mandalay can truly be called a City of a Thousand Pagodas. Some were old and in ruins, weathered by time till they were almost one with the wild plants that overgrew them. But others were newly built, topped in gold that glistened under the hot sun. They were guarded by gigantic whitewashed monsters, with golden teeth and bright vermilion tongues.'

George Rodger, 1943

Mandalay Hill, with its 1,729 steps and under whose shadow the city lies sprawling, gives Mandalay added distinction. When you eventually reach its 954ft peak (always assuming you haven't taken the recently constructed lift or been driven up most of the way on the road carved out in 1993), past the drinks, cheroot and betel vendors and fortune tellers, you have a superb panoramic view all round. The crenellated walls of the old palace with its wooden spire on one side and the long line of the distant Shan Hills on the other make a truly magnificent sight. And all the while, the huge, golden **Shweyattaw Buddha** stands guard, his right hand pointing to the city way below. At the foot of one of its two southern staircases, there are *chinthe* with permanent curls in their manes. *Zaungdan* cover the steps all the way up the hill; every step bears the name of a donor who earned merit by paying for it. At the very top are four Buddhas on each side and the wish-fulfilling **Two Snake Pagoda** (*Mway-hniq-kaung-hpaya*) and a precinct guarded by ogres. Visitors are now charged an entrance fee of US$4 (or K400 if you're lucky).

Mandalay Hill has four covered approaches. On the southwestern slope are the **Peshawar Relics**, sacred relics of the Buddha, which were discovered near Peshawar in 1909 and donated by the Government of India to the Burmese people. Near the southern approach stands the **Kyauktawgyi Pagoda** (US$3 entrance fee) built by King Mindon in

1878, having taken 25 years to complete. The Buddha image here was carved out of a huge single slab of marble brought from the nearby mines of Sagyin. Legend has it that the marble block was so big that 10,000 men had to be employed for 13 days to transport it from a canal to the site of the pagoda. Round the shrine are figures of 80 disciples of the Buddha, 20 on each side. To the east is the **Sandamuni Pagoda**, constructed on the site on which the temporary palace of King Mindon stood while the new palace was being built. This pagoda is also known to have been raised over the graves of the crown prince and some other members of the royal family, who lost their lives in the palace rebellion of 1866 when there was an attempt to assassinate King Mindon. It enshrines an iron image of the Buddha cast in 1802 by King Bodawpaya and brought from Amarapura 72 years later and marble slabs inscribed with commentaries on the *Tripitaka* (the three baskets of notes from Buddha's teaching).

Northeast of the Sandamuni Pagoda lies the **Kuthodaw** (Royal Merit) **Pagoda**, also known as the Maha Lawka Marazein Pagoda. Modelled on the Shwezigon at Nyaung-U (Pagan), it was built by King Mindon in 1857. In the eyes of Burmese Buddhists, the Kuthodaw — the 'world's largest book' or 450 Pagodas — holds pride of place in Mandalay, for there are over 729 monoliths of white marble on which the *Tripitaka* have been inscribed. The inscriptions were made after the Fifth Buddhist Synod convened at Mandalay in 1871-2. It is said it took 2,400 monks six months to recite the entire text. Each slab has a small temple erected over it, making the Kuthodaw a vast and venerable pagoda. The entrance fee is US$3.

South of the Kuthodaw lie the imposing ruins of the **Atu-mashi Kyaung** (The Incomparable Monastery) which dates from the same period (1857) and was built by King Mindon at a cost of 500,000 (five lakhs) rupees. The building was of wood covered with stucco on the outside, and its peculiar feature was the fact that it was surmounted by five graduated rectangular terraces instead of the customary *pya-that* (wooden spires). In it was enshrined a huge image of the Buddha made of the silken clothes of the king covered with lacquer, and its forehead was adorned with a huge diamond, which was presented to King Bodawpaya by Mahanawrata, governor of Arakan. In the building four sets of the *Tripitaka* were deposited in large teak boxes. During the troubles following the British annexation of Upper Burma, the valuable diamond disappeared, and the whole building, together with its contents, burnt down in 1890. The monastery was also renowned for the many ecclesiastical conventions which took place within its walls. All that remains of this great monument, which drew rapturous accounts from travellers who saw it in its former glory, are the brickwork platforms and the carved compound gates. As one anonymous English traveller wrote in 1885:

'In Mandalay, King Mindon erected a monastery — the like of which there is not, the great Incomparable — which possesses a beautiful hall, unquestionably the finest in all Mandalay. It would be no great stretch of truth to say that it is the finest in the world. The building is composed of a series of bold terraces, seven in number, rising one above another, the central one being the highest. The golden hall is carried on thirty-six pillars, some of which are seventy feet high, the ceiling reaching its greatest elevation in the high central terrace. And there a colossal figure of Gautama sits, mediating beside a golden throne intended for the King. The boldness of the general design, the noble proportions of the immense hall, and the great height of the golden roof soaring over the throne and the statue, fill the mind with surprise and pleasure. Pillars, walls, and roof are richly gilt, glass inlaying heightening the brilliancy. When the Viceroy comes to Mandalay to promulgate the decree which announces the future organisation of Burma, the ceremonial will probably be held in this noblest of throne rooms.'

By the side of the 'Incomparable Monastery' stands the superb **Shwenandaw Monastery** (known to the Burmese as the *Shwe-kyaung-gyi*) which contains a replica of the royal throne. It is said that Thibaw would come here to meditate; indeed the couch he used to sit on can still be seen. Inside were once some masterly examples of glass-mosaic craftsmanship, though most have been lost through the passing of time. The Shwenandaw Kyaung was originally an apartment of the Royal Palace; it was also the place where King Mindon passed away. His successor King Thibaw, believing the building to be haunted by Mindon's ghost, ordered it to be disassembled and moved to its present location in 1880. The Shwenandaw Monastery, which was built at a cost of about one lakh and 20,000 rupees, is a wonderful archetype of mid-19th century Burmese woodcarving with an array of stunning *nagas* (serpentine dragons); it is also a supremely relaxing place to wander around and to watch the novice monks peering curiously and timidly through the exquisitely carved wooden portals. Entrance fee: US$3.

The *Shwe-kyaung-gyi* is arguably Mandalay's finest example of a monastery. Ordinarily of teak, a Burmese monastery is always oblong in shape and the inhabited portion is raised on posts or pillars some 8 or 10ft above the ground. They are never more than one storey high, as it would be an indignity to a holy monk to have anyone over his head.

A flight of steps leads up to a veranda, which is usually adorned with carvings or plaster figures of *nats* or ogres. From the raised floor rises the building with tier upon tier of dark massive roofs capped at intervals with tapering roofs or *pya-that*. Monasteries are in many cases ornamented with the most elaborate carving (eg: the Nataunt Monastery in Pagan). Interior accommodation is very spartan — against the wall are arranged Buddha images, manuscript chests, small shrines, fans, various

Yankintaung, Mandalay. 'The Hill that is free from danger', where the Lord Buddha spent 136 of his previous lives. The Peace Pagoda.

Nat-pwe (Spirit Festival), Mandalay

Scenes of Upper Burma. Top: Water buffalo cool off in the Irrawaddy River.

Bottom: Maymyo, the old summer retreat of the colonialists

Scenes of Monywa, Upper Burma. Top: Strange sight at Shwebataung!

Bottom (left and right): Ogres (bilu) guarding the Hpo-win-taung Caves

Novice monk at the doorway of Mandalay's Shwenandaw Monastery

gifts of the pious and religious artefacts. In many monasteries there is a special room for the palm-leaf scribes, often detached from the main building, as are the cook-room, bathing-houses and, perhaps, a guesthouse.

Other attractions

Mandalay's original teak **Royal Palace** (known in its heyday as 'The Golden City' or 'The Centre of the Universe') is no more, but parts of it have been reconstructed. Built in 1857 by King Mindon, it formed a perfect square: 1¼ miles (2km) square to be precise. The walls were 27ft high and 10ft thick with gates and wooden spires and with a 225ft wide and 11ft deep moat all around. Each side had three gates and the palace itself was divided into 144 square plots: 16 square plots for the palace, the rest for the royal staff. In these 16 square plots there were 114 buildings: the eastern ones for the kings, the western ones for the queens. On the left side stood the clock tower and on the right side the tooth relics tower. In 1885, under the reign of King Thibaw, Mandalay was occupied by the British and the Royal Palace, having become a British military area, was renamed Fort Dufferin. The palace remained under British rule until 1945 when the Japanese invaded and seized control. The British, however, bombed the palace and a series of fires razed it to the ground. Only the city walls, the moat, the towers, the mausoleum and the raised platform, on which the palace was built, survived.

In recent years the SLORC has embarked on the task of recreating this once-wonderful palace. A number of buildings have been reconstructed including the great audience hall and the watch tower. The latter, known as the Nan-Myint Watch Tower, measures 108ft from the base to the top, and was finished in July 1990 at a cost of just over K2 million. Reconstruction work on the Lay Thein Gate (the entrance to the northern wall of the palace) took almost eight months to complete and cost K800,000, while the U Htake Gate of the eastern wall has also been renovated. Visitors to the palace are charged an entrance fee of US$5, plus $3 to see the museum.

Within the enclosure of the Royal Palace lies the mausoleum erected over the remains of King Mindon, who died in 1878. Before he died, he left instructions that his body should be buried and not cremated, thus violating the time-honoured custom of burning the dead bodies of members of the royal family. Close by lies the tomb of Sinbyumayin, the only daughter of the notorious Nanmadaw Me Nu, chief queen of King Bagyidaw, who was Mindon's second queen and mother-in-law of Thibaw. She died in Rangoon in 1900 and her body was permitted to be buried near Mindon's tomb. The chief queen of Mindon, Nanmadawgyi, who died in 1876, was also buried in the palace stockade, the third tomb to be erected within the sacred precincts of the Royal Palace.

A wungyi *(chief minister of state) and his wife in court dress*

Right in the heart of Mandalay stands the **Shwekyi-myint Pagoda**, built by King Minshinzaw, exiled son of King Alaungsithu (1114-1167) of Pagan. This shrine has two especial attractions. The image is the original one consecrated by the builder himself and has now become the repository of many images of the Buddha salvaged from the palace at the time of the British occupation in 1885: images made of gold and silver, adorned with invaluable precious stones, representing the collections of successive monarchs. There is also a small golden palanquin (a covered litter for one person, usually carried by four or six men) and outside, on a veranda, a wooden palanquin used by a lesser queen. There are numerous Buddha images in the quadrangle of the pagoda, and rows of *nats* with lamps on them. The Shwekyi-myint is perhaps the most serene and beautiful pagoda in Mandalay.

On 85th Street, just south of Zegyo Market, stands the **Setkya-thiha Pagoda**, where the Buddha image was cast at the command of King Bagyidaw at Ava in 1823 (just before the outbreak of the Anglo-Burmese War in 1824) and subsequently shifted to Amarapura in 1849. Thirty-five years later it was brought to Mandalay when the third war broke out and the Burmese monarchy became extinct. Measuring 16ft 8in, this huge bronze image is artistically crafted. The temple, which is on an elevated masonry platform, was badly damaged during the war but has since been renovated. In the courtyard of the pagoda there are numerous images of the reclining Buddha and also the sacred *Bo* tree (banyan tree, under which the Buddha reached Enlightenment) planted by former Prime Minister U Nu in an enclosure to the right of the entrance.

A little to the northwest of the Setkya-thiha Pagoda lies the **Eindawya Pagoda**, built by Pagan Min in 1847 on the site of the palace in which he resided before he ascended the throne. Heavily gilded, this beautifully proportioned shrine houses a chalcedony (a type of quartz mineral mixed with opal) Buddha image said to have been brought from Bodh Gaya in India in 1839. For 45 or 90 kyat, a fortune-teller in the pagoda precinct will read your palm.

To the south of the city is the much-venerated pagoda which is variously called the **Maha Muni** (Exalted Saint or The Great Teacher), the Hpaya-gyi (Great Pagoda) and the Arakan Pagoda. The 12½ft high seated image, which is heavily overlaid with gold leaf (and consequently badly misshapen), dates back to ancient times and was brought over by the son and heir of King Bodawpaya in 1784 from Myohaung in Arakan State. It is the largest bronze Buddha image in Burma. Legend has it that the Burmese had tried three times previously (but unsuccessfully) to steal it from the Arakanese. Bodawpaya, whose capital at that time was Amarapura, also built a road paved with brick from the capital to the eastern gate of the pagoda. Remains of this paved King's Highway can still be seen. The original temple was destroyed by fire in 1884 and the present pagoda, with its terraced roof of gilded stucco, is of more recent construction. In the courtyard is a small building housing six bronze figures, Khmer statues brought back from Arakan State at the same time as the Maha Muni image (there were originally 30 figures, but the remaining 24 were melted down by King Thibaw and cast into cannons for his struggle against the British). These figures have had a chequered past: they had been appropriated by the Siamese from Angkor Wat to Ayutthaya in 1431, and then by the Burmese to Pegu. From there the Arakanese King Razagyi had them removed to his own state, only for them to end up eventually in Mandalay. The courtyard also contains a five-ton traditional Burmese gong and various inscription stones brought there for safekeeping by King Bodawpaya. The government has spent a fortune renovating the pagoda, museum, garden, turtle pond, fish pond, clock tower, shops and roads. Entrance fee: US$4. Women are banned from approaching close; only men may climb on the image to apply gold leaf.

On 63rd Street, between 28th and 29th Streets in the Aung Daw Mu Quarter, stands the recently renovated **Aung Daw Mu Pagoda**. There are two glass mosaic stupas, one big, one small — the bigger one is beautifully adorned with weird-looking ogres. There are three stunning Buddha images: the main one is particularly resplendent. Women must pay homage on the right side, men on the left. In the pagoda precinct is an image of the Lord Buddha preaching to his five disciples.

Five miles (8km) due east of Mandalay stands **Yankintaung** — the 'Hill that is free from danger', a mere 426 steps to the top. Of the Buddha's 547 previous incarnations, 136 of them were spent as various animals on Yankintaung. Amongst the myriad of wonders are four stone fish (*Ngayantmin*), which people come from far and wide to pour water over and make a wish, and the *Lwanzedi*. *Lwan* means to miss somebody and King Mindon, while he was separated from his queen (Nanmadaw Me Nu), missed her so much that he built this stupa and gave it the name *Lwanzedi*. There is the King Buffalo stupa (*Kywe-minzedi*), with its eight statues of buffaloes, one for each time that Buddha incarnated as this creature, and the *Chan-tha-ayezedi* (peace pagoda) with a globe on top, followed by three terraces, leading up to the *hti*. The pagoda is surrounded by pictures and images of the *Pyittaing-daung*, the doll that never falls over (a favourite children's toy). At the top of the hill is a giant standing Buddha giving prophecy.

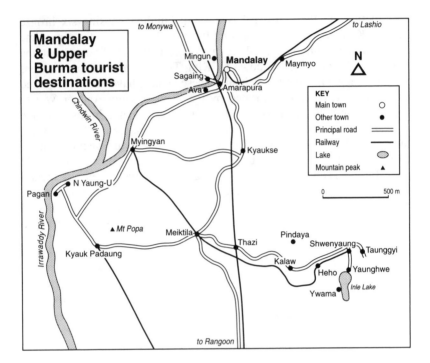

AMARAPURA

'In the course of the forenoon we reached the city of Amarapoorah, which, including the suburbs, extends four miles along the south-eastern bank of the river, and teems with religious buildings of various shapes. The palace, as seen from the river, appears a confused assemblage of buildings, glittering with a blaze of gilding.'

Capt Hiram Cox, 1821

Getting there

Lying nearly seven miles (11km) south of Mandalay, the ancient capital of Amarapura is accessible by local taxi (which will cost you K1,200 for the day, including excursions to Sagaing and Ava), private car or public bus. Bus 8 passes through Amarapura on its way to Ava; it departs from the corner of 84th and 27th Streets. Another alternative is the bus which goes to Sagaing from between 84th and 85th Streets.

History

Amarapura — the name means 'The City of Immortals' and is not Burmese but Pali — was described in its heyday as 'a microcosm of Burmese civilisation with a concentration, not only of the wealth, fashion

The Sacred White Elephant, 'Hsin-byu-daw'

and beauty, but also learning and scholarship'. As a capital it was founded by King Bodawpaya in 1783, the year after he came to the throne, and it superseded Ava. However, Bodawpaya died in 1819 and his grandson Bagyidaw shifted the capital back again to Ava in 1823. That was not the end of Amarapura though, for in 1841, during the reign of Tharrawaddy (the brother of Bagyidaw), it became the capital once more. Sixteen years later, with King Mindon in power, Amarapura for imperative astrological reasons was finally displaced by Mandalay.

What to see

Unlike its successor, Amarapura has little to show for its past glories. All that remains of Bodawpaya's palace are just two buildings, the **Royal Palace Tower** (Pangon) and the **Royal Treasury Building** (Shwedaik). The city walls have been demolished. There are also the tombs of King Bodawpaya and his grandson King Bagyidaw. Bodawpaya's body was burnt on the site of the so-called tomb, and the ashes were placed in a velvet bag and thrown into the Irrawaddy. Likewise, Bagyidaw's body was cremated on the site of his 'tomb' and his ashes also thrown into the river. The body of Bagyidaw's brother, Shwebo Min, suffered an identical fate.

In the Amarapura city area lies the **Ba-gaya Monastery**, built in 1785. It is noted for its collection of Pali manuscripts written on palm leaves (downstairs), its myriad Buddha images (upstairs) and a vast collection of various antiques.

The **U Bein Bridge** (named after the former town mayor) was constructed out of materials salvaged from the forsaken Ava Palace. The bridge, the longest made from teak in the world, is about three-quarters of a mile in length (3,967ft) as it crosses the Taungthaman Lake; it takes about 15 to 20 minutes to walk it. Repair work on the bridge started in February 1989 and was completed just over a year later at a cost of K400,000. At the head of the bridge stands the Taungmingyi Statue.

If you do decide to wander over, you'll end up at the **Kyauktawgyi Pagoda**, which was built by King Pagan in 1847 in the style of the Ananda Temple. Unlike the Ananda (which was constructed by Indians), the Kyauktawgyi is wholly the work of Burmese craftsmen and is the best preserved of the numerous religious buildings in the deserted capital of Amarapura. The temple itself is raised a few feet from ground level and has broad steps and huge doorways; unlike the Ananda, it has wooden beams or rafters. The stone image is seated on a high platform and there are also 88 stone figures of the disciples of the Buddha at the back and 12 of *manussiha*, twin-bodied mythical creatures half-man and half-beast, all around. The Kyauktawgyi is noted for its frescos in the four porches. These represent religious buildings in various styles of architecture, built or repaired by Pagan Min at Sagaing, Amarapura, Ava, Pakangyi, Prome and Rangoon, and the planets and the constellations according to Burmese ideas of astronomy. The human figures depict the dresses and customs of the period.

Re-crossing the bridge you'll come to the **Patodawgyi Pagoda**, which was built by King Bagyidaw in 1820 (some sources quote 1816) and is one of the largest of its kind. It goes up in a series of five terraces finishing up with a small *sikhara* (beehive-like dome, a spire of North Indian type) and a finial. On white marble panels on the three lower terraces are illustrations and scenes from the *Jataka Tales* (stories of the lives of the Buddha), while there is also an inscription stone relating the history of the pagoda and a large brass bell.

Besides the twin pagodas, the **Shwe Kyetyet** (Golden Fowl's Run, named, because, according to the legend, the place was once the habitat of the Buddha-to-be, who in one of his former lives was born a Golden Fowl) and **Shwe Kyetka**, which were originally built by King Asoka but subsequently repaired and enlarged by a king of Pagan in the 12th century and which are located on the banks of the Irrawaddy opposite Sagaing, there is one small but interesting pagoda called the **Nagayon** which has a distinctive architectural feature embodying the motif of a hooded snake. Amarapura also boasts a Chinese joss-house, which has stood since the time of King Bodawpaya. Legend has it that when King Mindon switched the capital to Mandalay, the Chinese stuck fast and refused to move with the king.

The nearby village of **Kyithunkhat** is renowned for its craftsmen who cast Buddha images in bronze; gongs and cymbals are also manufactured here. Amarapura is home to a number of silk and cotton weavers and it is here where many a silk *longyi* is turned out.

AVA

Getting there

If you want to go on your own, take bus 8 which passes through Amarapura on its way to Ava. You could always jump on a pick-up which is heading for Sagaing, get off before it crosses the Ava Bridge and follow the dusty road to the Myitngeh River where a 'ferry' will take you to the other side. From there, hire a horse-cart to the ruins.

History

'Ratanapura, the City of Gems, Inwa or Ava, the Fish-pond; such are the varying titles by which this city that was a capital for four and a half centuries is known to Burmese history, and of these the Fish-pond long preceded the City of Gems.'

After the disintegration of the Kingdom of Pagan, Ava emerged as the capital of the Burmese kings, having been founded by Thado Minbya in 1364. It remained the capital for more than 300 years until King

An outdoor court scene

Bodawpaya moved over to nearby Amarapura. Ava enjoyed another brief spell as the King's City during the reign of Bodawpaya's grandson Bagyidaw, as it did subsequently on two further occasions. Ava was on an artificially created island which was formed by linking the Irrawaddy and Myitngeh Rivers by a canal. The name *Ava* actually means 'lake's entrance'.

What to see

Unlike Amarapura, Ava's city walls can still be seen, and near the northern gate, opening out on the Irrawaddy, they remain practically intact. From here you have a marvellous view of the Ava Bridge and the river itself flowing by the pagoda-studded hills of Sagaing.

Little remains of the palace area save for a 90ft high masonry watch tower, the **Nan-myint** built by King Bagyidaw, which was shaken by the earthquake of 1838 and used to be regarded as the Burmese 'Leaning Tower of Pisa'. Now, it stands grimly in a yellow coat (body) with a red cap (roof), having been 'straightened out' by the government. Nearby is an impressive example of Burmese architecture, the **Maha Aung Mye Bonzan Monastery** which was built in 1818 by Bagyidaw's chief queen for her favourite *sayadaw* (chief abbot). Unfortunately, the 1838 tremor damaged this structure as well and what is left today is the result of renovations undertaken in 1873 by Sinbyumashin, queen of Mindon. It is a dome-like construction, with a seven-tiered spherical top. Inside there is the room where the *sayadaw* resided and a Buddha image on the original glass mosaic pedestal. Curiously enough, it has a teak floor. Approach steps, two on each side, three in front and one at the back, lead up to the monastery. Outside there is an inscription giving the name of the monastery and carved figures of a peacock, a hare, the sun and moon and some *chinthe*. The Maha Aung Mye Bonzan Monastery still stands today because, unlike most of the monasteries, it was constructed out of masonry and not wood.

On a rough white stone, set up on the site of Let-mayun Prison ('Hand shrink not'), is an inscription: 'in the prison of horror which stood here, sustained in his faith in the Lord Jesus Christ, and by the devotion of his heroic wife, endured unrecorded sufferings from June 1824 to May 1825'. It marks the incarceration of the first American Baptist missionary, Dr Adoniram Judson, whose horrific experiences are recalled in spellbinding fashion by fellow-prisoner Henry Gouger in the latter's extraordinary book *The Prisoner in Burmah: Personal Narrative of Two Years' Imprisonment in Burmah* (1860).

SAGAING

Getting there

One of the most beautiful spots in Burma, Sagaing is accessible from Mandalay by taxi or private car.

It is a most scenic route from Mandalay to Sagaing as you cross the Ava Bridge, about a mile long and the only bridge spanning the Irrawaddy. Built by the British in 1934 at a cost of well over a crore of rupees and destroyed by them eight years later as they retreated before the advancing Japanese troops, it was eventually repaired in 1954. For 'security reasons' photography is forbidden. On your way, you may be stopped by officials (as indeed you will whenever you travel on the roads in Burma), allegedly to pay 'customs charges' (the Burmese humorously refer to them as 'official beggars'). If you travel at the weekend, you will notice many people from the various townships sweeping and cleaning the roads. These citizens are obliged to tidy the streets every Saturday and Sunday without any remuneration. Under feudal-style regulations, the military claims an absolute right to call on the population to work on infrastructure projects. The workers are not paid since they are 'giving their labour' (*lok-a pay*).

History

Like other capital cities, Sagaing, preceding Ava, experienced a brief, chequered history. Athin Kaya, a Shan chieftain, made Sagaing his capital in 1322, when he set himself up independently, having freed himself from the overlordship of the Shan Kingdom of Pinya. It was his grandson Thado Minbya who transferred the capital to Ava and became its first king. Alaungpaya's son Naungdawgyi installed his capital again at Sagaing for four years (1760-64) but when he died, Ava once again became the seat of royalty. The name *Sagaing* has two possible meanings: either the 'start of the rounding of the river', or 'the branch of the sit tree (Albizzia procera) leaning over the river'.

Historically, that would have been the end of Sagaing were it not for the bloody scenes that took place between August 9 and 11 1988. Some 340 students and monks were gunned down and dumped into the Irrawaddy River (those who didn't die immediately were, according to by-standers, swiftly finished off with rifle butts). A few days later on Naukchinkyun Island at least 20 bodies were washed up — though the actual total massacred was many more than that. The one-time capital Sagaing had, some 224 years after its fall, witnessed an even darker hour.

What to see

The best views of Mandalay and the Irrawaddy River are from the **Ponnyashin Pagoda**, which is reached by a long staircase (not dissimilar to that of Mandalay Hill, only fortunately somewhat shorter and, for some inexplicable reason, with only one *chinthe* for protection). Another mystery is why the area is known locally as *Thayetpinseik*, which literally means 'Mango Tree Jetty', as there is not a single mango tree to be seen.

The Ponnyashin was built by U Ponnya (from whom its name comes), who was the minister of the founder of Sagaing, Athin Khaya and is dominated by two vast Buddha images. Legend has it that the spirit of the minister Ponnya still makes his daily dawn offering of alms food at the shrine earlier than anyone else — a unique honour conferred on him by the king — and if you go there before dawn with your offering, you will find that someone has already been there before you. Thus the pagoda is known as the **Hsun-u Ponnyashin**: 'Shrine of the earliest dawn offering'.

NB: There is a charge of US$3 to visit the pagodas on Sagaing Hill and the surrounding areas. If you claim to be an ambassador, diplomat or VIP, you can pay in local currency (K20).

Standing beside the Sagaing Kaunghmudaw Road is the **Hsinmyashin Pagoda** (The Lord of Elephants or Pagoda of Many Elephants) which was constructed by King Mohnyin of Ava in 1429. Originally called Ratna Ceti, it was destroyed by an earthquake in 1485 and renovated by King Mingaung II of Ava. However, another tremor razed it in 1955 and it was subsequently rebuilt. As the name implies, it is surrounded by innumerable statues of elephants and enshrines relics from Sri Lanka.

Located about six miles (10km) northwest of Sagaing is the **Kaunghmudaw** (Rajamanicula, Yazamanisula or 'Pumpkin') **Pagoda**. Built by King Thalun in 1636 to commemorate the re-establishment of Ava as the royal capital, this hemispherical pagoda (the only one of its type in Burma), with three circular terraces and a base circumference of 400ft, was modelled on the Mahaceti Pagoda in Sri Lanka. It has a vast dome, reaching 151½ft, with a *hti* on top which has a diameter of about 17ft 7in. Along the base are hollowed-out recesses housing 120 figures of *nats* or *devas*. This remarkable pagoda enshrines a left lower tooth relic of Buddha brought from Sri Lanka and King Dhammapala's emerald begging bowl, and has 812 stone posts, 4½ft high with niches for oil lamps on all the four sides for worshippers to *pu-zaw* (make puja) with lights, like candles in a Catholic church. There is also an 8½ft high marble stone inscription, in Burmese script, in one corner of the innermost yard, relating details of the construction of the pagoda. Recently renovated, this vast, white, bell-shaped stupa is an awesome, dazzling, imposing sight. Inside, the Buddha image with glittering lights adds to the splendour and aura of this wonderful pagoda.

The **Nga-datkyi Pagoda**, to the west of Sagaing, was built in 1657 by

Minye-nandameik, son and successor of King Thalun of Ava, and houses the largest sitting image of Buddha in Upper Burma. One of the most celebrated pagodas in Sagaing is the unfinished **Tupayon**, sponsored by the Ava King Narapati in 1444, which stands 90ft high and is unusual in that it is circular in plan with three storeys, marked by vertical or dormer window-like hollows with niches, enshrining a number of small Buddha images. It was destroyed in the 1838 earthquake and partially restored (though never completed) 11 years later. In a shed next door is a rich collection of inscription stones dating from the 14th and 15th centuries. The Tupayon has been described as a 'pagoda of very rare type in Burma and of peculiar architectural interest as marking a certain phase in the development of these structures'.

The **Aungmye-lawka Pagoda** (also known as the Eindawya Paya), built in 1783 by King Bodawpaya on the site on which his residence stood before he ascended the throne, stands on the river front, not far from the Tupayon. Its distinguishing feature is that it is wholly built of sandstone and designed to emulate the Shwezigon Pagoda at Nyaung-U (Pagan). It has a slender, tapering spire and is cylindrical in form with five pairs of *chinthe*.

The **Datpaung-su Pagoda**, whilst not as old as most of the others, houses relics collected from all the pagodas which were dismantled to make room for the construction of the railway through Sagaing. The **Umin Thonzeh** (30 caves) **Pagoda**, built by Padugyi Thingayaza (chief of the *Sanghas*), houses 30 images of the Buddha in a crescent-shaped building on the side of Sagaing Hill. Padugyi Thingayaza also constructed the **Badamyazedi** (in 1300) — it was repaired by the late Hsinbyumya-shin, queen of Mindon — which resembles pagodas of the Mandalay period. It is cylindrical in form, and its bell-shaped dome is covered with glass mosaic. Its original type may well have been changed to its present-day appearance by reconstruction and numerous repairs.

One of the most celebrated monasteries nestling on the slope of a hill is the **Pa Ba Kyaung** with a sign in Burmese which reads 'Of the original nine, this is the first'. It is over 900 years old and enjoys a wonderfully peaceful location. Approaching it, you may well hear the chanting of novices, in the traditional semi-recumbent posture, with their legs tucked in and poised on their elbows, taking their lessons in Buddha *dhamma* (Buddhist doctrine) from the *sayadaw* or some other learned monk.

On the right bank of the river lies a rather dilapidated old fort, where the Burmese put up a last-ditch effort against the British forces in 1885 during the operations culminating in the annexation of Upper Burma. If you climb the old wall, you can see the Irrawaddy, Ava Bridge and the hills of Sagaing and Mandalay. In the nearby village of **Ywataung**, a couple of miles out of town, live numerous silver-workers who, for generations, have produced silverware from their forges.

MINGUN
Getting there
Ask your trishaw driver to take you to the banks of the Irrawaddy (at the bottom of 26th Street or B Road) and hop on to one of the many boats that ply the muddy waters: it's best to start early in the morning before the heat becomes intolerable. You can either take the communal boat with all the locals (though you'll have to wait till it's completely full) at a cost of K10 one way, or hire your own boat (bargain hard). The outward trip, which offers a marvellous insight into life on the Irrawaddy, can take up to 90 minutes, though the return leg can be done in half the time. Mingun itself is a village located on the west bank of the Irrawaddy, roughly 7 miles (10½km) north of Mandalay.

Disembarking at Mingun, you first pass through the Methodist Infirmary (Daw Oo Zoon) which is home to 70 old ladies and 31 gentlemen. The friendly staff here take pleasure in showing tourists around, and in return you can make a donation and receive a certificate.

What to see
Mingun has two remarkable landmarks, both projects of King Bodawpaya: the **Mingun Bell and Pagoda**; both are candidates for the *Guinness Book of Records*. The construction of the Mingun (Pahtodawgyi) Pagoda began in 1790 and was to have been the largest in the world (at 492ft high — as intended by the king — it would have been no less than 65ft taller than the vast chedi at Nakhon Pathom in Thailand). It took years to build (nobody is quite sure how long), by which time many labourers had died and, even worse for the king, money had run out. So in 1813 he abandoned his scheme, leaving little more than a vast pile of bricks. The plan was a total fiasco and had a devastating effect on the community, as villagers fled to escape being called upon to continue the construction. Another tale has it that building was stopped because a prophecy had been circulated to the effect that the king's life would end with the completion of the structure. Whatever the reason, the mass of brickwork to this day remains a huge memorial of human vanity and folly.

In 1838 an earthquake struck and part of the building collapsed; today you can still see a huge fissure in the giant mound of brickwork. Guarded by a pair of dilapidated and misshapen brick *chinthe* and square in plan, the Mingun Pagoda rests on five receding terraces with porches projecting slightly on all four sides. The bottom terrace is a square of 450ft and the top terrace 230ft. Above the main square block are three receding terraces which have small square panels decorated with colourful glazed plaques. In a building close by are plaques glazed in green, brown and yellow which depict scenes from the five Buddhist Councils.

Today it is still possible to climb the 162ft to the very top, and local kids will follow you all the way. You have to leave your shoes at the bottom, which makes the ascent rather uncomfortable. Within the pagoda, according to the *Royal Chronicle of Burma*, 1,500 figures and images of gold, 2,534 of silver and 36,947 of 'other materials' lie buried. All you can actually see inside the pagoda is an uninspiring Buddha image accompanied by a foul and musty smell of bats' droppings.

Mingun may not have the largest pagoda in the world, but it does have the biggest uncracked bell, 14 times the size of that of St Paul's. There is a larger bell in Moscow (one-third bigger), but that one is flawed. Cast in 1790 (some say 1808) to be dedicated to the Mingun Pagoda, the Mingun Bell is 12ft high, weighs 90 tons and has a diameter at its outer lip of 16ft 3in. It's possible to crawl inside, and pray that none of the entourage of giggling kids rings it while you're underneath! Not surprisingly the bell fell off during the earthquake of 1838 and it lay on the ground until 1896 when it was re-mounted. It is now covered by a shelter open on all sides.

'King Bodawpaya who reigned in Amarapura City in 1782-1819 had an idea to hang a bell near Mingun Pagoda which was his merit at Mingun region. On 5th waxing of Kason, 1170 M.E. (1808 A.D.) casting of the bell was started in a great pomp and ceremony. It was Nandakyawthu, Minister of Forge, who patronized the bell casting. It is said that the bell is made of bronze and some bits of gold and silver inside. The weight of it is 55.555 viss (90.52 tons).

'The bell was completed in Nayon, 1173 M.E. (1811 A.D.). To move such massive bell to Mingun Pagoda was a big burden. But the Myanmar people's intelligence is very great and smart. The management to shift the bell was easy like this.

'People dug the soil beneath the bell and took it out. Then they made a canal in which two barges could pass well to the river. Similarly, they also canalized from the opposite bank to the fixed point. After digging the canals, they built the barges which were 120 feet (36 metres) long below the bell and guilded them. In Waso-Wagaung (July-August), the canals were flooded by the river and so the bell was successfully carried to the permanent place in the barges.

'The bell was hung on three parallel bars of wood covered with metal plate. Those bars were on two upright posts which were of teakwood covered with stucco on the outside. The bell cannot swing to and fro. The British gazettes expressed that two carts could drive and turn well under such voluminous Mingun Bell. Moreover, the diameter of the outer lip is 16 feet 3 inches, the diameter above 4 feet 8 inches of the inner lip 10 feet, the height on outside 12 feet and the diameter of the inner top 8 feet 6 inches. The thickness of the bell is from 6 inches to 12 inches and the weight of it is roughly about 80 tons the English estimated.

Mingun Bell: the largest uncracked bell in the world

'However, according to the measurements of the bell shown in "Kon-baung-set Maha Raja-wun" (Great History of the Konbaung dynasty), the diameter of the outer lip is 5 metres, the girth 15 metres, the height 6 metres and the weight 90.52 tons (91972.56 kilograms).

'The brick-posts sustaining the bell were crashed by earthquake on 23rd March, 1839. So the bell also fell nearly onto the ground and a few bits of it cracked. It was lifted by logs on the surface of the earth. In 1896 A.D., a Scottish officer of the Ayeyarwady Steamer Company shifted the bell from its original hanger onto the double iron-bars supporting with the steel-posts. The bell has been covered over by a "pyatthat" or pavilion of wood with 16 pillars open on all sides. Now it is maintained by the Archaeology Department.

'It is claimed to be the world's third biggest bell in Myanmar Encyclopedia Vol. 2 although Mingun Bell is said to be the world's largest one in Amended List of Ancient Monuments in Myanmar, Sagaing Division, Serial-5: published by the Archaeology Department. But "Guinness Book of World Records", March 1982 expresses, "At present, the heaviest bell in use is Mingun Bell which is 101.4 tons weigh and in Mandalay District in Myanmar".'

Myanmar Review

Just as you leave the boat and reach the bank there is a small white pagoda, **Pondaw-hpaya**, only 15ft high which was designed as the working model for the giant pagoda. Downstream from the Pondaw-hpaya lies the **Settawya Pagoda**, a hollow vaulted shrine built in 1811. There is a footprint here of the Buddha in brick and stucco.

A few hundred yards from the bell is the **Hsinbyu-meh** (Mya-theindan) **Pagoda**, built by Bagyidaw in 1816 in memory of his wife Princess Hsinbyu-meh when he was still crown prince. Modelled on Pagan's Sulamani Temple, it is of a circular construction with seven concentric terraces designed to represent the seven mountain ranges surrounding Mount Meru, the legendary home of the gods. There are four flights of steps on the four sides and the white marble figures in the niches of the balustrades are supposed to be the mythical monsters who stand guard on Mount Meru. This too was damaged during the earthquake but was restored by King Mindon in 1874. From the top terrace you have a panoramic view of Mingun.

MAYMYO

'And in Maymyo, too, there are those who will not hear a word against the place. According to them, Simla, Ootacamund and other stations in the East are all very well, but for an ideal resort give them Maymyo.'

Elizabeth Visits Burma, 'Jeff', 1910

Getting there
Some 42 miles (67km) northeast of Mandalay lies the hill station of Maymyo, and whilst it is possible to get there and back in one day (by pick-up truck or even train), it's far more sensible to stay overnight. If you manage to go on your own, it can take up to 2½ hours to reach and maybe 1½ to 2 hours to get back. The local pick-up costs K100 one way and departs from the corner of 32nd and 82nd Streets (the authorities will try and put you on a tourist bus — but insist on the public pick-up, it's more fun). The train, which can take anything up to five hours, isn't recommended. Around town you can hire a bicycle, a horse-drawn carriage (a sort of mini stagecoach) or even travel in a wooden bus.

History
Situated at around 3,500ft (roughly 1,100m) above sea level, Maymyo took its name from Colonel May (*Maymyo* literally means 'May Town') of the 5th Bengal Infantry Regiment which was stationed in the town in 1886. Because of its pleasant cool climate (and strawberries) it served as a summer resort for the British government in Burma.

Where to stay and eat
As with the Strand Hotel in Rangoon, Maymyo's very own colonial

masterpiece, the Candacraig, is alas no longer what it was; it has been gutted by the SLORC and is presently being renovated. Established in 1904 in the style of an old Scottish manor as a holiday retreat for British employees of the Bombay Burmah Trading Company, it has subsequently suffered an ignominious decline, not to mention numerous name changes in the intervening years. It appears to have been called the Maymyo Government Rest House, the Maymyo Inn and — now that the government has renamed the town Pyin U Lwin — the poor old Candacraig has become the Pyin U Lwin Government Rest House or *Thiri Myaing* (Magnificent Copse). However, the name 'Candacraig' still stands defiantly over the threshold and to all the stagecoach drivers, indeed to every non-military Burmese citizen, the Candacraig remains the Candacraig and the town forever Maymyo. Even the roast beef, Yorkshire pudding, strawberries and raspberries are still on the menu. With vast colonial rooms, foul-smelling Asian-style showers and a tennis court, the Candacraig charges US$12 for an economy room, $24 for a standard size room and $30 for a double.

The top hotel in Maymyo used to be the Cherry Myaing, originally the British governor's residence and subsequently the state guesthouse for high-ranking officials and foreign dignitaries. This is back to SLORC use only. Next best is the **Nann Myaing**, while basic accommodation is provided by the **Gandamar Myaing**, **Yuzana Myaing** and **Thazin Myaing Hotels**. These generally charge between US$15-25 a night. At all costs avoid the recently constructed Royal Parkview Hotel — neither royal nor offering a park view — where the dampness may give you pneumonia. Restaurants include the **Shanghai** on the Mandalay-Lashio Road — avoid the 'beggar's chicken' — and the **Hong Kong Chinese Restaurant** and **Happy Restaurant**, both on the Maymyo-Lashio Road. Hilltribe souvenirs can be purchased from 'Dream Merchant Tribal Souvenir Shop', No 4, Mandalay-Lashio Road, Block No 6 and from Mohammed Ali, No 45-46 Main Quarter, Maymyo.

What to see

Maymyo's 17 square miles are practically hedged in by low hills, the highest being One Tree Hill at 4,021ft. Eucalyptus, silver oak, pine, chrysanthemums, coffee, pineapples, strawberry milkshakes, cabbages and cauliflowers make it seem more like a village in rural Kent than *Pyin U Lwin* in Upper Burma.

Of principal interest are Maymyo's vast **Botanical Gardens**, laid out by Sir Harcourt Butler, governor of Burma, established in 1914 and located just south of town. The gardens are dominated by the Kandawgyi Lake, which is bisected by a small golden stupa called *Hsu-taung-pyay-cut-kyaw-zedi*.

At the **Chinese Temple** (*Tayoke-hpaya*), visitors are invited upstairs into the prayer room to receive the so-called 'Three Treasures' from a

Sino-Burmese Buddhist monk. These consist of 'the Heavenly Portal', 'the Divine Mantra' and 'the Symbolic Seal'. The ceremony itself takes the form of kneeling in front of a Chinese Buddha image, clasping your hands together in a rather peculiar way, bowing countless times and repeating the phrase *U Typhoo Me Loo*. This supplication should be uttered in times of crisis and the Chinese Buddha will come to one's aid.

Out of Maymyo, proceeding along the Lashio Road, the unsuspecting foreigner passes hordes of Japanese-made cars — without number plates — which are to be smuggled across the border into China. The Japanese impose a strict limit on the number of motor vehicles which can be exported directly from Japan to China. To bypass this formality, and to earn themselves a few extra million dollars with which to purchase arms and military equipment, the government acquires the cars themselves and deviously sells them on to their Chinese allies over the border.

One hour off the Lashio Road beyond Wetwun village (15 miles/24km southeast of Maymyo), where three streams, three cliffs, three caves, three gullies, three pits, three hills and three waterfalls come together and where *peik-chin* trees grow in abundance, are the **Peikchinmyaung Caves** (Catkin Creeper Caves).

'The cave was originally formed from rock rifts. The rocks are lime stone rocks. Just as a prophesy says that 'one of the three caves will gain fame' the State Law and Order Restoration Council, with the help of the people, have now developed the cave into the Pein Chin Myaung Maha Nandamu Cave. It is now being frequented by numerous pilgrims.'

The cave abounds in Buddha images (see front cover), many neon, and one stupa. One of the images is similar in style to the Maha Muni in Mandalay, and there are also statues depicting various tales from the life of the Buddha. There are countless stalactites and historians say that the rocks date from 345 to 395 million years ago and the cave itself from 230 to 310 million years ago. You can eat outside the cave at the Nann Myaing Restaurant. Car parking costs K10, car tax K15 and camera tax K25. Bring a torch, as some people have been known to find themselves trapped in the cave during a power failure!

A **waterfall** (*Pwei-gau*) five miles (8km) from town on the Lashio Road is another popular destination. Further out of town lie the **Anisahkan and Wetwun Waterfalls** (seven and 15 miles/11km and 24km out respectively), whilst 35 miles (56km) out on the Maymyo-Lashio Road is the famous **Goteik Viaduct**, built between two forest-studded plateaux of the Shan Hills and across a vast, deep gorge. An astonishing feat of engineering, this railway bridge crosses the valley at a height of 870ft. Maymyo also has a **market**, where many local hill people from Shan State in their stunning costumes can be seen. There is an excellent view of the surrounding area from the **Naung-kan-gyi Pagoda** on the hill top.

MONYWA
Getting there
Monywa (pronounced 'Mon-ywa'), the commercial centre of the Chindwin Valley, lies 84 miles (136km) northwest of Mandalay in Sagaing Division and takes some three hours to reach by car. Located by the banks of the Chindwin River, it is a dusty town — not in the least modernised — with a fascinating background. Monywa's economy is wholly dependent on illegal trade with India.

History
The town was actually founded during the Pagan period, and was only given the name Monywa in 1888; the name apparently coming from the expression *Mon Thama* (shortened to *Mon*) meaning Cake Sellers and *Ywa* (village). Prior to that, it was just a sleepy little village (though according to research, the surrounding areas were the dwelling places of mankind as long as a million years ago). Monywa is indeed recorded in Pagan inscriptions and King Thalun's Royal Register. Subsequently it was a village in Alon District during the Konbaung Dynasty. When King Alaungpaya led his troops in the 1750s to Manipur, the Burmese Armed Forces passed through Monywa. The town of Alon was formerly called Badon, and grew to a sizeable village with a big market during the late Konbaung period. The municipality of Monywa was constituted on April 25 1888 and the town was made the headquarters of the Lower Chindwin District. At that time the population was just 2,000 with 345 houses and two wards. Today Monywa is a thriving trading city with a population of more than 100,000, 18 wards and six markets.

Where to stay and eat
Monywa town is a hive of activity, all hustle and bustle by the banks of the Chindwin; maybe you'll come across old Ma Hla San who has been selling her flowers every day for the past 50 years. Or sample the best plum juice in Burma — and the worst Indian restaurant in the land, Yi Yi Win. The **Monywa Hotel** (US$30) is the only accommodation available to tourists. Built in chalet-style with plenty of shrubbery, it has adequate rooms but ghastly bathrooms.

Monywa's two 'best' restaurants are the **Pann Cherry Chinese Restaurant** on Bo-gyoke Street and the **Dagon Restaurant** on Myinmu Road. Both, alas, are fly-infested, overpriced and the latter serves the dreaded 'Deep Fried Fighting Ball'. For breakfast, I recommend **Zawtika Cold Drinks & Bakery** and for cold drinks, **Kanbawza Cold Drinks**.

What to see
The **Thanboddhay Temple** (also known as the Mo-hnyin-thanbuddhe

Temple), lies seven miles (11km) southeast of the town. A recent construction, it was built in 1939 by Mo-hnyin Sayadaw (Agga Maha Pandita), who had started it with a donation of just £10; now it is worth millions. It houses literally thousands of Buddha images: all in all there are reckoned to be 582,357. The Thanboddhay Temple attracts worshippers from all over the land.

Kyaukka village, about ten miles (16km) to the east of Monywa, is famous throughout the country for its lacquerware. Kyaukka lacquerware is cheap and not as good as that of Pagan but is more durable, since artisans use the 'coiling' rather than the 'matting' technique for manufacturing. In the village stands the **Shwe-Gu-Ni** (Gold Red Cave) **Pagoda**, which was founded in the 14th century and given its present name in 1638 during the reign of King Thalun. It is 108ft tall, contains 17th century frescos and an invaluable gold-leaf Buddha image. It is one of Burma's many 'wish-fulfilling' pagodas. North of Kyaukka is the Htan Za Lote Waterfall, where visitors must pay a K15 car tax and are fined K50 for swimming!

West of the Chindwin River in Min-Zu village tract among the Townships of Yin-Mar-bin, Sa-lin-gyi and Pa-lei, is **Hpo-Win Hill** (*Hpo-win-taung*) with its famed caves, a sandstone mountain housing numerous carvings of pagodas, images, pavilions and various other ancient woodcarvings. It derived its name from the *zawgyi* (alchemist-cum-magician) Hpo Win who, as legend has it, haunts the hill.

The **Hpo-win-taung Caves** are one of the most fascinating sites in Burma; there are estimated to be over four million Buddha images in the area (446,444 in the Hpo-win-taung Caves) and the caves were home once to the pre-Burmese Halin cave-dwellers. Nearby lies **Shweba-taung**, sandstone hillocks with many stone Buddhas, a giant sandstone elephant and a frog. There are also two recently renovated giant standing Buddhas called Aungchantha, decoratively painted on the outside, and the Chanthagyi image. Little kids and monkeys will guide you through the natural caves, a wonderful insight into Burmese culture, beliefs and superstitions. (Watch out, the monkeys are not pets and can be quite aggressive. They have been known to snatch food packages from one's hand.)

To reach the caves, you have to cross the Chindwin River to a place called Nyaungbingyi and then drive for about 20 minutes. The fare is K25 depending on the size of the vehicle, whilst individuals pay K1. The hills are located 12 miles (19km) from the east bank jetty.

Situated in Budalin Township, about two miles (3km) east of the river, is **Twinn Hill**. According to geologists, this was the crater of an extinct volcano about five to seven million years ago.

In the northeastern part of Monywa is the **Leh-di Monastery** which was constructed in 1886 by Leh-di Sayadaw, a scholar of Burmese literature and scripture. Today the monastery serves as a large monastic university. The Leh-di Inscription Hall built in 1925 features 806 upright stone slabs on which are inscribed scriptures in Burmese and Pali.

The only pagoda of interest in town is the **Shwezigon** (Gold Victory), which has a half-gold, half-brown stupa surrounded by four ogres. The stupa itself is beautifully painted with Jataka scenes at the bottom. There is a giant sitting Buddha image in the state of meditation, and in the pagoda precinct, a bo tree with two glazed stone fishes underneath. The pagoda, noted for its fine plaster carvings, is guarded by two vast *chinthe* with extraordinarily long whiskers.

Southeast of Monywa is the **Bodhi-tahtaung**, the '1,000 Banyan Trees Monastery', whilst the **Hsu-taung-pyay Pagoda** (Wish Fulfilment) dates from the Pagan period (11th century AD).

KYAUKSE AND VICINITY

'For tropical beauty, Kyaukse, with its canals and roads shaded by splendid trees, vies with Ceylon. It is a garden of delights.'

The Land of the Gold Pagoda, F Deaville Walker, 1935

About an hour south of Mandalay lies Kyaukse, famed for its elephant dancing festival (*Hsin ka-pwe*) every October. Indeed, all those entering Kyaukse are greeted by the sight of two stone elephants at the roadside. The town is dominated by two dams (*Kyaukse* means 'rock dam'), where Burmese ladies wash, men fish and children frolic in the water. Both dams are protected by *nat* shrines under the guardianship of Hseh-daw-shinma *nat*.

Four Buddha images stand on a vast mountain overlooking Kyaukse, which, apart from its numerous pagodas, is also home to some of the most superstitious people in the whole of Burma. To the inhabitants of Kyaukse, the number '9' elicits gasps of horror. So put out are they by this number, that should, for example, a bus be set to depart with nine people on board, it won't budge until either:

(a) one of the passengers has got off,

(b) an extra passenger has got on, thereby increasing the total to a 'lucky' ten, or

(c) most bizarrely of all, a rock has been placed on the bus, which is promptly given the name 'Mr Rock'.

With ten 'passengers' on board, all will supposedly be hunky-dory, though judging by the current record of Burmese modes of transport the vehicle will break down regardless. Were the bus to depart with nine people on board, a horrendous fate would lie in wait (a fate as unthinkable, perhaps, as the bus actually reaching its destination on time).

Kyaukse's most sacred pagoda is the **Shwe-mok-taw**. There are no less than nine stupas bearing the same name in the area, the most famous being located near the market. Half-way up Kyaukse's Shwethalyaung Hill stands the **Kyauk-thinbaw** or 'rock ship', a meditation centre in the form of a ship. Near the ship are 19 Buddha images known as *La-ba-muni* or 'wealth statues'. The Burmese believe if you pray to these you will become rich. You can drive to the Kyauk-thinbaw, but from there to the top of the hill, where the Shwethalyaung Pagoda stands, you must go on foot.

Ascribed to Asoka and repaired subsequently by King Anawrahta in about 1028, the **Shwethalyaung Pagoda** enshrines a replica of the tooth-relic of Ceylon. Carrying the sacred relic, the royal elephant (*Hsinma-Yintha*) was sent off by the latter king to indicate the spot where it should be enshrined. On reaching the summit of the Shwethalyaung Hill, the elephant knelt down, thereby denoting the site where the pagoda was to be built.

Leaving Mandalay and crossing the Myitngeh River, you arrive after about 30 minutes at **Paleik**. Paleik has no less than 325 stupas, its most extraordinary construction being the **Mway-hpaya** (Snake Pagoda), with 17 stupas in the pagoda precinct and (now) two live pythons, one donated by a monk. Inside the pagoda is a Buddha image dating from the Konbaung Dynasty. On excavating the site, the locals found three pythons curled round the Buddha image — the one actually on the Buddha's head was a female, who went on to lay nine eggs. Of the three snakes, two died and one was reincarnated as a nun. The last python used to curl itself nonchalantly beside the statue of Lord Buddha, a neon image built in ancient pre-Pagan style. The deceased python was cremated and three small gold stupas constructed in remembrance of the three pythons.

About 15 minutes' drive from Paleik is the village of **Sintkaing**, home of the **Hpa-lin-bo Pagoda** which is guarded by two fearsome-looking *chinthe*. The Hpa-lin-bo (literally 'Frog-husband-carry on back') marks the site of the residence of the founder of Pagan, King Anawrahta, immediately before he was gored to death by a wild buffalo in 1077. An evil omen was seen at this spot — a female frog carrying the body of her dead husband on her back. The Hpa-lin-bo has a small reclining Buddha in the position of relaxation, an image of the Buddha preaching to his five disciples, a footprint of the Buddha and a gold-plated statue called **Mann-hpaya**, which was worshipped by King Anawrahta himself.

Chapter Eight

Pagan and Vicinity

The pagoda-studded plains of Pagan

'The ruins of the old city lie in a broad arc ten or twelve miles long on the left bank of the Irrawaddy, which glistens like a band of pale satin between green fringes. This is the "Dry Country", the Tattadesa of 11th- and 12th-century inscriptions. Part of it is duneland, torn by ravines and swept into

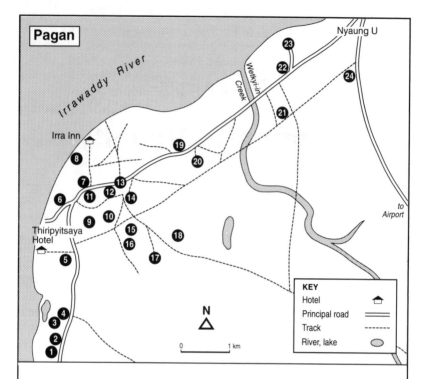

1 Somingyi Monastery
2 Abeyadana
3 Nan-hpaya
4 Manuha
5 Mingalazedi
6 Gawdawpalin
7 Mahabodhi
8 Bu-hpaya
9 Nathlaung Kyaung
10 Thatbyinnyu
11 Shwegugyi
12 Pitakat Taik

13 Sarabha Gateway
14 Ananda
15 Shwesandaw
16 Shinbin-tha-lyaung
17 Dhammayangyi
18 Sulamani
19 Upali Thein
20 Htilo-minlo
21 Kubyaukyyi
22 Kyansittha Umin
23 Shwezigon
24 Sapada

queer forms by the hot wind; part is sandy plain, with a scattering of bean-fields and sugar-palm plantations; most of it lies uncultivated, with goats browsing among stunted bushes and euphorbia. In the villages which straggle along the river-bank and the stream-beds the light drifts down through a leafy filter of tall shade-trees — the pippala with quivering foliage, the acacia with mottled yellow bark, and the tamarind gnarled and pitted by a thousand years of slow growth.

'The walled city occupied only a small part of the huge area demarcated by the ruins, doubtless because at the time of its greatness it expanded far beyond the original defenses and its security was felt to be so unquestionable that no new walls were needed: Pagan in those days was majestically entitled Arimaddanapura, "the city that tramples down its foes".'

A B Griswold, 1964

Getting there and around

Depending on where you are coming from, six options are available: plane, private bus/car, public bus, riverboat or train. Myanma Airways flies daily from Rangoon and Tuesday, Thursday and Sunday from Mandalay. The cost of a one-way ticket Rangoon-Pagan is US$80 on a twin-prop (F-27), US$90 on a jet (F-28). Mandalay-Pagan costs US$35 on an F-27, US$40 on an F-28. Air Mandalay has daily flights from Rangoon (US$93) and Mandalay (US$42) to Pagan.

The public bus from Mandalay leaves at around 0400 and costs K250. The riverboat from Mandalay takes between 10-14 hours and sails every Thursday and Sunday, departing at 0530 from the Gawwein jetty (at the west end of 35th Street). A cabin costs US$30, deck US$10. Private bus/car from Mandalay takes about six hours; from Prome over six hours. Train is not recommended, as there is no station at Pagan. You would have to take the train from Rangoon or Mandalay to Thazi and then catch the public bus from Thazi to Pagan.

Once in Pagan, go your own way by horse-cart (bargain madly for the fare) or rent a bicycle for about K15 an hour (make sure the brakes work and the tyres are full, and take a pump with you, just in case). A Burmese friend, map, sun-hat, water-bottle and torch are also recommended.

General description

No other capital of Burma, either before or after, has approached the magnificence of Pagan in the days of its greatness. Its ruins are still the most impressive in the country. If you climb to the top of one of the pagodas, you will see ruined pagodas in every direction, pagodas of every shape and size, and there is practically nothing else in sight but these remnants of Pagan's founder King Anawrahta (1044-77) and his successors. Of the secular buildings not a trace remains, though there must have been a very considerable population. The palace of the king, the monasteries of the monks, and the dwellings of the people built of wood and bamboo have all disappeared: nothing remains but countless pagodas, ranging from the majestic Ananda down to the humblest stupa.

All the great religious buildings, which make Pagan today such a wonderful scene of desolation, were constructed between 1057 and 1227. The Ananda was built by one of Anawrahta's sons, so not only is it one of the earliest, it is also one of the most remarkable. The religious zeal which for two centuries kept a whole people so absorbed in building pagodas, temples and monasteries is remarkable enough in itself, but it is still more remarkable that in the 11th century the Burmese should have been able to construct such a temple as the Ananda. The diversity of form and excellence of architectural skill has never been equalled since. The succeeding centuries have produced nothing to rival the relics of Pagan.

Where to stay and eat/shopping

As Mandalay had the Mandalay and Mya Mandala Hotels, so had Pagan the Thiripyitsaya and Irra Inn (renamed the Ayeyar Hotel by the SLORC). The only kind word to be said about either is that they enjoy scenic locations by the banks of the Irrawaddy. Other than that the service, particularly in the Thiripyitsaya (which attracts all the large tour groups and affluent/military Burmese) is surly and the rooms and meals dreary and overpriced.

The Thiripyitsaya and Irra Inn are both in 'Old' Pagan, as is the cheap and ghastly Co-Operative Inn. That's a plus: 'New' Pagan — whither all the inhabitants of 'Old' Pagan were relocated Khmer Rouge-style at gunpoint in May 1990 — is a satellite town, created some say to prevent people from witnessing Ne Win on his frequent visits to his astrologer in Pagan, others say to create a sort of tourist theme-park.

The privately run **Thande Hotel** is much improved. It consists of five cottages with 20 rooms and costs US$42 a night including breakfast. The **Myathida Hotel**, Main Road, New Pagan is cheap at US$8 for a single. On the main road to Nyaung-U is the **Golden Express** (US$36-$84, including breakfast), built in chalet-style with air conditioning and fridge. The newly constructed **Paradise Guest House** (US$8-$15 for fan-cooled rooms) in Old Pagan is recommended.

Pagan's most exclusive restaurant is the **River View**, a modern yet raj-like construction owned by Skyline Travel of Bangkok (ie: military) and quite out of place. The River View is some way out of town and you need to hire a horse-cart: make sure the driver waits for you and, as ever, bargain hard. You may need to reserve a table in advance (not because the restaurant will be fully booked, but to make sure the chef remembers to go to market that day).

Other restaurants include **Ever Queen** (also sells 'antiques') in Old Pagan, near the city gate, the **Nation** on the main road and the **Myayadana** which serves Burmese fare, whilst there is a pleasant little noodle shop near Nyaung-U Market called the **Sein Yatana Restaurant**.

Pagan is the home of lacquerware and you won't be able to escape from it anywhere. If you feel inclined to buy, go to U Kan Tun, Daw Hla Myaing & daughter Ma Moe Moe, 6/1 Khanlaung Quarter. This is one of the rare non-state owned shops, so you can haggle like mad. You can also settle up in cigarettes and whisky, swop items or change money. Nyaung-U Market has the usual collection of comestibles, cosmetics, *longyi* and smuggled goods.

Pagodas and temples

It is obviously impossible to visit all the pagodas and temples during your stay in Pagan. Most guidebooks tend to classify the structures according to their location. There are five main areas: Pagan village (near the two main hotels), Nyaung-U (near the market and northwest of the airport), Minnanthu (southwest of the airport), Myinkaba (south of Pagan) and Pwasaw (situated between Myinkaba and Minnanthu). However, since Pagan is essentially a place for those with a keen interest in history and architecture, it may be more useful to categorise the buildings according to their architectural style.

Independent tourists must pay an entrance fee of US$10 (dollars or FECs) and register at Pagan's National Museum before they are permitted access to any of the sites. An additional charge of US$3 is levied for every extra night exceeding two nights.

Stupa whose dome is modelled on a reliquary (a receptacle for relics)

A fine example of this is the **Bu-hpaya**, which stands on the brink of the Irrawaddy in Pagan, above rows of crenellated terraces, not far from the Irra Inn. The bulbous dome resembles that of the **Nga-kywe-na-daung** (an early bulbous stupa located in the south part of the old city of Pagan, c11th century), assuming the form of a cylindrical relic casket. Above it stands a bold convex band upon which rises a tapering stupa finial. Tradition attributes the Bu-hpaya to King Pyusawhti of Pagan who reigned from AD 168 to 243, though stylistically it may be ascribed to about the 11th century. According to tradition, it was constructed on the spot where a gigantic *Bu* or gourd creeper grew. Within its precincts is a shrine dedicated to the God of Storms (*Mondaing Nat*). It was completely destroyed during the 1975 earthquake but has subsequently been restored in the shape and size of the original.

Stupa whose dome is modelled on a tumulus (ancient burial mound)

Located by the banks of the Irrawaddy at Nyaung-U and accessible both by land and water, the **Shwezigon** is one of the holiest pagodas in Burma since it is believed to contain the frontal bone and a tooth of the Buddha. It is a solid, cylindrical structure resting on three square terraces, a prototype of Burmese stupas. It has a bold waistband round the bell-shaped dome, above which rises a series of concentric mouldings ending in a finial and crowned by a *hti*. Its construction was begun by King Anawrahta on the site chosen by setting a tooth of the Lord Buddha from Ceylon in a jewelled *pya-that* shrine on a white elephant and letting the animal roam. Where the elephant rested, there the site was chosen. Anawrahta left the pagoda in an unfinished state and it was completed by Kyansittha in just seven months and seven days.

Around the terraces of the pagoda, set in panels, are enamelled plaques illustrating scenes of the previous lives of the Buddha. On each of the four sides of the pagoda is a small temple enshrining a standing Buddha, 13ft high. On either side of the east approach is a square stone pillar with Mon inscriptions on all four sides dedicated by King Kyansittha. Figures of the 37 *nats* can be seen in a rather dreary shed at the northeast corner of the pagoda precinct.

Stupa of a Sinhalese type

Southeast of the Shwezigon is the **Sapada Pagoda**, which was built in the 12th century by Sapada, a native of Bassein, who had been ordained a monk in Ceylon and who founded a sect at Pagan on his return to Burma. The pagoda was constructed after the model of a Sinhalese shrine, and is the prototype of similar structures in the province. The Sapada's distinctive feature is the cubical relic-chamber above the bell. It is a landmark in the history of Buddhism, and commemorates the religious relationship between Burma and Ceylon (Sri Lanka).

Temple based on north Indian model

The most celebrated temple both in Pagan and Burma itself is the **Ananda**, which was built by Kyansittha in AD 1090, and constructed according to a plan furnished by Indian Buddhist monks. It symbolises the endless wisdom (*Ananta Panna*) of the Buddha. The name *Ananta*, which was later changed to *Ananda*, was the name of Buddha's cousin.

The proportions of the Ananda are majestic: it forms a square of nearly 200ft, broken on each side by the projection of large gabled vestibules which convert the plan into a perfect Greek cross. These vestibules are rather lower than the main mass of the building, which elevates itself to a height of 35ft in two tiers of windows. Above rise successively diminishing terraces, the last of which just affords sufficient breadth for the spire which crowns and completes the edifice. The lower half of this spire is in the form of a mitre-like pyramid adapted from the temples of India; the upper half is the same moulded taper pinnacle that completes the common bell-shaped pagodas of Pagan. The gilded *hti* caps the temple at a height of 168ft (51m) above the ground.

The interior consists of two vaulted and high but narrow corridors running parallel to each other along the four sides of the temple. They are connected by low and narrow passages and further intersected by four large corridors into which access is obtained through the porticoes. In the centre is an enormous cube, on the four sides of which are deep and high niches enshrining four colossal standing Buddhas. Each Buddha rises 31ft high above his throne, which itself measures almost 8ft in height. Of these images (which represent the four Buddhas who have attained nirvana), only those on the north and south are the original ones; those on the east and west are copies made 100 years ago to replace the originals which were destroyed by fire.

Other interesting features of the Ananda are the numerous glazed terracotta tiles ornamenting the base and the receding terraces which represent the Jataka stories. Each of these 1,500 plaques is inscribed with a Mon legend. The inner walls are a honeycomb of niches (80), made by Indian artists, in which are set small stone Buddhas in various postures. The western sanctum of the temple enshrines the lifesize statue of its founder Kyansittha. You will notice that the king's face is not Burmese, for his mother was an Indian lady. In the porch on the west face are two footprints of the Buddha placed on a pedestal. The king was so entranced with the Ananda he broke the mould by executing the architect, and buried alive a child to provide the building with a guardian spirit.

Temple of central Indian type
Southeast of the Bu-hpaya Pagoda stands the **Mahabodhi Pagoda**, built by King Htilo-minlo in AD 1215 and based on the temple at Bodh Gaya in Bihar which commemorates the spot where the Buddha attained Enlightenment. It is the only one of its type in Burma. The basement is a quadrangular block of no great height, supporting a tall pyramidal spire. The finial is a small slim stupa. The entire structure is covered with niches bearing seated Buddhas and interspersed with ornamental panels and mouldings.

Temple based on south Indian model
At Minnanthu, about three to four miles (6km) southwest of Nyaung-U, stands the **Sulamani Temple** which was built around AD 1183 by Narapatisithu. It consists of two storeys, set back one behind the other, each crowned by terraces ornamented with battlemented parapets; small stupas at each corner surmount a deeply moulded cornice set with glazed plaques of different sizes and patterns. In plan each storey is a square and four porches facing the cardinal points project from each, the porch

on the east face being larger than the rest. This temple, which in plan resembles the Thatbyinnyu, affords superb views of Pagan.

Cave temples based on Indian model

Situated close to the Shwezigon Pagoda is the **Kyansittha Umin**, a low brick building half underground and half above. Despite its name, it has been attributed to Anawrahta. The interior consists of long and dark corridors, some walls of which are ornamented with frescos dating from the 11th to 13th centuries. Those dating from the 13th century were most probably painted during the Mongol occupation of 1287 and represent Mongolian people, nobles, captains and warriors.

Ordination hall

Northeast of the Ananda Temple is the **Upali Thein**, named after a celebrated monk, Upali, and dating back to the second quarter of the 13th century (though repaired in the 17th century). It is a structure of fine proportions enclosed within brick walls and is rectangular ·in plan, containing a hall with a Buddha image placed on a pedestal near the western end. The roof is ornamented with a double row of battlements in simulation of wooden architecture, and its centre is surmounted by a small, slim pagoda. The arches on which the superstructure rests are well built and the brilliant frescos covering its walls and ceilings are in a fair state of preservation. These date from the late 17th or early 18th century.

Library

West of the Ananda, within the city walls, is the **Pitakat Taik** which was built in 1058 by Anawrahta to house the 30 elephant loads of Buddhist scriptures in Pali which he had brought from Thaton. The structure was repaired in 1783 by King Bodawpaya. It measures 51ft square and 60ft high with the entrance on the east and perforated stone windows on other sides. The inner cell has a corridor round it. The Pitakat Taik's chief peculiarity is its approximate simulation of architectural forms in wood: that's to say it is covered by five multiple roofs in a style similar to that of the Mandalay Palace, and ornamented with peacock-like finials in plaster carving.

Other pagodas and temples

There are scores of other pagodas and temples, the most interesting of which are located at Pagan. These include:

Htilo-minlo Temple Constructed around AD 1211 (some sources quote 1218) by King Htilo-minlo. Htilo-minlo (1210-34) was also known as Nantaungmya, meaning 'many entreaties for the throne', because his mother had so often entreated that he might succeed to the throne. The temple, a magnificent creation, was built on the spot where the white

Hpo-win-taung Caves. These magnificent caves contain, it is claimed, 446,444 Buddha images.

Kyaiktiyo, the Golden Rock Pagoda, the magnificent gold-encrusted boulder supported by one hair of the Lord Buddha

Lisu village near Mogok, Upper Burma, villager and baby

Lisu mother with her baby, Mogok, Upper Burma

umbrella had bowed down before him as a youth. It is the last of the series of great temples at Pagan. There are four Buddhas facing the cardinal points on the ground floor as well as on the upper storey, which is reached by two staircases built in the thickness of the walls.

Thatbyinnyu Temple Approached through the crumbling city walls, this temple stands 201ft high (the highest in Pagan) and dominates all others in majesty of line, offering stunning views of the Ananda Temple. Meaning 'omniscience', the Thatbyinnyu was built in 1144 by King Alaungsithu after the model of the temples in northern India. It has five storeys: the first and second were used as the residence of monks; images were kept on the third; the fourth was used as a library; and on the fifth a pagoda was constructed containing holy relics. The building is thus a combination of a stupa and vihara and its history is recorded on its walls. Like all the structures of Pagan, the Thatbyinnyu has suffered badly from tremors and the ravages of time, having been restored on numerous occasions.

Shwegugyi Temple Golden Cave Temple, located northwest of the Thatbyinnyu, it was built in 1131 by Alaungsithu after the model of the Buddha's sleeping chamber. Standing on a high brick platform, this temple faces north and access to it is by a flight of steps at the northwest corner. The Shwegugyi's history is recorded on two stone slabs set in the inner walls; it apparently took just seven months to complete.

Nathlaung Kyaung This is the sole remaining Hindu temple in Pagan and was built by King Taungthugyi in AD 931 (over a century before the introduction of the Southern School of Buddhism from Thaton). Partly in ruins, it is dedicated to the god Vishnu and is decorated on the outside with stone figures of the ten *Avatars* (past and future incarnations), Gautama Buddha being the ninth. Occupying the centre is a huge square brick pillar, around which there is the usual circumambulatory passage, vaulted over; this pillar supports the dome and *sikhara* above.

Gawdawpalin Temple Almost equidistant between Pagan's two best-known hotels, the Gawdawpalin was constructed by Narapatisithu (1173-1210) in order to commemorate the ceremony of paying homage to the manes (deified souls) of his ancestors, and its general arrangement resembles the Thatbyinnyu. It has a vestibule on the east, but unlike the Thatbyinnyu, the upper storey is reached by narrow stairs built in the thickness of the walls, and Buddha images are placed against the central cube on all sides on the ground floor. Both the *sikhara* and stupa are elongated but the temple is only 180ft high. The Gawdawpalin was severely damaged during the 1975 earthquake and its restoration, one of the most major ever undertaken, was completed in the 1980s. It offers splendid views of the Irrawaddy and the plains of Pagan.

Shwesandaw Pagoda This is a cylindrical stupa with five terraces, the first to be built by King Anawrahta after his conquest of Thaton in 1057. Enshrined inside are some sacred hairs of the Buddha. The chedi, rebuilt over 60 years ago, fell down in 1975 and was restored in 1977, painted yellow (it was originally white). From here, you have a marvellous view of the sunrise. This pagoda is also known as the Mahapeinne or Ganesha Pagoda, from the fact that each of the four corners of its lowest terrace is guarded by three Hindu gods, Brahma, Vishnu and Siva, the third being often identified with Ganesha.

Shinbin-tha-lyaung In a brick shed, within the confines of the Shwesandaw Pagoda, lies a 60ft long reclining Buddha (in the sleeping position) which dates from the 11th century. Unlike the recumbent image of the Buddha in the Manuha Temple, its head points to the south, whereas that of the Manuha Temple points to the north, a position assumed by Gautama Buddha when he was lying on his deathbed between two *sal* trees at Kusinara.

Mingalazedi Pagoda Built in 1274 by Narathihapati and located just south of the Thiripyitsaya Hotel, this pagoda is noted for its beautiful terracotta tiles with Burmese legends around the terraces. It stands on a low square basement with a broad staircase on each side. It has fine proportions and indicates the high watermark of Burmese religious architecture, because it was constructed ten years before the king fled from Pagan at the Mongol invasion.

Dhammayangyi Temple Built by King Narathu (1163-65), this temple is similar in plan to the Ananda, following the Mon style, but only the outer corridor is accessible as all the entrances to the inner ones are for some unknown reason blocked by brickwork, which is reputed to be the finest in Pagan. It is the biggest building of its kind in Burma, and attached to it are two inscriptions dated respectively 1205 and 1253. King Narathu, incidentally, was also known as the *Kalagyamin* or the 'king killed by the kalas'; while the construction of this temple was in progress, Narathu was assassinated by some kalas (foreigners), who were probably natives of Chittagong, and the temple itself was never completed.

Kubyaukkyi Temple Located at Myinkaba and built in 1113 by Rajakumar, son of Kyansittha, this temple consists of a square basement surmounted by a *sikhara* with curvilinear roofs resting on terraces. The interior has a sanctum around which runs a vaulted corridor adorned with niches enshrining stone Buddha images. The architecture of this temple is typically Mon, and some of the paintings in the sanctum are among the earliest still in existence in Pagan.

Manuha Temple Built by Manuha, the captive king of Thaton, in 1059, this square structure contains three seated Buddha images and a vast reclining image representing the Buddha in the position of parinibbana. The central roof collapsed during the earthquake, in the process badly damaging the largest, seated Buddha, though it has subsequently been repaired.

Nan-hpaya Temple Close to the Manuha, this delightful brick temple served as the residence of the captive Mon king, Manuha. It is built of brick and mud mortar, surfaced with stone, and is square in plan with a porch projecting on the east face. Flanking the sanctuary in the main building are four stone pillars, on the sides of each of which are carved triangular floral designs and the figures of the Brahma holding lotus flowers in each hand. Like other earlier temples at Pagan, the Nan-hpaya has perforated stone windows to admit light into the building. The arch pediments over the windows and the carvings of the frieze are fine examples of architectural motifs in stone. The interior of the Nan-hpaya is unusual. It is a hollow square, but the four stout pillars which support the superstructure seem to have been remnants of a central pillar pierced through and through by two intersecting tunnels.

Abeyadana Temple This temple faces north and consists of a square basement surmounted by a stupa with a pronounced relic-chamber and a tall spire; the porch on the north has three entrances. The basement is ornamented with perforated stone windows, and there is a vaulted corridor running round the central block. In the latter there is a deep recess forming a sanctum on the north, and in it is enshrined a large brick image of a seated Buddha. The most interesting aspect of the Abeyadana are the paintings with which the inner faces of its walls are decorated. They represent the Brahminical gods and divinities of the Mahayana pantheon. Scenes from the Jataka with Mon legends cover the walls of the front hall. The temple was built by King Kyansittha on the spot where his wife Abeyadana waited as he sought refuge during one of his flights from the wrath of Sawlu.

Somingyi Monastery Built in AD 1218, this is one of the typical monasteries of the Pagan period and is situated south of the Thiripyitsaya Hotel. It consists of a brick-enclosed platform surrounded by a lobby on the east, a chapel on the west and small cells on the north and south, all of which are connected by narrow passages. The chapel is a small square two-storeyed building with a single door opening on the east, connecting it with the central platform by a passage. In the lower chamber of the chapel, on a brick pedestal, the remains of an image were found placed against the west wall.

Nandamannya Temple Located at Minnanthu, east of the Sulamani, this temple has a small vaulted chamber with only one entrance on the east. The interior walls are decorated with fine frescos. Inside there is a seated image of the Buddha in a state of disrepair. The temple was built by King Kyazwa in 1248.

Thambula Temple Just south of the Nandamannya, this temple was built in 1255 by Thambula (Sumlula), wife of King Uzana. It is a square building with a circumambulatory corridor running round the central square pile sustaining the *sikhara* above. It is adorned with frescos and mural writings. Thambula is a misreading of *Sumlula*, 'The Moon of The Three Worlds', which is the briefest Burmese rendering of the Pali *Tilokacandadevi*.

Lay-myethna Temple Southwest of the Thambula and built in 1223 by minister Anandathura, this badly neglected temple rests on a high platform and faces east. The interior walls are decorated with frescos and the exterior is all painted white. It is topped by an Indian-style spire, similar to the Ananda.

Hpaya-thonzu In between the Thanbula and Lay-myethna Temples lies the Hpaya-thonzu (literally 'Pagoda-three-holy objects'), consisting of three distinct small square temples with vaulted corridors and porticoes, joined together by two vaulted narrow passages leading from the one into the other. There is a pedestal in each sanctum, but the images have disappeared and their exact nature is not known. The walls of the corridors and the vaults are covered with beautifully painted and well preserved frescos. The half-decorated middle sanctum and the plain walls of the western temple indicate that the work was abandoned before completion. The date of the foundation of the temple is not known, but it can safely be attributed to the late 13th century.

Dhammayazika Pagoda Located at Pwasaw and built by Narapatisithu in 1198, this is a solid circular pagoda similar in style to the Shwezigon but its design is elaborate and unusual. The three lower terraces, which are adorned with terracotta tablets illustrating the Jatakas, are pentagonal, and at the base of each side there is a small temple with a square basement enshrining a Buddha image. They are all built on a raised platform enclosed within a wall, and there is an outer circuit wall which is pierced with five gateways. There are some ink inscriptions on the interior walls of the projecting porches.

Stroll down to the banks of the Irrawaddy; take a trip on the river in the direction of the Shwezigon, past children frolicking in the murky waters as their mothers do the daily washing. You may come across the

Nataunt Monastery, with its nine novice monks, two *phongyi* and interesting woodcarvings and frescos dating from the 11th century, some of the earliest mural paintings in existence in Pagan. Then there's the **Myazigon**, a small white stupa and monastery. Eventually the Shwezigon itself appears: this time, of course, from a different angle. You can moor the boat here, try some fishing and wander up to the pagoda, not forgetting to remove your shoes at the bottom. Cross over to **Zaylan Island**, where the fishermen work at night for four months each year, retreating to the centre of the island when the river rises. Selling their catch at Nyaung-U Market, the 11 fishermen earn K400 a day in total between them. They'll greet you with typical Burmese hospitality, so bring along some cigarettes as a gift. This river journey, just like the one to Mingun, offers a rare glimpse into a world that few travellers are privileged to experience.

Archaeological museum

Opened in October 1979 at a cost of K1.4 million, this rather dull museum features a rectangular open hall housing inscriptions and stone sculptures, and an octagonal structure with a spire-like skylight exhibiting smaller antiquities. Of no great interest, it serves as a fair introduction to the history of Pagan. Foreigners must come here to pay their US$10 Pagan entrance fee, plus an additional US$4 (cash or FECs) to visit the museum alone. Open daily (except Mondays and public holidays) from 0930 to 1500.

'This realm of Pagan is so named because it is the fairest and dearest of lands. It is also called Arimaddana because its people are warriors who vanquish their foes, and even its name is terrible. Its folk are free from pain and danger, they are skilled in every art, they possess the tools of every craft, they are wealthy, the revenues are past telling and the land is full of useful things. Truly it is a land to be more desired than the Himavanta. It is a glorious realm and its people are famed for their splendour and power. The monastery I have built stands to the east of the capital.'

Thus reads an inscription recording the donation of a monastery by a princess in 1343. Nostalgia, perhaps, for in 1287 Pagan had been overrun by Kublai Khan, just as, 703 years later, the *Tatmadaw* stepped in so savagely to relocate the villagers.

MOUNT POPA

'Popa mountain detaches itself from surroundings, thirty or forty miles to the east; it is faint violet and rises from a slightly undulating wooded plain. It is a great place for game and nats. Most powerful nats or spirits live there, and if you go shooting you get nothing, unless you offer some of

your breakfast as a peace-offering to these spirits in the morning. This has
been found to be true over and over again by those who have shot there.'

W G Burn Murdoch, 1908

About 50 miles (80km) southeast of Pagan rises the sugar-loaf Mount
Popa (*Popa* is Sanskrit for flower) 4,981ft high, like a massive,
misplaced pillar. It was created from a violent volcanic eruption way
back in 442 BC to become the dwelling place of the gods. For 700 years
from the 4th to 11th centuries, every king had to make a pilgrimage here
to consult the spirits before his reign could begin. Even today, Mount
Popa is considered the earthly font of power for the mystical world of
the *nats*. A shrine to the Mahagiri *nats* (the blacksmith Nga Tin De and
his sister Shwemyet-hna, 'Handsome and Golden Face', guards of
Pagan's Sarabha Gateway) stands halfway up the steep path to the
summit, which itself is covered with pagodas and other religious
structures. According to legend, they perished in flames as a result of the
evil designs of the local king. Henceforth the 4th century King of Pagan,
Thinli-kyaung, made Mount Popa the official home of the brother and
sister spirits with the intention of providing a national centre for *nat*
worship.

As Maung Htin Aung describes so evocatively in his book *Folk
Elements in Burmese Buddhism*:

'It was near the time of the full moon, and according to the English
calendar it was December. The fields had been reaped, the harvest had been
successfully gathered, and the people were in festive mood. The images of
the two "Nats" were put on golden palanquins and attended by the king
himself, they were carried along the road to Mount Popa. Red was the
colour associated with "Nat" spirits and red flags and red streamers were
carried by the people taking part in the procession and by the people who
lived along the route. Everyone danced and sang, and when the procession
halted at villages on the way, food and toddy-wine flowed free. The
procession reached the summit of Mount Popa on the full moon day and a
golden "Nat" shrine, newly constructed, awaited the two images. The
images were set up in the shrine with great pomp and ceremony, and the
king proclaimed that the village on the slope of the hill, Popa Ywa, was
given as a perpetual fief to the two "Nat" spirits. As spirit mediums danced
in abandoned joy, hundreds of white oxen, white horses, and white goats
were sacrificed to the "Nat" spirits.

'It was the ninth month of the Burmese year, and it seemed so propitious
that the month associated with the magic number nine should now be
associated with the two "Nats". Both were now given by the king the title
of "Lords of the Great Mountain". The brother was given the title in a
Burmese-Pali form, "Min Maha-Giri". ("Min" in Burmese means "Lord",
and "Maha-Giri" in Pali means "Great Mountain".) The sister was given a
title in its pure Burmese form, "Taunggyi-Shin", "Taunggyi" meaning

"Great Mountain" and "Shin" meaning "Lord". However, the sister continued to be affectionately called "Shwe-Myetnha", "Golden Face". The king further ordered that the month be renamed "Nat-Taw", or "the month of the Royal "Nats", and fixed the full moon day in this month as the date of the annual festival in honour of the Popa "Nats". The name of the eighth month of the Burmese year, Tazaung-mon, means "the month of the Festival of Lights", and before the advent of the Lords of the Great Mountain the full moon day of this month was the occasion for the offering of lights to the gods of the planets in particular and to all gods in general. But the king now ordained that the festival of lights was to be held one month later, in the month of Nat-Taw.'

During the month of *Nayon* (May to June), Mount Popa is busy with pilgrims celebrating the annual 'Festival of Spirits'. Offerings to the *nats* have to be made of food which must not be fried.

So who are these *nats*, and what hold do they have over the Burmese nation? In Upper Burma, where even today the *nat* seems to have a powerful sway over the people, you find *nat-sin* (a shrine in honour of a *nat*) either at the main gate or at the centre of every village. The *nat-sin* is usually crowded with offerings — flowers, various kinds of fruits and sometimes even money.

It is remarkable to note that the inhabitants of Taungbyon, a village situated on the Shwetachaung Canal 20 miles (32km) north of Mandalay, are devoted adherents of the *nats*. Every house, every *zayat* (resthouse) is full of *nat-sins* and *nat-yokes* (*nat* images). Hence Taungbyon is often called *nat-ywa* (*nat*-village). The *nat* is a hero to them and they all pay regular homage.

The *nat* is a difficult customer to deal with, and even harder for the foreigner to come to terms with. He has many fancies and whims. He bullies weak-minded individuals but gives way to a strong-minded *lu-gyan* (villain). The *lu-gyan*, you see, might destroy his *nat-sin* and *nat-yoke*, steal his money and ill-treat his *nat-kadaw* (wife). Yes, *nats* also indulge in such things as love, courtship and marriage and enjoy polygamy with such liberality that many a Burmese king might have envied. The *nat* makes love to his sweetheart with all the assiduity and perseverance that characterises the action of an ordinary young man. He selects his bride from the spiritual standpoint, that is to say, he looks more to the spiritual beauty than to the physical. The *nat* pays his visits more often than his human counterpart. During the night the girl sees him coming, though nobody else can. He is smartly attired with plenty of perfume on his handkerchief. Courtship can be prolonged. After a few weeks, months or years, the date for the wedding is set. The *nat* usually sends one of his own wives as his representative at the wedding and the bride is given away by her parents or guardians. The wedding itself is conducted with great pomp and ceremony, at the expense of the bridegroom through his medium, the representative *nat-kadaw*. But beware — the *nat* is a jealous and, at times, weak being. Woe betide the youth who dares cross the path of his sweetheart!

The *nats* maintain their wives in two ways. They help their *nat-kadaws* in fortune-telling as they seem to know the past, the present and the future of the individual. Thus some *nat-kadaws* earn their livelihood as fortune-tellers. Others start a business or open a shop and the *nat* helps them to make a brisk sale of the goods with great profit. If they have no capital to start with, money is advanced by one of the old *nat-kadaws* referred to by the *nat*. *Nat-kadaws* are well protected by the *nat;* they are a powerful body greatly respected and obeyed and no one dares insult or maltreat them. For sure, *nats* are not to be trifled with.

This is just a brief insight into the lives and significance of the *nats*. Think about it as you climb Mount Popa, where the hordes of monkeys scurry hither and thither. When you eventually reach the top, it is rather disappointing: there are no interesting pagodas and the view does not match up to that from any of the temples in neighbouring Pagan. But a curse upon the traveller who speaks disparagingly of Mount Popa and its *nats*! Those wishing to know more about *nats* should consult Melford Spiro's *Burmese Supernaturalism: A Study in the Explanation and Reduction of Suffering* (Institute for the Study of Human Issues, Philadelphia, 1978).

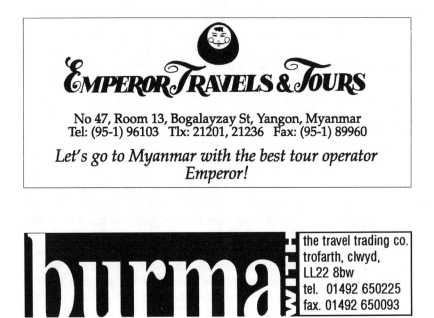

Chapter Nine

Prome and Shwedaung

PROME

'Prome itself possesses a most captivating situation. It stands rather high with the mighty Irrawaddy flowing silently at its feet, while across, on the opposite shore, it looks upon a glorious range of hills whose delicate wistful outlines are drawn out in the softest of lights and shades... The pagoda at Prome is quite one of the most beautiful in Burma. It is a golden one, but not nearly so large as the Shway Dagohn at Rangoon, but for its size it is quite as lovely. It stands like its Rangoon brother on a hill and overlooks with a benign glance the town beneath...

'The whole was intensely captivating, and struck one as possessed of a singular grace and charm especially when seen as we saw it in the soft sunlight glow which decked the golden company with crowns of radiance, while the tenderest of breezes shook the tiny tinkling bells on each golden Htee and caused them to ring a sweet melodious cadence. The date of this lovely shrine, the Shwe San-Daw as it is called, is said to be 441 B.C., a hundred and thirty years after the birth of Buddha, its age thus being 2,336 years.'

G T Gascoigne, 1896

History

Located by the steep banks of the Irrawaddy, some 5½ hours (161 miles/258km) northwest of Rangoon, lies the city of Prome, known to the Burmese as Pyay (the English name Prome came from the Burmese word *Pyay-myo*). Prome is actually two towns, both situated on the east bank of the river, where the Nawin stream flows into the Irrawaddy: the other one is the historic city of Sri Ksetra (Sri Ksetra is its classical Sanskrit name; the Burmese pronounce it *Thayay-khit-taya*). In reality the whole area is known as either Prome (to the British) or Pyay (to the locals). The actual name Sri Ksetra is found only in ancient texts and is used purely by students of history and archaeology.

One legend has it that the Buddha came to the area for the benefit of all creatures and stayed on a mountain to the northeast of Prome. He saw a lump of cow-dung floating in the sea. At that moment a snake came out of a clump of bamboo and moved up close to the Buddha's feet, behaving in a very reverent way. When the Buddha smiled, his disciple Ananda asked why. Buddha then prophesied that in later times five miracles would occur in that place: the earth would tremble; the sea would recede, leaving dry land; the mountain on which the Buddha sat would collapse, leaving a swamp; a river would appear; and a new range of mountains would arise. After these five miracles occurred, this snake would be reincarnated, named Duttabaung. One hundred and one years after Buddha had entered nirvana, this king would establish Sri Ksetra as his royal capital at the spot where the cow-dung was floating. He would be a patron of Buddhism, causing it to spread and flourish in this land. According to popular history, all five miracles did occur, just as the Lord Buddha had foretold. However, they all occurred as a result of the eruption of Mount Popa, thousands of years prior to the Buddhist era.

There is no record of the founding of Prome on the banks of the Irrawaddy. After Pagan became the capital, a number of people were probably sent back down the river to re-establish the former city of Sri Ksetra. But by that time the river had shifted its course considerably leaving the original site on higher ground far inland. Prome was thus built on the riverbank near the hill of the Shwesandaw Pagoda, positioned right between the rich lands of the delta in the south and the dry zone (of peanuts, cotton, tobacco, sesame seeds and toddy palms) in the north. Prome came under British rule in 1852 after the Second Anglo-Burmese War, but was completely destroyed by a terrible fire ten years later. Completely rebuilt, Prome today is euphemistically referred to as a 'thriving trading post', famous for its custard-apples.

Getting there

Unlike the road from Rangoon to Meiktila, the stretch from the capital to Prome is generally good and flat. Those with time on their hands can travel by boat or train. There are no boat schedules, but the journey from Prome to Rangoon, for example, takes two days and two nights, and costs under K100. Tickets can be purchased from an office located about 500 yards from the Pyay Hotel (turn left out of the hotel until you reach the river, then turn right along the banks of the Irrawaddy). For rail enthusiasts, the No 71-Up leaves Rangoon at 1300, arriving Prome at 2000; the No 72-Down departs Prome at 2200, reaching Rangoon at 0500. If you are coming from the north by car, stop off en route at a town called **Myay-deh**, 45 miles (72km) from Prome. Two eye-catching statues of Lokapala, spirit of music and peace and guardian of Mount Meru, will greet you outside the Kauk-ku-than Pagoda. You can also enjoy a superb Burmese meal at Daw Nyo's (Mrs Brown's!) restaurant in town.

Where to stay and eat

Prome has distinctly limited accommodation: there is the one government hotel, the Pyay on Strand Road, where the rooms, though sizeable and with air conditioning and fridge, have no washing facilities. There are only communal showers, ant-infested washbasins and disgusting toilets. Rates vary from US$15-30 (plus 20% taxes and not including breakfast), though at least you can pay for meals in local currency. A better alternative is the **Santhawda Guest House**, No 378 Lanmadaw, tel: 053 21676, which, although overpriced at US$12 (or K1200 if you manage to settle up in local currency), has air-conditioned rooms and reasonable showers. Forget both the Sakhanthar Guest House (opposite the Shwesandaw Pagoda) which is like a prison, and the appalling Myat Guest House.

The two best restaurants in Prome are the **Aungsi** and the **Thethant**, where an excellent meal costs around K60 per person. Just round the corner from the Pyay Hotel is the inappropriately named San Francisco Chinese Restaurant (No 775 Strand Road) which is filthy. Infinitely preferable are the **Ahpulay Chinese Restaurant** and the **Paradise**, located across the road from the San Francisco on the river. For *moun-hin-ga* I would recommend **Shweyinmar** (opposite the Santhawda Guest House) and for breakfast the **Aung Bawga** and **Yananthi Tea Shops**.

What to see

Around Hmawza (5 miles/8km south of Prome, where there is a rather drab archaeological museum) stands a trio of unusually-shaped ancient pagodas: the **Bawbawgyi**, **Hpayagy**i (Great Stupa) and **Hpayama**. Tradition ascribes them to the 5th century BC, but judging by their architecture, their construction could not have been earlier than the 5th or 6th centuries AD when Chinese, Cambodian, Talaing and south Indian influences were blended at Prome. The most fascinating is the **Bawbawgyi**, a solid brick structure over 150ft high. It rests on five terraces and is cylindrical in shape with a slight indentation in the middle. To reach it, you have to first drive to Hmawza and then take an ox-cart — it is not possible to go by horse-cart — for about one hour into the 'jungle'. This should cost you K350 (there and back) and is a real adventure.

Both the **Hpayagyi** and **Hpayama Pagodas**, which are more conical in shape, were said to have been erected by King Duttabaung in 443 BC. The Hpayagyi is the earliest stupa architecture in Burma and the largest conical shape.

Two other pagodas of interest are the Lay-myethna and Bebegyi. The **Lay-myethna**, a low brick construction, allegedly dates from the 9th century AD and consists of a vaulted corridor running around a central pillar in a style similar to certain pagodas in Pagan. Against the central pillar are embedded four sculptured stones facing the cardinal points.

The figures on the eastern and northern faces have been destroyed, but of those on the remaining sides, one is still in a fair state of preservation, while the other has broken away near the top. The unusual aspect about the Buddhas on the southern and western faces is that the right hand, instead of resting on the lap or pointing towards the earth, is outstretched.

The **Bebegyi** is a brick construction, surmounted by a *sikhara* with a single entrance facing the east. It is decorated with plaster carvings. The interior is covered with a vaulted roof, and in the wall facing the entrance a sculptured stone representing the Buddha in a sitting position is embedded, with the left foot not upon but below the right. He is flanked by two disciples in a prayer-like attitude wearing robes similar to those of Chinese or Tibetan monks, and having their legs drawn up like those of the Brahma in the Nan-hpaya in Pagan. At the foot of the stone is an inscription probably in Pyu script but barely legible. Judging by the inscription and its architecture, the Bebegyi can be assigned to the 10th century AD.

Down a side road lies the **Kanbaung *Nat* Shrine**, which dates back about 60 years. Here stand 12 *nats*, though by far the most important are the brother and sister (ogre and ogress) Saw Bya Thakhingyi and Ma Saw Oo, who originally came from Arakan State. Each day locals offer food to the *nats*; they must also seek permission from the *nats* to take their photographs. If they don't ask, legend has it, then the photos will turn out blank.

Prome Town's crowning glory — and indeed one of the most sacred pagodas in the whole of Burma — is the stunning **Shwesandaw** (Royal Gold Hair) **Pagoda**. To many Burmese Buddhists, the Shwesandaw is the third most revered pagoda in the land, after the Shwedagon in Rangoon and the Shwemawdaw in Pegu. Said to have been erected in the 6th century BC by two brothers, Ajjika and Bhallika, it contains four hairs of the Buddha, one tooth, a vest, shawl and belt. There are two large lion statues in front of the entrance to the staircase that leads up the hill (though, for a fee of K3, you can take a lift) and the entry gate is a spired pavilion. The staircase itself is an enclosed corridor, roofed over, with spired pavilions interspersed along the way with stalls on both sides. There is an ambulatory terrace on the level just one tier below the terrace of the momument. The Shwesandaw is four feet taller than the Shwedagon and in shape differs both from Rangoon's masterpiece and the Shwemawdaw. In fact the lower part (from the ambulatory terrace up to the bell) resembles the Shwezigon in Pagan, that is to say a typical Burmese stupa. There are assembly halls for paying reverence on the terrace around the monument, and looking out from the compound itself are stunning views of the Irrawaddy and the surrounding areas. There is a charge of K25 to take photographs (professional photography is not permitted).

Head-shaving of a Buddhist monk at Prome's Shwesandaw Pagoda

The annual festival, when the pagoda is visited by thousands of pious Buddhists, is held in November.

From the Shwesandaw one sight stands out above all others, and that is the 219ft tall Buddha image in pink robes poking through the **Hsehdatgyi** (Ten-Storey) **Pagoda**. It is claimed to be the tallest statue of Buddha in Burma, having been originally constructed in 1919, and is too large to have a roof on it. Legend, in fact, relates that every time a roof is built to house the image, the wind blows it off.

By the market is the **Shwehpon-pwint Pagoda**, which in design is similar to the Sule Pagoda. At the eastern gate it is guarded by two Western-style *chinthe*. It was built during the reign of King Duttabaung to enshrine two Buddha statues brought by sons of the king. The pagoda was destroyed in the First Anglo-Burmese War and later renovated by King Bagyidaw.

Finally, for wonderful panoramic views of the city and the Irrawaddy, drive up to **Mingyi-taung** (Hill of Kings). There you will find the **Bay-da-yi Cave**. There are three caves: a hermit in the left cave, the shrine with the Buddha image in the centre, and on the right Bay-da-yi. In days gone by the area was forested and inhabited by Kehpaduda. One day a doe came, drank the hermit's urine and gave birth to a girl named Bay-da-yi, who was adopted by the hermit. Bay-da-yi was the mother of King Duttabaung. This makes King Duttabaung's 'grandfather' a female deer — surely the only monarch in history who can boast such ancestry! Khin Myo Chit gives a splendid account of this tale in *A Wonderland of Burmese Legends*.

SHWEDAUNG

About 15 minutes drive from Prome (or eight miles south) on the right bank of the Irrawaddy lies the town of Shwedaung, which rose to importance after the occupation of Pegu by the English. Past records and travellers' tales mention the old town of 'Shwe-doung' or 'Shwe-doung Myoma', which is now just a village, some miles further south on the same bank of the Irrawaddy opposite Padoung. In 1863-64 Shwedaung could not even boast a population of 5,000 inhabitants; by 1877-78 that figure had swelled to 13,588. Formerly a great silk weaving centre, today Shwedaung is home to two outstanding pagodas, a major Chinese-built textile mill and an oil exploration base, and is famous for its plaid cotton *longyi*. The chief products of the area are rice, vegetables, tobacco and palm-trees. There is one hotel in town, the Shwedaung, though very few tourists have ever been tempted to stay.

The most unusual pagoda is the **Shwemyet-hman** or Gold Glasses **Pagoda**, which houses the only image in the world of the Buddha wearing spectacles. In years gone by, the local people removed the glasses but various disasters ensued and so now they do not dare take off the spectacles. The original pagoda was built by King Duttabaung of Sri Ksetra in 443 BC, according to the legend, but in the intervening years was covered by vegetation and subsequently discovered on clearing the site by the commissioner of Shwedaung, Zeyanandameik, who donated a pair of solid gold glasses. The present image was built in 1865. The spectacles that the Buddha wears now are apparently the fourth pair: the first were stolen, the frames of the second, donated by U Mae, were enshrined in the body of the statue, the third were offered by a British D C during the colonial rule to cure his wife's eyesores and the fourth donated by a rich Burmese. They weigh six viss or 24lb of solid gold.

Some 12 minutes down a side road stands the **Shwenattaung** (Golden Spirit Mountain) **Pagoda**. The Buddha himself is claimed to have visited this spot in BE (Buddhist Era) 104 (one year after attaining Enlightenment) and prophesied that there would be a venerated pagoda constructed here. Legend has it that the pagoda was built portion by portion by humans and *nats*. Prince Thuratapa, son of King Paukkan, was responsible for part of its construction in the Buddhist year 283 (over 2,000 years ago). The pagoda was originally 16½ft high, but during the reign of King Thihathu of Prome it was raised to 33ft, and later King Kyanyit raised it to 44ft. Then King Duttabaung raised it to approximately 90ft. Thanks to donations the height went up to 115½ft. During the Buddhist year 1220 (1858) a severe earthquake shook the area and the umbrella fell to the ground. After the *hti* had tumbled down, the pagoda was renovated by means of further donations to its present height of 122ft. The Shwenattaung, profusely gilt and shining in the sun, stands out conspicuously on the first hill of a low range overhanging the Shwenattaung plain. The annual festival is held in the month of *Tabaung* (March), when some 20,000 worshippers assemble, living for eight days in temporary sheds or *zayat* erected on the plain, occupying their time making offerings, attending a *pwe* or a wrestling match and, of course, buying and selling goods.

Chapter Ten

Inle Lake Region

The Inle (pronounced 'In-lay') Lake region consists of the lake itself with its floating market, gardens, villages and celebrated 'leg-rowers', Taunggyi (the capital of Shan State), Heho (the airport), the hill-station of Kalaw and Pindaya (with its famous caves).

Getting there

In theory, Heho Airport is well served by flights: from Rangoon and Mandalay (daily except Thursday on Myanma Airways; daily on Air Mandalay), Kengtung (daily except Saturday), Lashio (Tuesday, Wednesday, Friday and Saturday), Loikaw (Thursday and Sunday), Mong Hsat (Tuesday, Thursday and Sunday), Tachilek (daily except Wednesday and Friday) and from Chiang Rai by Thai Flying Service. Prices are Rangoon to Heho US$93, and Mandalay to Heho US$42.

If you're coming from Pagan, you'll pass through the towns of Meiktila and Thazi, the latter serving as the railway junction for trains to Rangoon and Mandalay. The journey from Pagan to Meiktila takes about three hours. You may well stop off for lunch at a village called Yinmapin in Shan State which has a Chinese restaurant called Shan Lay. From Yinmapin it's another two hours to Kalaw, a scenic route which at the same time is reminiscent of both the Swiss Alps and West Sumatra. In fact you're in the Shan Hills and as you climb, passing cotton plantations, the road twists and turns past houses resembling those of the northern Thai hilltribes. If you're lucky you may even catch the odd glimpse of an elephant splashing about in the Shan River.

KALAW AND THE HILLTRIBES

'The peacetime hill station of·Kalaw seemed the best place for a rest. The hotel there, we had been told, was the most attractive in all Burma, and the most likely place for a bath and a good dinner. We found it standing back in its own grounds, the entrance to the drive shadowed by a tree so thick with pink blossom there was no room on the boughs for leaves. The pattern of the pink-padded boughs against the blue sky was the most beautiful thing I had seen in Burma. The hotel itself was like a private house set in an old-world English garden. There was a rockery, crazy paving, a goldfish pond, and flowerbeds crowded with snapdragons, mignonette, saxifrage and delphiniums. It took me back with a jolt to the pre-war tranquillity of country homes in Sussex.'

George Rodger, 1943

Nestling in the heart of the pine-studded Shan Hills at 4,319ft (about 1,300m) above sea level is Kalaw, a former British hill-resort littered with colonial-style houses. Meaning 'pan' because of the shape of its location in the mountains, Kalaw has a population of around 25,000 and is surrounded by craggy slopes, numerous hilltribes and a large military base. In 1935 F Deaville Walker in his book *The Land of the Gold Pagoda* remarked: 'Kalaw has developed into a health resort and holiday hill-station for Europeans and Americans.' And indeed for many years Kalaw vied with Maymyo as the most popular hill-station in Burma.

At present Kalaw boasts just one hotel for tourists — but, as George Rodger described so eloquently over 50 years ago, what a hotel! For the **Kalaw Hotel**, a sprawling colonial-style Tudor mansion, is wholly out of character with a country in Southeast Asia. But here it has stood since about 1915. Originally a resthouse solely for the British, it is now managed by the privately owned Eastern Yoma Estate Investment Company. Improvements, cheaper prices and European cuisine — a great advance from the days of Tourist Burma — are to be hoped for. A new two-storey hotel should be open by September 1995. The best restaurant in town is the **Dragon** (Naga) **Restaurant**, a Chinese eatery on the main road near the petrol station.

Kalaw is a cool peaceful town with a fascinating market where the various hilltribes come to buy and sell their goods: vegetables, fruits, flowers, and even skewered eels are amongst the many items on offer. In the area there are five main tribes (not including the Intha who are based in and around Inle Lake):

Pa-O The women wear black dresses and turbans, the men a black jacket and trousers. The Pa-O are Buddhists of Karen stock and speak a Tibeto-Burman language.

Palaung They are noted for their colourful hats which they weave themselves and which vary according to their marital status. Married women wear a hat with white beads, a purple or blue jacket with red facing and a collection of thin lacquer bands around the waist. Single women, though, wear a fenced woollen cap and a thick red-striped *longyi* with an embroidered green jacket. At work however the velvet jacket is replaced by an embroidered cotton one and the hat by a band around the forehead to support the load of the basket carried on the back. About six miles (10km) northeast of Kalaw lies the Palaung village of Tawyaw with a population of around 150-200. The Palaung are Buddhist and speak a Mon-Khmer language.

Danu They dress like the Burmese, though they speak a different dialect. One mile (1.6km) from the Kalaw Hotel lie two Danu villages: Pinmagone and Ohnbin. The Danu are Buddhist.

Taungyo The women wear black skirts and brass rings on their legs and the men wear black jacket and trousers similar to the Pa-O. There are Taungyo villages around Kalaw and near Heho. They are mainly farming peoples of Tibeto-Burmese stock.

Padaung This is the famous tribe of the 'giraffe-necked' women who wear up to 28 brass rings on their neck and rings on their arms and legs. The rings were originally worn to stave off would-be kidnappers or protect them from tiger bites. The men dress in similar fashion to the Pa-O. The most interesting villages are located in the Loikaw area of Kayah State about 96 miles (155km) southeast of Kalaw (see the section on Loikaw). The Padaung, Kayah, are a sub-group of the Karen and are Buddhist/animist.

Visits to all the above tribes can be arranged either via a guide or through the Kalaw Hotel's charming and helpful staff.

For a good view of Kalaw and the surrounding areas go up to the Theindaung, a Buddhist monastery located on the hill near the market.

PINDAYA

The journey from Kalaw to Pindaya takes about 1¼ hours (though it's only 28 miles/45km). If at all possible ask the driver to stop off at the village of **Pwe-hla** en route. Around 2,000 hilltribe peoples live here, Pa-O and Danu, and there is also a primary school with 95 children and four teachers. They're sure to give you a warm welcome in their very best broken English.

Pindaya, situated at 3,880ft above sea level, is home to around 20,000 inhabitants and is essentially a farming community producing tea, cabbages, ginger, yams, potatoes, avocados, pineapples and oranges. The main hilltribe in the area are the Danu. The locals are absolutely charming, some of the most hospitable you will encounter on your travels throughout Burma. Pindaya lies beside a beautiful lake called Natthami-kan (Angels' Lake). It is very relaxing to simply sit beside the lake and watch the locals fishing, washing and playing in the water. Transport is by horse-cart.

Tourists are accommodated in the **Pindaya Hotel** which, like the Kalaw Hotel, is now under the auspices of the Eastern Yoma Estate Investment Company (EYE Hotel Chain), so things can only get better. There is one decent restaurant in town, a Chinese place called **Kyintlight**.

Tourists essentially visit Pindaya for its celebrated caves (**Shwe-umin** or Golden Cave), formed 200,000 million years ago, though both the spontaneous charm of the people and the scenic location have enormous appeal. The caves themselves are stocked full of Buddha images (apparently 8,094 in total) many covered in gold leaf and carved by the locals at the end of the 17th century in a variety of styles. There are also numerous stalactites and stalagmites. The prayer hall building (*tazaung*) was constructed by U Khanti, the hermit and architect of Mandalay Hill, the stupa inside the cave by King Alaungsithu in the 12th century (bring a torch if exploring). Every March a festival, *Tabaungpwe*, is held and there are shows and parties throughout the area. For a more detailed account and map of Shwe-umin and the nearby Alegu Pagoda (built in 1493), consult U Maung Maung Lwin's leaflet entitled *SELF-GUIDE to The natural cave-museum of Pindaya* (December 1993). Two other places of interest in the vicinity are the Shwe Ohnmin Pagoda and the Padah Lin Caves, where archaeologists have been excavating a neolithic site.

NB: There is a charge of US$5 for tourists who visit the Pindaya Caves.

INLE LAKE

The drive from Pindaya to the jetty at Inle Lake takes remarkably long, bearing in mind the actual distance covered: on the map it doesn't look very far at all. The approximate journey time is 2½ hours as you travel through Aungban (Garland of Victory), Heho (past the airport) and the junction town of Shwenyaung, finally arriving at Yaunghwe. Still, it's a scenic mountainous route past water buffalo, some working, some grazing and some being ridden by kids, horse-carts, ducks, lotus flowers in waterpools, farmers at work in the rice-fields — and always a multitude of curious, smiling faces.

Some tourists decide to stay at Yaunghwe's **Inle Inn** or at the **Golden Express Hotel**, No 19 Phaungdaw Pyan Street, which belongs to the same chain of hotels as in Pagan and Mandalay and has 11 rooms with accommodation for 26, but there's no particular reason to spend the night here. The Golden Express provides a motorboat for a trip on Inle Lake at a charge of US$25 for six hours. There is also the **White Elephant Guest House** (Hsin-byu), No 33 Mingalar Quarter, which provides an English-speaking guide and boat trips on the lake. Five floating

Water buffalo: an integral part of Burmese agricultural life

bungalows and a golf course are planned for 1996.

Inle Lake — meaning 'little lake' — is home to four big villages on the lake itself, though there are 200 in all on and around the lake. It is 70 miles (112km) from one end to the other (which lies in Kayah State) and 30½ miles (49km) from Yaunghwe to the famous Phaung-Daw-U Pagoda. The lake reaches a depth of five metres though this obviously diminishes during the dry season. The 'people of the lake' are the Intha of which there are approximately 70,000, hailing originally from the Tavoy region of Tenasserim. They began migrating to the lake area as early as the 14th century, completing their resettlement during the 18th century. To survive, they became fishermen and developed their unique style of leg-rowing and catching fish in conical traps. Their wives planted floating gardens and grew all manner of crops: tomatoes, aubergines, chillies, beans, maize, potatoes, limes, bananas, oranges and flowers, which they sold at the market. And since the land fronting the lake belonged to the Shans, they were forced to build their homes and villages on the water itself. Thus sprung up the villages of Ywama, where the floating market is held once every five days, and Thala, a weaving centre of fine cloth.

Departing from the jetty (where there is a shabby restaurant serving fried noodles, fried rice or ghastly fishballs) and having paid your entrance fee of US$5, you pass through a narrow canal before coming out on to the lake proper. Inle Lake elicits mixed emotions: one guidebook, for example, describes it as 'outrageously picturesque'. For me, however, it doesn't really compare with, say, Lake Maninjau in West Sumatra. Still the leg-rowers and floating gardens are unique, though make sure you arrive on the day when the floating market takes place, otherwise the trip isn't half as interesting.

Eventually you reach the **Phaung-Daw-U Pagoda** where the famous boat festival is held each October. Built at the beginning of the 18th century, the Phaung-Daw-U houses five extraordinary Buddha images. These are scarcely recognisable as they have been disfigured by layers of gold leaf which men stick on both for good luck and as an act of piety. Women are not permitted to do so, for Burmese Buddhists are afraid of harming Buddha's (and man's) *hpon* (potency).

As you near the villages and the pagoda, you will be pestered by touts and vendors offering Buddha images, opium weights, bananas and lotus flowers. At the hand-weaving centre you can purchase Shan shoulder-bags, cloth and *longyi* but they're all overpriced.

TAUNGGYI

Taunggyi (Great Mountain) is one of the few disappointing towns in Burma. As the Shan capital it's a much more affluent (and thus more Westernised) city than most in the land and the people scoot about on brand-new motorbikes and wear jeans not *longyi*. Affluence has come from smuggling, black market trading and opium trafficking and, as its centre, Taunggyi is markedly wealthier than either Kalaw or Pindaya. Consequently the locals are far less friendly: in fact they'll barely give foreigners a second glance. They're more concerned with zooming about on their motorcycles, seeing what's on at the cinema and, of course, making money. Taunggyi itself is not dissimilar to many a northern or northeastern Thai town: long, drab and characterless. It has no charm, few smiles and even fewer sights.

Another former British hill-station, Taunggyi is about an hour's drive from Inle Lake and situated at 4,690ft (1,430m) above sea level. The region (consisting mainly of 'traders', a frequently expressed Burmese euphemism) is home to roughly 150,000 people and is famed as the main cheroot-growing area in the land.

Tourists invariably stay at the **Taunggyi Hotel**, which is located a long way from the town centre (but that's not such a disadvantage). It's a large, rambling, smelly place which used to boast some of the most decrepit bathrooms in Southeast Asia. Now that the hotel has also been taken over by the EYE Hotel Chain, the character of another colonial masterpiece will be lost forever.

In Taunggyi itself there is little to do, just the Shan State Museum (open 0900-1530 Monday to Friday) which is of no particular interest, General Aung San Park and the inevitable market, with very much a northern Thai flavour to it. You soon notice the difference between

Taunggyi and, say, Mandalay, for here there is an abundance of quality goods, fruit, vegetables, fish, meat. At times you'd hardly believe you were in one of the most destitute countries in the world. At the daily market there is always a fascinating array of hilltribe costumes, and indeed of most interest in the vicinity are the various hilltribes: for example the Pa-O, who live in Paya Phyu and Pantin, two miles out of Taunggyi.

In the southwestern part of Taunggyi stands the **Yat Taw Mu Pagoda** which features a large standing Buddha. There is also a new pagoda about two miles (3km) south of town, built in 1985 and called the **Hsu-taungpyi**, which means 'Wish Fulfilling' or 'Lucky Hill' Pagoda. As the name implies, Buddhists from all round come here to make a wish (though the wish should remain a secret, many Burmese have confessed to me that their sole desire is to win the state lottery!). There are several Buddha images in this pagoda, including one of the Buddha entering into the nirvana position: feet on top of each other, left hand on the side and right hand by the head. From the Hsu-taungpyi you have a marvellous view of the surrounding area.

Less than a mile further out lie the **Montawa Caves**, which were formed by an underground river. The entrance to the caves contains numerous Buddha images and inscriptions. If you fancy exploring them, bring a torch.

Taunggyi is famed for its Tazaung-daing Balloon Festival. As the Burmese nursery rhyme has it: 'Old man bent and double, don't die so soon. For watch again the *pwe* at next Tazaungmon's full moon.' To quote from a 1930 source:

'Gifts of honey are presented to the monks and maidens sit up all night to weave the yellow robes worn by the pongyis. In memory of the expedition with which queen Maya the Mother of the Buddha had a monk's robe woven for her son when she perceived from the Nat world, her son discarding the royal robes, the cloth must be woven in a single night. By the aid of relays of workers the cloth is woven and ready by the morning. All through the long night much merriment prevailed. The sending of fire balloons up the sky and illumination made during this month is said to be an offering to Sulamuni. There are five munis or sages. They are Sakya muni, (the Buddha), Canda Muni, Cula muni, Sulamuni and Dussa muni. Sulamuni is said to be in the Tavatimsa Nat World.'

I am indebted to Patricia Herbert for unearthing the following evocative article (c 1970) by San Yi entitled *The Multiple Festival of Tazaungmon*, an excerpt from which I have cited below:

'After the Thadinkyut Light festival we have the triple feasts of Tazaungdaing; which is a festival of the lights, but not a religious feast, as at Thadinkyut. The lighting this time, is more or less an old pagan custom, before Buddhism had come to Burma. It is an offering to the Nats, especially to Maha-Wina-Ya-Ka-deva (Vishnu), who had just awakened from his long sleep. It is also called the "Ta-wa-reinda Pwe" (Tavatimsa festival) and this feast is enjoyed more in Lower Burma than we do up here, in Upper Burma.

'Huge fire balloons made of rice paper or rags, in different shapes and sizes, sometimes containing gifts, are sent up as offerings to the devas. They sail majestically up, and stay sometimes, for quite half an hour, in the still air to rival with the stars above. As usual, like in the Light festival, houses and streets, pagodas, zayats are all lighted up, more so in Rangoon; since now there is no more rain to spoil the effect as in Thadinkyut. This gay festival of lights occur in the eighth month of the Burmese Lunar Year (about mid-November) since the Monsoons, the rains and storms of the season are over, and the cold season begins.

'The skies are blue, with nary a dark cloud to mar its smiling surface. The sun shines brightly all day; and great sparkling stars adorn the dark velvet skies at night. It is said that all the stars of the Constellation are visible, and are at their brightest on these cool nights of Tazaungmon. The weather is at its best, so much that there is an old Burmese saying the Tazaungmon rain is worth a lakh of gold pieces! As it gives the paddy plants the much needed boost for ripening...

'The Tazaungmon Full Moon excels all the full moons of the year. It is the fairest of them all. The deep dark azure sky is a clear background for the gloriously bright moon, and the stars rival the sparkle of the most flawless diamond and gleam and shine in all their scintillating glory. The air is cool and fragrant with the scent of the Yuzana flower...

'On full moon nights too young men armed with bagsful of gooseberries, hurl them at the houses of pretty girls of their choice, and the girls undaunted, retaliated from their hiding nooks and windows, midst gay banter, teasing and laughter. I suppose this is the origin of the phrase "playing gooseberry".

'The night is full of sounds of insects and call of the little owl, and most of all the "Here I am" ditties of the poor crickets that creep out of holes in hordes to give themselves up to be eaten, especially at this time of the year one sees them in masses under electric highway lights and brightly-lit places. Fried with pounded ginger and garlic makes quite a delectable dish.

'So Tazaungmon in fact is a multiple of Traditional Feasts, full of innocent fun, mixed with religious fervour and generous gaiety.'

Taunggyi is also the home of cheroots. At the **Ma-Oak cheroot factory** northeast of the market, you can watch Burmese girls hard at work. Each girl earns K4 for a roll of 100 cigars (which takes roughly 45 minutes to produce); if they're lucky they'll manage 1,000 cheroots a day — a whopping K40. The girls (45 of them) toil from 0800 to 1600; to earn enough money to feed themselves and their families, many of the girls are obliged to take cheroots away to roll at home. Tobacco is shredded with tamarind juice and some nuts and left to dry for two days before wrapping the cheroot. A filter is made from the dried outer skin of the maize cob.

HEHO

Tourists don't stay at Heho (an hour's drive from Taunggyi), but they do fly there. Heho is the domestic airport for the Inle Lake region, though of much greater interest is the market held every five days. This is a rotating **market** and each day it moves from town to town, so make sure you see it at either Heho, Taunggyi, Kalaw, Ywama (the floating market on Inle Lake) or Yaunghwe (and sometimes even at Shwenyaung). The market is vast, offering all kinds of fruit and vegetables; they even sell cattle (one buffalo apparently goes for K15,000: this is where the euphemistically termed 'informal trade' comes into play). All the hilltribes are here in their different costumes: Pa-O in black and dark blue with orange trim and with what appear to be brightly coloured tea towels on their heads, Taungyo women with red-stained lips and teeth and clad in short black dresses sequinned with shells, Danu and Shan in khaki and brown, and Intha men (the 'people of the lake') in plaid sarongs and Intha women in bright flower prints. As Mi Mi Khaing observes in *The World of Burmese Women*:

'The five-day bazaar system is an ancient institution in these northern parts of Burma. Marco Polo, travelling through these parts bordering on China and Burma in the 13th Century, remarked on a regular bazaar to which hill peoples from the surrounding higher regions walked down. The description holds true of bazaar meets in the Shan States of today... All capitals held their bazaars on the same day, and other towns within a radius of about 25 miles held bazaars on days in between. Even in a cosmopolitan town like Taunggyi where there is a bazaar every day, Bazaar Day is noticeable. The swell on every 5th day, with country folk, fresh produce and 5-day-orientated town-wives makes its own hum.'

THAZI

'... Thazi is neither nice nor pretty. Thazi is fourteen miles from Meiktila and is important only because it is a junction for the Myingyan Branch Line and for the new Kalaw Railway. Also it is the place of refreshment for travellers, coming and going from Rangoon to Mandalay. On arriving at the station, one is besieged by Burmese women coolies, of the lowest class, who jump upon the foot-boards long before the train stops and start clamouring for the luggage.'

Rosamond E Park, 1916

If you're not flying or being driven back to Rangoon, you'll have to get to the railway junction at Thazi: 'get to' being the operative words.

From Heho it's a terrible journey. It may not look very far on the map — indeed as the proverbial Burmese crow flies it is only about 50 miles (80km) — yet it's an exhausting and bumpy ride of 4 hours 20 minutes, with perhaps an hour's stop for lunch in Kalaw. And the fun doesn't end in Thazi's grim railway station office, where you have to wait for the Mandalay to Rangoon 'express' to stagger through. For now it is time to embark on your return leg to Rangoon, which could easily take 11 hours at a cost of US$33. Thazi's sole accommodation is the **Moon Light Rest House** — but there's no reason to spend the night in what amounts to little more than a railway junction. After all, who in their right mind would sleep at Clapham Junction?

Leg-rower of Inle Lake with his unique conical net-cage

Chapter Eleven

Other Destinations

UPPER BURMA

Mogok

'The legend of the Mogok gems is that a female naga, a snake-dragon, had intercourse with the son of the Sun-spirit, and several eggs resulted. One of them broke at Mogok, "and became iron and ruby in that country". The scholars of the *Glass Palace Chronicle* criticise the legend: "Not a shadow, not a hint appears in the books of the existence of a son of the Sun-sprit", "Even if there were real union between the Sun-prince and the female naga, either a spirit or a naga should have been born, after the kind either of the father or of the mother. That a human son was born" (as the legend tells of one of the eggs) "is contrary to reason. As for the statement that one egg broke in the land of Mogok and became stone, iron and ruby, it is worth while considering whether in other places also the divers kinds of gems were the result of the breaking of a naga egg. Not a shadow, not a hint appears in the books that in all these places a naga egg broke. This being so, it should be regarded as a figure of speech." '

Major R Raven-Hart, 1946

'WELCOME TO RUBY LAND' (*Mogok Yadana Myay*) — the sign which greets all visitors who have survived the gruelling seven-hour drive from Mandalay to Mogok. In fact you have not yet arrived in Mogok, but in Kyatpin ('Cha-pi'), the preceding town. *The Glass Palace Chronicle of the Kings of Burma* (quoted by Major Raven-Hart above) refers to 'the land of Mogok Kyappyin', yet locals relate that the valley used to go under the name of *Kyauk-pyin* (literally 'slab of stone'), the term used for the flat stone on which *thanaka* paste is produced. Major Raven-Hart, in his book *Canoe to Mandalay*, is one of the few travellers to mention the town: 'There was only one town on the route (Kyatpin)... It was at a street corner in Kyatpin that we nearly ran into what looked like a sweet-stall, all pink paper and tinsel: it turned out to be a bier, complete with coffin', but he does not explain the meaning behind the name.

It is a wonderfully picturesque yet bumpy route which leads from Mandalay to the valleys of Kyatpin and Mogok. Both Kyatpin and Mogok have the feel of Swiss Alpine villages — but surrounded by stupas and pagodas. The Mogok Motel serves smugglers and foreigners alike, with its cafeteria, souvenir shop and dining room complete with Shan and Chinese song-birds. The room rate for foreigners is a combination of dollars and kyat — US$9 plus K450, including breakfast which consists of a fried egg sandwich and a cup of sweet tea. Inevitably for a state-run establishment, the service is lousy, the dining room and decor drab and the showers bereft of hot water (the rooms do at least have TV). In a town like Mogok, where winter temperatures drop to freezing, hot water would be pleasant. Mogok does not appear to have any restaurants, though Kyatpin has two, of which the Myoma (a costly K170 per person) is infinitely better than the Shwe Bamar.

Mogok, thronging with traders and Military Intelligence, has the atmosphere of an affluent smuggling town, indeed almost of a frontier post, though Namkham, on the Chinese border, is more than 100 miles away to the northeast. As with the northern Shan capital Lashio — another smugglers' route — locals are more concerned with striking deals than smiling at foreigners. For all that, Mogok is one of the most captivating regions in Burma. The town, with its pagoda-studded mountains, extends round the banks of a lake — *Myo-leh-in*, 'Mid-town lake' — in the hollow of a magnificent valley, 2,640ft in altitude.

The **Phaung-Daw-U Pagoda** has two replica Buddha images of Inle Lake's Phaung-Daw-U which are also badly misshapen, and one marble image in the style of the Maha Muni. In the large precinct is a glass mosaic stupa with a circular basement of unusual design.

The **Than-ban-than-bok-daw-zedi** ('The one who knows everything' pagoda) contains Buddha images which are kept under lock and key inside the basement of the golden stupa and which are richly endowed with rubies and emeralds.

There are truly spectacular views of Mogok from the **Chan-tha-gyi** (Great Prosperity) **Pagoda**, which has a stupa made up of gold plates and 'tinkly temple bells'. A rich array of precious stones is on display inside, and these will eventually be embroidered on to the diamond bud (*sein bu*) above the *hti*. Overlooking the lake is the **Kaunghmudaw**, named after the famous pagoda in Sagaing, similar in structure to its namesake but much smaller.

Kyauk Pya-that Zedi, perched on the top of a hill and reached via a bumpy mountain road, is Mogok's crowning glory. At the foot of the hill is the Kyauk Pya-that Monastery, encircled by small stupas with a seated Buddha image and a *zawgyi* atop a rock, kneeling on one leg. Similar in appearance to Loikaw's Taung-kweh-zedi, the Kyauk Pya-that is best viewed from afar — the area near the local school offers the most stunning vantage point.

A rocky road leads up **Spider Mountain** (*Pingu-taung*); cars can go roughly half way, from where you have to walk to the summit. There are images of Buddha's eight conquests and a peculiar reclining Buddha in the position of entering nirvana, the head resting on the right palm and clothed in a strange robe. At the very top of the mountain is a glass mosaic stupa. In the colonial era the British called the area Ruby Mountain when they came to plunder rubies, jade and teak and established the Ruby Mines Company in Mogok in 1889. The present abbot (U Hteik-khazara) is unable to confirm this tale, nor can he shed any light on the sobriquet Spider Mountain (given when the unnamed king built the pagoda). The mountain is also known by another name, *Hsin-bu-taung*, meaning 'where the elephant came to pay homage'. The current pagoda pre-dates Mandalay Palace, but no one is sure of the exact history (archaeologists are still trying to determine the date). It is only possible to drive halfway up the hill, from where you must walk to the top. Those who make it are rewarded with a stunning view of the entire plateau.

'He pointed his walking-stick towards a slope where a network of deep ravines made the shape of a web.

'"That steep hill over there's called Pingau Taung," he said. "It means the Hill of the Spider. There's a legend that a giant spider keeps watch there over the biggest ruby in the world."'

Mogok: The Valley of Rubies, Joseph Kessel,
translated from the French by Stella Rodway, 1960

Meiktila

There's not a great deal to see in Meiktila, whose name, pronounced 'Meik-hti-la', makes it sound more like a town situated somewhere north of Inverness. Tourists tend to stop over at the Wun Zin Hotel, en route to Pagan (from Mandalay; or vice versa). Complete with tennis court, the Wun Zin Hotel has airconditioned rooms with a fridge but foul bathrooms and room rates which vary from US$20-30. You can, however, relax on your balcony overlooking the splendid man-made Meiktila Lake, the highlight of a trip to this town. Tourists can also stay at the higher-grade Meiktila Hotel, Kyi-Kone Quarter, Rangoon-Mandalay Road, which is now run by a private company called Aung Sithu International Ltd. The rooms (US$42 a night including breakfast) have been upgraded and for K222 per person you can enjoy a decent Burmese meal. The town itself boasts one excellent Chinese restaurant called Seng Hein Restaurant. Transportation is by horse-cart. Bring a torch with you: there are nightly power failures.

Meiktila Lake was built in pre-Pagan times, most likely during Sri Ksetra's prominence in the 7th century AD. It was fed by the Chaungma (main stream), which received its waters from numerous auxiliary streams originating in the range of hills southeast of Mount Popa. Two of these streams that run north and south at Meiktila were dammed to form the lake. A 19th century inscription describes the lake as:

'Four-sided... its perimeter is 10,000 tas (15,800 feet); 300 streams and 250 streamlets flow into it. The area drained by these feeders is 3 *yuzanas* (40.5 square miles). The surface of the lake measures 10,000 *tas* on the Northern, Eastern, and Southern sides. The area irrigated by the lake is capable of being sown with 10,000 baskets of seed paddy. One thousand pairs of buffaloes were originally set apart to be used in connection with the lake. In the rainy season, the depth of the water is 18 cubits and 3 maiks (about 20 feet); and the surface of the lake measures 1,500 tas from east to west, and 1,300 from north to south.'

Meiktila Settlement

Toungoo

Roughly equidistant between Rangoon and Meiktila (and consequently a reasonable place to overnight), Toungoo's past is far more interesting than its present. It's an ugly, dull town, bereft of restaurants (save for the Happy Chinese Restaurant with a distinctly unhappy loo) and with just one hotel, the Toungoo (US$10-25). The No 19-Up departs Rangoon at 0740, arriving Toungoo at 1825; the No 20-Down leaves Toungoo at 0550, reaching Rangoon at 1720.

The town wallows in a glorious past, a particularly informative account of which is given in John Stuart's *Burma Through The Centuries*, 1909. In 1280 two brothers built a stockade round their village on the hill-spur *taunggnu*, and thus founded Toungoo; probably ferocious slave-raids from Karenni made the stockade a necessity. In the next two centuries Toungoo was ruled by 28 chiefs, of whom 15 were murdered. You can still see the city walls surrounded by the moat and the toddy palm groves (planted by Pyanchi, 1368-77) where King Tabinshwehti is said to have enjoyed his 'relaxation'. Tabinshwehti's name translates approximately as 'Sole Gold Umbrella'; he was so called because 'there were such prophecies about him that Minkyinyo had gold umbrellas erected over his cradle'. He was supposed to have been the reincarnation of a prince put to death by his father Dammazedi (1472-92), king of Pegu.

Tabinshwehti became king at the tender age of 13 (some say 15) and keenly partook in toddy-drinking and cock-fighting. Unfortunately, the incompetent Tabinshwehti met a painful and particularly humiliating end — one tale has it that he was assassinated whilst sitting on the 'toilet' during a bout of dysentery. As Stuart remarks of the king of 'Taungu':

'Tabeng Shwehti was still only thity-six years of age, but... he gave himself up to debauchery, and became incapable of any duties. A nephew of James Soarez became his boon companion, and supplied him with liquor, until the king became a confirmed drunkard.'

The renowned Burmese historian G E Harvey relates a different, but equally uncomfortable demise:

'Tabinshwehti went to live at Pantanaw in Maubin district in the care of Talaing chamberlains... some of the chamberlains, having sent away their loyal colleagues on a pretext, lured Tabinshwehti from Pantanaw into a jungle saying a white elephant had been traced, and there one evening his sword-bearers cut off his head...'

History of Burma, 1925

At the age of just 35 or 36, he became the Tabinshwehti *nat* spirit.

Toungoo's most famous pagoda is the **Myazigon** which houses a portrait of the ancient monarchs, while just outside the town lies a **Japanese World War II cemetery**.

Pakokku

Northeast of Pagan on the west bank of the Irrawaddy lies the town of Pakokku. Coming from Mandalay, you have to cross the Chindwin River at Prima by 'zed ferry'. At the jetty site stands the **Htihlaingshin Pagoda** with a large silver and glass mosaic stupa and housing a small Buddha image. Built by King Kyansittha, the pagoda, with its several large *chinthe* and surrounded by trees, offers scenic views of the Chindwin.

As you inevitably wait for your ferry — there are supposed to be two per day at 1100 and 1500, costing K150 per car — you can enjoy a Burmese meal at Pakokkutha Restaurant for about K60. The private bus from Mandalay to Pakokku costs K80. If you intend travelling from Pagan, there are ferries at 0700, 1000, 1300 and 1600 (all times BST).

The major disadvantage of Pakokku is the appalling standard of accommodation. Words fail to describe the horror that awaits the unwary foreigner. There are three choices: the Tha Pye Nyo Guest House No 1 (K180 a double; disgusting), the Tha Pye Nyo Guest House No 2 (K75 a single, K150 a double; dire) and the least of three evils, the Thu Htet San Guest House (K125 a single, K250 a double; grim). For breakfast, try the Shwenyaungbin Tea & Coffee Shop.

Seventeen miles before Pakokku in the locality of Pakangyi stands the **Sithu-shin Pagoda**, guarded by two giant brown *chinthe*. It was built by King Alaungsithu to enshrine a tiny Buddha image — the size of the king's four fingers — given to him by Sakka, Lord of the Heavens. The Sithu-shin has a vast precinct, a golden stupa under renovation, several silver stupas and Buddha images in various postures. It is a very beautiful and tranquil pagoda.

In the town itself is the **Shwegu Pagoda**, famous for its woodcarving and housing a Buddha seated on a lotus throne. However, Pakokku's most celebrated pagoda is the **Thiho-shin** (*Thiho* is Burmese for Ceylon), where a festival is held every April, July and October. There are a number of Buddhas but the noted Thiho-shin image stands in the main chamber flanked by two copies. It was brought from Ceylon (*Thiho-gyun*, the island of Ceylon) by King Alaungsithu and is said to have been constructed of ten kinds of wood: *thabye, thayetkan, bodhi, nantha, sandagu, tin-yu, kathit, thakut, kokku* and *tein*. It has been heavily disfigured by gilding. There are also relics of the Buddha contained in a glass casket and a museum with many images of the Lord Buddha and various antiquities. The pagoda has a large precinct, inside which you must take off your shoes (it is easy to jump out of a jeep or car which has parked inside a precinct and forget to remove your shoes!).

Magwe

Seventy miles south of Pagan lies the singularly drab town of Magwe (or Magway). It does, however, enjoy a pleasant riverside location directly opposite Minbu. And it does have the Mya-tha-lun Pagoda.

Almost uniquely, Magwe boasts an air-conditioned guesthouse called Gon (pronounced 'Gohn' and meaning 'dignity') at No 322, 19th Street, Ywathit Quarter, tel: 063 21966. It must be one of the best provincial guesthouses in the land. Some tourists have been charged an exorbitant K1,000 a night for a single or double room, but the normal rate is K500, which the manager will reduce to K400 if you bargain hard. Even so, this is expensive by Burmese standards, particularly as the showers leave a good deal to be desired. A much cheaper alternative is the Yar Zar Guest House, which has fan-cooled rooms costing K50 for a single, K100 a double and is not too bad.

For restaurants, I recommend the Chitte Htamin-zain — the only Indian restaurant in Magwe — run by a delightful lady called Daw Nyein. A meal here costs just K50. The Thahtay-tha Tea Shop and LJP Tea Centre are fine for breakfast.

Built in 1929 and renovated in 1972, the **Mya-tha-lun Pagoda** is guarded by two fearsome-looking sand-coloured *chinthe* and is approached by foot or car. Perched on the banks of the Irrawaddy, it enshrines an emerald couch of the Buddha which was presented to him by two *bilu* (ogre) brothers — some say four — Baw Kyaw and Baw Yaw, who had brought an offering of *zibyu-thi* (*Emblica officinalis* or Eastern gooseberry) and *hpanga-thi* (*Terminalia chebula*). Both fruits belong to the myrobalan family and are seen held in the fingers of the Buddha. Curiously *hpanga-thi*, which is eaten in salads and is extremely bitter, is also the nickname for the inhabitants of Magwe. The pagoda's gold stupa is currently under renovation. The couch (*tha-lun*) assumes great importance in Burmese history. It was used by royalty for conducting informal audiences and was also presented to the *sayadaw* of a monastery as an act of merit, since it was associated with the reclining Buddha image, symbolising the entrance into nirvana.

Situated next to the number two middle school, and very difficult to locate, is the **Shinbin Min-deh Pagoda**, built in 1727 but of no especial interest. Next to the pagoda, however, is the **Mintekyaung Monastery**, which is home to one *sayadaw*, six *phongyi* and four novices. Built before World War II in the style of the Pagan period, it was occupied by the Japanese who subsequently burnt it down. It was rebuilt 20 years ago by the present *sayadaw* and is a wonderful place to meet local kids and monks.

Taungdwingyi and Beikthano

Famed for its literary figures, Taungdwingyi is situated about 40 miles southeast of Magwe. Of especial interest is the **Shwe Indaung Pagoda**, built about AD 996, with a long *tazaung* with glass mosaic pillars. Newly gilded in 1992, the stupa has five terraces and is unique in shape in Burma. The beautiful, elongated stupa is constructed in a style called *myepaukzedi,* which means 'coming straight from the ground'. The particulars of the history or tradition of the pagoda are unknown, but its importance is attested by an annual festival.

On a hillock and in a state of disrepair stands the **Yakhaing Hpayagyi**, built about AD 996 by Minbyaung-Mingyi, who ordered the troops who had just returned from Arakan to bring one brick each for constructing this shrine.

Twelve miles out of Taungdwingyi, north of Kokkogwa Village on the road between Magwe and Taungdwingyi, is the ancient Pyu site of Beikthano, the 'Vishnu City'. With its city wall shaped like a rhombus, each side measuring about two miles, Beikthano dates from the 3rd to the 5th century AD, earlier than that of Sri Ksetra. Archaeologists have excavated 25 sites, an account of which is related in Aung Thaw's fascinating book *Historical Sites in Burma.*

Beikthano's most celebrated pagoda is the **Shweyaungdaw**, built by Pandwa Minthami, the Ruler of Beikthano, who subsequently became a Queen of Duttabaung. Both King and Queen were Pyu, a race which was predominant in the Irrawaddy valley long before the Burmans were welded into a nation. The northern side of the pagoda is guarded unusually by two elephants — rather than *chinthe* which guard the other sides — because the Buddha was an elephant in a previous incarnation and there were many elephants in the area. There are also eight white chickens on the stupa, as legend relates that Buddha also lived as a white chicken in nearby Kyet-pyudaw (White Chicken) Village. This fascinating and beautiful pagoda with fine ancient woodcarvings enjoys an utterly tranquil location and is in the custody of the Abbot of the Shweyaungdaw monastery, U Wisitanyana.

Scenes of Mogok, Upper Burma. Top left: Lord Buddha image on Spider Mountain
Top right: Lisu mother and child

Bottom: Lisu villagers practise their tribal dancing.

Aungmingala-hpaya, Hermit Mountain, near Kyaiktiyo, Lord Buddha preaching to his five disciples

Scenes of Loikaw, Kayah State. Market traders, Thiri Mingala Bazaar, Loikaw

Top left: Market time, Loikaw Top right: They start young in the cheroot factories of Loikaw!

Bottom: Bartering for chillies in the bazaar

SHAN STATE
Kengtung

'The moment Scott got over the Salween he was in territory subject to, or claimed by, the Sawbwa of Kengtung...

'They took fifteen days altogether on the journey, and at length came within sight of the important town of Kengtung, ten miles off, with the curious "One-tree pagoda near it," a pagoda from the top of which grows a tree, known all over the country.'

Scott of the Shan Hills, G E Mitton, 1936

Getting there

Kengtung is served by Myanma Airways from Rangoon (Monday, Wednesday, Friday and Sunday) and Heho (daily except weekends). Access is also possible on package tours from Mae Sai in Thailand via the Burmese border town of Tachilek, 104 miles (167km) to the southeast, and by charter flight on Thai Flying Service from Chiang Rai and Tachilek. However, Kengtung and Tachilek are often closed to foreigners as a result of continued fighting between the SLORC and opium warlord Khun Sa.

Where to stay and eat

Tourists are accommodated at the **Kyainge Tong Hotel**, built in bungalow-style with spacious rooms, acceptable bathrooms and minibar. Rates are US$30 (standard), US$36 (superior), and breakfast is K120. The hotel, which is better than most in Burma, is surrounded by stupas and a building site, where work is underway on the Kyainge Tong New Hotel. Kengtung boasts an outstanding restaurant, the **Golden Banyan Chinese Restaurant**, and the friendly **Lokthar** (Chinese) **Restaurant**. Opposite the cinema is the passable **Aung Tha Bye Burmese Restaurant**.

What to see

Capital of eastern Shan State, Kengtung is picturesque but dull. The area's main attraction is the many ethnic groups, including, amongst innumerable others, Akha, Shan, Khun (clad in horizontally striped green *longyi*), Lawa (black outfits), Lahu (black dresses with wavy patterns), Lishaw (similar to Khun), Shan-gyi (Big Shan, the most elegant of all in their yellow blouses, *longyi* and head-dress with green stripes) and Lu (silver bangles on their elbows and wrists and a black head-dress).

The **Maha Myat Muni** (Wat Phra Sao Loang), Kengtung's most venerated temple, is incongruously located on a roundabout near the hotel. As motorbikes whizz round the temple, the Lord Buddha smiles serenely. The Pagoda Board of Trustees writes:

'From the sacred shoulder to the tip of the toe (the image) was casted in copper. From the lowest part of the holy neck to the sacred summit of the holy head was casted in gold & silver alloy (A mixture of 1 Viss & 70 ticals of pure gold with 17 Viss of first class quality silver).'

The image, which despite its name does not resemble the famous Maha Muni, took four years to be cast (Mandalay, 1920) under the auspices of Saya U Tit.

'The Buddha image was casted in copper (Except the holy neck and head) from 1282 KE and completed in 1287 KE. It took them 1½ months to transport it from Mandalay to Kengtung. At that time TaKaw-Kengtung road was not a motor-way yet. The road was not a motorable road. Perhaps it was a road designed only for bullock-cart. It was because of the difficult communication that the Buddha image has to be transported in parts. From Mandalay to TaKaw, a tiny village situated on the eastern bank of the Salween River, it has been transported by lorry and from TaKaw to Kengtung by means of bullock-cart...

'It is also believed that anybody who has visited and pay homage to this Lord Buddha image earns extraordinary merits and is sure to come back to Kengtung town once again...'

The walls and pillars of the Maha Myat Muni have gold paintings on a red background and there are Shan inscriptions round the base of the temple. There are four entrances. Opposite the temple on one side is the Ho Khoang Monastery of Pariyatt; on another side stands the Wan Phat Kyauk Monastery, the doors of which are inlaid with beautiful woodcarvings.

The golden stupa that dominates the skyline belongs to the **Sunn Taung Pagoda**, the most fascinating feature of which is a series of wall paintings; gold on brown, they depict the ten lives of the Buddha which immediately precede his final incarnation as Prince Siddhartha, when he attained enlightenment. These, known in Burmese as the Ten Great Birth Stories, are often referred to in shortened form for ease of memorising as:

1. *Tay* short for Pali Temiya jataka (no 538)
2. *Za* short for Pali Janaka jataka (no 539)
3. *Thu* short for Pali Suvanna-sama jataka (no 540)
4. *Nay* short for Pali Nemi jataka (no 541)
5. *Ma* short for Pali Mahosadha jataka (no 542)
6. *Bu* short for Pali Bhuridatta jataka (no 543)
7. *Sa* short for Pali Canda-kumara jataka (no 544)
8. *Na(r)* short for Pali Narada jataka (no 545)
9. *Wi* short for Pali Vidhura jataka (no 546)
10. *Way* short for Pali Vessantara jataka (no 547), the best loved and best known of the ten, which inculcates the virtue of generosity and supreme self-sacrifice.

The Sunn Taung (Wat Zom Kham) Pagoda stands on Zom Tong Hill, 4,200ft above sea level, and was renovated for the fifth time in 1951. After work was completed (in 1957), its base measured 84ft and its height 226ft — its original dimensions in 157 BE were '3 fathoms and two cubits' (base) and 'five fathoms' (height). The *sein bu* contains diamonds, rubies, sapphires, pearls, gold, jade and cat's-eyes.

The tree referred to by Lady Scott (G E Mitton) belongs to the celebrated **Thit-tabin-daung-hpaya** (One Tree Hill Pagoda) and is reputed to be 282 years old. The monastery close by, which was established in 1886, is called **Zowmmoon Matyan** and contains five images, copies of Inle's Phaung-Daw-U and one ceramic image in Siamese style donated by Thailand. On the wall hangs a Shan traditional drum.

In the centre of town is the **Maing-pyin Monastery** containing a multitude of images. In the precinct stands a large jackfruit tree and two stupas, one with four images encircling it at the base.

Naung-Tong Lake is extremely picturesque, but smelly. On the lake is the Keng House Floating Restaurant and adjacent the Mini Zoo — entry charge three kyat; don't bother. Also eminently missable are the hot springs, located just out of town.

Kengtung has several Catholic churches: the **Roman Catholic Mission** is the most picturesque with its mountainous backdrop. The orphanage next door is home to 85 orphan boys, mainly from the hill tribes, who work in the vegetable garden by day. The Divine Providence Foundation has 40 sisters from eastern Shan State and 30 would-be sisters from as far afield as Henzada and Moulmein. Sister Magdalena Chit from Bassein is in charge. She is charming and speaks excellent English.

Finally, a stroll down the golf-course is a pleasant way to spend the time waiting for your domestic flight.

Lashio and vicinity

'It was dusk when we drove through the town and sped on our way to Lashio. Signposts flashed past us; we did not need to read them — the main road was clear and metaled all the way; side roads were gravel tracks.

'When we saw a small van stranded by the roadside with an Englishman standing beside it, an old instinct of road courtesy pulled me up and I (Outram) stopped to ask if he wanted any help.

'"No, thanks," he smiled. "I work here."

'I laughed and let in the clutch. "Oh, I didn't know. Cheero!"

'"Cheero," he replied. "Where are you going?"

'"Lashio — and China!"

'"No, you're not!" he cried.

'"What?"

'"You're on the wrong road. You're heading for Taunggyi, and it's a devil of a long way, too!"

'Driving gaily out of Hsipaw, we had branched right along the metaled road instead of going left on the gravel road.

'Our courtesy stood us in good stead, for Mr. Forbes insisted on our staying to dinner and spending the night at his tung oil estate.'

'Burma Road, Back Door to China', Frank Outram and G E Fane, *National Geographic Magazine*, November 1940
Visitors early in December 1938, the two authors give a superb account of Lashio and the infamous Burma Road.

Getting there

The northern Shan administrative centre of Lashio is accessible by plane from Rangoon (Tuesday, Wednesday, Friday and Saturday), by train or car from Mandalay (via Maymyo), or over the Chinese border. The majority of foreigners, trying to succeed where writers Paul Theroux and Miles Kington failed, opt for the rail journey.

Trains normally leave Mandalay Station early in the morning, between 0530 and 0545 and take up to 14/15 hours; the return leg departs from Lashio at around 0500, arriving in Mandalay at about 1900. The homeward journey has been known to take 17 hours. If you go from Mandalay or Maymyo, you have to buy your ticket in US dollars or FECs (a return costs about US$23), but if you travel from Lashio to Maymyo or Mandalay, you may be able to pay in local currency (the officials at Lashio are quite out of touch). Lashio to Maymyo costs just K56 one way, to Mandalay K76. Locals pay K66.

The drive from Mandalay takes approximately eight hours (via Maymyo): permission is needed and your papers will be checked at Nawnghkio. From the road you can take photographs of the Goteik Viaduct — the only way possible, as photography is banned by the government — but from that distance they fail to capture the awesome nature of the structure.

Since Lashio has been closed to tourists for years, it has conjured up all manner of mysterious images. As Lashio's city gates are locked from 1800 to 0600, who knows what happens inside? If the *Working People's Daily* is right, then the area is overrun by so-called 'insurgents'.

'The world of insurgents is a narrow and a gloomy world. They live in darkness as if they are living in a savage age. They become arrogant when they are at liberty to use their weapons as they like. They become sadistic. They take delight in torturing others. They become insane with lust. Culture and civilization has abandoned them so that they know not their father nor their mother. A bad end awaits those who cling to obsolete style depravities and delight in swimming in seas of blood in a gloomy world. Those who fear to see light will ultimately get crushed by the Tatmadaw and punished by the masses.'

And so Lashio kept its gates — and secrets — closed from the West until October 12 1992. It might as well have stayed that way: the train journey is a nightmare, bitterly cold at times, the carriages rock from side to side, crawling along at 30mph, and the town itself offers little, save for a glorious Chinese Temple.

As the train zigzags up to Maymyo — one and a half hours by car, but five by rail — you are wantonly tossed backwards, forwards and sideways through the four famous 'zigzags' (*lon-toe*), thence over the Goteik Viaduct, past the town of Kyaukme, famed for *lap'et,* green tea and its springtime Shan Festival, and eventually on to Lashio. Countless times the train grinds to a halt, countless times hawkers peddle their wares, and when you do eventually reach your destination, you can't see a thing. The Mandalay to Lashio 'express' has no lights.

The only reason for travelling to Lashio by train is to witness the wondrous Goteik Viaduct, one of the most amazing constructions in the world but a disappointment in so far as photographs are not permitted. According to officials, this is because there is a military camp at the bottom of the gorge — but seeing as that is 870ft below, you are unlikely to reveal any of the *Tatmadaw's* secrets to the Western world. Others say that the Burmese are so proud of their viaduct (which actually was built by the Pennsylvania Steel Co of USA in either 1899 or 1901 following the design of Sir A M Rendel & Co of London), they are afraid that the 'colonialists', armed with a photo, might copy it! The Goteik — the second highest viaduct in the world — is said to have cost £113,200 and was constructed with 4,300 tons of steel and iron and over 1,000,000 rivets.

'From the shingle bed of the river the scene is very impressive. Almost perpendicular cliffs surround you as the eye slowly mounts to the point from which, far beyond the ordinary angle of vision, the delicate tracery of the viaduct rises high into the air without offending.

'Truly the Goeteik gorge is an amazing sight tempting to the use of superlatives, and one which no visitor to Mandalay should fail to see.'

R Talbot Kelly, 1912

Where to stay and eat

Most foreigners are accommodated in the newly constructed, state-run **Lashio Motel** (US$48 a night including breakfast). All rooms have two beds, a sitting room, TV, fridge, and bath (take care the taps don't come off in your hand and flood the room). The hotel is very spacious with a patio and a separate dining area (grotty and characterless), but exceptionally noisy (there must be a disco/karaoke bar next door). The hotel has a souvenir shop, selling items at grossly inflated prices. Alternative (and cheaper) accommodation is provided by the **New Asia Hotel** (near the markets), the **Yadana Theingi Hotel** (K200/300) and the

Parkway and **Mao Shwe Li Guest Houses**. For food, I would recommend the **Mi-Tha-Zu Indian Restaurant**, whilst traditional Shan cuisine is available at the **Panthe hkauk-hsweh-zaing** which serves delicious beef salad (*ameh-tha-thok* in Burmese, *hlyan-phyan* in Chinese).

What to see

Lashio is noted for its scenery, mountains, markets and hill tribes. The best views are from the Mya Kan Tha (Pleasant Emerald Lakes) Recreation Centre, which is a wonderfully tranquil spot to relax, admire the vista and enjoy a plate of fresh papaya in the surrounds of a grove of eucalyptus trees. The northern Shans of Lashio are much friendlier than the southern Shans of Taunggyi (they have had less exposure to Western influences) and the markets are fascinating, though the town itself is unspectacular.

Lashio's masterpiece is the **Chinese Temple** (*Tayoke-bon-kyaung* or *Kwan Yin San*), arguably the finest in Burma, on a hillside overlooking the town. Inside are three Buddha images on the lotus throne, and at the back a statue of the Lord Buddha's mother. The temple is guarded by two Chinese warriors riding dragons, whilst inside the precinct is a model of Mount Meru in the middle of a turtle pond. From the top of the temple — the biggest in the land — you have a wonderful view of the locality.

Just outside the *Tayoke-bon-kyaung,* guarded by two grey stallions, is a Chinese spirit shrine next to the tomb of the abbot who founded the temple (Yin Gwan Abbot). Inside is the tomb of all subsequent abbots who have been cremated. There are several niches: those covered up contain the ashes. The higher the niche, the more senior the abbot.

Of Lashio's pagodas, the **Yanaungmyin** (also called the Pawdawmu or Sunlun) is of little interest, likewise the **Myo-U Zedi**, a small glass mosaic stupa at the entrance of the town. The unpronounceable **Tha-thana hnahtaung nga-ya** contains 28 Buddha images. In the pagoda precinct is the recently constructed (March 25 1992) **Kaba-aye zedidaw** (World Peace Pagoda). At the four cardinal points stand four devas. As well as being a meditation centre, it offers a great panoramic view.

The most imposing pagoda is the copper-gilded **Man Su**, perched high up and with a wonderful vista. According to Burmese legend it was built by Asoka, but there is no evidence of its real age. There is also the **Jameh Mosque**, built in 1952.

Lashio's celebrated **hot springs** (*Yay-bu-san,* natural hot water sulphur baths) are situated three miles out of town, near the airport. The locals come to bathe in the morning and evening. It is very atmospheric — if you fancy a dip, bring your swimming costume. You will certainly be the star attraction. However, the water is extremely hot — one pool, in fact, is boiling. They say if you put an egg in, it'll be cooked in five minutes! There is an entrance fee of K15, plus K15 for the car, and the baths range from K45-200-300.

Hsipaw

Roughly 40 miles southwest of Lashio (as the Burmese crow flies), Hsipaw is home to the most sacred pagoda in the Shan States — the **Bawgyo Pagoda**, six miles out of town and once the centre of the richest of all northern Shan medieval princedoms. Permission is needed to visit, as it lies beyond Nawngkhio. Tradition relates that King Alaungsithu reached Hsipaw in his royal barge in 1113 and built the Bawgyo. He had brought four Buddha images with him to pay respect to the Shan peoples and they are housed on all four sides of the central pillar. On the east side is the Yadanar Man Aung (the Buddha who conquered haughtiness), on the south side is the Yadanar Nyan Aung (the Buddha who has wisdom), on the west side is the Yadanar Zan Aung (the Buddha who has miracle powers) and on the north side is the Yadanar Yan Aung (the Buddha who conquered his enemies). In the grounds are two magnificent ogres and the Indian Champak Tree, which is famous for never exceeding the pagoda in height. There is a five-day pagoda festival in February.

On the main street of Hsipaw there is a very good Chinese restaurant.

LOWER BURMA

Moulmein and vicinity

'By the old Moulmein Pagoda, lookin' lazy at the sea, There's a Burma girl a-settin', and I know she thinks o'me...'
Mandalay, Rudyard Kipling, first published on June 22 1890

As your boat crosses the Salween River past the silver pagoda, Gaung-hsay-kyun-hpaya, on Gaung-hsay-kyun (Shampoo Island), you espy a golden stupa. It is Kyaik-than-lan, Kipling's Pagoda, the locals say, in Moulmein. You are not 'On the road to Mandalay' and there are no 'flyin'-fishes' in sight, just Moulmein, one of the most enchanting locations in all Burma.

'Maulmain is extremely beautiful, and has often been called the queen of British Burma. It is embosomed, on both sides of the river, with grand ranges of hills, which are clothed with rich jungle forests to the height of 4,000 feet, except in one direction, where the scene is diversified by a range of limestone rocks taking rugged and picturesque forms, and containing immense caves, which are the wonder and admiration of all visitors. The town is widely scattered, and is built on undulating ground; from different points of which there are exquisite views of the river and its adjacent mountains, with golden pagodas and monasteries peeping out from elevated ridges in the midst of luxuriant foliage.'
Personal Recollections of British Burma And its Church Mission Work In 1878-79, Right Rev J H Titcomb, 1880

Getting there

Moulmein, capital of Mon State and located at the mouth of the Salween River, was the British administrative centre in the first half of the 19th century. It is occasionally accessible by plane: for reasons best known to themselves (since Moulmein is Burma's third largest city), Myanma Airways flies just twice a week, on Wednesday (35 minutes direct from Rangoon) and Saturday (via Tavoy). In theory, therefore, you could also reach Moulmein from the south. In practice, you'll arrive by car or train.

The 'Road to Moulmein' — as opposed to Kipling's 'Road to Mandalay' — has deteriorated alarmingly and would assuredly have upset the old master. It is little short of diabolical. Travellers these days will sample mouthfuls of dirt and grit, experience a constant stream of straggling lorries throwing up snowstorms of dust, witness 'voluntary' labour repairing every possible stretch of the road in preparation for 'Visit Myanmar Year 1996' and the sight of prisoners in chain-gangs working in the stifling heat on the quarry and by the roadside.

It is possible that you will reach the river crossing at Martaban (known as Mottama to the Burmese) in about eight hours (punctures and errant goats permitting). En route you can stop off for lunch at Kyaikto, which has a decent Chinese restaurant called Panyoma. Once at Martaban, you are confronted with a typically Burmese problem: is there a ferry (known to the Burmese as a 'zed ferry') to transport you and your car over to Moulmein? Well, that all depends on what time you arrive in Martaban and on the depth of the river. If you're in luck, the car ferry will be ready and waiting, and the journey will take 40 minutes. If you decide to leave the car at Martaban and go by normal ferry, it'll take 30 minutes. If you wish to hire your own boat, the crossing will take just 20 minutes and cost you K120, but then your car, of course, will still be in Martaban. There is also a rail line running from Rangoon to Martaban (via Pegu, Kyaikto and Thaton), with trains scheduled to run as follows:

Rangoon dep 0300 Moulmein arr 1045 (No 81-Up, express)
Rangoon dep 0400 Moulmein arr 1130 (No 89-Up, post)
Rangoon dep 0800 Moulmein arr 1550 (No 83-Up, express)

Moulmein dep 0800 Rangoon arr 1610 (No 84-Down, express)
Moulmein dep 1145 Rangoon arr 1900 (No 82-Down, express)
Moulmein dep 1245 Rangoon arr 2015 (No 90-Down, post)

Where to stay and eat

Moulmein boasts the finest sunsets — and pomelos — in Burma, and, more surprisingly, one of the finest hotels, the **Mawlamyine** on Strand Road, tel: 22560/21976. Renovated in bungalow style and enjoying a wonderful location by the water's edge with views of Shampoo Island, the Mawlamyine has air-conditioned rooms, TV, fridge and cold water. The service used to be lousy, though since November 1994, when the

Mawlamyine was handed over to the so-called private sector (allegedly a rich army officer), this has changed. Room rates are US$35 for a single, US$40 a double (plus 20% in taxes). Owing to the bungalows' riverside position, an evening invasion of frogs, grasshoppers, moths and friends takes place. But that's a small price to pay to watch the myriad boats plying the waters, to glimpse the stunning sunset, the curiously named Gaung-hsay-kyun — or simply to play with the ever-smiling children of Moulmein. (The Thanlwin Hotel on Lower Main Road, Bo Kone, US$15-25, is not recommended.)

The late writer Mi Mi Khaing, who was born in Ye some 90 miles south of Moulmein, reveals the meaning behind the name **Shampoo Island**, in her wonderful book *Burmese Family*:

'Hairwashing is part of the New Year's rituals because the noblest part of the body, the head, must be in a clean condition at this time. In the days of the Burmese kings, there was a ceremonial washing of the King's hair at the New Year, called the tha-gyan daw gyi. The water was always brought from the clear springs of Gaung-se kyun, the island lying dark and green in the Moulmein river. The island had a special sanctity because it was believed to hang suspended from the heavens by an invisible cord. When the island passed into British territory after the first Burmese war, however, the waters of Gaung-se kyun were no longer used for this sacred purpose, and substitute clear water was got from the Irrawaddy.'

It costs K150 to hire a boat to Shampoo Island — ask one of the kids by the waterfront. On arrival, an English-speaking monk or abbot will show you round and relate the fascinating history of the island, which emerged about 2,006 years ago, just before the birth of Lord Buddha. Buddha is believed to have visited the area himself and presented eight hairs to some hermits. These hairs are now enshrined in the eye-catching silver stupa known as **Sandawshin** (Holy Hair). The ancient kings of Burma and Siam (and important personages) came to the island to wash their hair before their coronation in sacred water obtained from a well (you can still see the well today). These days Gaung-hsay-kyun is known locally for its meditation centre.

'How on earth they built that pagoda — ! And there is another on the tiny island nearest to Moulmein: the marvel here is not the difficulty of access but the perfect placing — it is again a holy place, "Head-Wash Island", springs here having given the water used for the yearly Royal headwashing at Ava, until the island became British and Irrawaddy water had to be used instead.'

Canoe To Mandalay, Major R Raven-Hart

Pomelos, pagodas, sunsets, Shampoo Island, the best coffee shop in Burma (Ngwe Lwin Oo Coffee Shop on Roman Road, run by a delightful old Burmese gentleman called U Naing Hok Shein, but only open in the evenings) and the finest mangoes in Burma. Known as *dasu-may,* meaning 'forgotten tress', legend has it that this type of mango is so delicious, that a woman forgets her tresses in the ecstasy of its taste! Moulmein, verily, has it all — except one decent restaurant.

Both the Chinese restaurants in town — the Peking and Badamya (directly opposite one another) — and the Burmese Daw Pu are ghastly. If you like attentive service but aren't too fussy about the quality of the food, you could try the Chitte Koko Maung Restaurant. For breakfast, the Kismir Teashop by the riverfront near the Shwemyaing Bridge is tolerable, however I'm not sure about the food at the Mawlamyine Hotel since neither 'Fish Water', 'Fried Finger Fish', 'Stewed Pork with Pickled Bumboo Shoots' nor 'Rabbit Green Sour Soap' caught my fancy.

What to see

'The three friends transferred themselves into a smaller ship which took them eastward across the Bay to Moulmein where, on a day Rudyard never forgot, "Aleck" set up his tripod and photographed first the elephants at work, and then a view of the sea from the terrace beside an old pagoda hung with bronze bells that the worshippers smote with stag-horns. "I should better remember what the pagoda was like," wrote Rudyard, "had I not fallen deeply and irrevocably in love with a Burmese girl at the foot of the first flight of steps.'
Rudyard Kipling: His Life and Work, Charles Carrington, 1970

Though no one can say for certain, Kipling's pagoda was in all probability the **Kyaik-than-lan,** and it is one of the most beautiful in the land. Originally constructed in AD 875, it is similar in structure to the Shwedagon and offers stunning views of the river and the surrounding areas. There is a lift to take you up, and you can then climb to the very top. The name *Kyaik-than-lan* is said to be a corruption of *Kyaik-shan-lan* (or *Kyaik Sem Lum*), the shrine commemorating the defeat of the Shans or Siamese. The pagoda has twice been enlarged — once by Pon-nu-rat, king of Moulmein, and again in 1538 by Wareru, king of Martaban. When Tenasserim was ceded to the British after the First Anglo-Burmese War of 1824, the Kyaik-than-lan was in ruins and was repaired by U Taw Le, an Extra Assistant Commissioner, with funds collected by public subscription. It measures 152ft in height and 377ft in circumference at the base. At the top of the west entrance to the right is the famous bell, whose inscription in English is barely legible:

'This Bell is made by Koonalenga, the priest, and weighs 600 viss. No body design to destroy this Bell: Moulmein, March 30th, 1855. He who destroyed to this Bell, they must be in the great Heell and unable to coming out.'

Next to the Kyaik-than-lan is Moulmein's **Maha Muni Pagoda**, with an image identical to that of Mandalay. Nearby is a monastery, the **Sein-don mi-baya kyaung**, which has some fabulous woodcarvings, excellently preserved. The monastery was built by one of Mindon's queens, Sein-don Queen. In 1985 it celebrated its one hundredth anniversary.

The town's other celebrated pagoda is the **Uzina**, a wish-fulfilling pagoda with a reclining Buddha, which was built in the 3rd century BC over a hair of the Buddha. It was repaired about 100 years ago by Uzina of Moulmein. The Uzina has some remarkably well-carved, life-size figures representing the four objects, the sight of which determined the Lord Buddha to become a hermit — a decrepit old man leaning on a staff, a man suffering from a loathsome disease, a putrid corpse, and a recluse in yellow garments, with features expressive of resignation and absence of worldly care. There are 21 neon images of the Buddha, 18 surrounding the three principal ones. One is seated and two standing, which is most unusual.

Located between these two pagodas is the **Aungthiekdi Stupa**, one-third gold, one-third silver and one-third white. From this stupa you have superb panoramic views.

In the vicinity of Moulmein is **Taungwaing** (Circle Mountain). Up the mountainside stand statues of the Lord Buddha and his 500 disciples (monks). The statues go all the way up the mountain and make an incredible sight.

Kyaikmaraw Town is home to the **Kyaikmaraw-hpaya**, an unusual square-shaped construction of glass mosaic. From the outside it looks quite ordinary, but inside are some wonderful columns inlaid with marble tiles, glass mosaic and a singularly beautiful Buddha image seated with his legs stretched out in the 'Going to Leave' or *Kywa-myi-han* position. This is similar to the image of the Buddha in Mergui's Thein-daw-gyi and is sometimes referred to as the Image of the Seated Buddha. The Kyaikmaraw Pagoda was built by the Mon queen Ba-nya-htaw in BE 817. The queen possessed a white elephant and was therefore known as Sinbyushin Ba-nya-htaw. The pagoda precinct also contains a museum with many Buddha images, *chinthe, hintha* birds (the Mon symbol) and old currency. You can eat at a number of food stalls opposite the pagoda entrance for around K40.

About one hour 40 minutes (88km) south of Moulmein on the coast lies **Kyaikkami** (pronounced 'Ji-ke-mee'), where, for K45, you can enjoy a fine Burmese meal on the beach at Annawa Restaurant. Once a popular seaside resort for the colonialists, when it was called Amherst, Kyaikkami is best known today for its **Yay-leh-hpaya** (the 'In the middle of the water pagoda'), where 11 hair relics along with 21 small Buddha images are enshrined.

The pagoda, which juts out into the sea, has been recently renovated at a cost of over 140 lakhs (one lakh equals 100,000 rupees) in an unfortunately gaudy fashion, with tacky souvenir stalls selling cheap souvenirs. Legend has it that the pagoda came floating from the sea and was stranded on the present ridge of rocks. It derives its sanctity from the fact that, owing to cross undercurrents, the basement of the shrine is never touched by sea water even at high flood. Women are not allowed inside the pagoda precinct, and have their own prayer hall. Once a beautiful and sacred shrine, the Yay-leh-hpaya today appears to be little more than a tourist trap very much in the mould of 'Visit Myanmar Year'.

Near Kyaikkami are two quaintly-named islands — Green Island and Onion Island — each boasting a lighthouse.

'Amherst... is situated on the point of an estuary into which the waters of the river Salween discharge themselves, after receiving its large tributaries, the Attaran and the Gyne, near to Maulmain, about twenty-five miles up the river. The climate was salubrious, the land high and bold to the seaward, and the view of the distant hills of Balloo island very captivating.'

Henry Gouger, 1860

Not far from Kyaikkami is the beach resort of **Setseh**, which is completely unspoilt and only frequented by locals. You can stop off here for a while, enjoy the sun and sea and a vast coconut for a mere K15. Also located in the vicinity is the World War II cemetery of **Thanbyuzayat** (literally 'Tin Rest House'), where there are 3,771 graves of Allied prisoners-of-war who perished whilst constructing the railway to Thailand under the command of the Japanese. The cemetery is situated about one and a quarter hours south of Moulmein and is meticulously maintained by the Commonwealth War Graves Commission.

Two towns of great interest in this area are Mudon and Thaton. **Mudon** is on the way from Moulmein to Kyaikkami — it is 18 miles from Moulmein — and boasts one of the most tranquil spots in all of Southeast Asia, Kangyi (Big Lake).

Before reaching Mudon, you will notice the Kyauktalone Mountain, with numerous pagodas perched on top. Mudon's Kangyi and its pagoda (Kangyi-hpaya or Kangyizedidaw) are sheer bliss. You can sit by the lake, watch the children frolic in the crystal-clear waters and sample *bu-hi-gyaw* (fried gourd dipped in chilli sauce) and *pebin-bauk-gyaw* (fried beansprouts). With its glorious golden pagoda said to have been constructed in the lifetime of the Buddha glinting in the sun, its 'tinkly temple bells' and mountainous backdrop, the Kangyizedidaw and lake are sights unsurpassed in all Burma. Mudon's best restaurant is the Shwin-pyaw-pyaw which serves such delicacies as snake, eel and venison.

Roughly halfway between Martaban and Kyaikto is **Thaton**, which like

Toungoo is a town whose past is of far greater interest than its present (save for the stunning Shwezayan Pagoda). A former capital of the Mon Kingdom of Suvannabhumi under the rule of King Manuha, Thaton was captured in 1057 after a long siege by King Anawrahta, founder of the Pagan Dynasty, thereby enabling him to gain control of Lower Burma. Anawrahta brought the Mon king of Thaton, Manuha and some 30,000 captives back to Pagan and the city was completely destroyed:

'Since the downfall of Manuha, the ancient city — most ancient, it would seem, of all the cities of Burma — has never again held up its head... Its life is in the past, and its glory has departed.'

Thaton's paragon today is the beautiful golden pagoda, the **Shwezayan**, which is guarded by two colourful *chinthe*. Built in the 5th century BC by King Thuriya-Candar Duttabaung, it enshrines four teeth of the Buddha. Situated nearby is the Thagya-hpaya or Mya-theindan, which has a square base, resembling the northern Indian style. Around the central and uppermost terraces are panels which were filled with plaques illustrating scenes from the Jataka Tales (stories of the Buddha's previous existences).

'With king and religion transplanted, Thaton fell into a decline, and soon lost her trade also, for the sea coast extended and left Thaton a dry inland town. However, it never lost its reputation as the old seat of religion — a soil which can grow rice, fruits and plantations of other crops in abundance; its easy access to the big towns of Moulmein and Rangoon; the Martaban Hills which were ranged behind the town, and over which waterfalls tumbled down to cross the red laterite roads as streams of clear water.'

Mi Mi Khaing

Kyaiktiyo and vicinity

'A few hours journey from Pegu is the little town of Kyaikto with its balancing pagoda of Kyaiktiyo which is built on the top of a boulder balanced on the edge of a precipice, and is more wonderful even than the Leaning Tower of Pisa.'

F Haskings, 1944

Suddenly, after trekking for three to four hours, as if from nowhere, appears a huge golden boulder, perched precariously on the hillside. It is Kyaiktiyo ('Ji-tea-owe'), the Golden Rock Pagoda.

Ascent by foot is not possible during the rainy season and not recommended during the hot season. On arrival at the base camp of Kinpun, tourists must first register with the immigration authorities. Independent travellers will be assigned their own personal armed guard, who is under strict instructions never to leave their side.

It is an invigorating 7½-mile trek up to the top (I suggest you purchase a bamboo pole at the bottom to assist you) and, if you feel so inclined, there are porters to carry your bags (strongly recommended). The porters charge K8 per viss (one viss is 3.65lb) and, my word, do they earn every kyat.

'Porters carry the pilgrims' luggage, and the carriers the pilgrims who are unwilling or unable to make the long climb on foot.

'Children are carried in cane baskets hanging from poles flung over the carriers' shoulders. Adults go up in hammocks, a strong cotton blanket tied lengthwise to a bamboo pole and carried by two men.'

Khin Myo Chit

Zayat (resthouses) and stalls line the entire route, selling an amazing array of souvenirs and Burmese medicines, including monkey's blood (*myauk-thwe*), python's gall (*sabagyi-thechay*) and seal's penis (*phantho*). When you reach Yay Myaung Gyi Camp ('Big Stream' Camp), you are a third of the way up and certainly entitled to a rest (and an excellent Burmese meal) at the Mi-Tha-Su Restaurant. From here to the top you will be cheered on by friendly Burmese fellow climbers and stared at by curious kids, who have assuredly never set eyes on a Westerner before. As Khin Myo Chit explains:

'Some of the climbs are quite steep and challenging, especially to the residents of the flat-lands. They have expressive names like "Shew-yin-so" ("Heaving Chest") and "Pho-pyan-taung" ("Old-Man-Turns-Back-Hill"). There is a flow of pilgrims going up or down the path. Those coming down hail the up comers with words of encouragement; "Come on, the pagoda is just ahead," or "You are doing fine — keep it up". At one of the stops, called "Myin-daw-mu" ("The View") pilgrims have a real glimpse of the Kyaiktiyo pagoda — something really exhilarating. The pilgrims then are convinced the trip was worth everything they had gone through.'

The Chinese, in fact, believe that if you climb Kyaiktiyo three times, you will become rich. Climbing Kyaiktiyo on foot achieves merit, which will assist you on the way to nirvana. Thus the SLORC-construction of a bumpy road up the Golden Rock reduces the amount of merit to be made. The ride costs K120 for a front seat on the way up (K90 for a back seat) and K90 for a front seat on the way down (K60 back seat), but still involves a 40-minute walk to the actual summit.

Derived from the Mon-Sanskrit, *Kyaiktiyo* means a 'pagoda shouldered on the head of a hermit' and the celebrated shrine is on the crest of the Paunglaung ridge (one of the ridges of Eastern Yoma). The diminutive Kyaiktiyo Pagoda, just 18ft high, is built on a huge boulder which balances precariously on a projecting tabular rock. The rock itself is separated from the mountain by a deep chasm which is spanned by an iron bridge, thus enabling the pilgrims (but not women) to pay close homage at its feet and to make merit by gilding the boulder with gold leaf.

Legend has it that in the time of the Lord Buddha, hermits resided in the mountains and after obtaining sacred hairs from the Buddha enshrined them in the pagoda on their respective mountains. But the hermit from Kyaiktiyo, reluctant to part with his share of the sacred relic, treasured it in his hair-knot. Only after finding a boulder resembling his head did he enshrine his cherished share in a pagoda built on it. For centuries the pagoda lay buried in the jungle, the wonderfully balanced boulder withstanding the rigours of wind, rain and earthquakes before being discovered in 1823 by Minhlathinkha-thu, the mayor of Sittang.

'Devotees throng the pagoda mostly in December. The climax of the pilgrimage is when you reach the peak tired and stiff; after paying homage you drink in the scenes around you. The night spent at the top is aching cold and the muscles ache as the cold raw wind comes whistling through the valleys upon you. One of the most lovely scenes which stays forever in you is that when you light candles and burn incense in the early hours of the morning, the pagoda platform drenched under the misty moon. Mists hang low and heavily along the inclines and valleys. However, only the tops of other mountains could lift their heads from the dense mist enveloping around them. And the peak on which you stand seems to tower above others finding yourself in the sea of white mists.'

'Kyaiktiyo In The Mists' by W M, *Burma Review*

There is just one hotel at the top, the Kyaikto, which has the effrontery to charge tourists US$24. The hotel has wafer-thin walls, sporadic electricity and only provides cold running water between the hours of 0600-0630 and 1800-1830. At other times, guests have a daily ration of two buckets of ice-cold water. There is no need to eat in the hotel: restaurants and food stalls abound in the vicinity of the pagoda. I particularly recommend the Kyu Kyu Win Restaurant. There are four essential items to bring with you: a torch, a sweater (as the evenings and mornings can be very cold), a cagoule and an umbrella.

Now that the government has recognised the value of Kyaiktiyo as a tourist attraction, they charge foreigners US$4 to register at Kinpun base camp, US$3 to enter the pagoda platform, US$3 for a camera and US$4 for a camcorder. They have also built a three-storey Dhammayon (congregation hall) and a circular platform, at a total cost of K5.4 million. There are four 14ft by 16ft rooms for members of the Sangha, one 40ft by 20ft hall for laity, a bathroom, four water closets on the ground floor, and one 70ft by 20ft hall, three water closets and two bathrooms on the first and second floors. The 214ft long and 20ft wide circular platform cost over K9,122,000 to construct. The government states that now 'women can pay obeisance more closely from the circular platform'. Alas, the building of the 'road', Dhammayon and circular platform — plus the various charges — all detract from what was once, for me, the most beautiful site in Burma.

Further up the mountain is U Ahbaw Cave, which contains an image of a Chinese monk who came from the Irrawaddy Delta and who practised at Kyaiktiyo for 26 years before attaining Enlightenment. Daily he would go out begging for food for up to 16 miles. Also on the mountain is a shrine to the guardian *nat* Mo Po Shin Gyi. An hour's stiff trek from Kyaiktiyo is the Hermit Mountain (*Yathe-taung*), which was named after a hermit called Eithsathara who practised on the mountain and also attained Enlightenment. In his memory a pagoda, Aungmingala-hpaya, was built during World War II by U Khanti, a hermit from Mandalay.

The word 'hermit' (*yathe*) is actually a misnomer: one imagines a hermit living a life more ascetic than a monk, seeing no one, eating only bread and water. In Burma, however, a hermit means someone living a life far less ascetic than a monk, taking no vows, able to handle money and beg for it, and wearing dark brown as opposed to saffron robes (see back cover photograph). As Max and Bertha Ferrars explain:

'They (the yathe) depend chiefly on alms, but cultivate gardens for themselves. Their appeal for alms is mute, they accept them in money as well as in kind, and they lay up a store for actual needs. They take food in the forenoon only. The yathe, who are few in number, live in forest caves or in derelict shrines, and shift for themselves, singly or in small colonies. The majority study, though they do not teach; some are illiterate. They receive a certain deference from the laity, and themselves defer to the yahan ("monk, follower of the perfect rule"). The yathe are the subject of a mild satire and burlesque in the plays; the yahan never. The robe is like that of the yahan, but dyed tan instead of yellow. Yathe mostly shave the head, but there is a class who wear the hair long. Certain of them use a headgear called dautcha, which forms a receptacle for an image of the Buddha. Some are addicted to mild forms of occultism such as alchemy and devising cabalistic diagrams for charms and tattoo-marks. These practices are under the ban of Buddhism.'

Burma, Max and Bertha Ferrars, 1900

The Irrawaddy Delta: Bassein

'Now we have wonderful theatrical pictures continually changing — bluey-green round pictures framed by the night, first on one bank then on the other, as the light sweeps from side to side, and always down its rays a continuous shower of golden insects seems to come rushing towards us. In the dark behind the lantern, the deck below is crawling with them. The trees we light up on the banks have the green of lime-lit trees on the stage, and the same cut out appearance. Fantastic boats suddenly appear out of the velvet darkness. They have high sterns elaborately carved, and the red teak wood and the brown bodies of the rowers pushing long oars glow in the halo of soft light; other figures resting on their decks are wrapped up in rose and white and green draperies, and each soft colour is reflected quivering in the ripple from the oars.'

From Edinburgh to India and Burmah, W G Burn Murdoch, 1908

Getting there

These days a newly constructed road, they say, leads from Rangoon to Bassein, but then maybe 'newly constructed' means something different in Burmese than it does in English. For the 118 miles (190km) journey takes over five hours. The route is often unpaved, dusty and very bumpy; occasionally it disintegrates into mere sand.

After crossing the Bayinnaung Bridge — opened in July 1994 — over the Hlaing River to Hlaingtha-ya, it's another one hour ten minutes to Nyaungdon to traverse the Irrawaddy. A frenetic scramble to board the ferry, then Setkaw, some 40 minutes away, emerges as the next port of call. From Setkaw to Bassein, count on three hours (including a drive over a stretch of railway line) — and a thick coating of dust.

Those with more time on their hands can make the journey from Rangoon to Bassein by water as W G Burn Murdoch did in 1906. A 'regular' double-decker boat leaves Rangoon at about 1600 every evening, reaching Bassein early next morning. Tickets are bookable at the Inland Water Transport Office in Rangoon. Bassein does have an airport but no flights, which is bizarre since it is the fifth biggest town in Burma. There are reports, however, that Bassein Airport is currently being renovated by means of 'patriotic labour'.

The highlight of the land route is a brief stopover at the town of Nyaungdon, which has three marvellous pagodas: the Nangangaye-hpaya-gyi with its giant Buddha image, the Mahazedi Stupa noted for its two large *chinthe* painted in red, green and white with black beards, and the Mohoke-hpaya-gyi, in front of which two smaller *chinthe* stand guard.

Where to stay and eat

Accommodation in Bassein used to be limited to the Pathein Hotel which looked like a prison from the outside and wasn't much better inside. It had pokey fan-cooled rooms with hard beds, foul bathrooms and frequent power failures. For these 'delights', tourists had to pay US$10 for a single room and US$20 for a double (plus 20% tax). Fortunately a new hotel, the **Kan-tha-ya** or New Bassein (Pathein) Hotel, has been completed. It enjoys a lakeside location and has the same rates as the Mawlamyine Hotel in Moulmein. A much cheaper alternative is the privately run **Delta Guest House** (US$5) near the cinema.

Good Burmese food is available at the **Shwezinyaw** and **Shan-Myanmar Restaurants**, while two restaurants offering Chinese fare are the **Golden Swallow** and the **Zee Bae-inn**. The best coffee shop in town is the **Nayi Soe**, though I would also recommend the **Shwe-la-tha Coffee Shop** and the **Oasis Cold Drinks Shop**.

General description

A quaint town, situated by the Ngawun River and thronging with bicycles, Bassein is the capital of the Irrawaddy Delta with a population (according to the most recent census of 1983) of 144,096. Bassein and the town of Henzada (see page 217 ff) are leading rice-producers in the delta, along with crops such as sesamum, groundnuts, jute, maize, pulses, tobacco, sunflowers, bananas, mangoes, coconuts, chillies, onions and a whole host of other vegetables. With so much water around, it is no surprise that the delta houses a number of fisheries, producing fish-paste, fish-sauce, dried prawns and, off Diamond Island at one of the mouths of the Irrawaddy, turtle's eggs (*leik-u*), considered a delicacy in Burma but not popular with environmentalists. The Turtle Island, just off the coast of Morton Point or Pagoda Point, south of Cape Negrais, is the leading producer of turtle's eggs in the region.

Bassein's two most celebrated industries are umbrella production and confectionery. Umbrellas can be purchased direct from the manufacturers: I recommend Yon Taseit Pathein Hti-zaing on Twenty Eight Pagoda Road. Prices start at K20 and go up to K1,800: there are all sizes available from the minute to the gigantic. Bassein's famous confectionery is *halawa,* made from a mixture of rice, sugar, coconut and butter.

History

The history of Bassein is uncertain. As the *British Burma Gazetteer* of 1880 notes:

'The town having been utterly depopulated in the time of the Burman conqueror Aloung-bhoora no trustworthy records are obtainable. It is by one account said to have been founded in AD 1249 by Oom-ma-dan-dee a Talaing Princess, whilst according to another it was in existence many years earlier.'

Another tale, apocryphal if Burmese historians are to be believed, records that Bassein 'is said to derive its name from the word "Pathi", the Burmese term for Muhammadans, as there were so many of them... A Muhammadan Princess named On-ma-dan-di had, according, to the legend, three lovers (presumably Buddhists), and she told each of them to put up a pagoda. One put up the Shwemoktaw, the second put up the Tagaung Pagoda, at the Southern edge of Bassein town, and the third put up the Thayaunggyaung Pagoda. The word "Bassein" is a corrupted form of Kusim, the Cosmin of the Portuguese and other early European writers.' Certainly travellers such as Ralph Fitch referred to 'Cosmin' as a port of considerable importance and found Rangoon (or 'Dagon', as it was then called) merely 'a small village'.

During the Second Anglo-Burmese War of 1852, Bassein played an important part, being home to a British fort, which included the site occupied by the Shwe-mok-taw Pagoda. All traces of these fortifications vanished years ago.

What to see
Bassein in the 1990s is dominated by the celebrated **Shwe-mok-taw Pagoda**, which started life as a small stupa about 7½ft high with a circumference of about 4½ft and dates back to around the time of 305 BC. It was named Shwe-arna or Grand Power and inside the Emperor Asoka enshrined sacred relics of Buddha along with a solid-gold bar, six inches in length. In the year AD 1115 Alaungsithu, king of Pagan, constructed a larger pagoda right over the smaller one, increasing the size to 36ft and renaming it Htu-par-yone. In 1263 King Smodagossa and his Queen Ommadanti (obviously the same princess referred to above as 'Oom-ma-dan-dee' or 'On-ma-dan-di') enlarged the pagoda to 130ft in height and changed the name to Shwe-mok-taw, meaning 'a bar of solid gold half a foot in length'. Following subsequent renovations, the pagoda reached its present height of 153ft. In memory of the three kings, a three-tiered sacred crown called a *shwe-hti* was placed on the top of the pagoda. The top tier is made of solid gold and weighs about 14lb, the second is of pure silver and the third (and largest) is of bronze. Both the silver and bronze tiers (as well as the entire structure) are thickly coated with gold leaf. The *shwe-hti* supports about 40lb of gold, 829 pieces of diamond, 843 pieces of ruby and 1,588 pieces of various other precious gems.

In the south shrine of the Shwe-mok-htaw reposes the famous Thiho-shin Phondawpyi statue of Buddha, one of four images which floated down originally from Ceylon (the others are at Kyaikto, Kyaikkami and Tavoy). Around the year AD 1418 Sri Prakkama-bahu VI, king of Ceylon, had four statues of the Buddha carved in order to help spread the word of Buddhism abroad. The four images were constructed from branches taken from the sacred banyan tree which were ground and mixed with cement composite. They were then placed on four wooden rafts and set adrift, with a vow that the statues would land where Buddhism took firm root. The one which landed in Tavoy is called the Shin Mokti, the one at Kyaikkami is in the Yay-leh-hpaya and the third is at Kyaikto, where it was named the Kyaik-pawlaw or 'the statue of the moving sacred mole'. The statue in the Shwe-mok-taw Pagoda originally ran aground at Phondawpyi, a seaside fishing village about 60 miles south of Bassein. During the reign of Shin-Sawbu, the sovereign-queen of the former Mon Empire, the statue was brought to Kuthima-nagara, the present day Bassein, and was placed in the Shwe-mok-taw precinct somewhere round about 1455. Stalls line the entrance to this magnificent pagoda, where there is also a reclining Buddha.

Hexagonal in shape with five terraces, surrounded by a number of small stupas and noted for its vast Buddha image is the **Tagaung Mingala Zedidaw**, which in former times was called the Tagaung Pagoda. It has eight pavilions (*tazaung*) and four entrances. According to the *AMENDED LIST OF Ancient Monuments in Burma* it was built in AD 984 by Samuddaghosa, king of the Talaings, and his Queen Ummadandi (yet another spelling of the same monarch), though the pagoda keeper relates a different history. Similar in style but smaller is the **Tha-Yaunggyaung Pagoda** (whose correct name in fact is the Thayaung Mahazedidawgyi). This pagoda is unusual in that it has three *hti* (umbrellas). It is located in a wonderfully peaceful, countryside setting.

The **Mahabodhi Mingalazedi** is at present under renovation: eventually the entire stupa will be covered by glass mosaic. Instead, you can visit the **Lay-kyun-yan-aung Pagoda** ('Four islands enmity conquer'), which is quite extraordinary in that it has been renovated by the SLORC in the style of the Ananda Temple at Pagan. Formerly called the Wish-Fulfilling Phaung-Daw-U, the pagoda has been enlarged and reconstructed around the old one.

In the precincts of the **Settawya Pagoda** stands a giant statue of the Buddha; close by the local people have constructed a new pagoda called the **Shwekyi-myint**. In December 1992, I had the great honour of helping lay the foundation stone, known as *panet* in Burmese.

One other pagoda of interest is the **Twenty Eight Pagoda** on Twenty Eight Pagoda Road (very near the umbrella shop): it is so called because it houses 28 statues of the Buddha. The Burmese believe that there have been 28 previous Buddhas. This pagoda's correct title is in fact *Hpaya ko-zu*, meaning 'Nine Buddhas' or 'Nine images' Pagoda.

Burma is renowned for its festivals, and one particularly enjoyable *pwe* takes place each year in Bassein on December 27: the Ni-gyaw-day Pagoda Festival. It relates one of the Jataka Tales, when the Lord Buddha came to preach to 550 Shan traders. On the way they were robbed, yet they still came to listen to the Buddha's preachings. The festival involves much dancing, singing and cheering with everyone dressing up in ethnic and formal costumes. A procession follows involving various modes of transport: an image of the Lord Buddha heads the parade followed in strict order by his 28 disciples, the Shan traders on bullock carts, numerous beautiful maidens (also on bullock carts, to accompany the traders) and, at the rear, the robbers or *dacoits*, as they are known in Burmese. As they proceed through the town, the

Native of Bassein celebrating the Nigyawday Pagoda Festival

dacoits re-enact the robbery. The whole performance is hugely entertaining.

Chaungtha

'A good beach in the East is somewhat rare. Besides, if you take a beach in the East too literally you may catch a crocodile, and that would be a pity. There are palm-trees, pink sunsets, and a gorgeous quietude.'

W J Grant, late Editor of the *Rangoon Times*, 1940

Such a beach is Chaungtha — without the crocodiles.

Getting there

If you glance at a map of Burma, the resort of Chaungtha looks tantalisingly close to Bassein: perhaps some 20 to 30 miles to the northwest (it's impossible to say exactly how far). But don't for one moment be fooled: it's a terrible journey.

It's hard to describe the route from Bassein to Chaungtha: dusty, exceptionally bumpy and with the certainty of at least one puncture on the way. It takes about 2½ hours in total, but it is extremely uncomfortable and not really recommended for cars (jeeps, maybe).

After 35 minutes, you cross the Ngawun River at Shwemyintin and arrive at Thanlyetsun (which takes 15 minutes) and then proceed to Chaungtha, continuously bounced up and down and caked in dust and sand.

Chaungtha itself is stunning: a deserted, undiscovered seaside paradise, where Burmese kids frolic in the sea without a care in the world, the Kyaukpahto Pagoda stands serenely and immovably on the beach and the fishermen haul in gigantic prawns. Every now and then a bullock cart meanders by over the sands as the sun sets behind a distant island.

Where to stay and eat

Chaungtha's location and way of life are truly idyllic, and at first glance the **Chaungtha Beach Hotel** (which you can book direct from Rangoon, tel: 042 22587) appears likewise. But you soon discover the truth: it's a state-run hotel and the service is appalling. Admittedly the well-appointed bungalows have TV, fridge and air conditioning, but often the rooms aren't made up, the toilets don't flush and you can't even tune in to TV Myanmar. Room rates are US$35 a day, and in true Burmese bureaucratic fashion, tourists are obliged to take breakfast (US$7), lunch and supper (both US$10) in the hotel, whereas locals can pay K350 for just a bungalow. As the surly manager gruffly remarks: 'Breakfast, lunch and dinner compulsory in hotel for tourist.' Although you will lose money, I suggest you ignore the manager's commands and head to Ywa-win-lan, Chaungtha's one street, which is littered with fine restaurants, tea and coffee shops, souvenir stalls, a pagoda and a hospital. The hotel manager will tell you: 'Very dangerous to eat outside. Unhygienic and security risk.' Nonsense: the *moun-hin-ga* is excellent and cheap, as are the *lap'et* and the many seafood dishes, and the local Burmese could not be more hospitable.

What to see

On a rock on the beach is the **Kyaukpahto Pagoda** with a Buddha image inside. Local children tend to congregate round here, paying homage, foraging for shells and crabs and diving off the rocks into the sea. The rare sight of a foreigner will send them into raptures of delight and they will show you around and take care of you. The town itself is unremarkable, though it may be of interest to have a look at the hospital which, like most in Burma, is dirty, very run down and suffers from a dire shortage of Western medicine. Pinned on the wall is a notice listing the cases of malaria in the area: the hospital staff are grateful for any donations. Nearby stands the **Pyilonechantha Pagoda** and a field where you can watch the locals skilfully playing volleyball.

From the beach at Chaungtha, take a boat for K5 to **Foh-ka-lah Island**, which has a population of around 200 who rely solely on fishing for their living. They sell their catch in the market at Bassein, making around K125 a day. However, there are fears that increased poaching by Thai fishing boats in the area will damage their livelihood — and indeed a Thai boat, captured for illegal fishing, was held off Chaungtha for some time. On Foh-ka-lah Island, on Palitaung (Pali Mountain), is the six-year-old Hsu-taungpyay Pagoda, which offers stunning views of the beaches.

Henzada

'You feel inclined to stop at Henzada for ever, it is so picturesque and fresh, and the walks by the river under the high trees are very pretty, and there's no dustiness or towniness.'

W G Burn Murdoch, 1908

Henzada lies in the middle of the delta region and has a more central location than Bassein. South of Henzada the Irrawaddy divides into numerous tributaries and thus the town is an important commercial centre. Henzada's history is not clear: it was supposed to have been founded in the earlier part of the 16th century by Talaing princes, on the right bank of the Irrawaddy which opposite to the town is split into several channels by large sandbanks. When Colonel Symes visited Ava at the end of the 18th century he found at Henzada 'evident signs of wealth but little cultivation'. On the annexation of Pegu the present Henzada district was called Sarawa (Tha-ra-waw) and shortly afterwards was divided into two, called Henzada — Hinthada to the locals — and Tharrawaddy. These days it is once again known as Henzada district.

According to the *Gazetteer of Burma*:

> 'In 1876 the population numbered 15,307 souls of whom about two-thirds are Burmese, the remainder being chiefly Talaing though Shan, Chinamen, Madrassees, Mahomedans, Indo-Europeans and Chin-Indo-Europeans are represented. It contains Court-houses, a Treasury, a Police Station, a Public Works Department Inspection Bungalow, a Telegraph Office, a Post Office, a small masonry Gaol or Lock-up with wooden barracks in which an average of 72 prisoners were confined in 1876, a Charitable Dispensary in which during that year 202 in and 2,041 out patients were treated, a fine market place or bazaar and three schools'.

The major drawback of Henzada in the 1990s is the utterly appalling state of the roads, making the journey to and fro unbelievably arduous. For all that, Henzada is a fascinating town with three interesting pagodas and the largest reclining Buddha in the land.

Where to stay and eat
The best accommodation is to be had at the **Dagon Guest House**, which costs K180 for a double room, is airy and spacious and has a decent shower. Unfortunately there is only electricity after 2000 and the manager is deaf. Tourists must register with the Military Intelligence on arrival, who insist on asking pointless questions like 'What is your father's name?'. The response 'father *mashi-bu*' or 'father no have' is not acceptable. Tough luck on orphans.

There are two good restaurants in town: the Shwe-naga (Chinese) and the Aung Myin (Burmese). The Country Boy Café is recommended for breakfast.

What to see
Near the guesthouse is the **Hseh-datgyi** (Ten-Storey) **Pagoda** which houses a truly vast sitting Buddha image. According to the pagoda trustees, the image was constructed in 1916 as a memorial for Leh-di Sayadaw (not the one from Monywa) by donations from his disciples and measures 76½ft tall. This seems to me a gross under-assessment — it is much bigger than that. Unfortunately the Burmese use a bizarre measuring system called *taung*; one *taung* equals 18 inches and the image is supposed to be 51 *taung* high. After much debate and calculating, we settled at 76½ft.

Located by a pond and surrounded by monasteries is the **Nga-myethna Pagoda**. It was built in 1815 by U Bu, *Myothugyi* of Myanaung, who had received the title of Kyawdin Nawrata from the Burmese King Bodawpaya, who had married his daughter, the Thetpan Mibaya. Owing to the erosion of the Irrawaddy, the shrine was removed and rebuilt on another site in 1887. Its present position is wonderfully tranquil. There are Buddha images at the eight cardinal points and a stunning neon Buddha at the northeast entrance.

By the river stands the **U Pay Pagoda**, built in 1804 by *Myothugyi* U Pay. The stupa is surrounded by 13 Buddha images; the main shrine has three, the centre one constructed in the style of the Maha Muni.

Twenty minutes out of Henzada in the village of Natmaw lies Burma's longest **reclining Buddha** with a name to match: Tilawka Oak Shaung Shin Thar Lyaung Hpayagyi. It measures 252ft in length and is thus 9ft longer than the one at Tavoy and 36ft longer than Mergui's. Its construction was started by two *sayadaw* from Henzada in 1910, U Thathana and U Marlar. However they only got as far as building the head before they died, and it was not completed until after World War II. In the precincts are a museum and a monastery.

ARAKAN STATE

'But in Rangoon the thoughts of the holidaymaker are not always on Amhurst. Some earnest souls swear by a romantic spot near Sandaway.'

W J Grant, 1940

Sandoway and Ngapali

The 'earnest souls' in questions were referring to Ngapali, the best known beach resort in Burma.

According to folklore, Ngapali was given its name by a homesick Italian, who thought the beach reminded him of Naples. In fact in Burmese the word *Ngapali* means 'fish who is wheedling, cajoling or deceiving', so nobody can say with certainty if the tale is true.

Pronounced 'Ngapalee' (like the English expression 'at the sea' said quickly), the resort attracts many more visitors than either Chaungtha or Setseh, particularly the more affluent members of Burmese society, but, despite being Burma's main seaside destination, is hardly in the Caribbean (or even Neapolitan) league. It enjoys an idyllic, peaceful, scenic location but is less intimate than Chaungtha. And since Ngapali itself has no real village to speak of, there is little atmosphere. To cap it all, the rich Burmese visitors (military, ambassadors, diplomats, VIPs and Chinese) are less friendly and a good deal more arrogant than those at Chaungtha.

Getting there

Ngapali is accessible via Sandoway's Mazin Airport: from Rangoon, there are flights on Tuesday, Thursday and Saturday (one way on an F-27 costs US$50; F-28 US$55. It is a 40-minute flight). From Akyab (Sittwe), there is a flight on Tuesday taking 45 minutes (F-27 US$50; F-28 US $55), whilst from Kyaukpyu via Akyab (35 minutes), there is a Saturday flight, costing US$30 on an F-27, US$35 on an F-28. Air

Mandalay has flights on Wednesday, Friday and Sunday between Rangoon and Sandoway (US$63 one way). The beach is closed during the rainy season, when flights are cancelled. Some tourists (and most locals) make the trip by road: a gruelling journey via Prome, whether you are coming from Upper or Lower Burma.

Where to stay and eat

Ngapali has three hotels: the old favourite is the **Ngapali Beach Hotel**, which charges between US$25-45 for beachside bungalows. Inevitably, this hotel is beginning to fray at the edges: the rooms are grubby and the bathrooms grotty. A notice on each door reads:

> 'There is a battery operated emergency light. The switch of which is located behind your bedside table. Please use it when the electric lights fail or when the town electricity supply is cut off at 10 pm everynight. Please switch off to conserve the battery.'

Electricity is only available between 1800-2200, so a torch is a must.

Breakfast is compulsory in the hotel for foreigners and, as with all military-run establishments, the receptionist is surly and inefficient. It is quite remarkable in Burma that every time a tourist checks into (or, for that matter, out of) a hotel, it is as though it has never happened before (this is also the case when buying train, boat and aeroplane tickets).

Directly to the right of the Ngapali Beach Hotel (looking from the main road) is the **Shwewar Gyaing Hotel** (US$10-40) which has a pleasant enough location but is much more down-market than its neighbour. To the left is the 'star' of the trio, the **New Ngapali Beach Hotel**, which charges an exorbitant US$60-100. All the rates are plus 10% service charge and 10% government tax.

Next to the New Ngapali Beach Hotel is an ice factory, which, in true Burmese style, produces no ice. This is because it used to receive its water supply from the Ngapali Beach Hotel, but for some reason refused to provide the hotel with ice. So in revenge the hotel cut off the water supply — and thus 'very little' ice is available in Ngapali.

There is no point in taking lunch or supper in the hotel: simply wander over to **Zaw Restaurant**, which is virtually opposite the Ngapali Beach Hotel (meals must be ordered in advance). The charming owner can also arrange visits to the three famous pagodas in Sandoway (the Andaw, Nandaw and Shwesandaw) and boat trips to the neighbouring islands. An alternative to Zaw Restaurant is the **Kyi Nu Yeik Restaurant** next door, run by a delightful couple U Tin Pe and Daw Tin May. Seafood (large prawns and crab) are particularly appetising and a speciality of the area. *Ganan-hin*, Arakanese crab curry, is especially recommended.

What to see

Past the two restaurants is a monastery called **Myabyin** which has a reclining Buddha in a state of disrepair; just two monks and three novices live in what is a rather sizeable compound. There are also two stupas, one made from glass mosaic, the other painted white. In the room where the monks eat is an image of the Buddha preaching to his five disciples.

About 2½ miles from the hotel is the **Lon-tha jetty** where the British landed during colonial times. On the jetty you can watch the local children skilfully catching fish for their supper.

Sandoway itself is rather a drab town with the inevitable market (which has a decidedly smelly fish section) but an interesting cheroot factory called **Na-yi dazeik Hsay-leik-hkon** (Watch Brand Cheroot Factory). However, the area has a deep religious significance to Burmese Buddhists, for it is here that the Lord Buddha lived three of his previous 547 lives: a king cobra (hamadryad), a partridge-king and a *sa-mari* (pronounced 'za-mari'). Most writers have taken *sa-mari* to signify a yak, but a visit to the pagoda in question (Shwesandaw) would have revealed a statue of a bird resembling a partridge and not a yak. As Judson explains, *sa-mari* is 'a fabulous beast, celebrated for its regard for its tail. Some say it is a bird'. The current Myanmar-English dictionary actually provides a drawing of the creature, which is a fabulous four-legged beast — not a yak — yet gives only one definition, a yak!

Legend relates that the Lord Buddha visited the region himself and pronounced that he had lived three of his past lives here and each of the three pagodas (Andaw, Nandaw and Shwesandaw) is said to contain one of his relics and not, as most books relate, relics of the animals concerned (though, of course, no one can say for certain).

Sandoway is a very ancient town, often mentioned in Arakanese history, and is said to have been at one time the capital of a kingdom (in all likelihood a petty chieftainship). Its original name was Dwa-ra-wad-dee which, according to legend, was changed to Than-dwai (or Thandweh), the name by which it is now known to the Burmese and Arakanese — Sandoway is an English corruption of *Than-dwai* — from its having been miraculously fastened to the earth by iron chains (*than* means 'iron', *tweh* or *dweh* to suspend).

After the capture of the town of Arakan in 1824, a force was sent southwards to attack Ramree and Sandoway. General Macbean arrived off the mouth of the Sandoway River on April 28 and reached the town two days later. Stakes had been placed across the stream in several places and stockades had been erected, but these were abandoned and Sandoway was occupied without resistance. For a few years after the cessation of the war, Sandoway was the headquarters of the troops garrisoning Arakan. Subsequently the headquarters were transferred to

Kyaukpyu, and two companies of native infantry dispatched to Sandoway. Eventually this force was withdrawn, being replaced by a detachment of the Arakan local battalion, and still later, when this was dispersed, the garrison was disbanded altogether.

It is in this hilly area on three mountains (Andaw, Nandaw and Sandaw) that the celebrated trio of pagodas is located. It is a stiff climb up to the **Andaw** ('Sacred double tooth') **Pagoda** which is under renovation and guarded by two cement *chinthe*. Built by King Minzetchok, king of Sandoway, in AD 761 and repaired by the inhabitants of Sandoway in AD 1848 (there is an inscription in Burmese which records that the pagoda was repaired, gilt and crowned by a new *hti* in 1210 BE or AD 1848), it lost its outer shell in 1865, and was again repaired. The Andaw is reputed to contain a molar tooth of the Buddha. In the pagoda precincts is a statue of a king cobra, an incarnation of the Buddha in one of his previous existences. Feasts are held thrice yearly during the months of March, June and October, each lasting one day. Those who attend (chiefly locals) move on for another day to the Nandaw Pagoda and for a third day to the Shwesandaw.

It is a steep ascent to the **Nandaw Pagoda**, which is perched on a hilltop and best reached by car. Guarded by Nandawtaung Bodaw *Nat*, the Nandaw, like all three pagodas, is under renovation. It was originally built by King Minbya (Meng Bhra) in AD 763 to enshrine a rib of the Lord Buddha (not of the partridge-king) and has four pavilions. It is visited principally by the local Buddhists during one of the three feast days in March, June and October.

A newly constructed path now makes the **Shwesandaw Pagoda** accessible by car, though if you decide to walk up you will be greeted by two cement *chinthe*. The pagoda was constructed by Minnyokin (Gnyo-kheng), king of Sandoway, in AD 784 and has been repaired by successive kings of Arakan, and, prior to the current renovation, by the inhabitants of Sandoway in 1876. In BE 236 Minister Damathuriya enshrined real hair relics of the Lord Buddha in the pagoda. A statue of a bird resembling a pheasant (see above) stands in the pagoda precincts. As with the Andaw and Nandaw Pagodas, there are festivals held for one day during the months of March, June and October.

Akyab

'Akyab is a charming place, situated at the mouth of the river Koladyne, which, rising in the far north, flows through 200 miles of British territory. The river is in its upper parts extremely picturesque, having little hamlets dotted here and there on the hill tops overlooking its banks, while in its southern course it is open to large boats for 140 miles. Immediately opposite to Akyab stands Savage Island, on which is a fine lighthouse. It is a most romantic spot, and one which, to myself, will be ever pleasant in retrospection from the remembrance of a delightful morning picnic under

Akyab, Arakan State: an Arakanese child selling lottery tickets

the hospitable superintendence of Mr. Hodgkinson and Captain and Mrs. Ransom... How charming it was to wander about this place, beholding glorious waves dashing in among the rocks, and breathing the breezes of the ocean, I cannot describe. I went to bed each night listening to the roaring of the waters upon the beach, dreaming that I was at home again on England's sea-girt shores.'

The Right Rev J H Titcomb, 1880

The capital of Arakan State, Akyab (known these days as Sittwe and pronounced 'Sit-tway') is one of the four districts forming the Arakan Division of Lower Burma and covers an area of 5,136 square miles. The town is situated on the sea coast at the mouth of the Kaladan River and is located on well-wooded, low-lying ground between the sea face and the Kaladan.

The origin of the name Akyab is supposed to be a corruption of the word *Akhyatdaw,* the title of a pagoda in the neighbourhood which was, in all probability, a landmark for ships in former times. Some historians have taken the Arakanese name Sittwe to mean 'where the war began' or 'where the armies encountered', since the British army encamped there in 1825, but this interpretation is not justified by the present spelling in Burmese. Akyab used to be known as 'The white man's grave' owing to regular cholera epidemics and malaria.

'When I got over to Burma and made some inquiries I was told that the Arakans were one ghastly impenetrable fever swamp, and that except for a month or two in spring it was almost certain death for a European to venture into the district.'

The Road I Travelled, A Boger, 1936

Originally a Mug (the former term for Arakanese) fishing village, Akyab was chosen as the chief station of the province of Arakan soon after the end of the First Anglo-Burmese War when the extreme unhealthiness of Myohaung (or 'old city'), the last capital of the ancient Arakanese Kingdom and subsequently the seat of the Burmese Governor of Arakan, rendered the removal of the troops and civil establishments a matter of necessity. The site, only 15ft above sea level at half-tide and with places actually below the high-water mark, was laid out with broad raised roads, forming causeways, with deep ditches on either side. Readily accessible by boats from the prosperous rice lands in the interior and with a fine harbour formed by the mouth of the river, Akyab soon became a significant trade emporium. Ships seeking rice cargoes would cast anchor and a large influx of people took place from Chittagong, Ramoo and Cox's Bazar in Bengal and from Myohaung. Thus the town rapidly increased in wealth and importance.

The area around Akyab used to boast an abundance of flora, fauna and trees, a large assortment of weird and wonderful creatures: pigs, hogs, sambur, barking deer, leopards, tigers, wild cats, jackals, elephants, rhinoceros, all types of birds, pigeons, snipe, pintails and fantails, pheasants, teal and duck, hawks, kites and fish-eagles, owls, snakes, oysters and, naturally, fish, the main food of Akyab. In fact altogether there were reckoned to be no less than 139 different genera of fresh, saltwater and sea fish. Rice is the staple crop grown in the region, whilst petroleum (oil beds) are situated in the eastern Boronga Island. The district also produces coal, laterite, sandstone and opium. And with its unique Arakanese culture, it is truly an unmatched region of Burma. In fact Burmese joke that to be born a true Arakanese, *Ya-khaing* to the Burmese, *Ra-khaing* to the locals, is to be born within sight of the rusty, steel-framed clock tower (*Na-yee-zin*) which stands in the centre of Akyab. The writer Hector Hugh Munro (Saki) was born in Akyab on December 18 1870.

'At Akyab in 1939 I met a man who had been so long in the East that he had apparently forgotten whence he had come, but it was surely somewhere north of the Trent. His every other phrase ended "But, of course, Akyab isn't Burma." In desperation I had to ask him why it was not. "Because it's Arakan." I might have thought of that all alone.'

A Brodrick, 1944

Getting there
Akyab is only accessible by plane: daily from Rangoon (one hour, costing US$80 one way on an F-27, US$90 on an F-28), on Saturday from Kyaukpyu (30 minutes, US$25 and US$30) and on Tuesday from Sandoway (45 minutes, F-27 US$50, F-28 US$55).

Where to stay and eat/shopping
Foreigners have a choice of three hovels: the inappropriately named Mya ('Emerald') Hotel, the Gisspa Rest House or the Sanpya ('Ideal') Rest House, another misnomer. None has 'en-suite facilities' of any description. Regarding the first-named, the communal ant- and mosquito-infested showers and toilets stink, the fans (only available in the triple rooms) creak and all the rooms are interminably noisy. However, the manager of the Mya Hotel is a qualified Bengali astrologer, speaks 'fluent' (but incomprehensible) English and is absolutely charming. Room rates are only K50 for a single and K100 for a double. More importantly, the manager and his associates can organise trips to Myohaung, the main reason for any visit to Akyab.

The Gisspa Rest House — named after the local river (and smelling like it, too) — has the same rates as the Mya and, though the staff are very friendly, the place is grim. The Sanpya Rest House is far from 'ideal'; in fact it is the most dire of all three. Construction of the (long overdue) new Sittwe Hotel seems to be taking an eternity.

'Externally the hotel did not look unprepossessing, but internally — I was told there was only one room vacant, and that was on the ground floor. I was led to it through the principal eating-room, where several English people were having tiffin. On the raising of a dirty curtain I saw the filthiest room it has ever been my lot to enter: the stained, discoloured walls had once been whitewashed; the mattresses that lay uncovered on two rickety wooden bedsteads effloresced a strong odour; there was plenty of evidence of other occupants of an indescribable nature. From one side of the room opened off a noisome cupboard, absolutely dark, and about the size of a large hearthrug. This was the bathroom! I stepped across and looked out of the window into a pestilential back-yard surrounded by high walls. For this accommodation the native in charge demanded eight rupees a night!'

G E Mitton, 1907

Like the accommodation, good restaurants in Akyab are in rather short supply. **Sein** (Chinese) **Restaurant** serves excellent *wet-u-gyaung-gyaw* (fried sausages), whilst near the mosque is the **Moe Pa Le Burmese Restaurant**. The most idyllic location is that of the **Lay Nyin Tha** (Peaceful Breeze) **Restaurant**, situated by the river. Here you can relax and enjoy a beer — or, for the Buddhists, a 'Sunkist' (fizzy orange) — and a snack.

Akyab, alack, is also not a shopper's paradise. However, for Arakan *longyi* and cheroots, I warmly recommend the Black Cat cheroot shop (Kyaung-net Hsay-baw-leik hsaing), run by a beautiful lady called Ma San San Aye, c/o U Ba Kyaw, House No 344, Strand Road, Kinbingyi Quarter. The best quality Arakan *longyi* — some of the most sought after in Burma — fetches around K480.

What to see

Akyab's most famous pagoda is the **Atula-marazein Pyilone-chantha Hpayagyi**, which was built by U Agga Sayadaw in BE 1255. Inside is a large bronze Buddha image with neon lights whose head contains nine different types of precious stone. It has a large, bustling pavilion with glass mosaic pillars. Directly opposite stands the **Ko Nawin Katkyawzedi** which, unusually, contains a golden stupa inside with a very large *hti,* encircled by eight small stupas. Next to the Atula-marazein is the **Kya-yoke Monastery** (Picture of Tiger) which has two stupas, one cylindrical with a Buddha image inside with a square relics box on top in Sinhalese style, the other in typical Burmese style. Close by is the **Than-bok-day Stupa**, with three terraces and encircled by small stupas. The **Thetkyamuni Pagoda** is an ancient pagoda with a vast Buddha image.

Perhaps of greatest interest in Akyab is the **Mahazeya Monastery** and the adjacent Adeiktan Sima (ordination hall). The monastery has Buddha

Ethnic groups in Burma. Top left: Akha lady, Kengtung Top right: Padaung lady, Loikaw

Bottom left: Ethnic origin could not be ascertained!, Kengtung Bottom right: Tattooed Chin lady, Putao

Scenes of Mergui, Lower Burma. The golden hti (umbrella) of the Thein-daw-gyi, the first view of Mergui glimpsed by Samuel White in 1677

'I sat in the upper veranda of the residence and looked westwards into the great bay.'
The clock tower, market street and Pataw-Patit, Mergui

Pagodas of Mergui. Top: The Pagoda which appeared by itself

Bottom: Nine Images Pagoda

Tiger standing guard outside the Kya-yoke Monastery, Akyab

images which are copies from Myohaung and a large pink Buddha image guarded by Thet Taw Shay Bodaw on the left and by a Brahmin fortune-teller on the right. The abbot is a delightful man called U Kula Rekhita Sayadaw.

The **Adeiktan Sima**, renovated in 1987, is filled with a myriad of different size Buddha images in various postures. It is guarded by two ogres: Ahlawaka on the left, Pannaka on the right.

The **Akyeik Pagoda**, built about 130 years ago, is said to contain a tooth relic of the Buddha, while located on a ridge called Akyatkundaw are three separate pagodas: **Dattaw**, **Letya-thalon** and **Let-weh-thalon**, which allegedly enshrine the hip and right and left shins of the Buddha.

The **Buddermokan Mosque** was said to have been founded over a century ago by two merchants of Chittagong in memory of a certain Budder Auliah, whom the Mussulmans regarded as an eminent saint. A fascinating account of this mosque is given by Colonel Nelson Davis, Deputy Commissioner of Akyab, in 1876 in a record preserved in the office of the Commissioner of Arakan:

'On the southern side of the island of Akyab, near the eastern shore of the Bay, there is a group of masonry buildings, one of which, in its style of construction, resembles an Indian mosque; the other is a cave, constructed of stone on the bare rock which superstructure once served as a hermit's cell. The spot where these buildings are situated is called Buddermokan, "Budder" being the name of a saint of Islam, and "mokan", a place of abode. It is said that 140 years ago or thereabouts two brothers named Manick and Chan, traders from Chittagong, while returning from Cape Negrais in a vessel loaded with turmeric called at Akyab for water, and anchored off the Budermokan rocks. On the following night, after Chan and Manick had procured water near these rocks, Manick had a dream that the saint Budder Auliah desired him to construct a cave or a place of abode at a locality near where they procured the water. Manick replied that he had no means wherewith he could comply with the request. Budder then said that all his (Manick's) turmeric would turn into gold, and that he should therefore endeavour to erect the building from the proceeds thereof. When morning came Manick, observing that all the turmeric had been transformed into gold, consulted his brother Chan on the subject of the dream, and they conjointly constructed a cave and also dug a well at the locality now known as Buddermokan.

'There are orders in Persian in the Deputy Commissioner's Court of Akyab, dated 1834 from William Dampier, Esq., Commissioner of Chittagong, and also from T. Dickenson, Esq., Commissioner of Arakan to the effect that one Hussain Ally (then the "thugyi" or village headman of Bhudamaw Circle) was to have charge of the Buddermokan in token of his good services rendered to the British force in 1825, and to enjoy any sums that he might collect on account of alms and offerings.

'In 1849 Mr R. C. Raikes, the officiating Magistrate at Akyab, ordered that Hussain Ally was to have charge of the Budermokan buildings, and granted permission to one Mah Ming Oung, a female fakir to erect a building; accordingly in 1849 the present masonry buildings were constructed by her; she also re-dug the tank.

'The expenditure for the whole work came to about Rs. 2,000. After Hussain Ally's death his son Abdoolah had charge, and after the death of the latter, his sister Me Moorazamal, the present wife of Abdool Morein, Pleader, took charge. Abdool Morein is now in charge on behalf of his wife.'

In the compound of the Deputy Commisioner is a stone inscription belonging to the Palace hill of Myohaung which dates back over four centuries.

On West Boronga Island stands the **Sandawshin Pagoda** which is said to have been erected in the lifetime of the Buddha over eight of his hairs. The tradition about Tapussa and Bhallika bringing these relics is identical to that attached to the Shwedagon in Rangoon. The current structure is relatively modern.

About 16 miles by boat on the way to Myohaung and situated on a low, steep and rocky hill opposite the village of Ponna-gyun is the **Urittaung Pagoda**. The original builder is not known, but it is said that on the hill where this pagoda stands the Buddha once lived in a former existence as a Brahmin of high birth and that on his death a pagoda was erected over his skull, which was found on the same hill. The pagoda was repaired by King Gajapati, of the Myauk-U dynasty, in AD 1521 when it had fallen into ruin and has subsequently been repaired by King Thadomintara in 1641 AD, by King Varadhammaraja in 1688 AD and in the middle of this century, when it was repaired and gilt by a private individual.

Myohaung

'It should be borne in mind that Mrauk-u, though less substantially built, was comparable in size and wealth to such Western cities as Amsterdam and London. Schouten... declares it the richest city in that part of Asia, exceeding in its resources both Pegu and Ayudhya, the capital of Siam.'
The Land of the Great Image, Maurice Collis, 1943

Situated about 40 miles from Akyab and the Bay of Bengal on the Shwenatpyin *chaung,* a branch of the Kaladan River, is Myohaung. The township covers 567 square miles: in 1891 it was transferred to the newly constituted Kyauktaw subdivision.

Myohaung was a former ancient capital, founded in 1433 by King Minzawmun. In fact it was known as Mrauk-U ('Mrow-Oo' is the approximate Arakanese pronouncing; the Burmese referred to it as Myauk-U, pronounced 'Myow-Oo') until the First Anglo-Burmese War

(1824-26), when it was renamed Myohaung (meaning 'old city') as the British moved their administrative headquarters to Akyab. Some writers claim that the name *Myauk-U* actually means 'monkey's egg' (the Burmese name for a root vegetable), but since Burmese is a tonal language both *Myauk* and *U* can have several meanings and there is no logical reason why the town should have been known as 'monkey's egg'.

It is interesting to note the following extract from Burma expert Maurice Collis' book *Into Hidden Burma*:

'I asked the name of it and was told, Mrohaung. The word "Mrohaung" means "old city". It was a place sixty miles up the Kaladan River.

'"The old city is called the old city," said I, laughing.

'"That's right," he said. "Not to speak of the history, the very name of the old capital is forgotten. Everyone calls it just Mrohaung. Even the British map makers could not be bothered to ascertain its real name and ignorantly copied down Old City."

'I begged to know its correct name. "Mrauk-u... The Monkey's Egg, though why that, I cannot tell..."'

On the conquest of Arakan by the Burmese in 1784, the town offered no resistance but yielded after the defeat of the Arakanese monarch in a general action fought some distance from his capital and became the headquarters of one of the four districts or provinces into which the country was divided.

In 1824, on the declaration of war with Ava, one of the points at which the kingdom was attacked was Arakan. On February 2 1825 the first British detachment crossed the Naaf from Chittagong and, after an arduous march, the whole division of British troops acting in Arakan under General Morrison, and the flotilla, under Commodore Hayes, arrived before the town of Arakan on March 28. The place was found to be strongly fortified, and the first attack was unsuccessful. However, the entrenchments were eventually carried by storm, but not without considerable loss.

The capture of this stronghold led to the immediate withdrawal of the entire Burman army and General Morrison cantoned the greater part of his troops in the town. When the rains came early in May, disease broke out in the cantonments and carried off more victims (including the general himself) than in any other part of the country in which British troops were engaged. Some say that the Arakan army was completely ravaged by disease; thus shortly after the end of the war, the troops were removed and the headquarters of the division stationed at Akyab. From this moment onwards, Myohaung faded away and today is remembered for its glorious past — its pagodas, temples, Buddha images, ancient city walls, lakes, hills, tranquillity and awesome scenery. To the Arakanese, Myohaung is as of great a significance as Pagan is to the Burmans. It is home to the majestic Shit-thaung Pagoda, finer, many would say, than any of the buildings at Pagan. A full account of Myohaung can be found in U Tun Shwe Khine's *A Guide To Mrauk-U: An Ancient City of Rakhine, Myanmar* (1992).

Getting there

There are three ways to reach Myohaung (which is only accessible in the dry season): by state or private motorboat service or by a special chartered boat. The state service costs K18 one way, K36 return (for an 'upper class cabin', shared unfortunately with the boorish military, VIPs, etc), the private motorboat about K40 per person, whilst a group of 20 tourists or more would have to negotiate the price for their own boat. Tickets are purchased from the Inland Water Transport Office in Akyab — if you want to travel to Myohaung independently, you will require written permission from the SLORC in Rangoon. The state and private services run as follows (Burmese Standard Time, BST):

Akyab to Myohaung

Monday:	state boat (with a night stop service at Myohaung), dep 0730 arr 1230
Tuesday:	private motorboat, dep 0700 or 0730 arr 1200
Wednesday:	private motorboat, dep 0700 arr 1200
Thursday:	state boat, dep 0700 or 0730 arr 1130. The boat then returns the same day: dep Myohaung 1300 arr Akyab 1800
Friday:	private motorboat
Saturday:	state boat (Kyauktaw via Myohaung)
Sunday:	private motorboat

Myohaung to Akyab (departs around midday, BST)

Monday:	private motorboat
Tuesday:	state boat
Wednesday:	private motorboat
Thursday:	state boat
Friday:	private motorboat
Saturday:	private motorboat
Sunday:	state boat coming back from Kyauktaw

Where to stay

If you wish to stay overnight in Myohaung, there are two resthouses: the Myanantheingi Rest House and the Kyawsoe Rest House. Both charge K50 a night for a single, K100 for a double. The rooms are extremely basic and the 'showers' not recommended for those suffering from arachnophobia.

What to see

Are there any locations in the world more idyllic than Myohaung, where the women still sit smoking Kipling's 'whackin' white cheroot', where you can still trace the old walls of the ancient city and the royal palace? Certainly you will find no people more hospitable, no market more fascinating, no village more tranquil than that of the 'lost city' of Myohaung.

Situated within eight miles of the Kaladan River, 48 miles north of Myohaung, is the **Maha Muni Temple**. Tradition ascribes this temple to Chandasuriya, king of Arakan, who built it to enshrine the image of the Buddha cast during the lifetime of the Sage himself in the 6th century BC. The image was removed to Amarapura in 1784 as a spoil of war after the conquest of Arakan by the Einshemin, son of Bodawpaya. Until the removal of the image, the Maha Muni was the most sacred shrine in Indochina. It has now been placed in the Maha Muni or Arakan Pagoda in Mandalay. This temple has passed through many vicissitudes and has been repaired many times, the last occasion being in 1867. For the Arakanese, the loss of the Maha Muni image was the end of the end. It was their head, their life-blood, their very soul.

In Mrunchaungwa village, three miles west of the Maha Muni on the top of a hill, stands the **Mrunchaungwa Pagoda**. Tradition ascribes the foundation of this small shrine to the pious Buddhist kings of old Dhannavati (Arakan) (4th century AD).

On either bank of the upper Kaladan River lies Kyauktaw, of which the most celebrated pagoda, the **Kyauktaw Zedi**, stands on a hill opposite Kyauktaw. It was erected by a fugitive queen of the Launggyet Dynasty (1237-1401) and repaired by the villagers in the middle of this century. Kyauktaw also has a number of stone images and a footprint of the Buddha cut in stone dating from the 14th century.

Myohaung's most famous temple is the **Shit-thaung Pagoda**, which is built on a promontory half way up the west side of the hill. Shit-thaung means 'The shrine of 80,000 images' and it was constructed by King Minbin, the 12th of the Myauk-U dynasty, who reigned over Arakan from 1531-1553. The Shit-thaung served as a place of refuge for the royal family and is more like a fortress than a pagoda, with numerous passages, tunnels and caves. Unbelievably atmospheric, it is one of the most wondrous constructions in Burma. As Dr Forchhammer explains:

'The Shrine is the work of Hindu architects and Hindu workmen; the skill and art displayed in its construction and ornamentation are far beyond what the Arakanese themselves have ever attained to: the entire structure is alien in its main features to the native architectural style.'

Situated 86ft to the northeast of the Shit-thaung is the **Andaw Pagoda** which was built by King Minbin (1531-1553) — full name Sirisuriyacanda-maha-dhammaraja — to enshrine a tooth relic of the Buddha said to have been obtained from Ceylon. Like the Shit-thaung, the Andaw too is a temple fortress and place of refuge.

Located 40ft to the north of the outer wall of the Andaw is the **Ratanabon Pagoda**, which was erected by King Minpalaung who ruled Arakan from 1571-1593. It rises in a number of concentric tiers and was built for purposes of defence, forming a link in the system of fortifications which protect the approaches to the palace from the north.

Opposite, and about 300ft to the northwest of the entrance to the Shitthaung, on a low elevation rise the **Dukkan-thein** and **Lay-myet-hna Pagodas**, built by King Minbin. These too are temple fortresses and places of refuge in war, chiefly for Buddhist priests. Both are constructed of massive stone blocks and layers of bricks over the roof. The **Lay-myet-hna** (Four-Sided Pagoda) is 150ft northwest of the Dukkan-thein.

Half a mile north of the Dukkan-thein is the **Pitakat-taik** or Library which was built by King Narapatigyi (1638-1645) to store the Buddhist scriptures which were brought over from Ceylon. It was originally ornamented with exquisite carvings in stone. Some 50ft to the north of the Pitakat-taik lies the enclosure of the **Linpan-hmaung** or **Laung-pwan-brauk Pagoda** which was constructed in the 16th century and also has some beautiful stone carvings. Fifty steps to the north are the ruins of the **Dipayon Pagoda**, made from stone also in the 16th century.

A stone's throw to the east of the Dipayon is the partly ruined **Anoma Pagoda** with an enclosing wall which was built in the 15th century. The shrine stands on the battlefield on which the Arakanese were defeated by the Burmans in 1784. A half-mile to the west of the Dipayon is the **Mingala-mraung Pagoda**, an octagonal solid stone spire overgrown with dense jungle, which was constructed by King Narapatigyi. There are inscriptions in Burmese which were set up by King Chandavijaya (1710-1731).

The **Jina-man-aung Pagoda** stands on a low steep hill and was built by King Chandasudhamma between 1652 and 1684. The façade of the porch exhibits some good stone carvings. Each of the eight corners of the pagoda is guarded by a lion or griffin, each with a double body and a head with whiskers and a beard.

Five and a half miles from Myohaung down an exceedingly bumpy road lies the ancient city of **Vesali** (The Shrine of Misery), founded in AD 327 by King Sandramuni. It is noted for its 22ft sitting Buddha image cast out of a single stone on a lotus throne dating back 1,666 years.

Southeast of Alezeywa on the steep Shwedaung Hill is the **Shwedaung Pagoda** which was built by King Minbin. Though small, this pagoda is historically important. To oppose the advance of the British soldiers, the Burmans set up camp — which is still traceable — in 1825 on the top of the Shwedaung Hill. A half-mile north of the Shwedaung Pagoda (Shwedaung-hpaya) on another small hill called Wunti-taung is the **Wunti-ceti**, the origin of which is unknown. It is first mentioned in

Arakanese history in the 14th century. It is a Hindu shrine with Hindu deities represented in the sculptures and is clearly very ancient, although the stone inscription is probably 14th century.

The **Sandhikan Mosque** was built of sandstone by the followers of King Minzawmun after he had returned from 24 years of exile in India in 1430. It is located 2½ miles southeast of the palace.

The **Sakya-manaung** and **Ratana-manaung Pagodas** are both ascribed to King Chandasudhamma, the 23rd of the Myauk-U dynasty, who reigned in Arakan from 1652 to 1684. The latter is a solid stone structure, octagonal from the base to the top.

West of Wa-zeh village on a steep and narrow rocky ridge is the **Letyo-dat Pagoda** (there are two pagodas of the same name). Tradition asserts that the bone of the fourth finger of the Buddha is enshrined in one of these pagodas erected in the 15th century AD.

On the Peinnugun, another small hill to the northwest of Wa-zeh, is the **Shwegya-thein Temple**, again built by King Chandasudhamma, who was also responsible for the construction of the **Lokamu Pagoda** between Byinze and Kyauk-yit villages. In the spacious temple court, shaded by mango and tamarind trees, the pilgrims who intended to visit the distant Maha Muni Pagoda (48 miles to the north) used to assemble. The Lokamu was repaired by Chit San of Wa-zeh and the public.

Another pagoda usually visited by pilgrims on their way to the Maha Muni is the **Parabho Pagoda**, which is reached by crossing the Parabochaung. Standing on the banks of a tidal creek, the Parabho was built by King Minrajagyi, the 17th king of the Myauk-U dynasty, in 1603 and was repaired by the first Burmese Governor of Myohaung in 1786.

An ancient pagoda, now sadly completely demolished, is the **Moktaw Pagoda** (also called the Shwemawdaw Pagoda). It was built at the first foundation of Myohaung, but only the basement of the original pagoda remains. A smaller pagoda, which was built on it, has also fallen into ruin.

Standing on the central hill which rises behind the village of the same name is the **Mahati Pagoda** which was built in the 12th century by the Arakanese King Koliya. The pagoda contains an image of the Buddha which was also finished in the 12th century, as well as stone inscriptions and sculptures. Mahati village was once the site of a considerable town.

The celebrated **Kyauk-nyo** or 'Dusky stone' image stands on top of the southernmost hill of Mahati village. It was reputed to have been set up by King Koliya in 1133. The **Mi-gyaun Rock inscription**, five centuries old, in Burmese characters and language, covers 21ft of rock and is situated on the west side of the hill on which the Kyauk-nyo image stands. A mile to the north of Mahati village are the remains of the **Paungdaw-dat Pagoda**. The original pagoda was built by Chulataingchandra in AD 954 to enshrine the thigh-bone of Ananda, the well-known disciple of the Buddha. It was repaired in 1591 by Minpalaung, the 16th of the Myauk-U dynasty. There is an inscription in Burmese which records this fact.

One mile north of Kamaungdat village and ten miles due south of Laung-gyet is the **Kado-thein** which was built by King Chandavijaya (1710-1731) in 1723. This is the gem of the art of stone-sculpture in Arakan and lay buried in the jungle until around 1890. It is constructed entirely of stone and is square with the corners indented. There are fine carvings in stone and also two inscriptions recording the grants of land to the inmates of the monasteries in the neighbourhood of the pagoda. Glazed tiles have been found nearby.

Dr Forchhammer concluded:

'Myauk-U has at all times been an unhealthy place; the plain on which the city now stands has in ancient times often been selected as a site for a capital, but as often abandoned owing, as the Arakanese chronicles state, to "men, elephants, horses, and cattle dying of pestilential fever."'

But that was eons ago. Today the area of Myohaung, like Pagan, stands as yet another wonderment of Burma. For where else in the world can you bathe in two vast lakes — Anoma-kan and Let-seh-kan — surrounded by hills, pagodas and ancient city walls, and watch the sun go down behind the Shwedaung-hpaya?

KACHIN STATE

Myitkyina

'There were single redstarts all along the road, and between Washaung and Chipwi I collected eleven dark thrushes and saw as many more, all single birds; in four years previously I had never blundered across any in Myitkyina, and only two in twelve years' collecting. We saw another a few days farther on and then no more till the end of our trip, and what to deduce from that I do not know.'

Far Ridges: A Record of Travel in North-Eastern Burma 1938-39,
J K Stanford, 1944

The dark thrush, according to Stanford, went under the Latin name of *Turdus obscurus*. Judging by the 'toilets' in Myitkyina's state-controlled Manaw Guest House, Stanford, former deputy commissioner of Myitkyina, was evidently psychic. Bertram Smythies in his marvellous book *The Birds of Burma* confirms that the dark thrush is indeed *Turdus obscurus*. Smythies further explains: 'Length 10 inches. Sexes differ... The female... utters a thin pipit-like zip-zip when disturbed.' Thrush-fanciers (the thrush is known as *mye-lu-hnget* in Burmese, by the way) may be interested to read that no less than seven other varieties can be found in Burma: *Turdus merula, Turdus boulboul, Turdus rubrocanus, Turdus naumanni, Turdus ruficollis, Turdus dissimilis* and *Turdus feae*.

Myitkyina — meaning 'Near Big River' and pronounced 'Myit-jee-na' (stress on 'na') — is the capital of Kachin State, which in 1994 finally came under the control of Rangoon. The Kachin had been fighting the central government for greater autonomy since 1962. Previous attempts to negotiate political settlements in 1963, 1972 and 1980-81 all failed because of Rangoon's insistence that the group first surrender its arms. Eventually, on February 24 1994, the Kachin Independence Organisation yielded to the State Law and Order Restoration Council.

Readers wishing to learn more about the Kachin should consult *The Kachins: Religion and Customs* by Reverend C Gilhodes, who writes:

'In the North and North-East of Burma are found the savage tribes, which the Burmese and after them the English call "Kachins." They call themselves Chimpaws; they pretend to come from the North, and that little by little they have succeeded in becoming the masters of the range of mountains, which they now inhabit, partly in Burma and partly in Yunnan.

'The Kachins, properly so called, comprise five principal tribes: the Marips, the Lathongs, the Laphais, the Nkhums and the Marans. We may add to them the Marus, the Atsis and the Lachyis, who live in the same countries and whose ways and customs are nearly the same. They worship a multitude of Nats or Spirits to whom they offer continually sacrifices of animals in order to appease them or secure their good will. They are living in a great number of villages presided over by a du-wa, who is a more or less influential chief according to his intelligence, but always looked up to, because, according to tradition, he descends from a race superior to that of the rest of men, and is the master of the land, which forms his territory.'

It is reckoned that the Kachin are 44% Baptist, 40% Roman Catholic, 5% Shamanist/Animist, 4% Church of Christ, 3% Anglican, 3% Buddhist and 1% Jehovah's Witnesses.

Getting there

The quickest way to reach Myitkyina is by Myanma Airways (UB) — there is only one non-stop flight a week from Rangoon, but there are three others via Mandalay and up to Putao. The non-stop flight takes 1½ hours and departs on a Wednesday (F-27 US$150 one way, F-28 US$165). The flight via Mandalay leaves on Monday, Friday and Sunday, continues up to Putao, turns round and returns to Rangoon via Mandalay. It is invariably delayed and, in bad weather, cancelled. On Wednesday there is a flight from Rangoon and Mandalay to Myitkyina via Bhamo — and back to Bhamo and Mandalay (but not Rangoon!). Total flying time is 185 minutes (BAST), but this does not take into account the late departure, the refuelling stops and possible mechanical failure en route.

The alternatives to Myanma Airways are train from Mandalay (be warned: 25 hours to cover 540km on a single track laid in colonial times), or boat and train (boat from Mandalay to Katha, train from Katha to Myitkyina).

Mandalay-Myitkyina: Monday and Friday, dep 1930 (takes 24 hours)
Myitkyina-Mandalay: Wednesday and Sunday, dep 1130 (24 hours)
(This is the 'Malikha-Mandala' MFF train, half-SLORC, half-private. Lunch and dinner boxes included in the ticket.)

Mandalay-Myitkyina: Sunday and Wednesday, dep 1930 (24/25 hours)
Myitkyina-Mandalay: Tuesday and Friday, dep 1130 (24/25 hours)
(This is the 'Meikha-Mandala' train, Sunthawda Co, and is privately operated. It has reclining seats, a dining car, fans that work and newer rolling stock.)

Reservations are necessary for both trains and you need to show evidence of permission from the Ministry of Tourism to be able to purchase tickets. The total return fare is US$40 — some proportion is payable in kyats according to which train company you use. A combination of outward on MFF and return on Sunthawda is possible.

General description

Noted botanist — and travelling companion of J K Stanford — Frank Kingdon-Ward, who made many a trek from Myitkyina, wasn't that taken with the town, describing it in his last book *Return to the Irrawaddy* (1956) thus:

'Myitkyina, though pleasantly situated on the river bank, is no earthly paradise. The hot weather is very hot, the rainy season very rainy. The river rises forty feet in the summer, and frequently threatens to burst its banks and sweep away the town — the crisis generally occurs about two o'clock in the morning.

'During the war the old town was almost completely destroyed, and the new one is no improvement on the old, being dirty, noisy, and already overcrowded. However, Myitkyina is not all bad, and it offers compensations for its shortcomings, including a delightful cold weather of about four months' duration. The plain is as flat as a pancake, but the mountains of the China frontier form a massive background to the east.'

Almost 40 years on, Myitkyina, I suspect, has scarcely changed since Kingdon-Ward's day, yet I rather like it. The climate is temperate at dawn and dusk, the location by the Irrawaddy enchanting, the varied hilltribes beguiling and the markets fascinating. And Myitkyina has assuredly the finest array of fruit in Burma. At the markets you will find a wonderful assortment of oranges (including the giant 'Washingtons'), apples, grapefruit, American (and presumably non-American) limes, pomelos, pineapples, avocados and *teh-thi,* a red fruit of Chinese origin with the consistency of an apricot. There are vast carp and frogs, countless vegetables, the celebrated Kachin *longyi* (about K230) and the much sought-after shoulder-bags in reds and greens, embellished with silver. The vendors and buyers are Burman, Kachin, Karen, Indian, Gurkhas, Rawan, Lishaw and a whole host of other ethnic groups, whose names escaped me. An engaging account of travel amongst the tribes in this district (Lisu, Maru and Lashi) is given in *The Fire Ox and Other Years* by Suydam Cutting.

Where to stay and eat

Foreigners must bear in mind that although Myitkyina is the Kachin State capital, Western-style accommodation simply does not exist. The **Manaw Guest House** is lousy but only charges K90 for a single, K180 for a double. The recently upgraded **YMCA** isn't much better and costs US$20 for a room with a toilet. The **Popa Hotel** (address: Railway Station, Myitkyina!) charges US$24 a single (K420) and is certainly the pick (misnomer) of the trio. It has spacious and clean fan-cooled rooms, communal bathroom and a large dining hall (shame about the trains, though).

Some of the best Shan noodles in Myitkyina are to be found at a stall located on the corner of Bo-gyoke Aung San and Zegyi Streets. It doesn't have a name, but is run by a charming lady called Daw Leh-leh Win. Close to the Manaw Guest House is the **Shwe Ein Zay Chinese Restaurant**, whilst three coffee shops worth a visit are **Lucky Cafe and Confectionary** (sic), **Phet Phu Yaung Coffee Shop** and **Shine Café**.

What to see

Since a majority of the Kachin are Baptist and Roman Catholic, it will come as no surprise to discover that Myitkyina only boasts two pagodas of note. The most celebrated is the silver **Andawshin** (The Owner of Tooth Relic Pagoda), or to give it its full title, the Thetkya Marazein Andawshin Pagoda. This beautiful pagoda contains a footprint of the Buddha and a glass mosaic stupa with a spired entrance, and has a number of monasteries in its precinct (including a Buddhist Missionary Monastery). There are two replicas from Beijing of tooth relics inside the stupa, which are only on show at festival time. However, as a special honour to the foreigner, the abbot U Aryawantha (from Pakokku) will open up the chamber to reveal the replicas (the originals are in China). The Andawshin was built in 1959 by U Nu to enshrine the tooth relics.

Although not as well known as the Andawshin, the **Hsu-taungpyi** (full name: Lawka-man-aung Hsu-taungpyi-zeditaw or Conqueror of the Pride of the World Wish-Fulfilling Stupa) is, in its own way, quite idyllic. Blessed with a stunning, tranquil location by the banks of the Irrawaddy and guarded by two sand-coloured *chinthe,* the Hsu-taungpyi — its shining golden stupa glinting in the midday sun — is one of the most serene and peaceful pagodas in the land. It was built by King Alaungsithu in 1113 and measures 75ft 10in. In the precinct is a banyan tree supported by bamboo poles which have been placed by devotees. Legend relates that as long as the tree is propped up, the life of the devotee will not end.

Myitkyina also boasts a Gurkha temple (Sheeri Shara Swathi Temple), a mosque (the Islam Central Mosque called Jaame Masjid, built in 1956 and located near the market), a *nat* shrine and a Chinese Temple. The splendid *nat* shrine is on the road leading to the ferry and has two unusual tiger guardians in front. The Chinese Temple (in Burmese Tayok-boutda-ba-tha hpongyi kyaung) has one abbot and just two monks and is similar to the Chinese Temple in Maymyo. It contains a display of statues of three Chinese heroes from three past kingdoms — Qwankon, his adopted son Kwanpin, and Chouchang. The nearby Chinese school is also of interest.

Across the Irrawaddy River from the Nanthida State Guest House can be seen — on a clear day — the 'Brassière' or Khin Than Nu Mountains, so called because the two peaks resemble the figure of a well-known voluptuous Burmese film star.

'There is yet another starting-point available, above Myitkyina. The Irrawaddy, like the Weser, has no source: instead, it is formed by the union of two streams, neither of which claims its name, and this confluence is some twenty miles above Myitkyina and a favourite picnic goal (you may quite probably meet wild elephants on the road, I heard). For two reasons I decided against it: one was that the river there was said to be shallow and rocky, unsuitable as a practice ground for an entire beginner; and the other was that I did not feel that 25s. for car hire was justified by the purely terminological exactitude of having started the river "where it begins".'

Canoe To Mandalay, Major R Raven-Hart, 1946

Oh, Major, what a skinflint you were! I would have willingly paid 25s and more to glimpse *Myit-hson* (River meet), where the two source rivers, the Mali Hka and Nmai Hka, converge to form the confluence of the Irrawaddy, Burma's life-blood (see *Chapter One, Geography*).

Myit-hson is located 27 miles (or 1 hour 20 minutes) north of Myitkina down a road that has not been touched since the end of World War II. Wander down to cool, craggy waters where locals pan for gold and stare in wonderment at one of the world's mightiest waterways. The source of the Irrawaddy is overlooked by a derelict state resthouse, burnt down by rebels in 1964, which the SLORC plans to convert into a hotel 'soon'.

Six miles from Myitkyina is **Kraing Naw Yeiktha**, which offers equally scenic views of the Irrawaddy, rocks and mountains and where there are restaurants and stalls. I think I could stay here for the rest of my life.

Bhamo

'... Bhamo, a town on the very frontier of the Chinese enigma, where caravans incessantly come and go through mysterious valleys and where people live on rumours from day to day... '

Joseph Conrad, August 1 1922

Bhamo — pronounced 'Banmaw' in Burmese — is the furthest point to which the Irrawaddy River is navigable by boat and the beginning of the main trade route into China. The Irrawaddy waterway is commercially navigable 900 miles inland and from Bhamo itself the name 'Upper Irrawaddy' is often used.

Getting there

For some, the idea of a boat trip from Bhamo to Mandalay (or vice versa) on the Irrawaddy River evokes Kiplingesque images of flying fish, tinkly temples bells and pretty Burmese girls sitting smoking whacking white cheroots.

Oh, how I wish! For me, it was 41 hours 40 minutes of sheer hell. No cabin, no bed, no food, no toilet, just the captain's table to sleep on, a watermelon hurled at me by a drunken soldier and a plastic bag in which to pee.

Maybe in the colonial era it was a romantic journey down (or up) the Irrawaddy, with servants to cater to your every whim. But in these days of SLORC control, that is but a dim and distant memory. The boats which ply the murky waters of the Irrawaddy are grotesquely overloaded (I heard the figure of one thousand travellers mentioned). Each passenger has his (or her) own 'plot' designated on deck on which to cook, eat, sleep, wash and live for the duration. There are only seven cabins on these ancient riverboats — hot, stuffy, claustrophobic and insect-infested they are too — and invariably allocated to Major so-and-so and his kowtowing entourage. Foreigners, thus, must either squat on deck Burmese-style or beg of the captain to be allowed to stay on the bridge, where at least it is less crowded, less noisy and there is a semblance of a breeze. But be warned: the captain's bridge is no mansion. It is permanently locked from the rest of the boat, so there is no access to the lower decks. This means no toilet nor washing facilities. You are obliged therefore to urinate into a plastic sack, which is then cast overboard (pray the wind is blowing in the right direction). Since you are under 'bridge arrest', you are unable to purchase anything to eat or drink and must either 'rest' on the outside upper deck or on the captain's 'desk', where a gruesome array of undiscriminating Burmese insects will partake of a better meal than will hapless you.

'I took my passage on the "Bazaar Boat" for the voyage to Bhamo from Mandalay. Not only does the traveller see far more of the country traversed, for the Bazaar steamer touches at many more places than the Express service and for a longer time at each, but also the life on board is one of constant pleasure and amusement. The "Bazaar Boat" is a travelling market. The entire upper deck, with the exception of the cabin accommodation, is fitted with little shops in which whole Burmese and Indian families live and eat and sleep. They travel backwards and forwards in this manner between Mandalay and Bhamo. Amidst their goods tastefully displayed, they sit on the floor of their shops and trade, for as soon as the steamer arrives at a stopping-place the village people hurry on board. It is thus that they replenish their little local village shops or their wardrobes.

'Every variety of article can be purchased on the ship from fine silks to children's toys, from sweetmeats to Manchester cottons; writing pads and tooth-powder, key-rings and playing cards; lamps and sock-suspenders...

'On the lower deck is piled cargo, and what a cargo! Amongst great cases and sacks of produce were two buffaloes, four ponies, two bicycles, a motor-car, endless tins of petroleum, and two dug-out canoes... '

East For Pleasure, Walter Harris, 1929

For non-masochists, Bhamo is accessible by plane: on Sunday from Mandalay (1 hour). On Wednesday there is a flight from Rangoon, which takes the circuitous route via Mandalay and on to Myitkyina (and back), ending up in Mandalay.

Those who do wish to sample the 'bizarre boat' pay a mere 180 kyat at the office of the Inland Water Transport Board (IWTB), which makes Myanma Airways seem like Swissair. The journey takes in the celebrated Irrawaddy defiles (rock-bound gorges), one of which Gwendolen Trench Gascoigne describes thus in her book of 1896 *Among Pagodas and Fair Ladies*:

'After leaving Kyoodan we entered the second defile. It is of an entirely different character from the first. The first is charming, riante, and sunny; the second is grand, stately, serious. The river appears to have cleft the mountains asunder, and winds in and out through a magnficent gorge, with the gaunt grey cliffs rising up sheer from the water's edge some two hundred feet. Sharp perpendicular rocks and crags stand out, and hang over the wild abyss beneath, as if they would hurl themselves down on any unlucky craft below. The shadows, the stillness, and the green forest-clad hills hovering above the crags, and the dark, lurid blue depths of the waters beneath seem to strike one with a sudden dumb awe; and a half eerie feeling possessed one, till one's eyes fell on a tiny ray of sunlight, which had crept down from the mountain tops and lay like a brilliant emerald on the waving, rustling bamboos, and then wandered on to the grey crags and rocks, till it left them arrayed in a robe of sheeny gold.'

The only interesting pagoda en route comes just after leaving Thabeik-kyin. The **Anya-thiha-daw Pagoda** (known to some as the 'Elephant Rock') is built on an island of an elephant-based stupa, half gold, half white. You can enter the basement which contains ancient Buddha images worshipped by kings of old. It was constructed by King Alaungsithu and is located just before the third ravine on the way down river towards Mandalay. Legend relates that the pagoda was erected on a raft, but one so loaded with earth and stones that it appears to be solid ground. It is the only stone pagoda in Burma, and though close to the water, is never flooded. The fish, apparently, are so tame that they come to be fed daily. They are dogfish, five feet long, and the pilgrims put gold leaf on their heads. When I sailed by, the pagoda looked deserted and not a fish (dog or flying) in sight.

A third way to reach Bhamo is to take the train from Mandalay (or Myitkyina) to Katha, there transfer to the boat, and sail up the Irrawaddy to Bhamo. The path from the jetty into town is rutted and extremely bumpy — a quagmire in the rainy season — and only to be undertaken by horse-cart. Ignore all offers from trishaw drivers.

Where to stay and eat
Considering it is a major smuggling junction to and from China, Bhamo is a surprisingly relaxed and tranquil town with a delightful riverside location. Foreigners are accommodated in the **Shwe-naga** (Golden Dragon) **Guest House**, which is more 'dragon' than 'golden'. It has grotty rooms at K100 a night and ghastly 'showers'. Restaurants in Bhamo are somewhat thin on the ground — your best bet is the **Sein Sein Chinese Restaurant**.

What to see
Bhamo is home to one of the most peculiar pagodas in Burma, the **Thein-maha-zedi-dawgyi**, located by a pond and guarded by two male *chinthe*. The stupa itself is of glass mosaic (silver) and built in ancient Burmese style, similar in its cylindrical design to the Bawbawgyi and Bebegyi in Prome. For some reason, Murray's *Handbook for Travellers in India, Burma and Ceylon* states, 'The Thein-dawgyi Pagoda resembles those of Siam in shape'. This is incorrect. There are eight small stupas encircling the main stupa at the cardinal points which represent the eight Burmese birthday corners. In the precinct is a museum depicting the life of the Lord Buddha and an old *hti*. The Thein-maha-zedi-dawgyi is unique, serene and quite beautiful.

The **Taung lay-lon dat-paung-zu zedi-daw** has four receding terraces with a prayer hall at the top with Buddha images. On the roof is a half gold, half white stupa encircled by eight small stupas. It was renovated in 1971 near the site of an ancient bell donated by King Mahathirithihathu in the 11th century. The ordination hall contains one large sitting Buddha image and one marble image, an ancient peacock and a small ancient marble Buddha. Introduce yourself to the charming abbot U Zagarabudi, who will offer you coffee, cakes, biscuits and a Burmese speciality called *pauk-pauk-hsok*, popped rice rolled into a ball with jaggery (like popcorn).

About two miles northeast of Bhamo (half an hour by horse-cart) lies the ancient pre-Pagan city of **Sanpa-nago**, the walls of which can still be seen. The ancient city is famous for the Shwe-kyi-na Pagoda, 'Where The Golden Crow Perches'.

'Good-bye, sweet Bhamo. You weep, and we weep; but we go with a hope we may return.

'... Even in pouring wet, Bhamo is beautiful. Good-bye again; we will tell all our friends at home that there is such a desirable quiet country on this side of Heaven, where the mansions truly are few, but the hosts are very kind.'

W G Burn Murdoch, 1908

Putao

'Twice a week the plane came in from Rangoon and Mandalay, and every Thursday it went on to Putao, 135 miles further north...

'Jean was anxious to see Putao — possibly she shared Saw Shwe Thaik's scepticism concerning the existence of Burma's icy mountains, and preferred to see for herself. So on the afternoon of New Year's Day 1953, she and Rutherford boarded the plane on its arrival, and were whisked northwards.

'It was a remarkably clear day, the dustless atmosphere sparkling, so that one could easily see a hundred or two hundred miles, and make out the most distant mountains quite clearly. They returned to a late tea, thrilled by what they had seen, and satisfied with the view of a glittering array of snowy peaks. I did not altogether envy them their quick trip to the edge of beyond. Several times I had done the journey between Myitkyina and Putao — 220 miles, on foot — taking twenty leisurely days over it, and revelling each day in the slowly changing landscape. I still think that North Burma is best seen from the ground.'

Thus wrote Frank Kingdon-Ward in his final book *Return to the Irrawaddy* in 1956. The most significant phrase penned by botanist Kingdon-Ward is 'the edge of beyond', for that assuredly sums up Putao, the northernmost town in Burma. Another of Kingdon-Ward's books, first published in 1930, was entitled *Plant Hunting on the Edge of the World* — the 'edge of the world' is Putao.

Other writers to have ventured to the edge of the world have been J K Stanford (*Far Ridges*, 1944), who joined Kingdon-Ward on one of his trips, and the celebrated Morse family. The extraordinary tale of the Morses — American missionaries in Putao — is told in Eugene Morse's remarkable book *Exodus to a Hidden Valley* (1974).

'We loved working and living on the fertile plain of Putao, in northern Burma, where we had spent more than fifteen years teaching and helping the local tribes create what was, for them, a paradise.'

This excerpt is taken from the first chapter of *Exodus to a Hidden Valley*, without doubt one of the most incredible stories of Burma. Twenty-five years on, locals still recall the Morse family of Putao.

Readers of earlier accounts of this region will come across the name 'Fort Hertz' and not Putao. Fort Hertz was named after William Axel Hertz (1859-1950) who was born in Moulmein of Danish-British descent and entered government service in 1886, serving in the 'pacification' campaign in Upper Burma and then becoming Deputy Commissioner of Myitkyina in 1903 and Commissioner in 1919. He served in Kachin Hill operations of 1914-15 and earlier campaigns and was involved in frontier negotiations with the Chinese. Fort Hertz was given as the name of the military police post at Putao, headquarters of the new district of Putao which was formed in 1914 in unexplored territory north of Myitkyina. The name commemorated Hertz's retirement and came to overshadow Putao as the name of the whole settlement. There were similar other Myitkyina Hill Tracts District names — Fort Morton (Sima) and Fort Harrison (Sadon) — but Fort Hertz lasted longest as the name assumed World War II importance.

Getting there

On landing at Putao Airport, the only evidence that you have not stepped back into the 19th century is a Burma Airways calendar of 1986 that hangs abandoned on the wall of the airport manager's 'office', a corrugated iron shed. The Burmese, you see, treat calendars as we treat pictures — as wall decoration and not for the date. If they don't have an up-to-date one, they will leave the older one there!

There are four flights a week to Putao: on Monday, Friday and Sunday from Rangoon via Mandalay and Myitkyina, and on Wednesday from Rangoon via Myitkyina. Excluding delays, the flying time via Mandalay and Myitkyina is 2 hours 25 minutes, via Myitkyina alone 2 hours 5 minutes. The problem, however, is that 'through tickets' do not exist in Burma. Thus in theory it is impossible to purchase a ticket Rangoon/Mandalay/Myitkyina/Putao or Rangoon/Myitkyina/Putao — at least for travel on the same day. All passengers are required to break their journey for a minimum of one day in either Mandalay or Myitkyina. Myanma Airways' (UB) system is not yet capable of securing a same-day passage from Rangoon to Putao. In theory, on arrival at Mandalay or Myitkyina, all the passengers disembark and a new load board to fly up to Putao. However, as with all things Burmese, it is possible to bypass the system — simply by staying put in your seat and refusing to get off when the plane touches down at Mandalay or

Myitkyina. This I proved by being the first Western tourist for many a year to fly the same day from Mandalay to Putao via Myitkyina. On touching down at Myitkyina, I did not leave my seat and insisted I be flown to Putao. If you intend doing this, you must ensure that your baggage is not removed at Myitkyina (or, as the case may be, Mandalay), since it goes without saying that baggage cannot be 'tagged' all the way through to Putao. A one-way ticket from Rangoon to Myitkyina costs US$150/165, from Mandalay to Myitkyina US$70/80, from Myitkyina to Putao US$40/45.

General description/where to stay and eat

Do not inquire about transportation to your accommodation — the answer will be *mashi-ba-bu* (there isn't any). It is a ten-minute walk to the **Tokyo Guest House**, owned by a charming Lisu couple with six mischievous kids. Similar in style to a northern Thai hilltribe house, with ducks, chickens and assorted farm animals running riot, a room here costs K45 a night. The toilet consists of an extremely deep hole in the ground at the back of the garden and washing facilities of an even deeper well plus bucket.

With a population of around 10,000, Putao is an ethnic hodgepodge: the state officials are all Burmans, but the majority of the inhabitants are Kachin and Lisu with a sprinkling of Rawang, Shan and countless other hilltribes. Apart from farming, there is little for the locals to do other than sit all day smoking and getting drunk on an exceedingly obnoxious Kachin version of rice whisky. The only work available, and quite bizarre it is too, is that involving the extension of the runway at Putao Airport, so that it can accommodate a Boeing 747. Locals (mainly female) have to walk seven miles a day to the site — and seven miles back home again — for a pittance of a wage, in return for work which involves the chopping up and lugging around of large, heavy stones. The head of Myanma Airways' Northern Division is extremely proud that a jumbo jet can land at Putao Airport (something that is not possible at Mingaladon Airport, Rangoon), since this is part of Kyaw Ba's master plan to turn Putao into a ski resort. When I put it to the UB chief that Putao had no accommodation, no transportation, no restaurants — and, perhaps, most importantly of all — no snow, he smiled and replied *kayt-sa mashi-ba-bu*, 'never mind'. He gave the same response when I asked him why Western tourists should come all the way to Putao in north Burma to go skiing, when they could go to Switzerland instead.

But I lie. Putao does have lodging: a guesthouse (see above) . It also has one 'restaurant' (**Sein Restaurant**), which offers mainly fried noodles and is the hang-out for local drunkards, but for sure there is no reliable transportation. Perhaps Kingdon-Ward had the right idea after all when he took Shank's pony from Myitkyina to Putao. There are only working bullock carts (whose busy owners understandably don't wish to transport tourists around), the peculiar 'trawler G', a kind of trailer drawn by a small engine (which generally isn't available) or bicycles. The latter are not easy to rent: you will have to ask the kind guesthouse owner if you can borrow his — but you must check the tyres and brakes. There is a steep hill leading down from the guesthouse, and if your brakes are not functioning, you will end up in the ditch.

As a result of its remoteness, prices in Putao are high. A cup of tea costs K20 and there is no bottled water available, though there are soft drinks. Near the Tokyo Guest House is the Yadana-bon lottery and tea shop (an interesting combination), where tea, coffee, Burmese pancakes (*bein-moun*) — and lottery tickets — are available. In the vicinity of the Taung-dan Tha-thana-pyu Pagoda (literally 'Hill-range making religion Pagoda') is the Township Co-operative Tea Shop, which offers tea and a very limited supply of juices. I recommend the grapefruit *phyaw yay* (grapefruit juice).

What to see

There are just two pagodas in Putao and the only one of any interest — and marginal interest at that — is the **Taung-dan Tha-thana-pyu** mentioned above. It consists of a white stupa with a golden *hti* encircled by eight small stupas over the eight birthday corners. At the entrance to the precinct is a miniature golden stupa with eight small niches housing eight different Buddha images. There is also a monastery of the same name, which has more than a suggestion of Buddhists trying to convert the Christian Kachin.

Of greatest interest in Putao are the two **markets**: one is near the guesthouse (on the way to the airport), the other is located in the opposite direction. The assorted hilltribes and their array of different languages are astonishing. You may even glimpse a Chin lady with her face completely tattooed. This ancient tradition is carried out to make the lady so ugly that no man would dream of leading her astray, and a successful operation it is too, judging by the hideous Chin lady I saw at the market closest to the guesthouse.

Apart from wishing to experience Kingdon-Ward's 'edge of the world', there is no reason to visit Putao. Unless, of course, you're bored with St Moritz!

KAYAH STATE

Loikaw

'A RELENTLESS EMBRACE of brass, the burden of beauty shouldered by a Padaung tribeswoman of Burma armors the neck in a coil that weighs about 20 pounds, and measures a head-popping one foot high. The loops, draped with silver chains and coins and cushioned by a small pillow under the chin, signal elegance, wealth, and position.

'But what is the anatomy beneath it all? Do the vertebrae stretch? Or do the ligaments binding them lengthen? Perhaps the disk spaces expand? An invitation to lecture at Burma's three medical schools enabled me to unravel the secret of the long-necked women.

'At the Rangoon General Hospital I tracked down the X rays of a Padaung woman admitted for diagnostic tests. As fans swished lazily overhead, the films on view boxes illuminated the mystery. The neck hadn't been stretched at all. In effect, the chest had been pushed down. Each added loop increased pressure downward on the vertebral column. Something had to give — and did, as an X ray's ghostly shadow shows. The clavicles, or collarbones, as well as the ribs, had been gradually pushed down. The result of this displacement: a neck that just looks elongated...

'"THE LAND of the giraffe women," as Polish explorer Vitold de Golish called it, lies in eastern Burma on a high plateau dimpled by terraced, paddy-filled valleys. Here live the Padaung, a tribe of about 7,000 members.

'Legend claims that the brass rings protect the women from tiger bites, but actually the practice of wearing them helps maintain individual and tribal identity.

'A brass rod a third of an inch in diameter is worked around a girl's neck at about 5 years of age by a village medicine man. After divination with chicken bones to determine the most auspicious date, several loops are twisted around her neck. Additional loops are added periodically.

'Rings worn on arms and legs may weigh a woman down with an additional thirty pounds of brass. Since leg coils hamper walking, the women waddle. Constrained from drinking in the usual head-back position, a ring wearer leans forward to sip through a straw. And the voices of wearers, wrote British journalist J.G.Scott, sound "as if they were speaking up the shaft of a well."

'After years of being straitjacketed in brass, the neck muscles atrophy. If the rings are cut off, a brace must support the neck until exercises rebuild the muscles.

'In past times the punishment for adultery decreed removal of the coils. The head then flopped over, and suffocation could follow.

'Two decades ago the encroachment of modern civilization prompted some women to remove their rings, though years of wearing them had left striations. The custom, indelibly inscribed in Padaung culture, persists and, according to University of Illinois anthropologist F.K.Lehman, shows sign of a resurgence.'

'Anatomy of a Burmese Beauty Secret', John M Keshishian, MD,
National Geographic, June 1979

Getting there

Capital of Kayah State, sandwiched in east Burma between the Shan and Karen States and Thailand, picturesque Loikaw can only be reached by the domestic airline. There are four weekly flights from Rangoon (Tuesday, Thursday, Friday and Sunday), which take 70 minutes and cost US$55 (F-27) or US$60 (F-28). On Thursday and Sunday there are also flights from Heho, 35 minutes away; the fare is US$30 (F-27) or US$35 (F-28).

General description

Two lakes, Naung-yar and Hti-nga-lian, a stream called Bilu-chaung (Ogre Stream) and a bizarrely shaped mountain Taung-kweh (Two Split Mountain) combine to make Loikaw another Burmese wonderland. A mere 20 minutes away by jeep or lorry lies the village of Hoa Ri Ko Khu, home of 74-year-old Daw Mu Suey and two other Padaung or 'giraffe-necked' ladies. Loikaw has no traffic, no pollution, simply lakes, streams and mountains with funny names.

Where to stay and eat

Visitors stay at the **State Guest House No 2** (No 1 being reserved for Secretary 1 and entourage), one of the finest (and cheapest) in the land. Clean, spacious rooms with 'bathroom' attached cost a mere K25 a night. There is intermittent running water and a tub provided in case the caretaker forgets to switch on the water. In front of the guesthouse is a park with eucalyptus trees, leading to Hti-nga-lian Lake — wander over and maybe you'll encounter the old Kayah (Red Karen or Karenni) lady who comes daily to graze her three cows. In the town you can eat at either **Yin Myo Chit Chinese Restaurant**, **Meik Set Burmese Restaurant** or enjoy a delicious bowl of noodles and soup for K20 at the nameless noodle shop opposite Shwekyaung.

What to see

The most wonderful vista in all Burma is from the top of **Taung-kweh**, home of the Taung-kweh-zedi. It is steep to climb, but the views are just imperious. Taung-kweh is two mountains connected by a bridge, looking out magnificently over the town of Loikaw. Down below is a newly constructed standing Buddha surrounded by the eight cardinal points denoting the days of the week.

The **Myonan Pagoda**, built in similar style to Pagan's Ananda Temple, is a glorious sight too, particularly at night when it is all lit up. Only men are permitted to climb to the top of the pagoda where there are fine views of the Taung-kweh-zedi and Bilu-chaung.

With the backdrop of Taung-kweh, Loikaw's market (**Thiri Mingala Bazaar**) is the most scenic — and fascinating — in the land. Assorted peoples of Burma, Kayan, Shan, Pa-O, come to sell their wares. Few but the Shans can speak English; you could have a word with U Sai Tun Shwe, Shop 3/4, who proffers strange Burmese medicine, or with the young Shan lad selling blankets and shoulder bags at the stall opposite. By this time, you deserve a cup of tea at the Shwe Tea Shop near the bazaar or at the Myodaw Tea Shop next to the Myonan Pagoda.

At the **Badamya** (Ruby) **Cheroot Factory**, run by a charming Shan/ Pa-O lady from Taunggyi called Daw Aye Aye Thein, you can admire the skill of the 30 girls who roll cheroots for eight hours a day. Each girl is paid 5 kyats for every 100 cheroots she rolls; some manage to make 800 a day and earn themselves K40. Three sizes of cheroot are available, small and medium (which cost K25 for 50), and large (K45 for 50). Incongruous as it may seem, you can actually watch the BBC World Service News on Daw Aye Aye Thein's TV!

Finally, in the wonderfully named village of Hoa Ri Ko Khu (pronounced 'Hwa Re Co Coo'), greet the elegant Padaung lady, Daw Mu Suey. She thinks she has been wearing her rings since she was a little girl of six — but that was a long time ago and she can't be sure. These days, little stirs in the village of Hoa Ri Ko Khu, for, as in the rest of Burma, they are patiently awaiting the arrival of the 20th century.

TENASSERIM DIVISION

Tavoy

'Tavoy, as a whole, apart from any individual characteristics which may have distinguished its town, certainly struck me as a spot where those native to the place and "to the manner born", might lead a very peaceful existence. Nature had placed within their reach a supply of delicious food, to be had without the asking. The bright green leaves of the plantain rose up in every direction, growing and multiplying unaided, besides bearing huge clusters of fruit all the year round. The glossy, thick-leaved Jack-fruit was also conspicuous; palms reared their tufted heads aloft, among them the much esteemed cocoa-nut, useful in more ways than one; there, too, the leafy tamarind stood waving its pinnate foliage in the evening breeze, proof against the scorching rays of the sun, even at midday.

'The women, as elsewhere, sat under their houses, busy with the looms, on which they spun garments of many colours and gorgeous design. The buffaloes grazed around, enjoying a peaceful existence, until summoned to the periodical contest in the arena. They found no lack of food, and were kept at night in a strong enclosure, secure from the prowling tiger...

'Yes, the aborigines must have led a happy, contented life in such a place; while the European grumbled, growled, and vilified everything, after the manner of his kind.'

Deputy-Surgeon-General C T Paske, 1893

History

The town of Tavoy was founded in 1751, though the region is noted in much earlier records and ruins of some nine cities exist in various parts of the district, notably at Old Tavoy or Myo-haung a few miles to the north. In 1752 the ruler of the country made overtures to the British to establish a factory in or near his new capital. During the First Anglo-Burmese War the garrison rose against the commander on the appearance of the British at the mouth of the river and handed the place over to the English, together with the second in command and his family, whom they had taken prisoner. For several years a detachment from Moulmein was quartered in the town which was gradually weakened and withdrawn.

At different periods Tavoy District formed part of the dominions of the Kings of Siam, Pegu and Ava, though its history is shrouded in obscurity. The first settlers were probably Siamese, but at a very early date a colony of Arakanese was established who had an influence on the language. The earliest written accounts of the region state that the Burman King Narapatisithu, who came more as a preacher of religion than a conqueror, founded Kyek-hlut in Khwe-doung Bay not far from the mouth of the Tavoy River in 1200, the first city ever built in this district. He also constructed the pagoda on Tavoy Point, the oldest of which there are any records, and was probably the first to place Buddhism on a permanent base in the region. Anxious to connect the foundations of their religion with the great Asoka, Buddhist writers assert that in 315 BC, the king ordered the construction of a pagoda in what is now the town of Tavoy.

Many years later the district was subject to the king of Siam and still later to the rulers of Pegu (from whom it passed to the kings of Burma), but it was continually suffering from invasions by the Siamese. Around 1752 the ruler of Tavoy set himself up as an independent prince and made approaches to the British government, which itself had made many efforts to obtain settlements east of Hindustan. The terms proposed, however, were too exorbitant from a pecuniary point of view and in 1757 Ensign Lister proposed a treaty to the then king of Burma, Alaungpaya, one of the terms of which was a pledge on the part of the English not to assist the king of Tavoy.

Soon after this, Tavoy again became a province of Siam but in 1759 it surrendered to Alaungpaya. The following year a British mission was despatched to Pegu to obtain, amongst other things, remuneration for the loss of a ship belonging to a Captain Whitehill which had been forcibly taken by the Burmese and employed against the king of Tavoy. From this time, until the Treaty of Yandabo in 1826, the district was torn by rebellions and incursions by the Siamese.

There are various legends as to how Tavoy (*Dawei* or *Daweh* in Burmese) acquired its name. Some say it was a corruption of a Siamese word meaning 'a landing-place for rattans'; another tale has it that Tavoy was so named because it was celebrated for its armourers, people coming from far and wide to buy swords (*dha* meaning 'sword' and *way* 'to buy') or even that a miraculous sword was once bought here. According to a fourth tale, Tavoy is a Burmese corruption of the Talaing word *Hta-way*, 'sitting cross-legged after the manner of tailors', and the town was thus called because the Lord Buddha was so found by the inhabitants on his visit to the area.

In 1994 Tavoy found its way into the international press as a result of the public outcry following revelations of forced labour on the construction of the rail-link between Ye and Tavoy. As the *Edmonton Journal* reported on September 7 1994:

'Although a project on the scale of the Ye-Tavoy railway has been rare, the U.S. State Department's recent annual report on human rights abuses in Burma says that the SLORC "routinely" uses forced labor for large construction projects, such as the building of roads, canals, and even hydroelectric dams. Many of these infrastructure projects are taking place in Burma's ethnic minority areas, including the Ye-Tavoy railway which is in Mon state...

'... With greater control over the border areas, the SLORC has now begun numerous infrastructure development projects in which, like the Ye-Tavoy railway, the local villagers are used as slave labor.

'So far the SLORC response to the charges of using slave labor is that all work is being provided "voluntarily" and is in lieu of taxation.

'They claim that the economic benefits of the infrastructure projects will also improve the living standards of the local people.

'Most of the economic benefits of the Ye-Tavoy railway, say many Burma watchers, have to do with a new natural gas pipeline being built between Thailand and Burma.

'It appears that the SLORC will use the new railway to transport soldiers and construction supplies into the pipeline area.

'The new $1.1-billion pipeline, being built by the French oil firm Total, will allow Burma to export large amounts of natural gas, providing hundreds of millions of dollars to a junta which spends an estimated 60 per cent of all state revenues on its military.'

General description

Tavoy is located by the banks of the Tavoy River. The various streams which unite to form the river have their sources in the southern slopes of the Mahlweh spur and in the western slopes of the main range in the extreme north of Tavoy district. At Tavoy Point, roughly 40 miles below the town, the river falls into the sea, but is only navigable for about 70 miles from its mouth owing to numerous shoals and low islands. During the monsoon season, ships take refuge all along the banks of the river under the lee of the islands which shelter the coast.

In the western township of Tavoy district, west of the town, is Maung-magan, which includes a group of islands known as the Middle Moscos Islands and the famous beach referred to as Maung-magan. The islands, in fact, are divided into three groups, the Northern, Middle and Southern, or in Burmese *Hein-zeh, Maung-magan* and *Laung-lon* respectively.

'The mainland, covered in dense tree jungle and palms, rose steeply from the sea. Moskos Island, clothed with cedars, lay lapped with shoal water creaming the coral reefs about its feet. Occasionally a turtle floated lazily past. As the sun rose above the great forest-clad hills the Maungmagan beaches gleamed white on the distant shore.'

Hunter's Moon, Leonard Handley, 1933

Getting there

Plane is the only way to reach Tavoy. There are daily flights from Rangoon (taking between 50 and 80 minutes), costing US$65 one way on an F-27, US$75 on an F-28. On Monday and Saturday there is a flight from Mergui, which costs US$35/40 and takes half an hour; on Wednesday and Saturday from Moulmein (US$50/55 — one hour) and on Thursday from Kawthaung (US$80/85, 1½ hours).

Where to stay and eat

Tavoy offers little accommodation and tourists may be obliged to stay at the **Sibin Guest House**, the resthouse for state officials. Reminiscent in some respects of a public school dormitory (but, at 15 kyat a night, noticeably cheaper than either Eton or Harrow), there are communal six-bedded rooms with a 'shower' and a 'toilet'. 'Shower' and 'toilet' both break the Trade Description's Act, as indeed do the words 'grim' and 'spartan'. Who would be a state official in Burma?

The best restaurants in town are the **Daw Khin San Restaurant** (Burmese) and the **Aung Chan Mya** (Chinese). There are alternatives: at the **Myamya San Restaurant** a meal for two (including drinks) comes to around K160 (just over £1). Directly opposite is the **Bay-da Restaurant**, tea and coffee shop. Near the Hpaya-shin-myauk Stupa is the **Beik lap'et-yay-zaing** (tea and coffee shop) which serves excellent *kauk-hnyin sanwin-makin* (baked sticky rice); close to the Kyet-thindaing Pagoda is the **Eye Restaurant and Tea Shop** and in the vicinity of Myanma Airways' office is the **Dollar Tea and Coffee Shop**. There is also the strangely-named **Spider Cold Drink** (shop) which has a giant plastic spider on the wall with a (fake) butterfly trapped in its web, the **Meikswe Tea and Confectionery** (tea/coffee shop) and the **Pwint Wa** (Yellow Flower) **Cold Drinks Shop**. Transportation around town is by horse-cart or trishaw.

What to see

Visitors to Tavoy don't come for the luxury of five-star hotels or haute cuisine — though it should be remarked that the celebrated and exceedingly smelly *seinsa ngapi* (shrimp paste) hails from this region. The quaint, serene town of Tavoy, with its tranquil riverside location, in some ways reminiscent of Moulmein, is one of the most beautiful in Burma and boasts three gems — the second largest reclining Buddha in the land, the unique six-fingered Buddha and the peculiar Kyet-thindaing Pagoda.

It is for none of these constructions that the town of Tavoy is most famed, however. That honour belongs to the **Shin Mokti Pagoda** built in 1438 by Sawthila, King of Wedi, enshrining an image of the Buddha built of the bodhi tree wood which he had miraculously obtained from Ceylon. The other three images are in Bassein, Kyaikto and Kyaikkami. Though the most celebrated and sacred pagoda in Tavoy, the Shin Mokti has no stupa and is not visually impressive.

Seven miles out of town stands Tauk-tein-taung (Very Bright Mountain). On the hill is the wish-fulfilling **Hsu-taungpyi**, which has two stupas: one silver, one half gold, half white. Round the pagoda are scenes from the Jataka Tales and a bo tree in one corner; the image itself is housed in the Kassapa Cave. There are panoramic views of the area: the watch tower offers a stunning vista of the Tavoy River, the pagoda's *zaungdan* and the surrounding plains. There is also a meditation centre, whose abbot *Sayadaw* U Eidar Wuntha has been teaching and meditating for over 20 years.

Located out of town is the second biggest reclining Buddha in Burma, the **Lyaung-daw-mu**, built in 1931. Its dimensions are vast: 243ft in length, 69ft in height, the face, sole of the foot and palm of the hand all measure 33ft, whilst the large toe is 13½ft long. Legend has it that in years gone by you could actually climb in through one nostril and out through one ear, but that is no longer possible.

In the town is the giant standing image known as the **Yat-taw-mu**, which is 41ft tall and has three green mosaic stupas. The **Shwe-taungza Pagoda**, in the process of being gilded, was built in 1762 by Maung Shin Zaw, a native of Tavoy who became *Myo-sa* (literally 'eater of the town' or governor) of his own birthplace under the title of *Shwe-taungza*. The pagoda has a large precinct but is in no way outstanding.

Every now and then the traveller in Burma comes across an unexpected jewel. Such is the little-known **Kyet-thindaing Pagoda**, built on the grounds of a cemetery in an utterly tranquil location. The pagoda contains many fascinating, but sadly dilapidated buildings housing a variety of Buddha images of different styles, some of Indian influence, others Burmese. There are three reclining Buddhas of varying proportions, a beautiful emerald Buddha and the only image in the land of the Lord Buddha with six fingers on his left hand. Legend has it that each time one of the fingers is removed, another grows back. On my visit to this idyllic yet run-down pagoda, I certainly counted six fingers! The origins of the Kyet-thindaing are unknown, though it has been ascribed to Asoka.

In the locality of Maungmeshaung in a vast precinct stands the **Shin-daweh Pagoda**, built in the 11th century by Shin Zaw and Shin Za, two disciples of Govinda Rishi, over a corporeal relic of the Buddha obtained from Shin Arahan. The main prayer hall contains a stunning neon image. The *hti* was knocked down in the monsoon of 1993. Adjacent to the pagoda is the **Mahabodhi Stupa**, recently constructed by ex-General Sein Win, and surrounded by 28 images of the Buddha.

Located in Tavoy Town is the **Hpaya-shin-myauk Stupa**, which is peculiarly shaped and painted light green. In the prayer hall are many images including a reclining Buddha, whilst in the pagoda precinct is a *nat* shrine. The silver stupa is surrounded by five *devas* (celestial beings), the most famous of which is Sakka, the lord of all celestial beings. Sakka is the Hindu god Indra, who appears in Buddhist scriptures as Sakka, but in Burmese as Thagya-min. He is the lord of the first and second levels of existence of the *nat devas* (the celestial beings), as opposed to the local Burmese *nats*. There is also a small and quaint Tavoy (Myanmar) **Baptist Church** in the town.

One of Burma's most famous abbots, *Sayadaw* Gaw-thi-tabi-wuntha, lives in the **Gaw-thi-tar Yama Monastery**, home to more than 150 monks. The *Sayadaw,* who claims to be around 87 years old, has for understandable reasons rejected repeated SLORC requests to appoint him the Chief Abbot of Burma. Visitors in need of assistance or interested in meeting the venerable *Sayadaw* should contact his deputy, *Sayadaw* Badanta U Thilawintha. In the monastery precinct stands a copy of the Maha Muni Pagoda, whose image is the same as those at Mandalay and Myohaung.

Mergui and the Archipelago

'After an hour or so the Dharacotta weighed anchor, and the journey to Mergui started. The coastline was beautiful and just as fine, if not finer, than any of the South Sea Islands that I have seen. I sat amazed at the wonderful panorama, as we threaded our way through the various wooded islands with white sandy beaches backed in some cases by casuarina trees and flowering jungle shrubs. I only wish I had the gift of writing a more vivid description of the journey, as I feel sure it would entice thousands of tourists to this land of fairy tales, instead of going to the South of France or the South Seas.'

A Merchant Adventurer among the Sea Gipsies: Being a Pioneer's account of life on an island in the Mergui Archipelago,
Leopold Ainsworth, FRGS, 1930

History

Mergui — Beik to the locals — is of a beauty unrivalled throughout the land. This out-of-the-way little town, once deep in the jungle of southern Burma, lay on the high road to Siam. It served as the port of Ayutthaya, the former capital situated north of Bangkok. At Mergui travellers bound for Siam disembarked and, transferring to small boats, proceeded up the river to Tenasserim. From Tenasserim a paved road led to Ayutthaya.

Lokanat: the celestial being believed to spread peace in the world

Mergui itself was Siamese at that period and the centre of a very lucrative trade.

In 1687 Mergui was the scene of a massacre of the British residents, many of whom were employed by the king of Siam as officials and customs officers. British trade had suffered badly as a result of a series of high-handed actions, and in April 1687 the Madras Council of the East India Company sent an ultimatum to the king of Siam, demanding an indemnity of £65,000 and threatening war if he did not pay.

The king of Siam was given 60 days to reply, and during those 60 days it was agreed that no act of hostility should be committed. In the meantime all the Englishmen employed by the Siamese were invited by the East India Company to resign. The most important person at Mergui at that time was a certain Samuel White, an Englishman who was to all intents and purposes the governor of the town. He immediately carried out the instructions of the East India Company's Council and paid off all the Englishmen in question. But before the 60 days had elapsed there was an unfortunate and disastrous breach of the truce. Captain Anthony Weltden, in command of two British ships, seized by force — and treacherously it must be said — a Siamese vessel lying in the anchorage. His impetuous act, to say nothing of its immorality, so exasperated the Siamese population that they massacred the British residents — 76 were murdered, 20 escaped. Samuel White fled, eventually passing away in Bath, England in April 1689. Near the landing-stage at Mergui a stone was laid in his memory.

It is written that Caesar Frederick, the Venetian traveller who visited Burma in 1569, described Beik as 'a village called Mergui in whose harbour there lay every year some ships, with veizina (Sappan wood) nyppa and benjamin'. Burma expert Maurice Collis, however, refutes this. In *Siamese White*, Collis states, 'In 1568 Cesare dei Fedrici pulled along the coast for eight days, looking for it in the maze of islands, and never found it'. In 1688 de La Loubère, French ambassador to Siam in 1685, asserted that 'The Port of Merguy, they say, is the most lovely in all India'. Two years earlier one of the Madras establishment had written 'There are abundance of Stragglers of all nations in Mergee'.

In 1780 the Siamese invaded the country but were defeated before Mergui and forced to retreat, but in 1821 it was again attacked by the Siamese and burned down.

During the First Anglo-Burmese War an expeditionary force under Lieutenant-Colonel Miles, having captured Tavoy, proceeded to Mergui. Heavy fire was opened from the town but was silenced by the guns of the ships. The troops, wading through the mud banks on the beach, escaladed the stockade from which the enemy had already fled. The town was found deserted but the people soon returned and showed themselves perfectly indifferent to the change of authorities. A small garrison of native infantry was left and from that time (1825 to 1948) Mergui became a British town.

But let us go back to 1677, the year of Samuel White's arrival in Mergui. White's extraordinary adventures are related in Maurice Collis' wonderful book *Siamese White*, first published in 1936. Collis describes in great detail and with an evocative atmosphere life in Mergui towards the end of the 17th century. In *Into Hidden Burma* (1954), Collis, who himself spent nearly three years in charge of administration at Mergui, writes:

'... there was a further reason which made my posting to Mergui even more lucky. The place was to provide... a literary subject so suited to me that my hesitations at last were to be put aside and I was to be able to realize the ambition of so many years. The story of Samuel White, one time Shahbander of the port, lay to my hand... Before coming to Mergui I had never heard of the man. As soon as I got there and perceived what an interesting old port it was, I began to wonder what its history might be...

'During the two years and eight months I lived at Mergui I visited every spot connected with White. Being convinced for good reason that his house had stood on the ridge, probably within the boundaries of my garden, or slightly below it to the south, it was easy to plot his movements and imagine the scene as he had beheld it during the eighties of the seventeenth century.'

To this day, local writers and officials remember Maurice Collis with great affection and as for Samuel White... well, the 'notorious interloper' of the 17th century has become a hero of the 20th century. They say that the ghosts of pirates massacred in White's time still haunt the 'House on the Ridge' and that Collis' 'Chinese Language Tree' (*ta-yok sa-ga*), mentioned in *Into Hidden Burma*, still hangs over the 'avenue gate'. By the water's edge stands a headstone bearing the following inscription:

'H... LYETH T... BODY OF MA...... .. SAM WHITE.......... THIS LIF....O DONI 1682...... ERGO RESURGAM.'

It is the headstone of Samuel White's wife Mary who died of dysentery complicated by a miscarriage in September 1682. As Collis relates in *Siamese White*:

'One of my predecessors at Mergui, Mr. J. S. Furnivall, made in 1917 the interesting discovery of her gravestone. Out walking one day in the town he noticed an Indian washerman pounding clothes on a slab in the manner of his country. His eye caught an inscription upon the stone...

'It was beyond question Mary White's headstone. Where her bones now lie, no one knows. Mr. Furnivall rescued the stone from the washerman... He set it up, strongly reinforced, at the entrance to the port under an ancient tree, where it now stands.'

Today the state insists that Mergui be called 'Myeik', though to the locals it is known as 'Beik' (actually 'Byeik' slurred to 'Beik'), from the local Tavoyan dialect which pronounces 'My' written combinations as 'By' or 'Ba'. The old Admiralty's chart refers to the town as 'Tenasary' (from the old name for Tenasserim), whilst in White's day — and even before — Mergui appeared as 'Mergen', 'Mergee', 'Merjee', 'Mergy', 'Merguy', 'Merghi', 'Merguim' and even 'Mirgim'. In fact, Butler's *Gazetteer of the Mergui District* (1884) states:

> 'By the Burmese the district is called Myatmyo but pronounced Beitmyo. The word "myat" literally means a fringe or border, and was probably given as a name to the Mergui district from its forming the outer fringe or border of the Burmese dominions. How such a name came to be transposed into English as Mergui I have been unable to discover; nor can I even suggest an explanation.'

Getting there

Unlike in White's time, when Mergui was reached by boat, foreigners these days arrive by plane. Readers of *Golden Earth* by Norman Lewis will not need reminding of his opinion of Mergui 'Airport':

> 'The airport was a prairie of burnt grass surrounded by bush. Snacks were being served in a palm-leaf shack, and an official who attached himself in an informal, almost abstracted way, led me to this and ordered cups of thick sweet tea, and hard-boiled eggs, for which he would not allow me to pay. A few soldiers were hanging about, and presently these scattered to various points of the perimeter, where they took up positions behind light machine-guns. An army lorry came charging up, loaded with more troops, who tumbled out and formed two ranks. They were smartly turned out in British uniforms, with knife-edge creases in the right places. Eyes were turned skywards in response to a faint throbbing and the Sunday-plane came into sight, glinting distantly. Dropping down gently, as if lowered on a thread, to land, it disappeared, absorbed in the heat-haze, from which it suddenly burst forth almost upon us. The plane, a Dakota, stopped, with its idly slapping propellers raising squalls of dust. A door opened and a military figure leaped down. Two officers ran forward, saluted and shook hands. One raised a Leica to his eye. There was a yelp of command, in traditionally unrecognizable English, followed by a smacking of butts as arms were correctly presented. A Brigadier had arrived to take over operations in the South.
>
> 'The normal seating equipment of the Sunday-plane had been removed to allow the carriage of more passengers and freight. We sat on what looked like theatre-queue stools, with backs. The airline had a reputation for keeping its planes in the air as much as possible and the floor was littered with the debris of several previous trips.'

The sun sets on the Irrawaddy River

The future of Burma. Top left: Street-side vendor on the 'Road to Moulmein' Top right: By the big bell, Kipling's Pagoda, Moulmein

Bottom: Frolicking in a creek, Mandalay

Norman Lewis was writing about the airport at Mergui as it was in 1951. Over 40 years later, the burnt grass, the bush, the palm-leaf shack, the thick sweet tea, the soldiers and the overloaded plane are still there. The only difference is that these days the soldiers wear Burmese not British uniforms, the plane is a Fokker not a Dakota, and the official makes you pay for his tea. Lewis also never mentioned the prisoners in chain-gangs labouring in the stifling heat on the runway: perhaps in his time, they weren't there.

Mice-infested Mergui 'shack' is served daily from Rangoon — in fact on Monday, Tuesday, Thursday and Friday two flights are scheduled. Flying time is 1 hour 5 minutes and costs US$90 one way (F-27), US$100 (F-28). On Monday and Saturday there are flights from Tavoy (50 minutes; F-27 US$35, F-28 US$40); on Tuesday, Thursday and Friday from Kawthaung, one hour away (F-27 US$50; F-28 US$55) and on Wednesday from Moulmein (1 hour 50 minutes (US$75 & US$85). The two red helicopters and twin-prop that come and go from Mergui Airport are, alas, nothing to do with Myanma Airways. They belong to a Texaco/Canadian franchise drilling for oil nearby and the Canadians are kept well apart from tourists and the citizens of Mergui.

Where to stay and eat
Mergui may be the capital of Tenasserim Division, but it is more renowned for the habitat of birds with edible nests than for accommodation for foreigners. The majority of visitors must suffer the indignity of the **Ein-Daw-Phyu Guest House** (White House Guest House — but no similarity with the building in Washington) at No 57, Kan Phya Main Road, which charges K100 for a minute single room and K200 for a double. The communal showers and toilets defy description. As Harold Braund wrote in his story entitled *Where the South Seas Begin*, 'Of tourist traffic there was virtually none: the quality of Mergui's hostelry saw to that'.

Visitors with the right 'connections' can stay at the government resthouse, *Annawa,* meaning 'sea' or 'ocean' in Pali, and the best located of any I know in Burma. It is situated next to the splendid Thein-daw-gyi Pagoda overlooking Mergui's clock tower, harbour and the island of Pataw-Patit. Spacious rooms with fan and mosquito net cost K500, though the shared bathrooms — watch out for the giant spiders — may not be to everyone's liking. But as you sit on the veranda, sipping plain tea and looking out as perhaps Samuel White did in 1677, you forget about the toilet.

Mergui boasts one of the best 'rural' restaurants in Burma: the **Bamboo House** (*Wah Ein*), which is clean, friendly and, as the name implies, constructed out of bamboo. I would also recommend the **Sakhan-tha** and **Welcome Restaurants** (Chinese), the **Karaweik Cold Drinks Store** and the **Black Cat** and **Meikset** tea/coffee shops. The

Karani Restaurant & Cold Drinks, run by a charming Indian gentleman, proudly asserts '1945 ESTABLISHED', whilst for breakfast, drop by the tea shop (no name) located at No 121, Zay-lan (Market Road). Mergui market itself, which is vast, is particularly interesting.

What to see
Marred only by the forced labour all round the town (noticeably at the airport and on the golf course), Mergui is the most scenic place in Burma. With its winding streets that go up and down in every direction and make motorbikes and bicycles prized items, its archipelago, the third largest reclining Buddha in the land and the most idyllic pagoda (the Paw-daw-mu-aung theik-di-gon), Mergui is a traveller's paradise.

The **Paw-daw-mu-aung theik-di-gon** ('Pagoda which appeared by itself'), overlooking the sea and rubber plantations, could not be more perfectly positioned. The approach through the rubber trees and stunning *zaungdan* is simply breathtaking. There are three golden stupas mounted on a four-sided shrine. The middle stupa is the biggest, constructed on a square basement. There are four golden stupas on the basement. The pagoda, which was renovated 40 years ago, enshrines one hair relic of the Buddha.

Curiously enough, I have only been able to trace one mention of this pagoda — in a book entitled *The New Burma* (1940) by W J Grant, late editor of the *Rangoon Times*. In his chapter 'Tavoy and Mergue', Grant writes:

'I don't know much about Tavoy. I have never been there, but I have been in Mergue. I have played golf there. The golf course shares a field with a pagoda. In front of the first tee there is a tank. A devil of a tank. My first ball went into it; so did my second; so did my third. By this time one of the caddies who could swim had recovered the first. And I'm hanged if it didn't go into the tank a second time!

'As a caddie has only one life I decided to walk to the second tee. It was a glorious afternoon. My companions were the highly placed officers of the good ship Juno. We played in pairs, and I had the chief engineer. A more amiable soul never rolled a putt. I think I took 79 for nine holes; he took 53. Pride shone in his quiet, grey eyes for the rest of the voyage. Never was human heart more triumphant, for he took golf very, very seriously. Round and round the pagoda we went, now seeing it from this angle, then from that. It crowned a green mound in the centre, and somehow I could not get away from the feeling that I was on holy ground. Around us grew tall palms and thick clumps of bamboo. It was the monsoon season, and all things were green and wet and solemn. A sense of remoteness prevailed. We might have been on an uncharted island of the Pacific. No wind, no sun, no movement; only a tropical luxuriance, a warm, engentling stillness. An afternoon I shall never forget.

'I remember watching a slow, grey cloud bow a cumulous head as it passed over the pagoda. Are clouds all Buddhists, or have they only an instinctive holiness?'

The **Hpaya ko-zu** (Nine Images Pagoda) contains the World Water Ordination Hall (*Kaba-lon-yay-thein*): a Buddha seated on a lotus throne in an ordination hall surrounded by a moat. *Yay-thein* means an 'ordination hall erected in shallow water'. The light orange global-shaped dome is topped with a *hti*. There is a light blue stupa encircled by small stupas with eight different animals, representing the days of the week: Sunday — galon bird, Monday — tiger, Tuesday — lion, Wednesday morning — elephant with tusks, Wednesday afternoon — elephant without tusks, Thursday — rat, Friday — guinea pig and Saturday — naga.

Mergui's most celebrated pagoda, and the one first glimpsed by travellers of old who arrived by boat, is the **Thein-daw-gyi** (Great Ordination Hall). Currently under renovation, it consists of a large ordination hall and a big golden stupa surrounded by four smaller golden stupas. There is a large sitting image of the Buddha in front of a reclining Buddha, and a peculiar image sitting on a chair (not unlike the celebrated image at Kyaikmaraw). There is also a preaching hall and museum. The Thein-daw-gyi offers a wondrous view of Mergui harbour and Pataw-Patit.

> 'I awoke before dawn and watched the sun come up behind the golden pagoda. My first impression was a jet-black cone gleaming with spirals of light, while below the town and harbour lay hushed in sleep. Gradually the sky turned to silver with sombre bands of cloud, the lights on the pagoda lost their radiance, and its slender spire, silhouetted against a silver sky, turned every shade of colour, from palest turquoise to flaming bronze, until the sun burst above the rim of the horizon, and the pagoda gleamed like plates of beaten gold.'
>
> *Hunter's Moon*, Leonard Handley, 1933

To the right of the Thein-daw-gyi, as you approach from the sea, is the **Bu-hpaya**, whilst another pagoda — the **Atula Lawka Marazein** — contains a huge sitting Buddha image surrounded by smaller images.

Of the many islands in the archipelago, the one closest to the port of Mergui, and consequently the best known, is **Pataw-Patit**. This island has been described many times by past travellers. In *Siamese White*, Collis first writes:

> 'After another ten miles the ship makes Pataw island, rising some eight hundred feet, the lower part covered with fruit trees, especially duryans, mangosteens and jackfruit.'

In *Into Hidden Burma*, Collis adds:

> 'Mergui was so tucked away from interlocking islands, that when you lifted
> your eyes to what lay beyond the wharf, it was not the open bay that
> confronted you but a water half a mile broad, bounded on its west side by
> an island called Pataw-Patit, and forming the anchorage known as Mergui
> harbour. From my vantage on the ridge I could see over the saddle of
> Pataw-Patit to other islands stretching to the western horizon, particularly
> King Island, twenty-five miles long and with peaks rising to three thousand
> feet...
> 'South of my grounds the ridge ended and below me were the roofs of the
> Nauk-le quarter of the town, whose edge was the mouth of the Tenasserim
> river with its fringe of mangrove swamp. Opposite here, the island of
> Pataw-Patit was covered with pagodas and monasteries.'

Pataw-Patit (the south end is called 'Patit') is just five minutes by boat
from the jetty and offers spectacular views of Mergui and the Thein-daw-
gyi Pagoda. The old chart referred to the island as 'Madramacon', the
name of a shrine on Patit, where sailors wishing safe passage came to
pay homage. On the island — or beach, to be more precise — they have
renovated what is claimed to be the third largest reclining Buddha in
Burma (now complete in a covered shelter). Whether or not this assertion
is true, I know not, but I do know that with a name consisting of 43
letters, it is certainly the longest in that respect. The Atularanthi-patit-
taung shwe-tha-lyaung-hpaya-gyi was built in 1956 (1317 BE), is 216ft
long and 57ft tall. Unlike the giant reclining Buddhas at Tavoy and Pegu,
you can actually go inside this one.

The ordination hall of the Kok-thein-na-yon Monastery contains a
reclining image, depicting, it is asserted, the Lord Buddha suffering from
dysentery, with his physician Ziwaka grinding medicinal herbs with
which to treat him. There is also an unusual image of the Buddha lying
on his deathbed surrounded by his disciples. One disciple, Ananda, is
standing, his back towards the Buddha, his hands covering his eyes. Also
peculiar is the donation box which is carved from a flying elephant.
Some of the images in the ordination hall are Siamese. The name 'Kok-
thein-na-yon' is the Burmese rendition of Kusinara, the village where the
Buddha died, and is often given to a shelter or resthouse.

In the precinct of the monastery is the Sulamani Stupa, which takes its
name from a stupa constructed by a Brahma in the abode of *devas*. The
stupa overlooks the Yay-dat-chaung (Naval Creek).

In the Kan-pya (pond end) quarter lies a large lotus lake, which locals
claim produces the country's biggest lotus flowers and leaves. Boat races
take place on the lake.

Residents of Mergui assert that their archipelago consists of some
4,800 registered islands. Yet one-time 'governor' of Mergui Maurice

Maybury wrote in *Swan-Song of the Heaven-Born*, the final volume of his trilogy *Heaven-Born in Burma*:

'While waiting in Rangoon I had learned a good deal about Mergui and was able to tell them something of the 804 islands, mostly uninhabited, which make up the Mergui Archipelago...'

There are islands with names such as 'Banana', 'Elephant' (shaped like an elephant sleeping!), 'Poor' (*Kyun-mweh,* since nothing can be grown there) and 'Entwined Snake' (*Kon-mway-kyun*). Topped with a white stupa, 'Entwined Snake Island' is so-called because it takes the form of two snakes intertwined.

After Kalakyun (passing the odd *ngabyan,* flying fish!) comes **King Island** with, as Collis, wrote 'its deep bays fringed with the richest fruit gardens in Indo-China'. King Island is known these days as *Kyun-suu,* 'Island gather together'. A white stupa *Than-thayar-aye-myo-u-zedi* (literally 'The pagoda at the top of the town, the end of rebirth') greets all visitors to King Island, home to a naval base that is strictly out of bounds to foreigners. The island, which became a township in 1981, has one guesthouse that is certainly better than the Ein-Daw-Phyu on the mainland. However the island is unlikely to appeal to tourists since there is no beach (Banana Island has one — but no accommodation), and all foreigners are required to take with them an escort of two armed guards and one Military Intelligence official. Of further discomfort to visitors is the hydro-electric power station (which doesn't function), built by 'patriotic' labour which, it is claimed, resulted in the death of 80% of the workforce.

Three miles due west of King Island lies **Maingy Island** — referred to as 'Mingyi' by the locals — which was named after A D Maingy, administrator of Tenasserim from 1825 to 1834. The island is 'home' to the Salon people, the so-called 'sea gypsies' (many in fact live on boats, as they are frequently attacked on land). Only about 400 still remain and they make their living by diving for pearls, ambergris, abalone, sea-slugs, shells and fish and climbing the precipitous rocks in search of edible birds' nests. Inhabitants of the archipelago, particularly the officials, speak slightingly of the Salon, whom they claim are addicted to opium.

There is no public or tourist boat to take visitors round the archipelago. Foreigners must hire a private/government boat, which costs a minimum of K6,000 (US$60) for one day.

'So much for the persons of this narrative. But I am forgetting — there is still one character left, Mergui itself. What happened there in the end? Has it had a history since? In a sense, it has had a history, for in 1765 the Burmese conqueror, Alaungpaya, descended upon it, slaughtered its inhabitants and incorporated it in Burma; and in 1824 the English frigates arrived again, this time to take and keep it. But in the sense of an important or dramatic history, it has had none. Its severance from Siam ruined it commercially. It became and has remained a little coastal port. The ordinary people there are the same as ever they were; there is plenty to eat and drink in that little paradise; but no more do personages from overseas pass through it and no one like White has sat on the ridge.'

Siamese White, Maurice Collis, 1951

FURTHER READING

A must for anyone interested in Burma is Patricia Herbert's superb annotated bibliography *Burma,* Volume 132 in the World Bibliographical Series, 1991, published by Clio Press of Oxford (tel: 01865 311350, fax: 01865 311358). This is available through Plymbridge Distributors Ltd, Plymbridge House, Estover Road, Plymouth PL6 7PZ, tel: 01752 695745, fax: 01752 695699, or can be found in good university libraries.

The author lists more than 1,500 works on Burma (books, booklets and articles) — commented on pithily and incisively, cross-referred and skilfully indexed. The entries are grouped under 30 subject headings. Besides the usual ones — history, politics, religion, economics — there are sections on art, flora and fauna, Western novels on Burma, and on war memoirs. If you do not know an author's name, you can find a work under its title or if necessary locate it by using the subject index. For the author, its compilation was 'like my feelings for Burma, an expression of love tinged with despair'.

Those intrigued by the excerpts from the various books on Burma will be interested in the *Traveller's Literary Companion to South-east Asia,* published by In Print Publishing Ltd, 9 Beaufort Terrace, Brighton BN2 2SU, tel: 01273 682836, fax: 01273 620958.

John Randall, 47 Moreton Street, London SW1V 2NY, tel: 0171 630 5531, fax: 0171 821 6544, has the best selection of books on Burma (especially secondhand, rare and out-of-print — as well as current titles).

Other antiquarian booksellers who occasionally come up with books on Burma are:

Bates and Hindmarch, Bridge Street, Boroughbridge, York YO5 9LA, tel/fax: 01423 324258

Clive Farahar, XIV The Green, Calne, Wilts SN11 8DQ, tel: 01249 821121, fax: 01249 821202

Hugh Ashley Rayner FRGS, Southstoke House, Packhorse Lane, Southstoke, Bath BA2 7DJ, tel/fax: 01225 840891

Ulysses, 31 & 40 Museum Street, London WC1A 1LH, tel/fax: 0171 831 1600

The *National Geographic Magazine* has also published — and continues to do so — some fascinating articles on Burma.

Travellers' tales

Ainsworth, L, *A Merchant Adventurer among the Sea Gipsies,* Nisbet & Co, 1930

Anderson, J, *The Irawady and its Sources,* Royal Geographical Society, 1870
Mandalay to Momien, Macmillan and Co, 1876

Bixler, N, *Burmese Journey,* The Antioch Press, Ohio, 1967

Cuming, E, *In the Shadow of the Pagoda: Sketches of Burmese Life and Character,* W H Allen & Co Ltd, 1897

Ellis, B, *An English Girl's First Impressions of Burmah,* R Platt, Wigan, 1899

Edmonds, P, *Peacocks and Pagodas,* George Routledge, 1924

Ferrars, M & B, *Burma,* Sampson, Low, Marston and Company, 1900

Gascoigne, G, *Among Pagodas And Fair Ladies: An account of a tour through Burma,* A D Innes & Co, 1896

Gordon, C, *Our Trip to Burmah: With Notes on that Country,* Baillière, Tindall and Cox, 1877

Gordon, R, *On the Ruby Mines near Mogok, Burma,* Royal Geographical Society, 1888

Harris, W, *East For Pleasure,* Edward Arnold, 1929

'Jeff', *Elizabeth Visits Burma,* Thacker & Company Limited, Bombay, 1910

Kessel, J, *Mogok: The Valley of Rubies,* (translated from the French), MacGibbon & Kee, 1960

Mitton, G, *A Bachelor Girl in Burma,* A & C Black, 1907

Murdoch, W, *From Edinburgh to India & Burmah,* George Routledge & Sons Ltd, 1908

Nickerson, M, *Burma Interlude,* Topgallant Publishing Co Ltd, Honolulu, 1981

Outram, F & Fane, G, *Burma Road, Back Door to China,* The National Geographic Magazine, Volume LXXVIII, Number Five, November 1940

Park, R, *Recollections and Red Letter Days: Being the Sojournings of two Pilgrims in the East,* privately published, 1916

Paske, C, *Myamma: A Retrospect of Life and Travel in Lower Burmah,* W H Allen & Co, 1893

Powell, J, *Mandalay to Bhamo,* American Baptist Mission Press, Rangoon, 1922

Raven-Hart, R, *Canoe to Mandalay,* Frederick Muller Ltd, 1946

Slater, R, *Guns through Arcady: Burma and The Burma Road,* Angus and Robertson Ltd, Sydney, 1941

Stanford, J, *Far Ridges: A Record of Travel in North-Eastern Burma 1938-39,* C & J Temple Ltd, 1944

Williams, C, *Through Burmah to Western China,* William Blackwood and Sons, 1868

Woodthorpe, R, *Explorations on the Chindwin River, Upper Burma,* Royal Geographical Society, London, 1888

History, politics & economics

Allott, A, *Inked Over, Ripped Out: Burmese Storytellers and the Censors,* Pen American Center, New York, 1993; Silkworm Books, Chiang Mai, 1994
Burmese Ways, Index on Censorship (File on Burma), Volume 23 (new series) No 3, July/August 1994, Index on Censorship, London, 1994

Amnesty International, *MYANMAR: Human rights developments July to December 1993,* Amnesty International, January 1994
THAILAND: Burmese and other asylum-seekers at risk, Amnesty International, September 1994
MYANMAR: Human rights still denied, Amnesty International, November 1994

Asia Watch, *A Modern Form of Slavery: Trafficking of Burmese Women and Girls into Brothels in Thailand,* Asia Watch and The Women's Rights Project, Human Rights Watch, New York, 1993

Aung San Suu Kyi, *Freedom From Fear,* Penguin, 1991
Towards a True Refuge, The Refugee Studies Programme with The Perpetua Press, 1993

Brodrick, A, *Beyond the Burma Road,* Hutchinson & Co, 1944

Christian, J, *Burma,* Collins, 1945

Clements, A & Kean, L, *Burma's Revolution of the Spirit: The Struggle for Democratic Freedom and Dignity,* Aperture Foundation, New York, 1994

Collis, M, *The Burmese Scene: Political, Historical, Pictorial,* John Crowther Ltd, (no date)

Cox, H, *Journal of a Residence in the Burmhan Empire, and more particularly at the Court of Amarapoorah,* John Warren and G and W B Whittaker, London, 1821

Fytche, A, *Burma, Past and Present,* (two volumes), C Kegan Paul & Co, 1878

Grant, W, *The New Burma,* George Allen and Unwin Ltd, 1940

Hall, D, *Early English Intercourse with Burma,* Longmans, Green and Co, 1928

Harvey, G, *History of Burma,* Longmans, Green & Co, 1925

Haskings, F, *Burma Yesterday and Tomorrow,* Thacker & Co Ltd, Bombay, 1944

Khun Sa, *His Life and His Speeches,* Shan Herald Agency for News, 1993

Kin Oung, *Who Killed Aung San?,* White Lotus, Bangkok, 1993

Lintner, B, *Outrage,* White Lotus, Bangkok, 1990

Matthews, B (ed), *Religion, Culture And Political Economy in Burma,* Research Monograph No 3, 1993, Centre for Southeast Asian Research, University of British Columbia, Canada, 1993

Maung Maung Pye, *Burma in the Crucible,* Khittaya Publishing House, Rangoon, 1952

Mya Maung, *Totalitarianism in Burma: Prospects for Economic Development,* Paragon House, New York, 1992
On the Road to Mandalay: A Case Study of the Sinonization of Upper Burma, Asian Survey, Vol XXXIV, No 5, May 1994, University of California Press

National Coalition Government of the Union of Burma, *Ye-Tavoy Railway Construction: Report on Forced Labour in the Mon State and Tenasserim Division in Burma,* NCGUB, 1994

Pe Maung Tin & Luce, G, *The Glass Palace Chronicle of the Kings of Burma,* (translated from Burmese), Rangoon University Press, 1960

Pointon, A, *The Bombay Burmah Trading Corporation Limited 1863-1963,* The Millbrook Press Limited, Southampton, 1964

Project Maje, *A Swamp Full of Lilies: Human Rights Violations Committed by Units/Personnel of Burma's Army, 1992-1993,* Project Maje, New Jersey, 1994

Scott, J (Shway Yoe), *Burma As It Was, As It Is, And As It Will Be,* George Redway, 1886

Silverstein, J, *Burma: Military Rule and the Politics of Stagnation,* Cornell University Press, 1977

Smith, M, *State of Fear: Censorship in Burma (Myanmar),* Article 19, London, 1991
Burma: Insurgency and the Politics of Ethnicity, Zed Books Ltd, 1993
Paradise Lost? The Suppression of Environmental Rights and Freedom of Expression in Burma, Article 19, London, 1994
Ethnic Groups in Burma: Development, Democracy and Human Rights, Anti-Slavery International, London, 1994
Censorship Prevails: Political Deadlock and Economic Transition in Burma, Article 19, London, 1995

Snodgrass, J, *Narrative of the Burmese War,* J Murray, 1827

Spearman, H (compiler), *Gazetteer of Burma,* (two volumes), Cultural Publishing House, Delhi, 1983

Stuart, J, *Burma Through the Centuries,* Kegan Paul, Trench, Truebner & Co, 1909

Tinker, H (ed), Burma: *The Struggle for Independence 1944-1948, (Constitutional Relations between Britain and Burma),* (two volumes), Her Majesty's Stationery Office, London, 1983-84

Weller, M (ed), *Democracy and Politics in Burma: A Collection of Documents,* Gvt Printing Office of the NCGUB, Thailand, 1993

Culture & art

Aung Thaw, *Historical Sites in Burma,* Sarpay Beikman Press, Rangoon, 1978

Forchhammer, E, *Notes on the Early History and Geography of British Burma,* Rangoon, 1883
Papers on Subjects Relating to the Archaeology of Burma including Arakan I, Mahamuni Pagoda II, Mrohaung III, Launggyet, Minbya, Urittaung, Akyab and Sandoway, Rangoon, 1891, rev 1895
Report on the Antiquities of Arakan, Superintendent of Government Printing, Rangoon, 1892

Fraser-Lu, S, *Burmese Crafts Past and Present,* Oxford University Press, Kuala Lumpur, 1994

Gilhodes, C, *The Kachins: Religion and Customs,* Catholic Orphan Press, Calcutta, 1922

Griswold, A, etc, *Art of the World: Burma, Korea, Tibet,* Methuen, 1964

Khin Zaw, *Burmese Culture: General and Particular,* Sarpay Beikman, Rangoon, 1981

Ma Thanegi, *The Illusion of Life: Burmese Marionettes,* White Orchid Press, Bangkok, 1994

Mi Mi Khaing, *Burmese Family,* Longmans, Green & Co, Calcutta, 1946
The World of Burmese Women, Zed Books Ltd, 1984

San Tha Aung, *The Buddhist Art of Ancient Arakan,* Daw Saw Saw, Rangoon, 1979

Geography, flora & fauna

Cox, E, *Farrer's Last Journey: Upper Burma, 1919-20,* Dulau & Co, 1926

Evans, G, *Big-Game Shooting in Upper Burma,* Longmans, Green, and Co, 1911

Kingdon-Ward, F, *Return to the Irrawaddy,* Andrew Melrose, 1956
Plant Hunting on the Edge of the World, Minerva, 1974 (see also Whitehead, J)

Pollok, F & Thom, W, *Wild Sports of Burma and Assam,* Hurst and Blackett Ltd, 1900

Smythies, B, *The Birds of Burma,* Oliver and Boyd, 1953

Whitehead, J (ed), *Himalayan Enchantment: An Anthology, Frank Kingdon-Ward,* Serindia Publications, 1990

Language

John, R, *Burmese Self-Taught,* Asian Educational Services, New Delhi, 1991

Okell, J, *First Steps in Burmese,* available from the School of Oriental and African Studies (University of London), 1989 (includes five cassettes)

Four volume modern course in Burmese (1994), consisting of: an Introduction to the Spoken Language, Book 1 (with 12 tapes); an Introduction to the Spoken Language, Book 2 (14 tapes), an Introduction to the Script (seven tapes) and an Introduction to the Literary Style (one tape). Total cost US$158, plus US$4 shipping and handling. Contact the Center for Southeast Asian Studies, 412 Adams Hall, Northern Illinois University, DeKalb, IL 60115, USA, tel: (815) 753 1651, fax: (815) 753 1771

Religion

Baillie, J, *Rivers in the Desert: Or, Mission-Scenes in Burmah,* Seeley, Jackson, and Halliday, 1858

Bigandet, P, *The Life or Legend of Gaudama The Buddha of the Burmese,* Truebner and Co, 1880

Byles, M, *Journey into Burmese Silence,* George Allen & Unwin Ltd, 1962

Herbert, P, *The Life of the Buddha,* The British Library, 1993

Holmes, E, *The Creed of Buddha,* The Bodley Head, 1949

Knowles, J, *Life of Mrs. Ann H. Judson, late Missionary to Burmah; with an account of the American Baptist Mission to that Empire,* American Sunday School Union, Philadelphia, (no date, 1830?)

Marrat, J, *The Apostle of Burma. A Memoir of Adoniram Judson D.D.,* Charles H Kelly, 1890

Maung Htin Aung, *Folk Elements in Burmese Buddhism,* Rangoon, 1959

Sayadaw U Pannavamsa *The Life of Buddha in Pictures,* Ministry of Trade, Burma, (no date)

Titcomb, J, *Personal Recollections of British Burma And its Church Mission Work In 1878-79,* Wells Gardner, Darton, & Co, 1880

Venerable Sayadaw U Janakabhivamsa, *Vipassana Meditation: Lectures on Insight Meditation,* Chanmyay Yeiktha Meditation Centre, Rangoon, (no date)

Novels & tales

Chan-Toon, M, *A Marriage in Burmah,* Greening & Co, 1909

Collis, M, *Siamese White,* Faber and Faber, 1951

Keely H & Price C, *The City of the Dagger and Other Tales from Burma,* Frederick Warne & Co Ltd, 1972

Khin Myo Chit, *Anawrahta of Burma,* Sarpay Beikman Press, Rangoon, 1970
A Wonderland of Burmese Legends, The Tamarind Press, Bangkok, 1984

Ma Ma Lay, *Not Out Of Hate,* (translated from Burmese), Ohio University Center for International Studies, 1991

Mannin, E, *The Living Lotus,* Jarrolds Publishers Ltd, 1956

Mimosa, *Told On The Pagoda: Tales of Burmah,* T Fisher Unwin, 1895

Orwell, G, *Burmese Days,* Penguin, 1989

Pereira, M, *Stranger in the Land,* Geoffrey Bles, 1967

Autobiographies, biographies & memoirs (including the wars)

Beamish, J, *Burma Drop,* Elek Books, 1958

Chapman, C, *Glints of Gold (Burma),* Lucknow Publishing House, Lucknow, 1943

Collis, M, *The Journey Outward: An Autobiography,* Faber and Faber, 1952
Into Hidden Burma, Faber and Faber, 1954

Denny, J, *Chindit Indiscretion,* Christopher Johnson, 1956

Doveton, F, *Reminiscences of the Burmese War In 1824-5-6,* Allen and Co, 1852

Gouger, H, *The Prisoner in Burmah: Personal Narrative of Two Years' Imprisonment in Burmah,* John Murray, 1860

Ludu U Hla, *The Caged Ones,* (translated from Burmese), The Tamarind Press, Bangkok, 1986

Maybury, M, *Heaven-Born in Burma,* (three volumes), Folio Hadspen, Castle Cary, 1984-86

Mitton, G, *Scott of the Shan Hills: Orders and Impressions,* John Murray, 1936

Morrison, I, *Grandfather Longlegs: The Life and Gallant Death of Major H. P. Seagrim,* Faber and Faber, 1947

Morse, E, *Exodus To A Hidden Valley,* Collins, 1973

Nu, U, *Saturday's Son: Memoirs of the former Prime Minister of Burma,* Yale University Press, 1975

On Kin, *Burma Under The Japanese,* Lucknow Publishing House, Lucknow, 1947

Rodger, G, *Red Moon Rising,* The Cresset Press, 1943

Rodriguez, H, *Helen of Burma,* Collins, 1983

Sargent, I, *Twilight over Burma: My Life as a Shan Princess,* University of Hawaii Press; Silkworm Books, Chiang Mai, 1994

Scott, J (Shway Yoe), *The Burman: His Life and Notions,* (two volumes), Macmillan, 1882

Seagrave, G, *Burma Surgeon,* Victor Gollancz, 1944
Burma Surgeon Returns, Victor Gollancz, 1946
My Hospital in the Hills, Robert Hale, 1957

Short, S, *On Burma's Eastern Frontier,* Marshall, Morgan & Scott Ltd, 1945

Stibbe, P, *Return via Rangoon,* Leo Cooper, 1994

Trant, T, (published anonymously), *Two Years in Ava: from May 1824 to May 1826,* John Murray, 1827

White, A, *The Burma of 'AJ',* BACSA, 1991

White H, *A Civil Servant in Burma,* Edward Arnold, 1913

General

Aung Aung Taik, *Under the Golden Pagoda: The Best of Burmese Cooking,* Chronicle Books, San Francisco, 1993

Bryce, J, *Burma: the Country and People,* Royal Geographical Society, London, 1886

Hla Pe, *Burmese Proverbs,* John Murray, 1962

Houtman, G, *Burmese Personal Names,* Dept of Religious Affairs, Rangoon, 1982

Huerlimann, M, *Burma, Ceylon, Indo-China, Siam, Cambodia, Annam, Tongking, Yunnan: Landscape, Architecture, Inhabitants,* B Westermann Co Inc, New York, 1930

Hunt, L & Kenny, A, *On Duty Under A Tropical Sun,* W H Allen & Co, 1883

Maung Myint Thein, *When At Night I Strive To Sleep: A Book of Verse,* The Asoka Society, 1971
Burmese Proverbs Explained in Verse, Rangoon, 1984
Burmese Folk-Songs, Writers Workshop, Calcutta, 1987

Mi Mi Khaing, *Cook And Entertain The Burmese Way,* Daw Khin Myo Chit, (no date)

Oolay (Conway Poole, M), *Ballads of Burma (Anecdotal and Analytical),* W Thacker & Co, 1912

POSTSCRIPT

'Democracy is not a mere form of government, nor even government by a majority. The statement that its purpose is to secure the greatest good for the greatest number is, like most simplifications, wholly inadequate and misleading. True Democracy is much more than that. It is an inner spirit, an attitude to life. It implies a spirit of toleration, an inbred hatred of oppression, the readiness to grant equal rights and equal opportunities to all. It implies that no one shall be allowed to enjoy an advantage at the expense of his fellowmen...

'I want to see Burma free — free from domination, free to manage her own affairs, free to develop in the way that best suits the genius of her people. This may seem to imply that I advocate absolute and complete independence. But now-a-days such a thing is impossible. The ends of the earth are so linked together that mankind has become, in a sense, one family. The solidarity of the human race is such that if one nation suffers distress or famine there are immediately worldwide repercussions. An international society is no longer a dream of the past, but a present urgent reality. We must therefore recognize that in the present state of the world an international authority is indispensible. How else can a small country like Burma, wedged in between powerful neighbours, enjoy the freedom she is demanding?'

Rev U On Kin, District Superintendent, Methodist Church,
Twante, Burma 1947

BURMA DIRECTORY

Political groups

All Burma Students' Democratic Front (ABSDF), c/o Aung Naing, UK, tel: 0171 289 2070
Europe, PO Box 6720, St Olavs Plass, N-0130 Oslo, tel: (42) 22 608597, fax: (42) 22 608598
Thailand, PO Box 1352, GPO, Bangkok 10501, tel/fax: (662) 587 2400

All Burma Students Relief Fund (ABSRF), 105 Harrowes Meade, Edgware, Middx HA8 8RS, tel/fax: 0181 958 2111

Amnesty International, 99-119 Rosebery Avenue, London EC1R 4RE, tel: 0171 814 6200, fax: 0171 833 1510

Asian-American Free Labor Institute (AAFLI), 1925 K Street, NW, Suite 301, Washington, DC 20006, USA, tel: (202) 778 4500, fax: (202) 778 4525

Asia Watch, *see* Human Rights/Asia

Burma Action Group UK (BAG UK), Collins Studios, Collins Yard, Islington Green, London N1 2XU, tel: 0171 359 7679, fax: 0171 354 3987

Burma Affairs Monitor, 3a Chatto Road, London SW11 6LJ, tel/fax: 0171 924 3147

The Burma Project USA, 10 Robertson Terrace, Mill Valley, CA 94941, USA, tel: (415) 924 6447, fax: (415) 381 1326

Burmese Relief Center-Japan, 266-27 Ozuku-cho, Kashihara-Shi, Nara-ken 634, Japan, tel: (07442) 28236, fax: (07442) 46254

Burmese Relief Centre, PO Box 48, Chiang Mai University, Chiang Mai 50002, Thailand, tel/fax: (53) 216 894

Christian Participation in the Development of Shan, Kayah and Karen State Communities (CPDSK), PO Box 260, Samsennai PO, Bangkok 10400, Thailand

Coalition for Corporate Withdrawal from Burma, Simon Billenness, Chair, Steering Committee, Franklin Research and Development Corporation, 711 Atlantic Avenue, Boston, MA 02111, USA, tel: (617) 423 6655, fax: (617) 482 6179

Committee for Publicity of People's Struggle in Monland (CPPSM), GPO Box 227, Bangkok 10501, Thailand

Democratic Voice of Burma (DVB), see ABSDF (Europe)

Federation of Trade Unions of Burma, U Maung Maung, Secretary, FTUB Co Ltd, GPO Box 1270, Bangkok, Thailand, tel/fax: (662) 300 0123

Human Rights/Asia (formerly Asia Watch), 33 Islington High Street, London N1 9LH, tel: 0171 713 1995, fax: 0171 713 1800; 485 Fifth Avenue, New York, NY 10017-6104, USA, tel: (212) 972 8400, fax: (212) 972 0905

Indigenous Women's Development Centre (IWDC), PO Box 169, Chiang Mai University, Chiang Mai 50200, Thailand, tel/fax: (53) 278 945

International Confederation of Free Trade Unions, Boulevard Emile Jacqmain 155/1, B-1210 Brussels, tel: (32) 2 2240211, fax: (32) 2 2015815/2030756

Karen Human Rights Group (KHRG), PO Box 22, Mae Sot, Tak 63110, Thailand, tel: (662) 332 7554, fax: (662) 332 1924

Liverpool Burma Support Group, 15 Menlove Gardens West, Liverpool L18 2DL, tel: 0151 721 1121

The Norwegian Burma Council, Josefinesgate 9, 0351 Oslo, Norway, tel: (47) 22567910, fax: (47) 22567920

Overseas Mon Young Monks Union, GPO Box 2122, Bangkok 10501, Thailand, tel: (662) 211 2346, fax: (662) 291 9396

Project Maje, 14 Dartmouth Road, Cranford, NJ 07016, USA, tel: (908) 276 8494

Radio Burma, PO Box 39, Bung Thong Luang, Bangkok 10242, Thailand

Representative Office of Kachin Affairs (ROKA), PO Box 822, Bangkok 10110, Thailand

The Seafarers' Union of Burma, Zaw Tun, Secretary, PO Box 34, Huamark Post Office, Bangkok 10243, Thailand, tel/fax: (662) 300 0123

Shan Human Rights Foundation, PO Box 41, Mae Hong Son 58000, Thailand

Shan State Association (USA), PO Box 1144, Washington Grove, MD 20880-1144, USA, fax: (301) 208 8012

Non-political groups & charities
Anti-Slavery International, The Stableyard, Broomgrove Road, London SW9 9TL, tel: 0171 924 9555, fax: 0171 738 4110

The Britain-Burma Society: c/o Mrs Anna Allott, Honorary Secretary, Sorbrook Mill, Bodicote, Banbury, Oxford OX15 4AU, tel: 01295 720142, fax: 01295 721664. Founded in 1957. Monthly lecture meetings held in London

British Association for Cemeteries in South Asia (BACSA), c/o Mr T C Wilkinson, MBE, Honorary Secretary, 76½ Chartfield Avenue, London SW15 6HQ

The Burma Star Association, 4 Lower Belgrave Street, London SW1W 0LA, tel: 0171 823 4273

Dr Cynthia's Clinic and Primary Health Care on the Thai-Burma Border, Dr Cynthia, PO Box 67, Mae Sot, Tak 63110, Thailand, tel: (55) 533644

Prospect Burma, 143 Rivermead Court, Ranelagh Gardens, London SW6 3SE, tel: 0171 371 0887, fax: 0171 371 0547

Religious organisations
The Britain Burma Buddhist Trust, No 1, Old Church Lane, London NW9 8TG, tel: 0181 200 6898

British Buddhist Association, 11 Biddulph Road, London W9 1JA, tel: 0171 286 5575

Centres of Burma studies & library collections
Center for Burma Studies, Adams Hall 410, Northern Illinois University, DeKalb, IL 60115-2854, USA, tel: (815) 753 0512, fax: (815) 753 0198

Department of South East Asia, School of Oriental and African Studies (SOAS), University of London, Thornhaugh Street, Russell Square, London WC1H 0XG, tel: 0171 637 2388, fax: 0171 436 3844

Oriental and India Office Collections (British Library), 197 Blackfriars Road, London SE1 8NG, tel: 0171 412 7873, fax: 0171 412 7858. Contact Patricia Herbert

Publications

Article 19, Lancaster House, 33 Islington High Street, London N1 9LH, tel: 0171 278 9292, fax: 0171 713 1356

Asian Survey, Institute of East Asian Studies, University of California, Room 408, 6701 San Pablo Avenue, Oakland, CA 94608, USA, tel: (510) 642 0978, fax: (510) 643 9930

Burma Alert, c/o Harn Yawnghwe, RR4, Shawville, J0X 2Y0, Quebec, Canada, tel: (819) 647 5405, fax: (819) 647 5403

Burma Debate, PO Box 19126, Washington, DC 20036, fax: (301) 983 5011

Far Eastern Economic Review, 25/F, Citicorp Centre, 18 Whitfield Road, Causeway Bay, GPO Box 160, Hong Kong, tel: (852) 508 4381, fax: (852) 503 1530

Index on Censorship, Lancaster House, 33 Islington High Street, London N1 9LH, tel: 0171 278 2313, fax: 0171 278 1878; USA, c/o Human Rights Watch, 485 Fifth Avenue, New York, NY 10164-0709

The Irrawaddy (Independent News and Information), PO Box 14154, Silver Spring, MD 20911, USA

PEN American Center, 568 Broadway, New York, NY 10012, USA

Bookseller

Randall, John (Books of Asia), 47 Moreton Street, London SW1V 2NY, tel: 0171 630 5331, fax: 0171 821 6544

AND FINALLY...

The Burman by Walter B Harris, FRGS, FSA

'It was a practical business Scotchman, long settled in Burma, who gave me in a few words a list of the bad qualities of the Burman — and finally confirmed my good opinion of these happy children of the East. "The Burman," he said, "has no stability and is never serious" — O lucky Burman. — "He pays no attention to business and has no ambition to be prosperous, and never thinks about the morrow" — O wise, fortunate Burman, how do you accomplish it? — "He laughs all the time" — Tell me your secret, Burman. — "He is too amorous" — Of course you are, and how can you help it when your women are so attractive? — "He seems to think life is made for pleasure" — Alas, alas, we cannot think that any longer. — "He won't put a suffering animal out of its misery" — Fie, fie, Burman, that is bad. We are so compassionate that we kill all our pheasants and our foxes while they are still strong and well, lest they should suffer later on. You must be kind, O Burman. — "He makes a bad domestic servant" — Of course you do, of course you do. So should I. — "Though by religion he is a Buddhist he is superstitious and believes in 'Nats', good and evil demons" — Naturally, because you know that they really exist, the naughty "Nats", in those wonderful jungle forests of yours.

'You propitiate them with offerings and build them little houses and shrines, and when they are troublesome you drive them out with great noises. How can you help believing in them? Keep your "Nats" and your faith. O delightful Burman! Perhaps in the end you will have to become like us, who believe in little or nothing — and my business friend added: "They are so foolish, the Burmans. My wife and I have tried over and over again to train them, but they can never understand our Scotch ways." — Of course you can't, dear Burman, of course you can't. Nor can I. The foreigner is taking most of what your country has to give but don't let him take your "Nats" or your "Faith" or your joyous laughter. Keep those, for they are invaluable.

'The foreigner will go home a rich man and will likely buy a deer-forest and men will call him "laird", but he will never laugh as you do and never have your great measure of faith or your happiness. Shut your ears to the music of the West. Be what God made you, the gayest and the most gracious of men and women, and if ever at times you are sad, go out and watch the children flying kites and the youths playing "Chin-lon" and thank God for the sunshine of your land and the sunshine of your hearts, for your joy of life, for the monks in their yellow robes, for your golden tipped pagodas, for the giant jungle trees and the bright colour of your clothes. Sit up all night at your festive Pwes and watch the little dancers, the clowns, the jugglers, and the marionettes. Go to the pagodas and hold your hands reverently before the image of the Buddha the Great Teacher, and trust in your next incarnation you may be a Burman over again — a delightful happy laughing Burman — just as you are to-day, and pray fervently that never for your sins may you be reincarnated north of the Tweed.' (1929)

NOTES

NOTES

NOTES

NOTES

NOTES

NOTES

284

INDEX

Accommodation 92-93
Addresses 91-92
Airlines 83-85, 88-91
Akyab 222-231
Alaungpaya, King 6, 95, 142, 151, 250, 264
Alaungsithu, King 44, 134, 163, 181, 192, 193, 201, 213, 239, 242
Amarapura 7, 8, 43, 126, 127, 129, 134, 136, 138, 139, 146, 232
  Ba-gaya Monastery 138
  Kyauktawgyi Pagoda 138
  Nagayon Pagoda 139
  Patodawgyi Pagoda 139
  Royal Palace Tower 138
  Royal Treasury Building 138
  Shwe Kyetka Pagoda 139
  Shwe Kyetyet Pagoda 139
  U Bein Bridge 138
Anawrahta, King 5, 59, 154, 157, 158, 160, 162, 164, 207
Arakan State 2, 4, 7, 26, 37, 40, 102, 126, 134, 135, 174, 194, **219-235**
Arakanese 37, 224, 225, 229, 230, 232-235, 250
Arrival 86
Aung San 13-18, 20, 23, 102
Aung San Suu Kyi 20, 23-25, 28-29
Aungban 27, 181
Ava 5, 6, 134, 139, 141-143, 217, 230, 250
  Bridge 141-142, 144
  Maha Aung Mye Bonzan Monastery 141
  Nan-myint 141
  Palace 138
Ayutthaya 6, 135, 229, 254, 256

Bagyidaw, King 7, 132, 134, 138, 139, 141, 148, 175

Bassein 102, 160, **210-216**, 253
  Shwe-mok-taw Pagoda 212-214
Beikthano 194
Bhamo 236, **240-243**
Black market 77-78
Bodawpaya, King 7, 106, 126, 129, 134, 135, 138, 139, 141, 144-146, 162, 232
Border crossings 85-86
Buddhism 38-40, 41-42, 64-65, 67
Burma Road 14-15, 198

Chaungtha **216-217**, 219
Chin 17, 36, 40, 246
Chindwin River 2, 3, 151-152, 192
Climate 2
Collis, Maurice 230, 256-257, 263-264
Currency 77-78
Customs 86-87

Danu 180, 186
Dates 3
Days 3
Departure 86-87
Drink 56-58

Economy 33-36
Embassies
  abroad 69-70
  in Rangoon 91

Festivals 42-45, 61-63
Food 53-55, 57-58
Fort Hertz 244

Geography 1-3
Golden Rock Pagoda (*see* Kyaiktiyo)
Goteik Viaduct 150, 198-199

Health 70-77

Heho 178, 181, 186-187
Henzada 212, **217-219**
Hermit 210
History 4-30
Hmawza 173
Hsipaw 201

Inle Lake 44, 178-179, **181-187**
  Phaung-Daw-U Pagoda 44, 182-183, 189, 197
Intha 182, 186
Irrawaddy Delta 120, **210-219**
Irrawaddy River 2-6, 9, 23, 36, 141-142, 144-145, 155, 158-160, 163, 166, 171-172, 174-176, 192-194, 203, 212, 217-218, 237-243

Jataka Tales 139, 153, 161, 166, **196**, 207, 253

Kachin 18, 26, 36, 37, 40, 238, 245
Kachin State 2, 17, 27, 33, 36, 102, **235-246**
Kaladan River 224, 229-230, 232
Kalaw **178-180**, 183, 186-187
Karen 11, 16, 18, 26, 36, 37, 40, 45, 179-180, 238
Karen State 2, 17, 18, 36, 248
Katha 120, 121, 237, 242
Kayah 37, 180, 248
Kayah State 2, 17, 37, 180, 182, **246-249**
Kengtung 195-197
  Maha Myat Muni 195-196
  Sunn Taung Pagoda 196-197
King Island 262-263
Kipling, Rudyard xi, 103, 105, 117, 120-122, 201-202, 204, 232
Konbaung Dynasty 6, 11, 151, 154
Kyaikkami 205-206, 213, 253
Kyaikmaraw 205, 261
Kyaiktiyo **207-210**, 213

Kyaikto 202, 207, 253
Kyansittha, King 5, 160, 161, 192
Kyatpin 188-189
Kyaukka 152
Kyaukse 4, **153-154**
  Kyauk-thinbaw 154
  Shwe-mok-taw Pagoda 153-154
  Shwethalyaung Pagoda 154
Kyithunkhat 139

Language 45-48
Lashio 11, 150, 189, **197-200**
Loikaw 27, 180, 189, **246-249**
Lower Burma 201-219

Magwe 193-194
Maingy Island 263
Mandalay 5, 9, 11, 14, 26, 60, 62, 66, 99, 100, 102, **117-135**, 139, 196, 236, 237, 241, 242, 244, 245, 254
  Atu-mashi Kyaung 129-130
  Aung Daw Mu Pagoda 135
  Eindawya Pagoda 134
  entertainment and shopping 127-128
  getting there and around 117-120
  Hill 8, 123, 126, 128-129, 181
  Kuthodaw Pagoda 129
  Kyauktawgyi Pagoda 128-129
  Maha Muni Pagoda 127, 134-135, 150, 189, 219, 232, 254
  Palace 27, 106, 132, 162, 190
  Peshawar Relics 128
  Sandamuni Pagoda 129
  Setkya-thiha Pagoda 134
  Shwekyi-myint Pagoda 134
  Shwenandaw Monastery 130-131
  Shweyattaw Buddha 128
  Two Snake Pagoda 128
  where to eat 126-127
  where to stay 125-126
  Yankintaung 135
  Zegyo Market 127, 134

Marionettes 100
Martaban 2, 4, 5, 8, 202, 204, 207
Maymyo **148-150**, 179, 198, 239
  Botanical Gardens 149
  Chinese Temple 149-150
  Peikchinmyaung Caves 150
Meiktila 119, 178, **190-191**
Mergui 42, 54, 205, 219, 252, **254-264**
  Thein-daw-gyi Pagoda 205, 259, 261-262
Mindon, King 8, 104, 107, 123, 124, 128-130, 132, 135, 138, 139, 141, 148, 205
Mingun 145-148
  Bell 7, 145-147
  Hsinbyu-meh Pagoda 148
  Pagoda 7, 145-146
  Pondaw-hpaya 148
  Settawya Pagoda 148
Mogok 33, **188-190**
Mon 4, 5, 26, 36, 37, 45, 110, 205, 207, 213
Mon State 2, 102, 202
Monywa 151-153
  Hpo-win-taung Caves 152
  Leh-di Monastery 152-153
  Shwe-Gu-Ni Pagoda 152
  Shweba-taung 152
  Shwezigon Pagoda 153
  Thanboddhay Temple 151-152
Moulmein 38, 120, **201-206**, 244, 250, 252, 253, 259
  Kyaik-than-lan Pagoda 201, 204-205
  Uzina Pagoda 205
Mount Popa 40, **167-170**, 172, 190
Mrauk-U (*see* Myohaung)
Mudon 206
Music 100-101
Myay-deh 172
Myit-hson 2, 239
Myitkyina 11, 15, 54, **235-246**

Myitngeh River 139, 141, 154
Myohaung 54, 134, 224-225, **228-235**, 254

Names (old and new, personal) 48-53
Nat 40, 41, 45, 59-62, 160, 167-170, 184, 277
National League for Democracy (NLD) 24-25
Ne Win (Shu Maung) 14, 19-22, 24-25, 158
Ngapali 219-220
Nu, U 13, 15-17, 19, 107, 134, 238
Nyaungdon 211

Orwell, George xi, 95, 110, 120-121

Pa-O 179-180, 184, 186, 248-249
Padaung 180, 246-249
Pagan 4, 5, 40, 102, 154, **155-168**, 172, 207, 230, 231, 235, 248
  Abeyadana Temple 165
  Ananda Temple 5, 138, 158, 160-164, 166, 214, 248
  Archaeological Museum 167
  Bu-hpaya 159
  Dhammayangyi Temple 164
  Dhammayazika Pagoda 166
  Dynasty 5, 37, 106, 139, 151, 153, 194, 207
  Gawdawpalin Temple 163
  getting there and around 157
  Hpaya-thonzu 166
  Htilo-minlo Temple 162
  Kubyaukkyi Temple 164
  Kyansittha Umin 162
  Lay-myethna Temple 166
  Mahabodhi Pagoda 161
  Manuha Temple 164, 165
  Mingalazedi Pagoda 164
  Myazigon 167
  Nan-hpaya Temple 165, 174

Nandamannya Temple 166
Nataunt Monastery 130, 167
Nathlaung Kyaung 163
Nyaung-U 159-160
Nyaung-U Market 159, 167
Pitakat Taik 162
Sapada Pagoda 160
Shinbin-tha-lyaung 164
Shwegugyi Temple 163
Shwesandaw Pagoda 164
Shwezigon Pagoda 40, 129, 144, 160, 166-167, 174
Somingyi Monastery 165
Sulamani Temple 161
Thambula Temple 166
Thatbyinnyu Temple 163
Upali Thein 162
where to stay and eat 158-159
Zaylan Island 167
Pagodas 41
Pakokku 192-193
Palaung 45, 179-180
Paleik 154
Mway-hpaya 154
Pataw-Patit Island 259, **261-262**
Pegu 4, 5, 6, 8, 21, 38, **111-115**, 135, 176, 202, 207, 217, 229, 250, 262
Kalyani Thein 114
Kyaikpun Pagoda/Images 114
Mahazedi Pagoda 112, 114
Shwegu-galay 114
Shwegugyi 114
Shwemawdaw Pagoda 102, **111-112**, 174
Shwethalyaung 112
Pindaya 178, **180-181**, 183
Politics 4-30
Population 36-38
Press 30-33
Prome 4, 5, 8, **171-177**, 220, 242
Bawbawgyi Pagoda 4, 173, 242
Bay-da-yi Cave 176
Bebegyi Pagoda 173-174, 242
Hpayagyi 173
Hpayama 173
Hseh-datgyi Pagoda 175
Kanbaung Nat Shrine 174
Lay-myethna 173-174
Mingyi-taung 176
Shwehpon-pwint Pagoda 175
Shwesandaw Pagoda 102, 171-172, **174-175**
Propaganda 30-33
Putao 236, **243-246**
Pwe 60-63, 99-100, 184-185, 277
Pyinmana 119
Pyu (people) 4, 174, 194
Pyu (town) 119

Rail 91
Rangoon 4, 6-8, 12, 14, 15, 16, 20-23, 62, 66, **94-109**, 114, 213
Alein-nga-sint Pagoda 108
Bo-gyoke Aung San Market 101-102
Botataung Pagoda 107
Chauk Htat Gyi Pagoda 107
Eindawya Pagoda 108
entertainment 99-103
Htaukkyant War Cemetery 109
Kaba-Aye Pagoda 107
Kohtatgyi Pagoda 109
Kyaik-kalo Pagoda 108
Kyaik-kasan Pagoda 109
Kyaikkale Pagoda 108
Kyauk-waing Pagoda 108
Mahapasana Guha 107
Mahawizayazedi 95
Meilamu Pagoda 108
National Museum 105-106
Nga Htat Gyi Pagoda 107
shopping 101-102
Shwedagon Pagoda 4, 6, 21, 22, 43, 45, 94, 95, 102, **103-105**, 107, 109, 110, 112, 114, 174, 229
Shwephonebywint Pagoda 97, 109
Sule Pagoda 21, 23, **105**, 175
where to eat 97, 98
where to stay 97

Religion 38-42

Sagaing 23, 123, **141-144**
  Aungmye-lawka Pagoda 144
  Badamyazedi Pagoda 144
  Datpaung-su Pagoda 144
  Hsinmyashin Pagoda 143
  Kaunghmudaw Pagoda 143
  Nga-datkyi Pagoda 143-144
  Pa Ba Kyaung 144
  Ponnyashin Pagoda 142-143
  Tupayon Pagoda 144
  Umin Thonzeh Pagoda 144
Salon 263
Salween River 2, 3, 196, 201-202
Sandoway 219-222
Setseh 206, 219
Shampoo Island 201, 203-204
Shan 5, 8, 37, 45, 182, 186, 195-197, 200, 214, 218, 245, 248-249
Shan State(s) 2, 6, 8, 11, 15, 17, 18, 34, 36, 37, 150, 178, 186, **195-201**, 247
Shwebo 6, 8
Shwedaung 176-177
  Shwemyet-hman Pagoda 176
  Shwenattaung Pagoda 176-177
Sintkaing 154
  Hpa-lin-bo Pagoda 154
Sittang River 3, 5
Sittwe (*see* Akyab)
Sri Ksetra 4, 171-172, 176, 190
Supayalat, Queen 8, 9, 11, 106
Syriam 6, 95, 105, **109-110**, 120
  Kyaikkauk Pagoda 109
  Kyauktan Yay-leh-hpaya 109-110
  Natsin-gone 109-110

Tabinshwehti, King 5, 111, 191-192
Taungbyon 43, 60, 169
Taungdwingyi 194
Taunggyi 66, 178, **183-186**, 197, 200, 249
Taungwaing 205
Taungyo 180, 186
Tavoy 5, 27, 54, 93, 182, 213, 219, **249-254**, 256, 259-260, 262
  Shin Mokti Pagoda 213, 253
Tenasserim Division 2, 7, 14, 27, 33, 37, 182, 204, **249-264**
Thakin 13
Thanbyuzayat 206
Thaton 4, 5, 37, 111, 163-165, 202, 206-207
Thazi 118, 178, 186-187
Thibaw, King 8, 9, 106, 121, 130, 132, 135
Time 3
Toungoo 5, 6, 118-119, **191-192**
  Dynasty 5, 6, 111
Tour operators 79-82
Travel restrictions 82-83
Twante **110**, 120

Upper Burma 188-194

Visas 68-69

White, Samuel xi, **256-259**

Yaunghwe 44, 181-182, 186
Ye 27, 203, 251
Ywama 182, 186
Ywataung 144